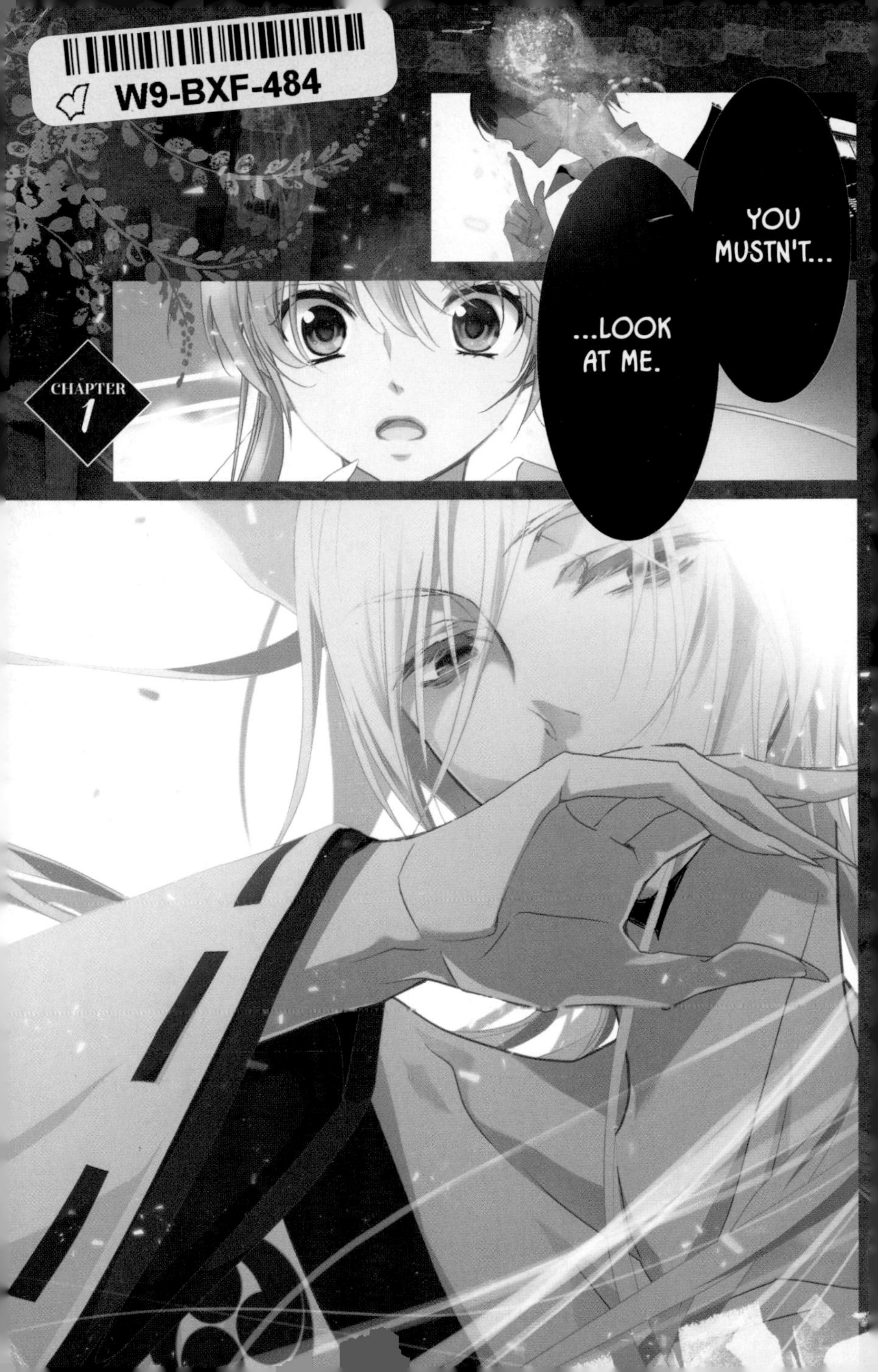
YOU MUSTN'T...
...LOOK AT ME.
CHAPTER 1

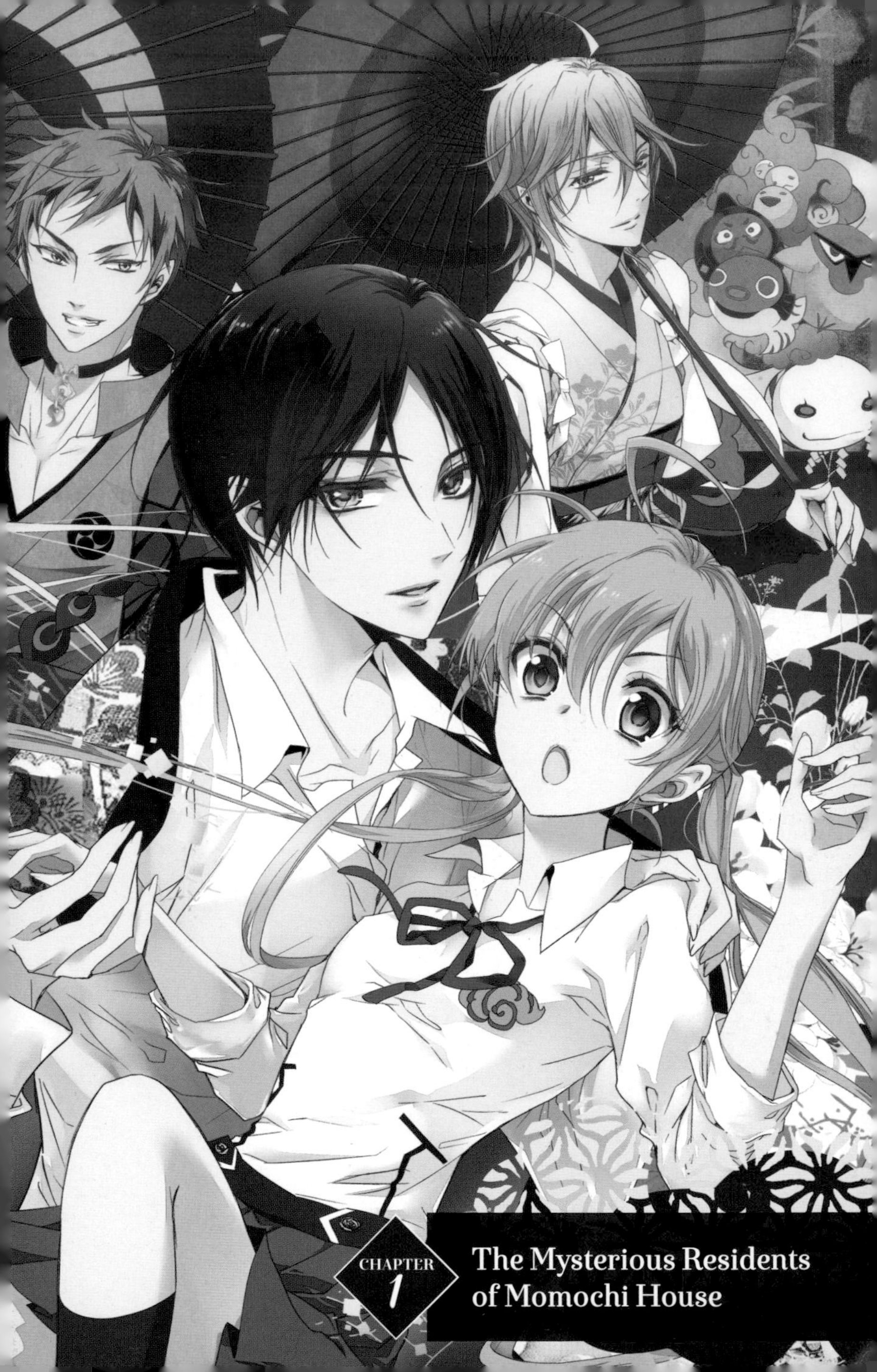

CHAPTER 1 The Mysterious Residents of Momochi House

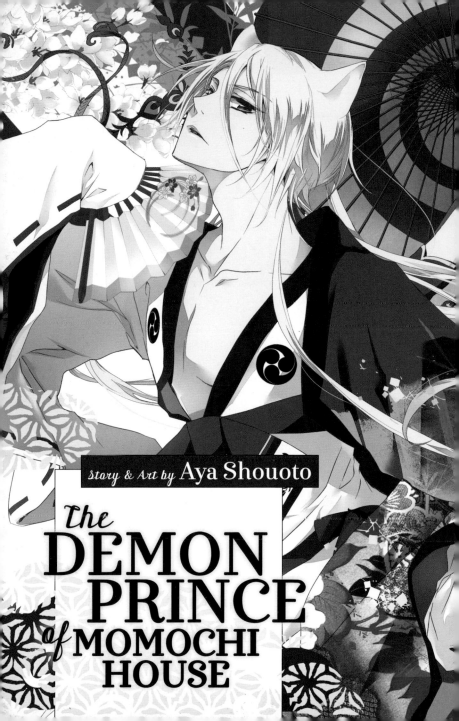

Story & Art by Aya Shouoto

The DEMON PRINCE of MOMOCHI HOUSE

The DEMON PRINCE of MOMOCHI HOUSE

1

Contents

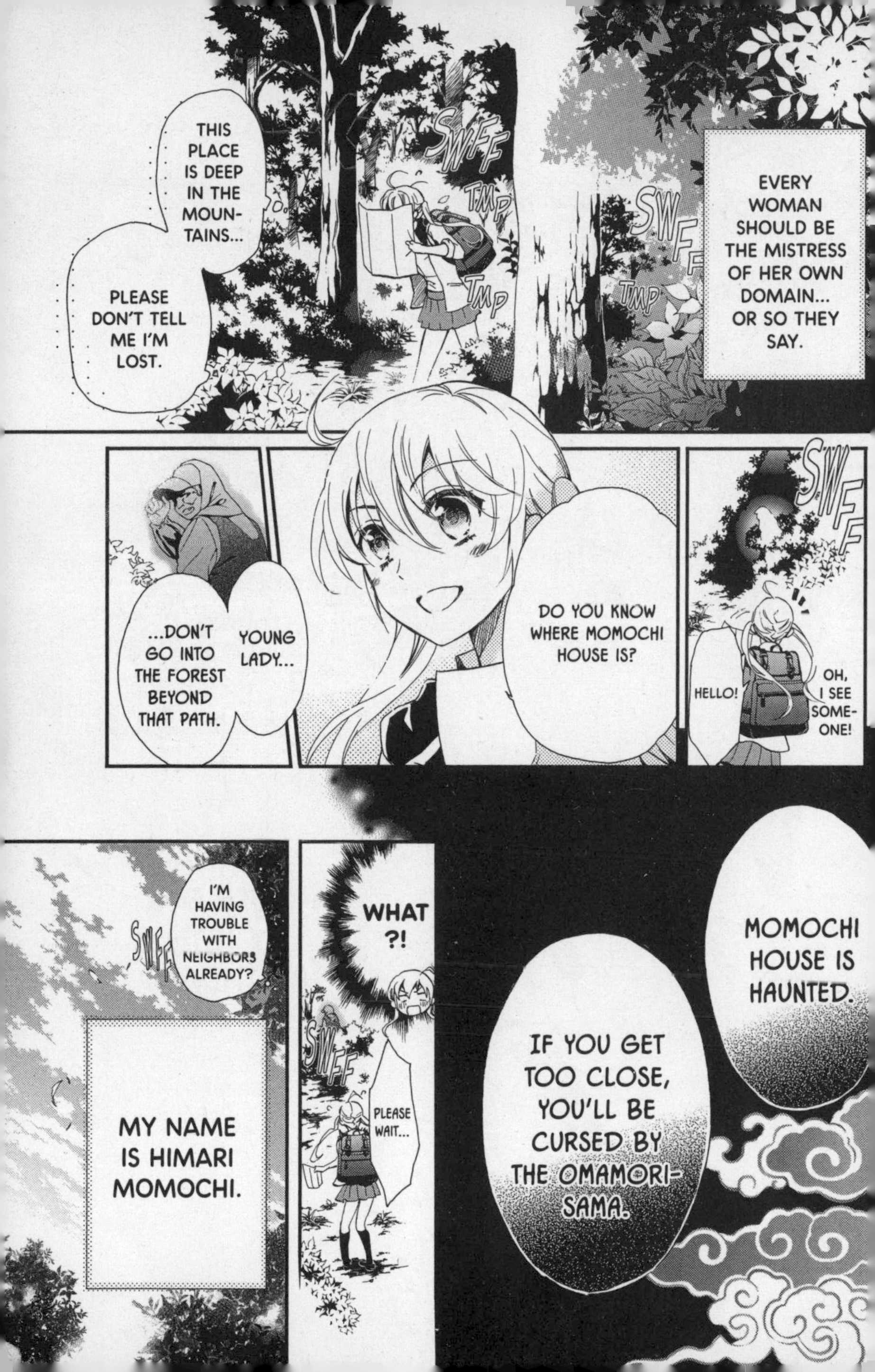
EVERY WOMAN SHOULD BE THE MISTRESS OF HER OWN DOMAIN... OR SO THEY SAY.
SWFF
TMP
TMP
SWFF
TMP
TMP
THIS PLACE IS DEEP IN THE MOUNTAINS...
PLEASE DON'T TELL ME I'M LOST.
SWFF
OH, I SEE SOMEONE!
HELLO!
DO YOU KNOW WHERE MOMOCHI HOUSE IS?
YOUNG LADY...
...DON'T GO INTO THE FOREST BEYOND THAT PATH.
MOMOCHI HOUSE IS HAUNTED.
IF YOU GET TOO CLOSE, YOU'LL BE CURSED BY THE OMAMORI-SAMA.
WHAT?!
SWFF
PLEASE WAIT...
I'M HAVING TROUBLE WITH NEIGHBORS ALREADY?
SWFF
MY NAME IS HIMARI MOMOCHI.

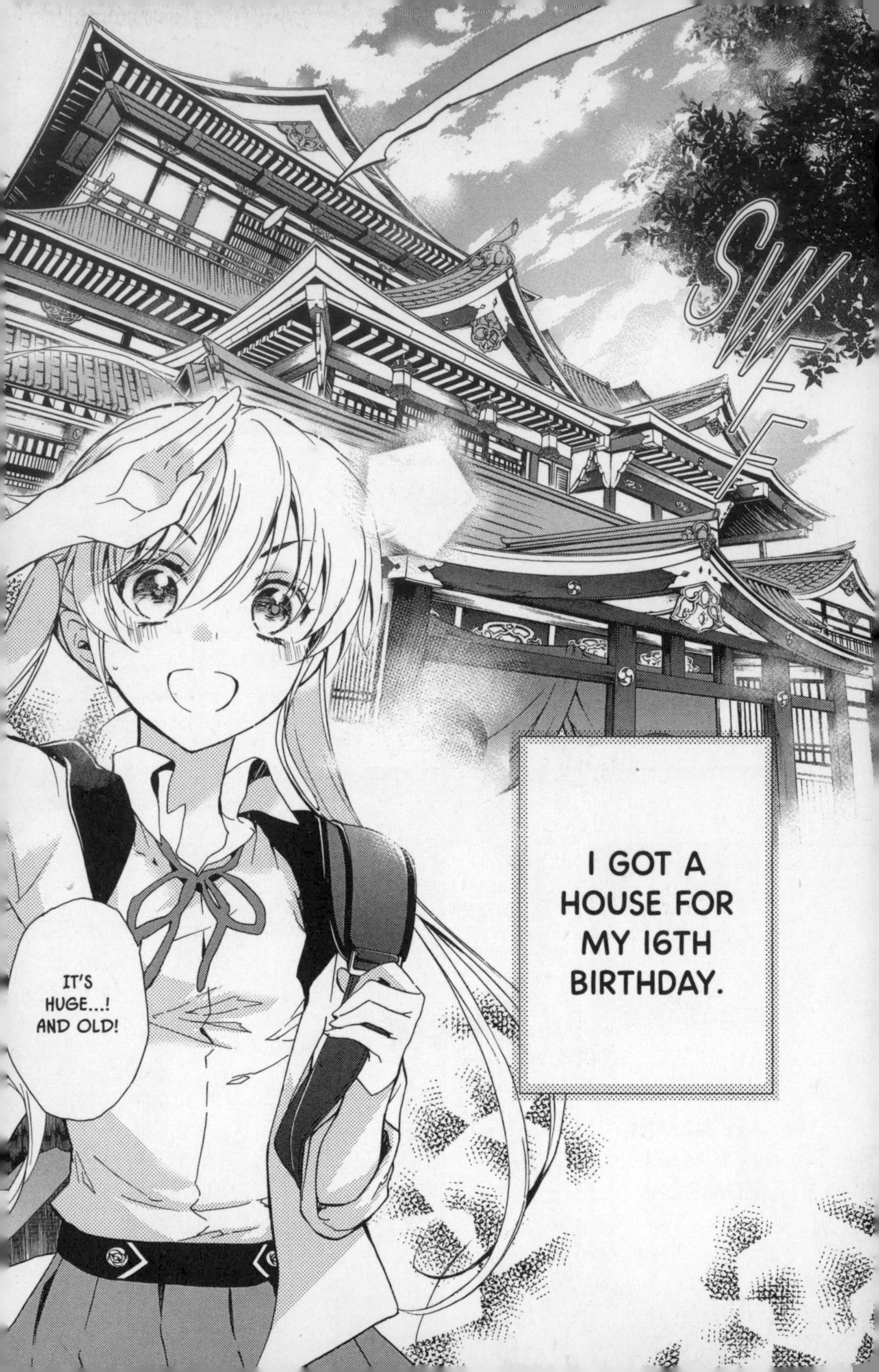
SWFF
I GOT A HOUSE FOR MY 16TH BIRTHDAY.
IT'S HUGE...! AND OLD!

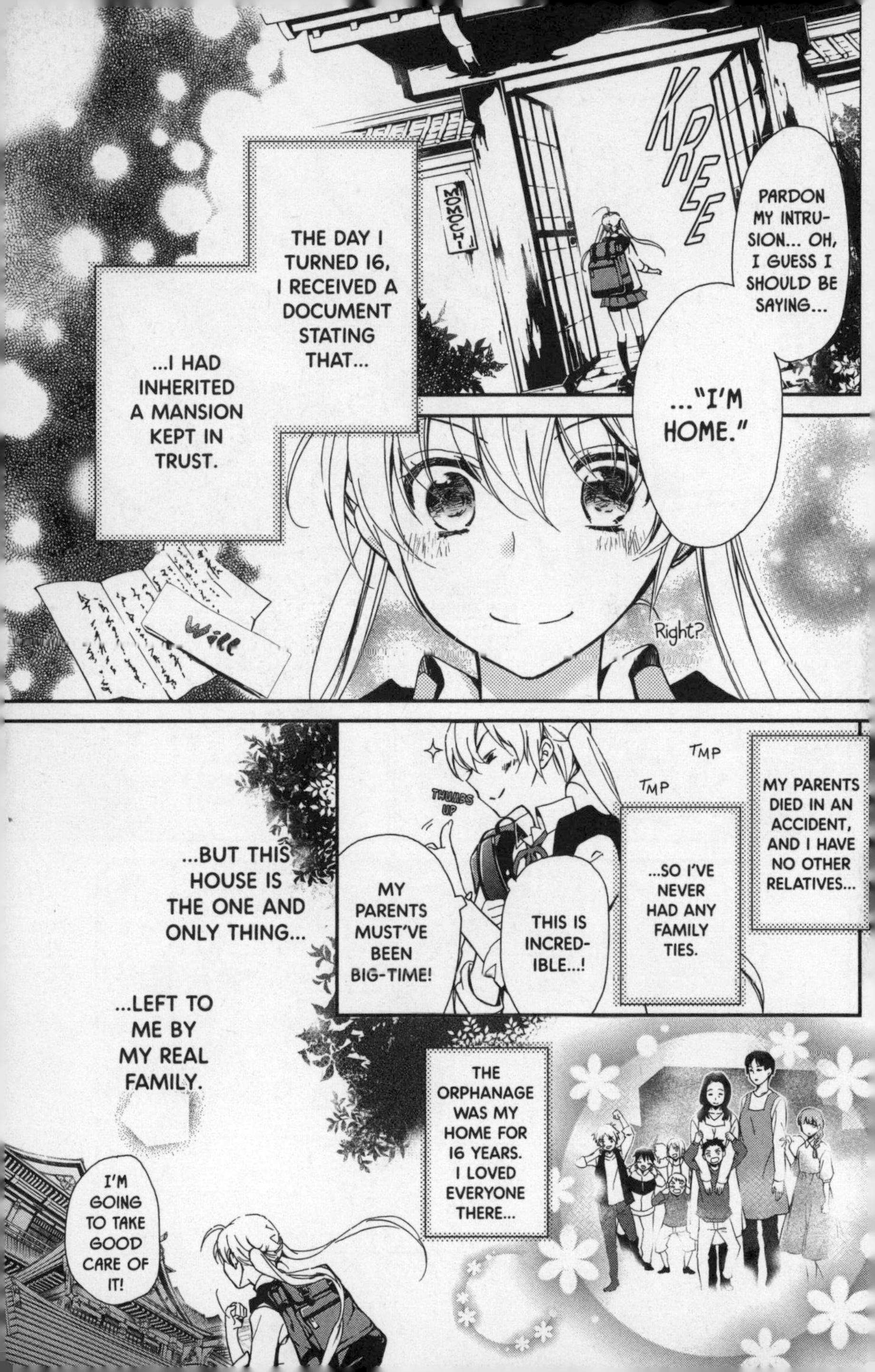
KREE
PARDON MY INTRUSION... OH, I GUESS I SHOULD BE SAYING...
MOMOCHI
THE DAY I TURNED 16, I RECEIVED A DOCUMENT STATING THAT...
...I HAD INHERITED A MANSION KEPT IN TRUST.
..."I'M HOME."
Right?
Will
MY PARENTS DIED IN AN ACCIDENT, AND I HAVE NO OTHER RELATIVES...
TMP
TMP
...SO I'VE NEVER HAD ANY FAMILY TIES.
THIS IS INCREDIBLE...!
MY PARENTS MUST'VE BEEN BIG-TIME!
THUMBS UP
...BUT THIS HOUSE IS THE ONE AND ONLY THING...
...LEFT TO ME BY MY REAL FAMILY.
THE ORPHANAGE WAS MY HOME FOR 16 YEARS. I LOVED EVERYONE THERE...
I'M GOING TO TAKE GOOD CARE OF IT!

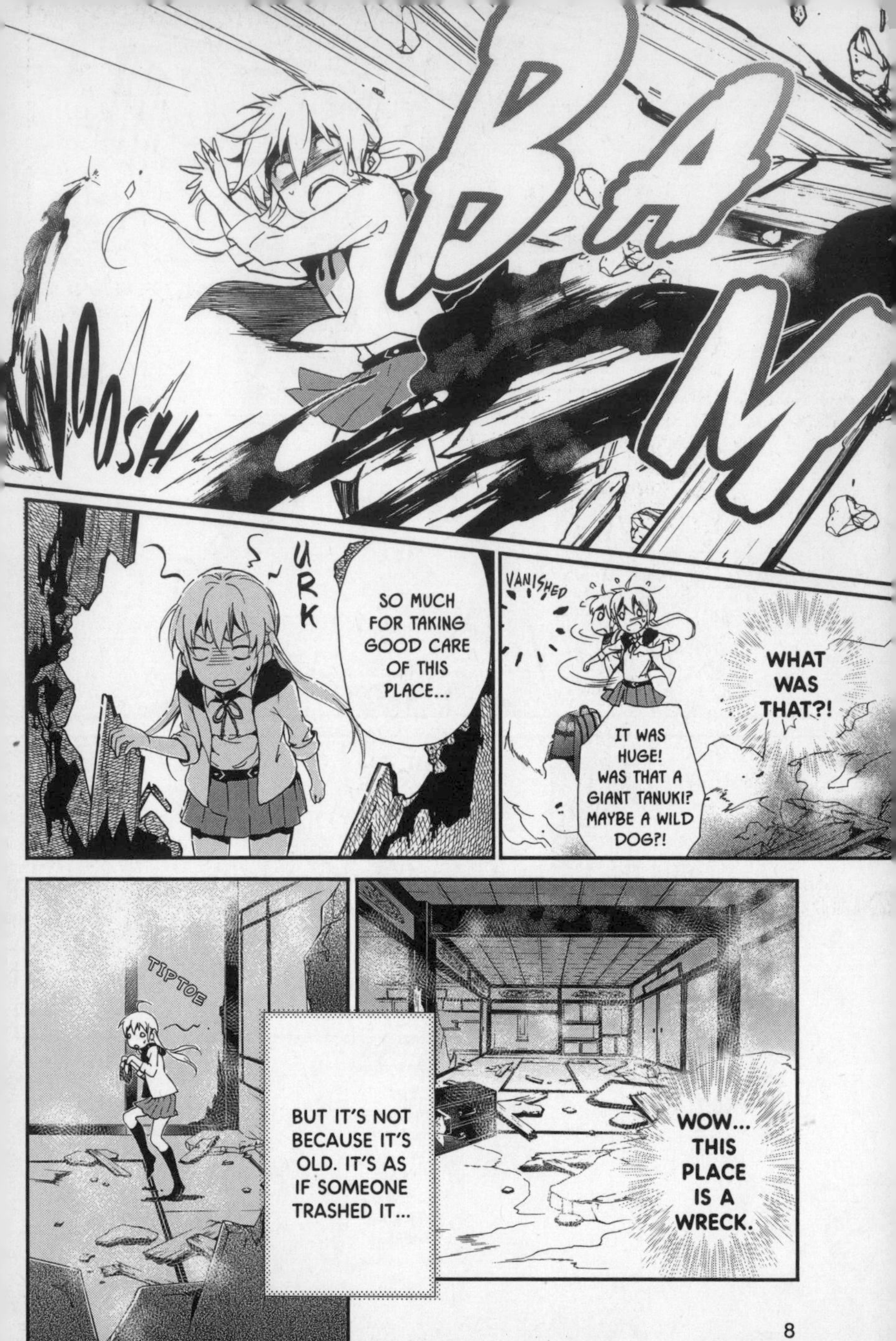
BAM
WHOOSH
VANISHED
WHAT WAS THAT?!
IT WAS HUGE! WAS THAT A GIANT TANUKI? MAYBE A WILD DOG?!
URK
SO MUCH FOR TAKING GOOD CARE OF THIS PLACE...
WOW... THIS PLACE IS A WRECK.
BUT IT'S NOT BECAUSE IT'S OLD. IT'S AS IF SOMEONE TRASHED IT...
TIPTOE

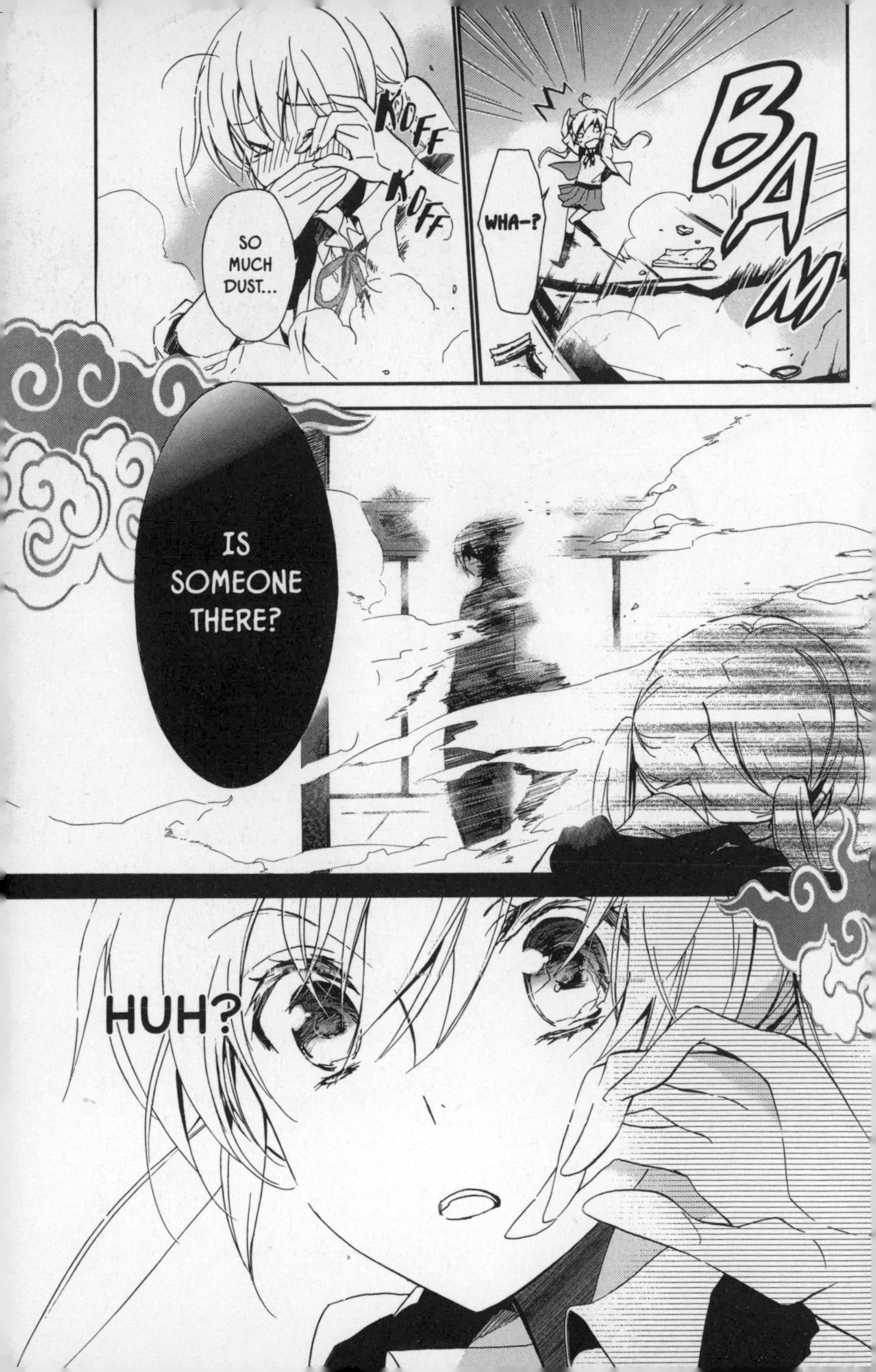
BAM
WHA-?
KOFF KOFF
SO MUCH DUST...
IS SOMEONE THERE?
HUH?

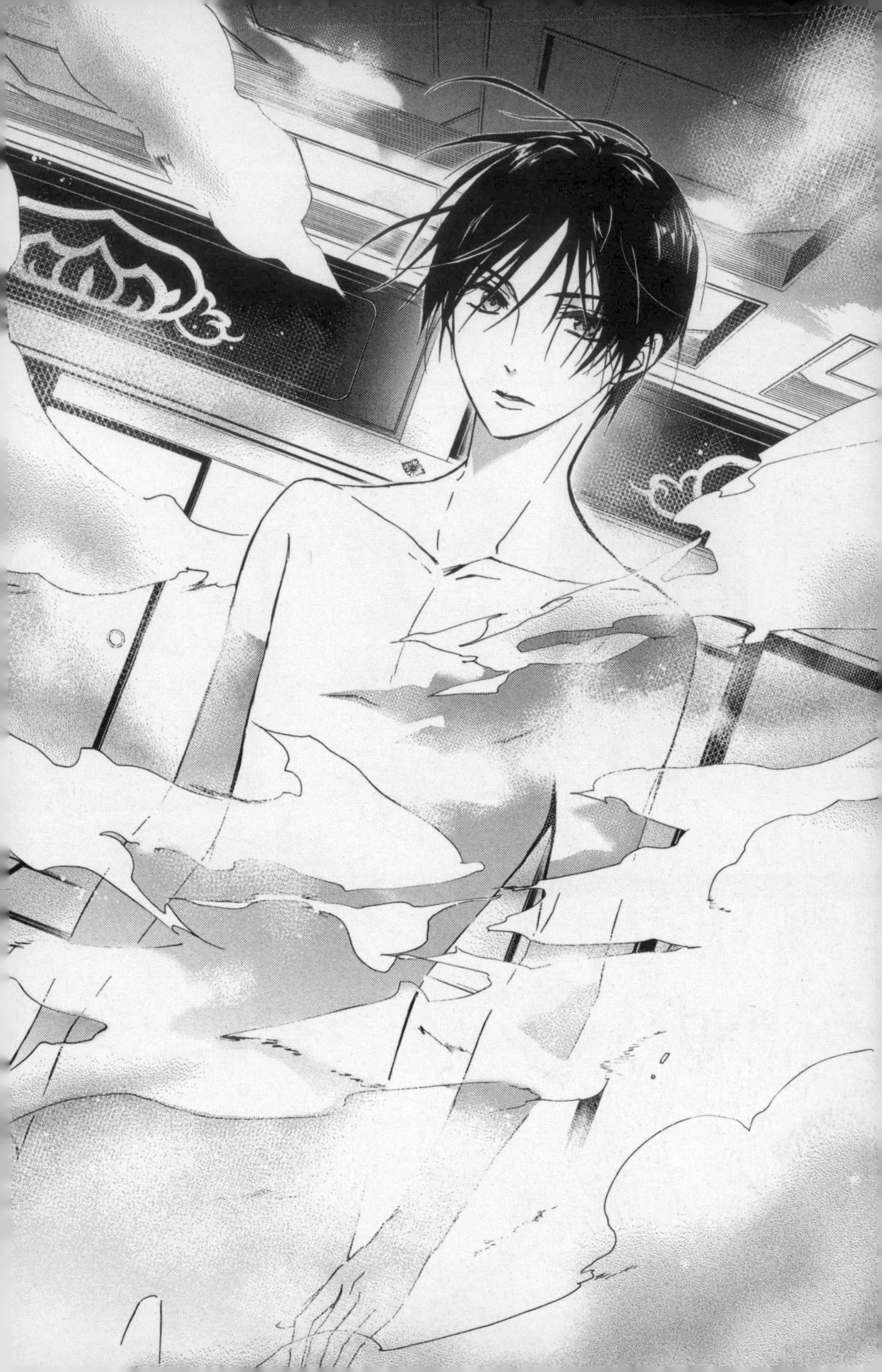

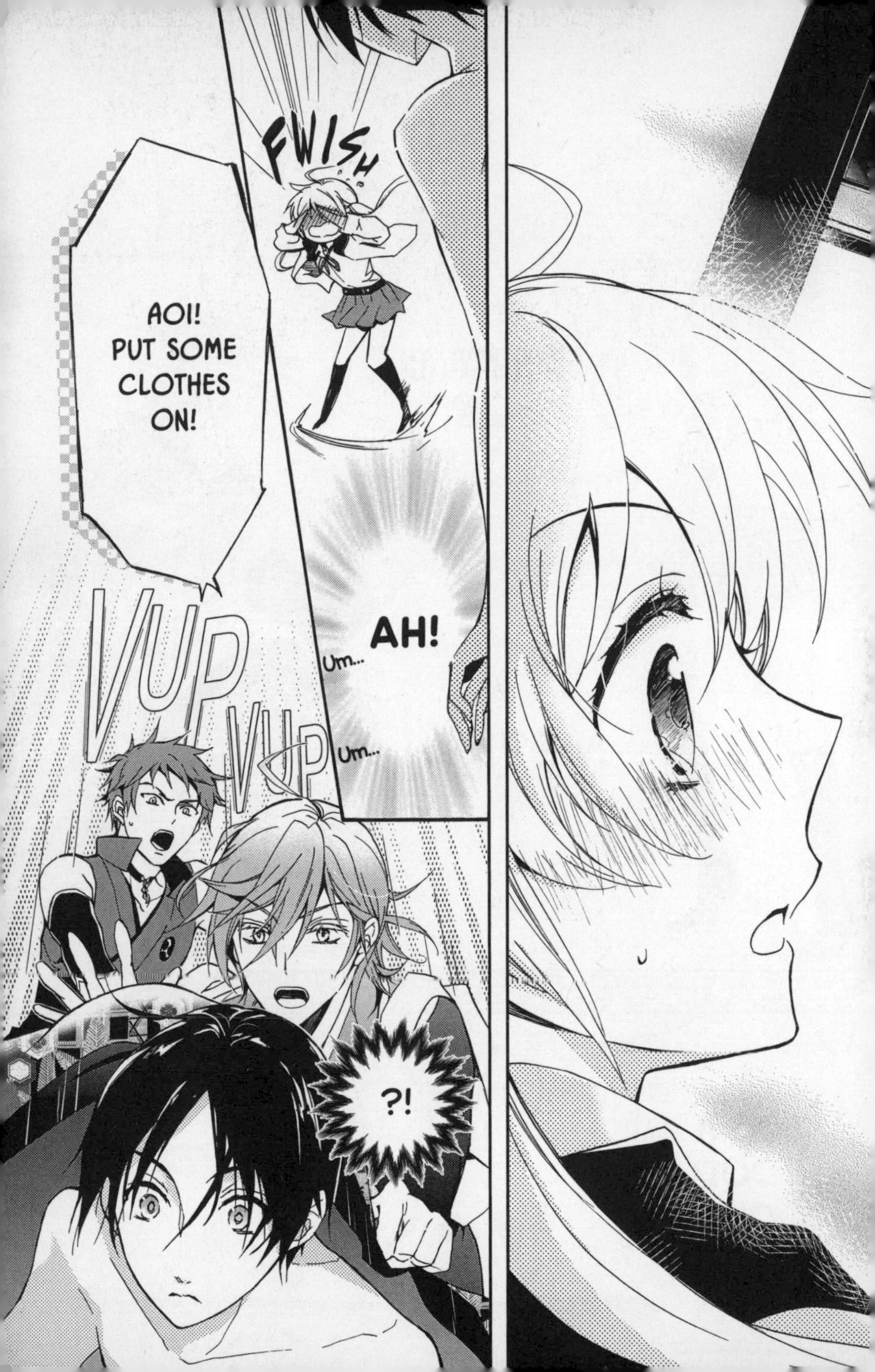
FWISH
AOI!
PUT SOME
CLOTHES
ON!
AH!
Um...
Um...
VUP
VUP
?!

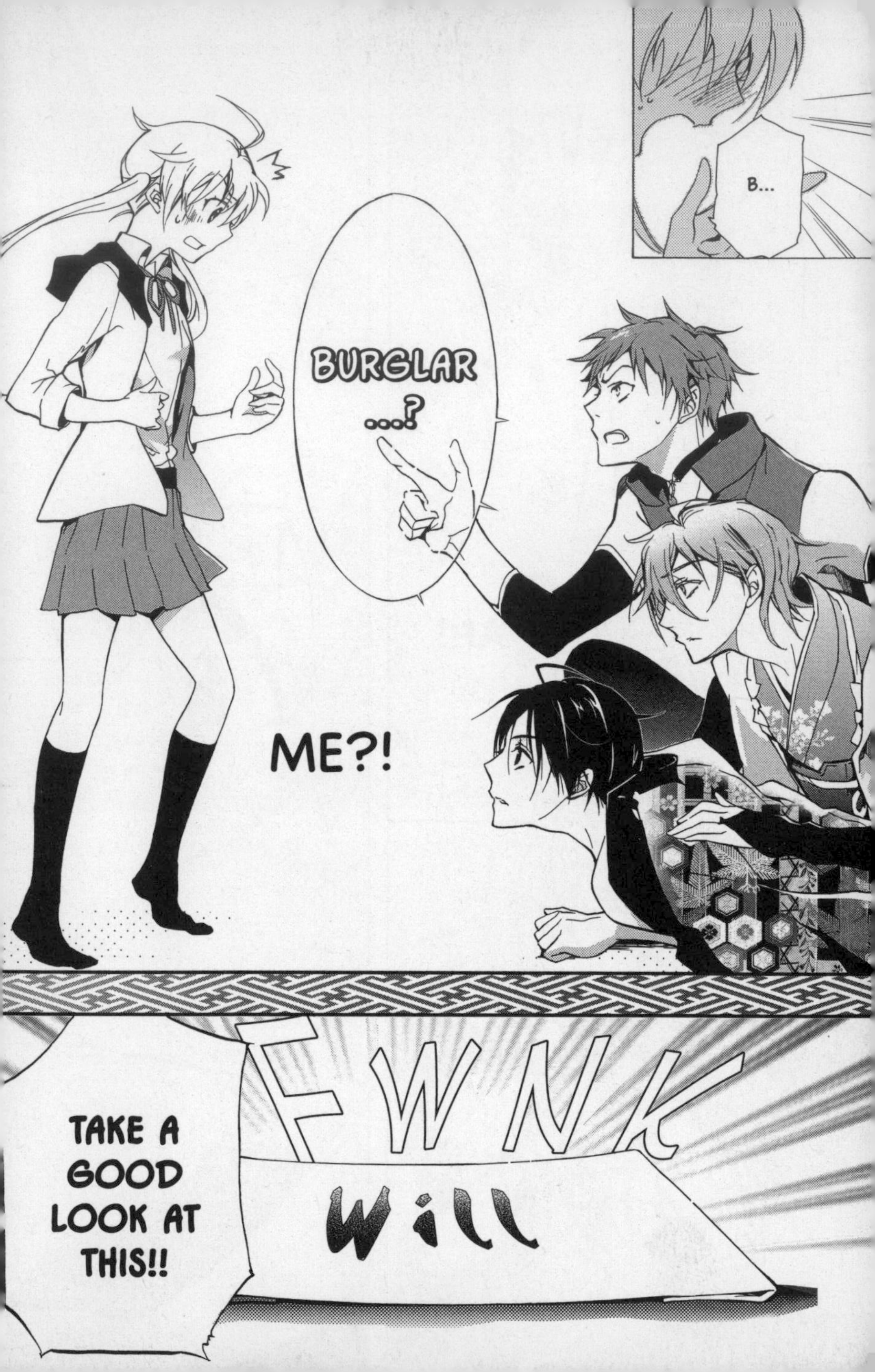
B...
BURGLAR ...?
ME?!
FWNK
Will
TAKE A GOOD LOOK AT THIS!!

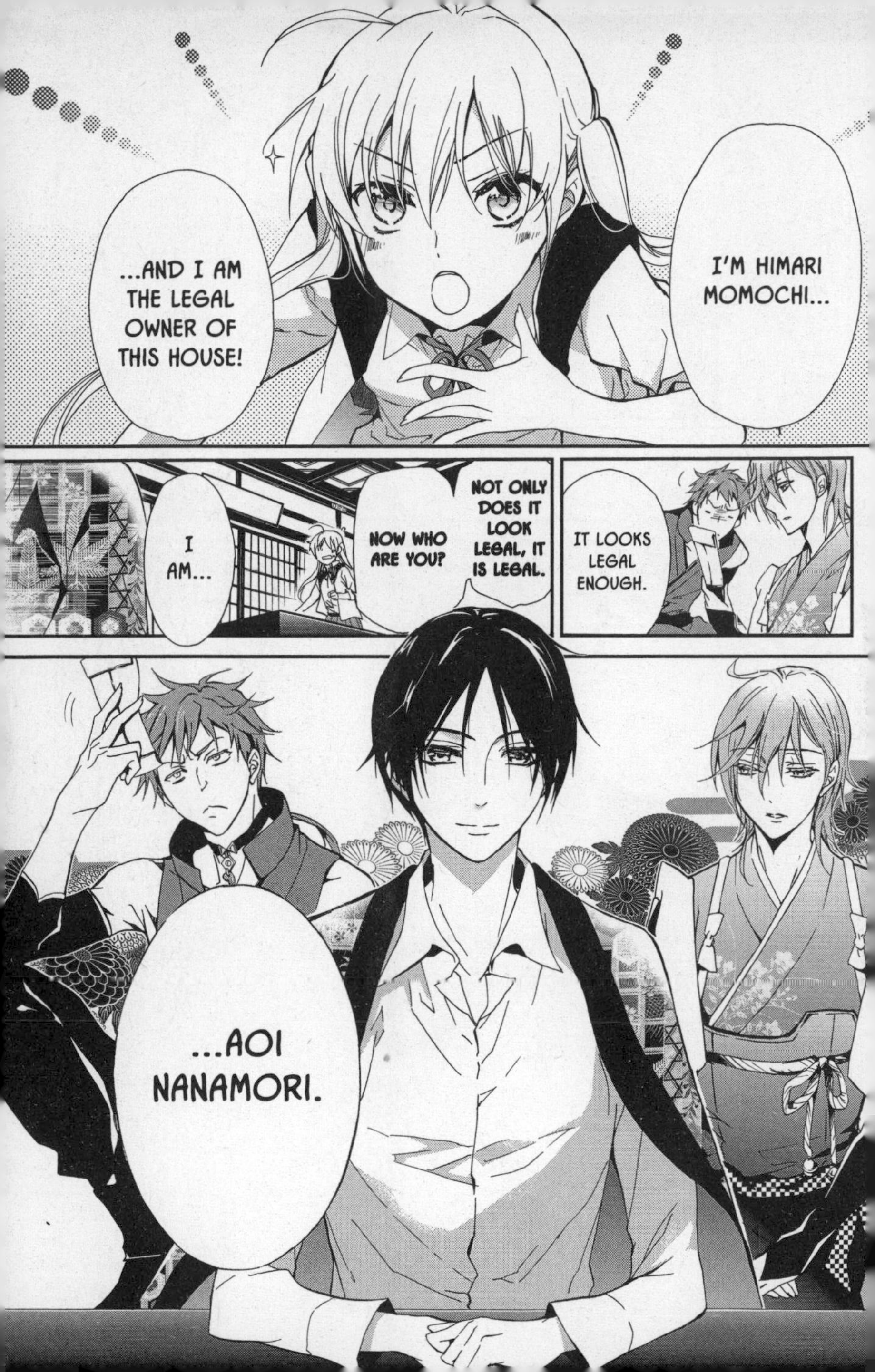
I'M HIMARI MOMOCHI...
...AND I AM THE LEGAL OWNER OF THIS HOUSE!
IT LOOKS LEGAL ENOUGH.
NOT ONLY DOES IT LOOK LEGAL, IT IS LEGAL.
NOW WHO ARE YOU?
I AM...
...AOI NANAMORI.

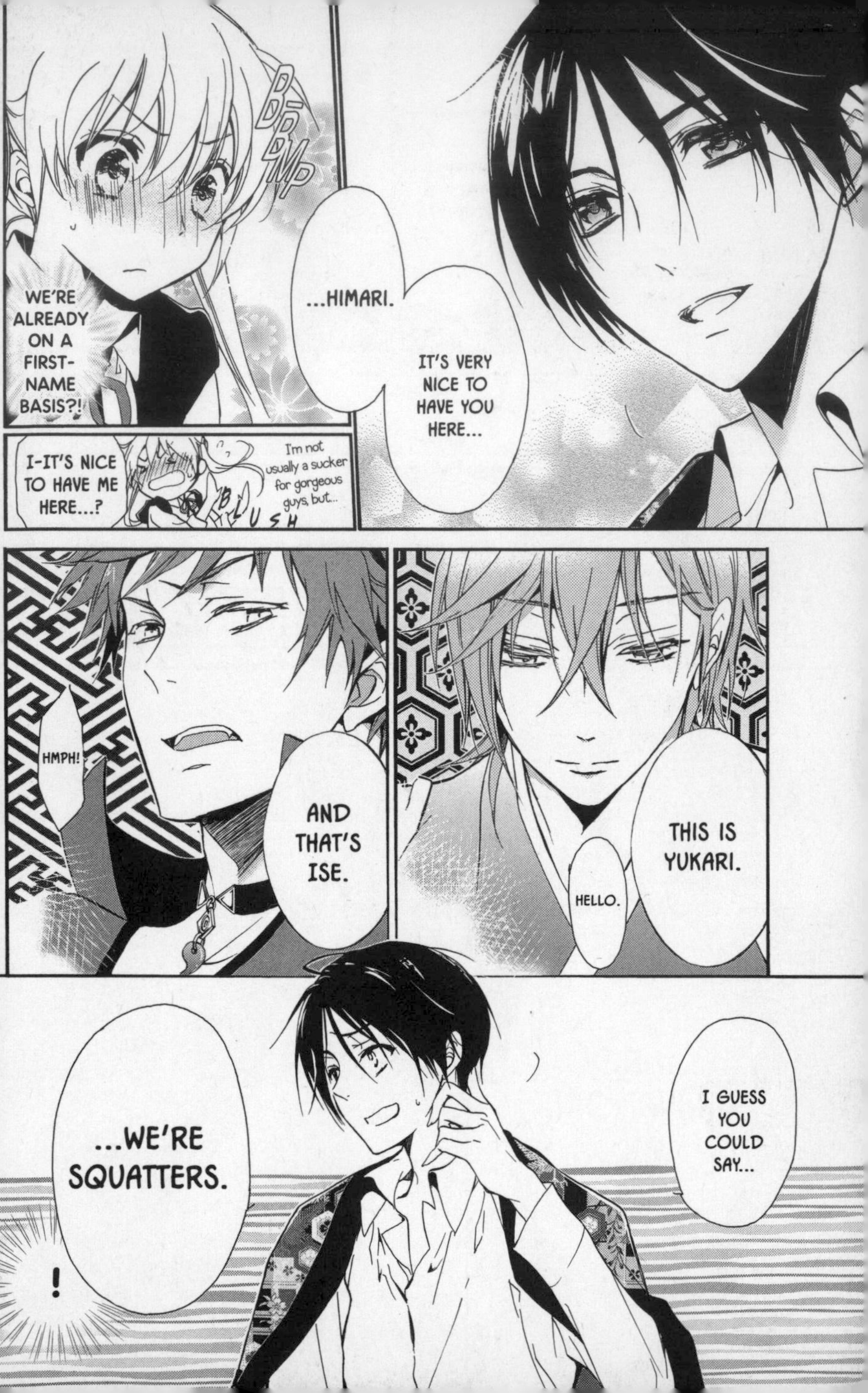
...HIMARI.
IT'S VERY NICE TO HAVE YOU HERE...
WE'RE ALREADY ON A FIRST-NAME BASIS?!
I'm not usually a sucker for gorgeous guys, but...
BLUSH
I-IT'S NICE TO HAVE ME HERE...?
THIS IS YUKARI.
HELLO.
AND THAT'S ISE.
HMPH!
I GUESS YOU COULD SAY...
...WE'RE SQUATTERS.
!

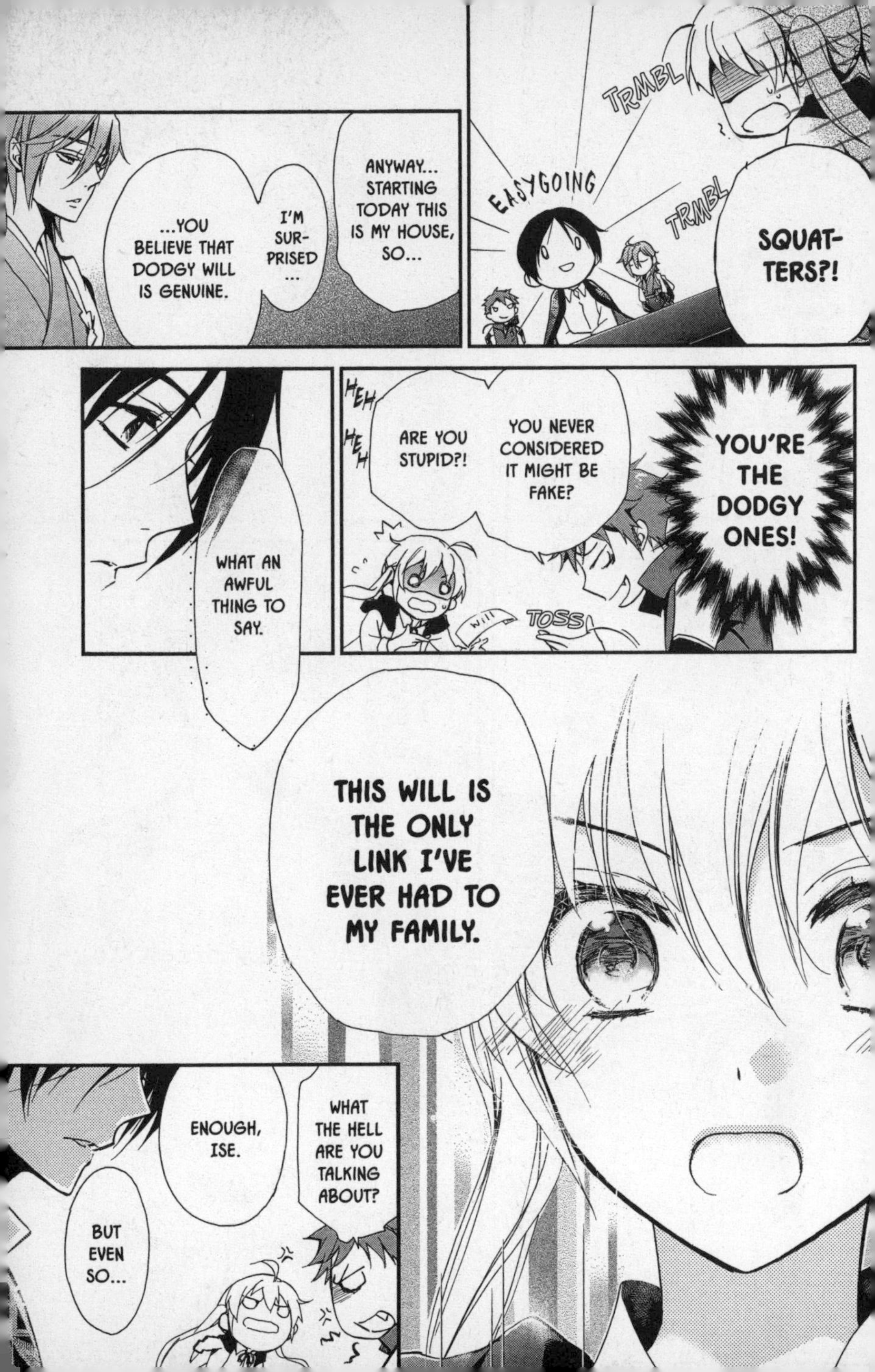
TRMBL
SQUAT-TERS?!
TRMBL
EASYGOING
ANYWAY... STARTING TODAY THIS IS MY HOUSE, SO...
I'M SUR-PRISED...
...YOU BELIEVE THAT DODGY WILL IS GENUINE.
YOU'RE THE DODGY ONES!
YOU NEVER CONSIDERED IT MIGHT BE FAKE?
ARE YOU STUPID?!
HEH HEH
TOSS
Will
WHAT AN AWFUL THING TO SAY.
THIS WILL IS THE ONLY LINK I'VE EVER HAD TO MY FAMILY.
WHAT THE HELL ARE YOU TALKING ABOUT?
ENOUGH, ISE.
BUT EVEN SO...

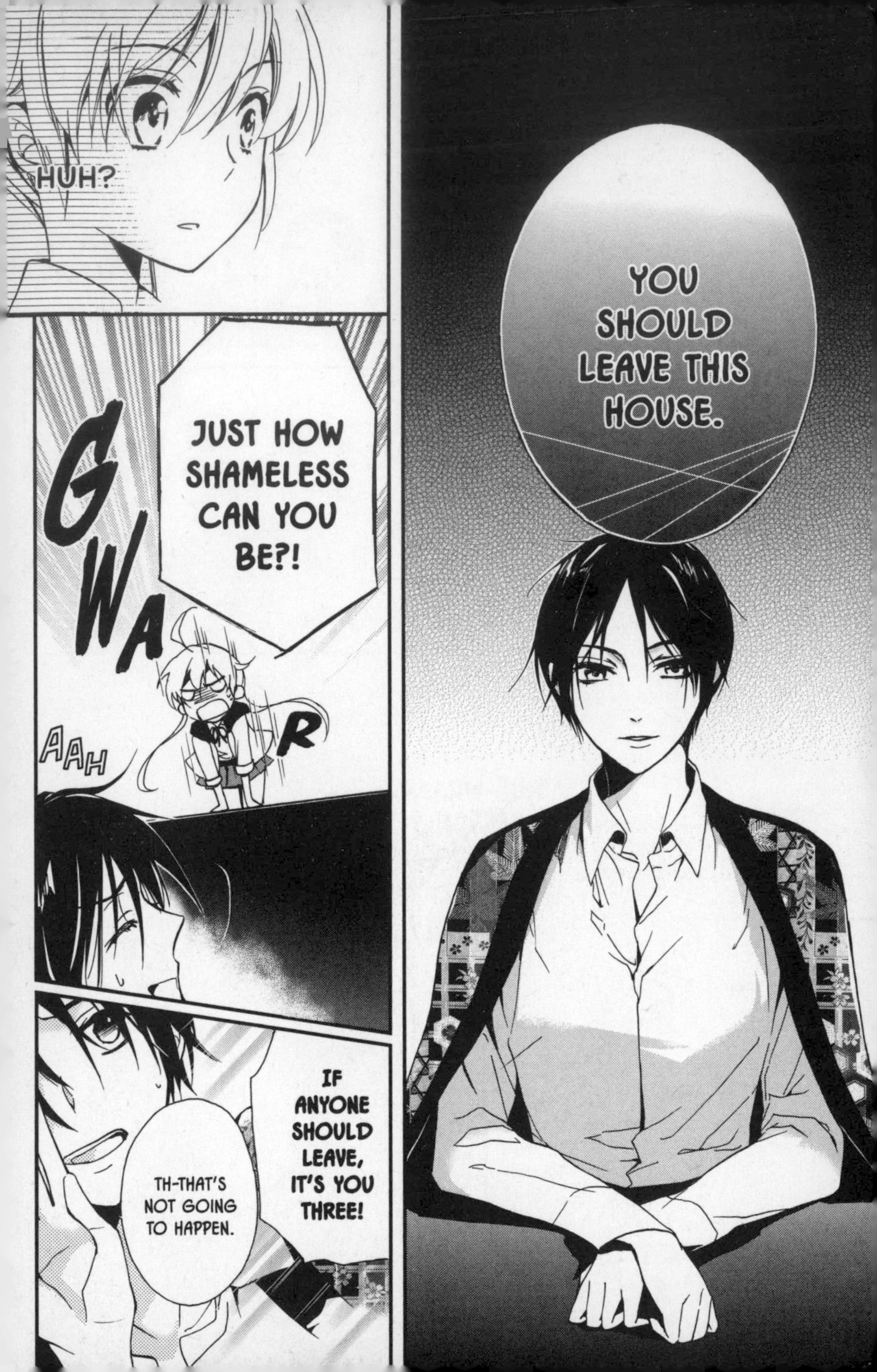
YOU SHOULD LEAVE THIS HOUSE.
HUH?
JUST HOW SHAMELESS CAN YOU BE?!
GWAR
AAH
IF ANYONE SHOULD LEAVE, IT'S YOU THREE!
TH-THAT'S NOT GOING TO HAPPEN.

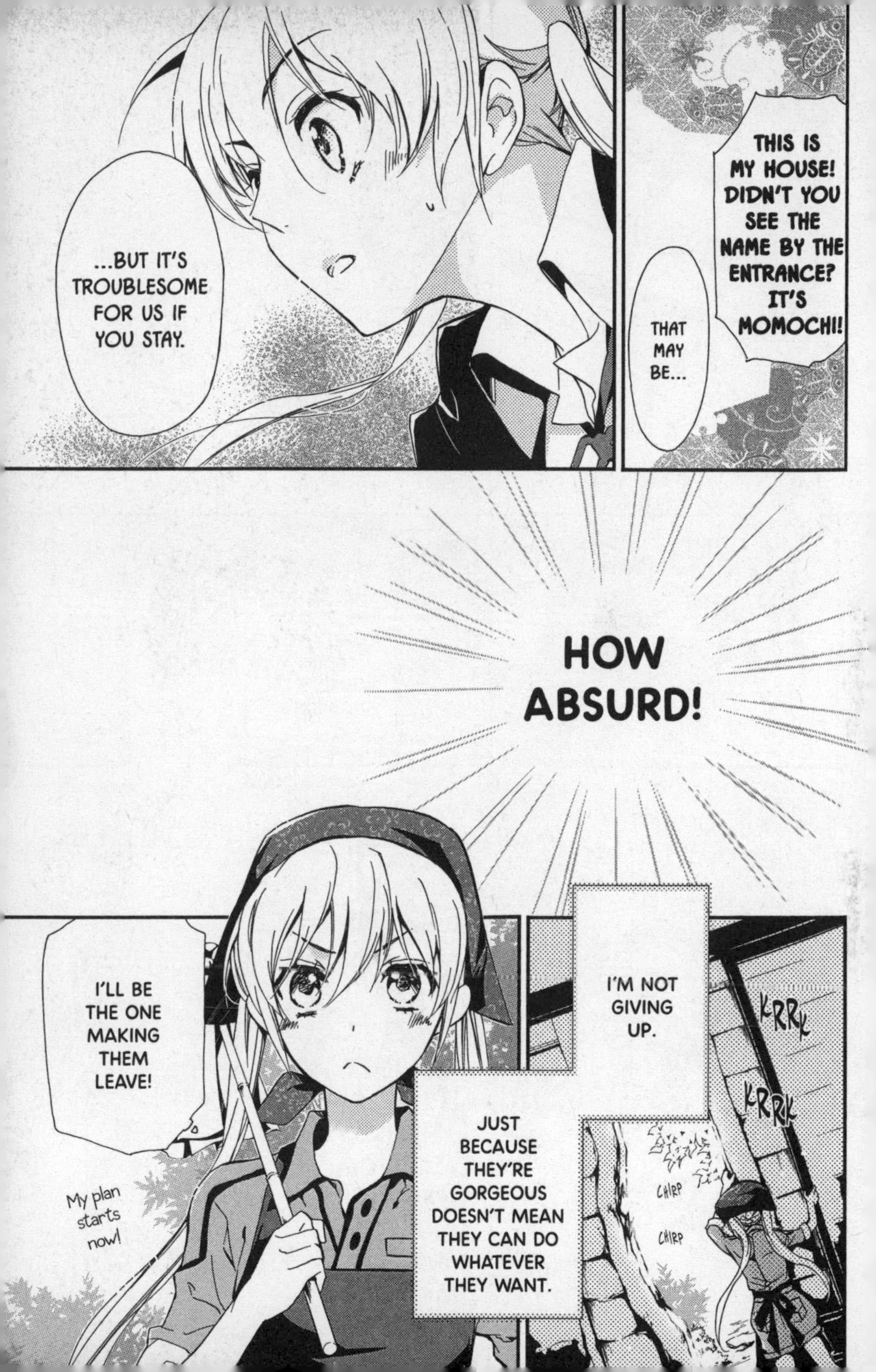
THIS IS MY HOUSE! DIDN'T YOU SEE THE NAME BY THE ENTRANCE? IT'S MOMOCHI!
THAT MAY BE...
...BUT IT'S TROUBLESOME FOR US IF YOU STAY.
HOW ABSURD!
I'M NOT GIVING UP.
KRRK
KRRK
CHIRP
CHIRP
JUST BECAUSE THEY'RE GORGEOUS DOESN'T MEAN THEY CAN DO WHATEVER THEY WANT.
I'LL BE THE ONE MAKING THEM LEAVE!
My plan starts now!

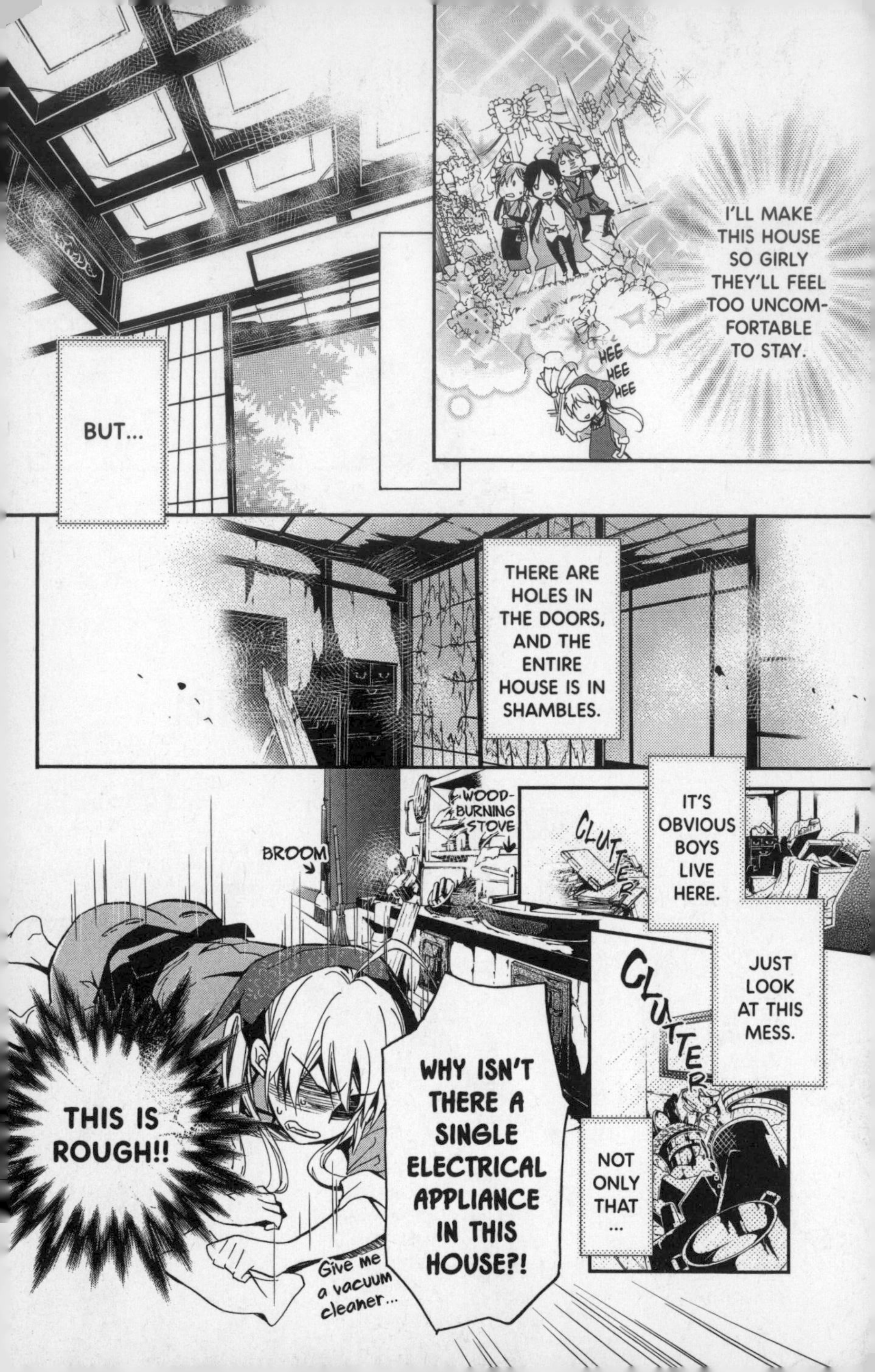
I'LL MAKE THIS HOUSE SO GIRLY THEY'LL FEEL TOO UNCOMFORTABLE TO STAY.
HEE HEE HEE
BUT...
THERE ARE HOLES IN THE DOORS, AND THE ENTIRE HOUSE IS IN SHAMBLES.
IT'S OBVIOUS BOYS LIVE HERE.
JUST LOOK AT THIS MESS.
CLUTTER
WOOD-BURNING STOVE
CLUTTER
BROOM
NOT ONLY THAT...
WHY ISN'T THERE A SINGLE ELECTRICAL APPLIANCE IN THIS HOUSE?!
THIS IS ROUGH!!
Give me a vacuum cleaner...

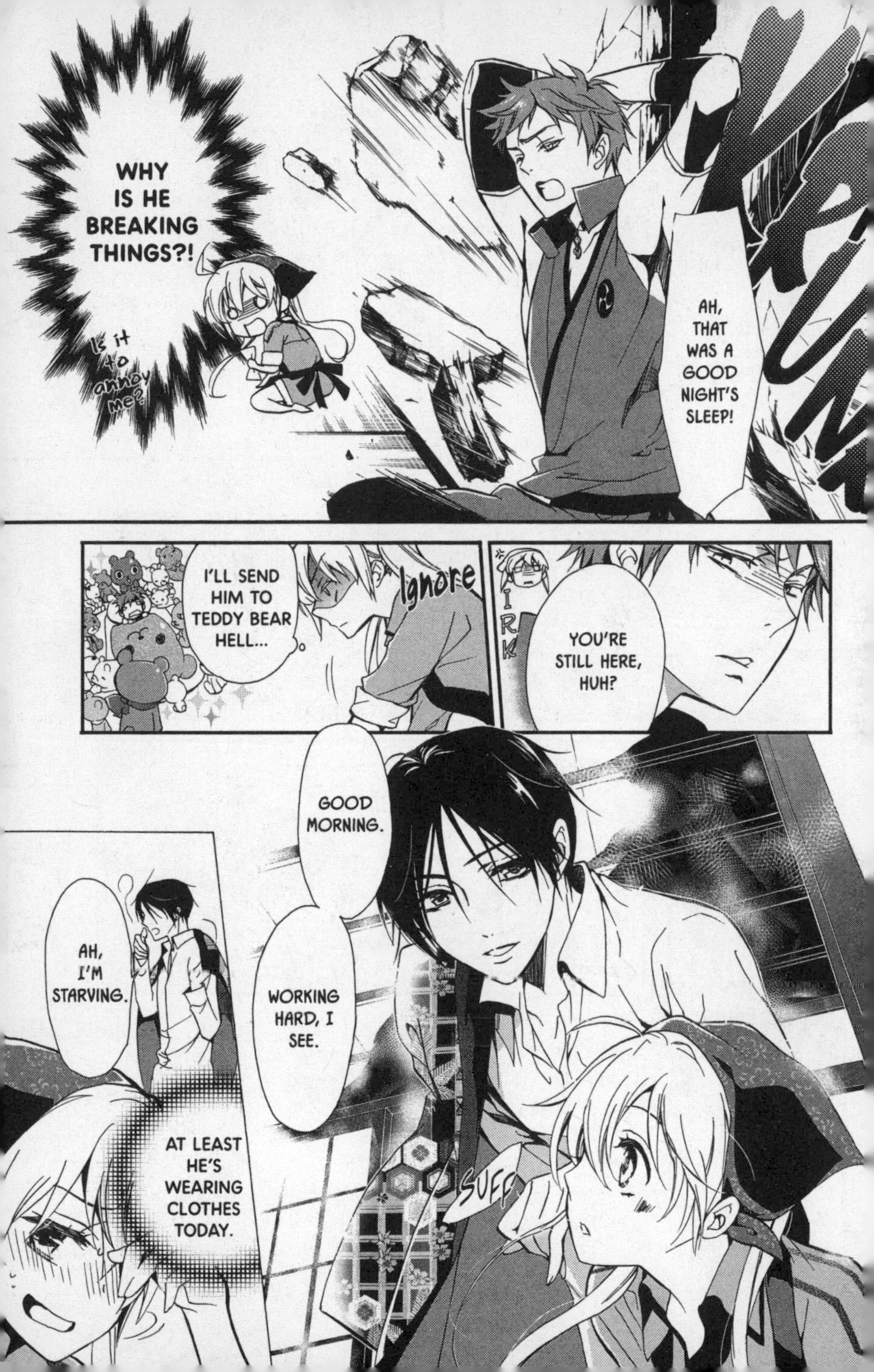
AH, THAT WAS A GOOD NIGHT'S SLEEP!
WHY IS HE BREAKING THINGS?!
Is it to annoy me?
YOU'RE STILL HERE, HUH?
IRK
Ignore
I'LL SEND HIM TO TEDDY BEAR HELL...
GOOD MORNING.
WORKING HARD, I SEE.
SUFF
AH, I'M STARVING.
AT LEAST HE'S WEARING CLOTHES TODAY.

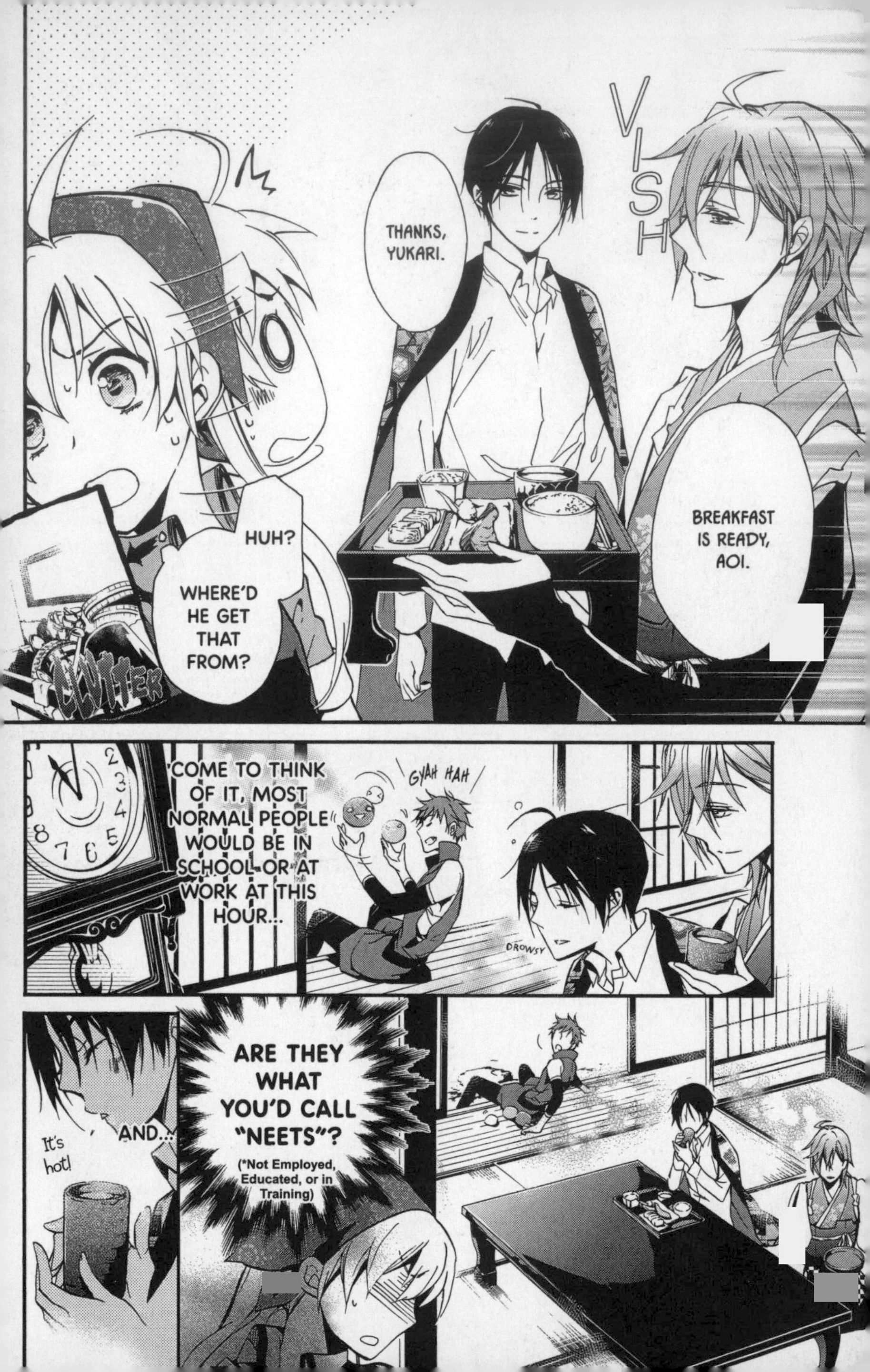
VISH
BREAKFAST IS READY, AOI.
THANKS, YUKARI.
HUH?
WHERE'D HE GET THAT FROM?
CLUTTER
GYAH HAH
DROWSY
COME TO THINK OF IT, MOST NORMAL PEOPLE WOULD BE IN SCHOOL OR AT WORK AT THIS HOUR...
ARE THEY WHAT YOU'D CALL "NEETS"?
(*Not Employed, Educated, or in Training)
AND...
It's hot!

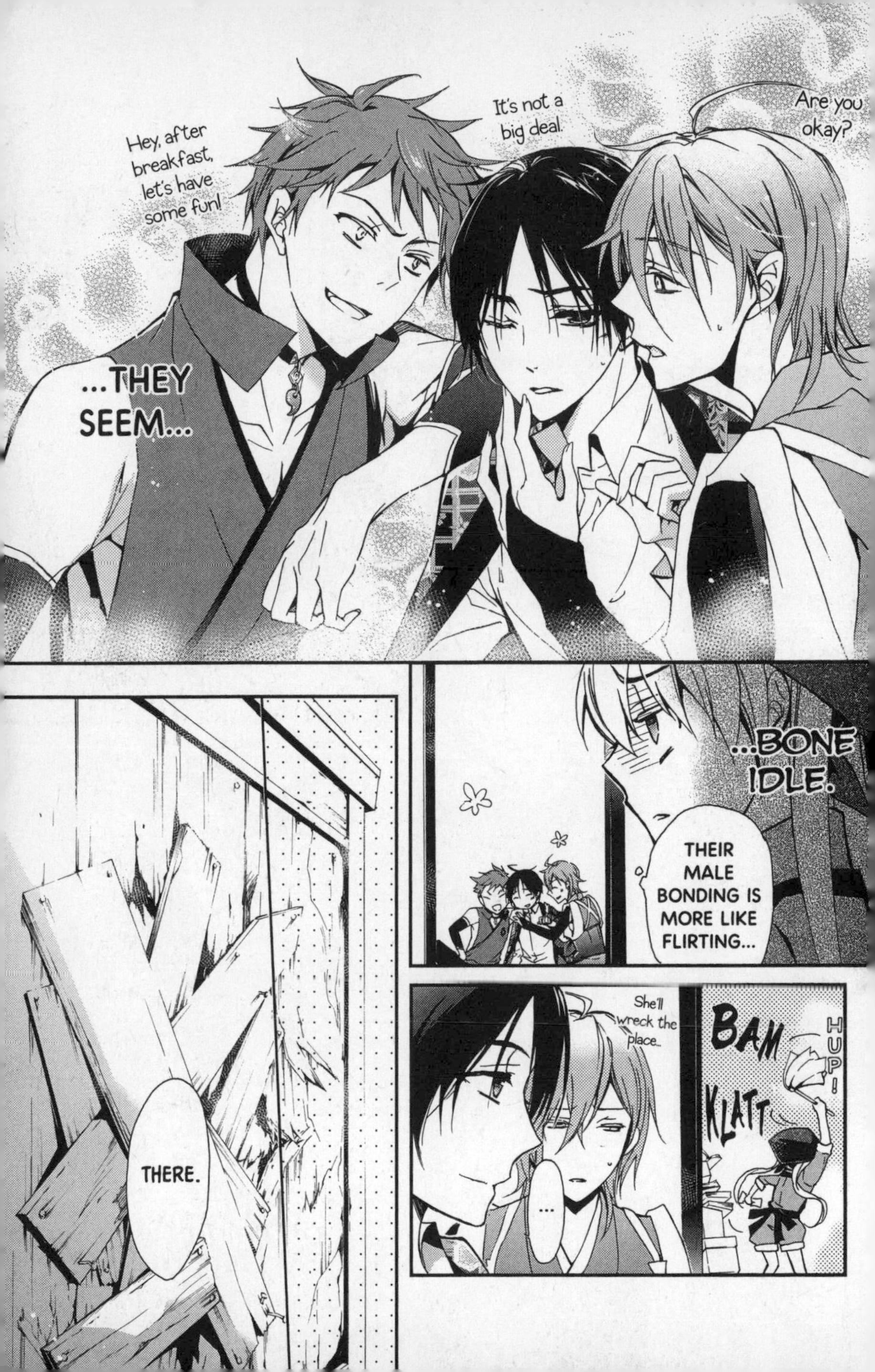
Are you okay?
It's not a big deal.
Hey, after breakfast, let's have some fun!
...THEY SEEM...
...BONE IDLE.
THEIR MALE BONDING IS MORE LIKE FLIRTING...
HUP!
BAM
She'll wreck the place..
KLATT
...
THERE.

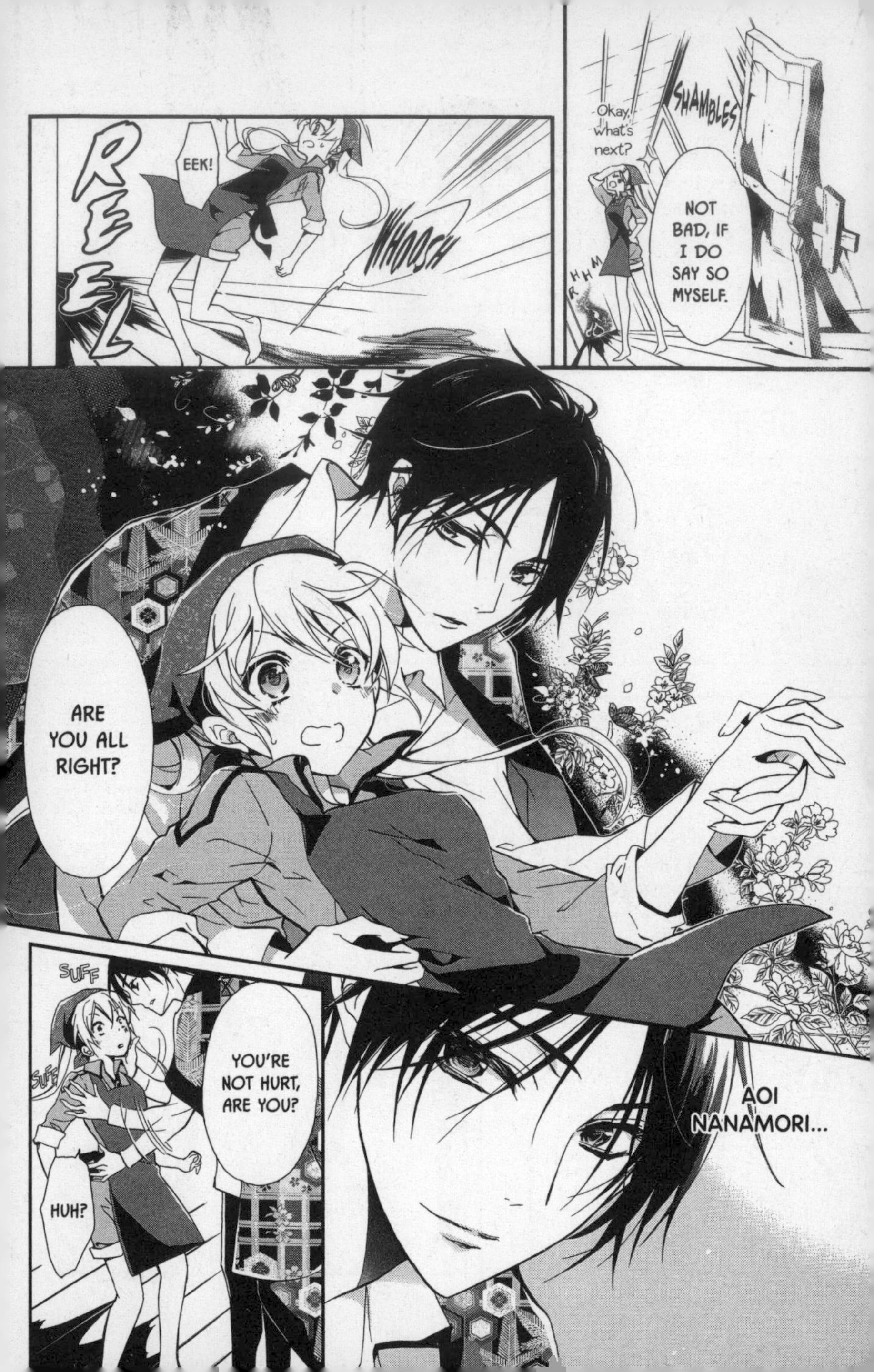
SHAMBLES
Okay, what's next?
NOT BAD, IF I DO SAY SO MYSELF.
EEK!
REEL
WHOOSH
ARE YOU ALL RIGHT?
AOI NANAMORI...
YOU'RE NOT HURT, ARE YOU?
SUFF
SUFF
HUH?

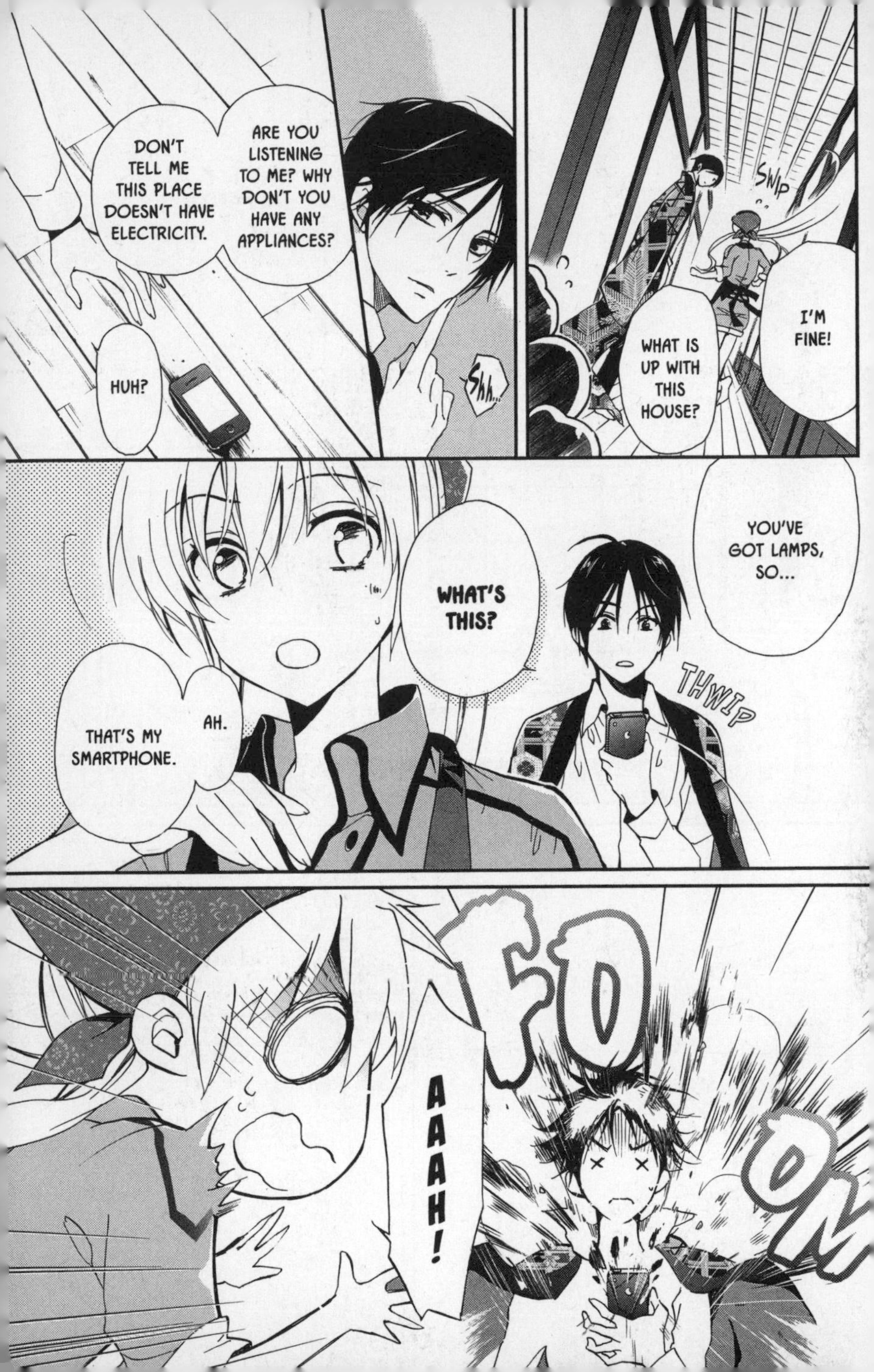
I'M FINE!
SWIP
WHAT IS UP WITH THIS HOUSE?
ARE YOU LISTENING TO ME? WHY DON'T YOU HAVE ANY APPLIANCES?
Shh...
DON'T TELL ME THIS PLACE DOESN'T HAVE ELECTRICITY.
HUH?
YOU'VE GOT LAMPS, SO...
THWIP
WHAT'S THIS?
AH.
THAT'S MY SMARTPHONE.
FOOM
AAAAH!

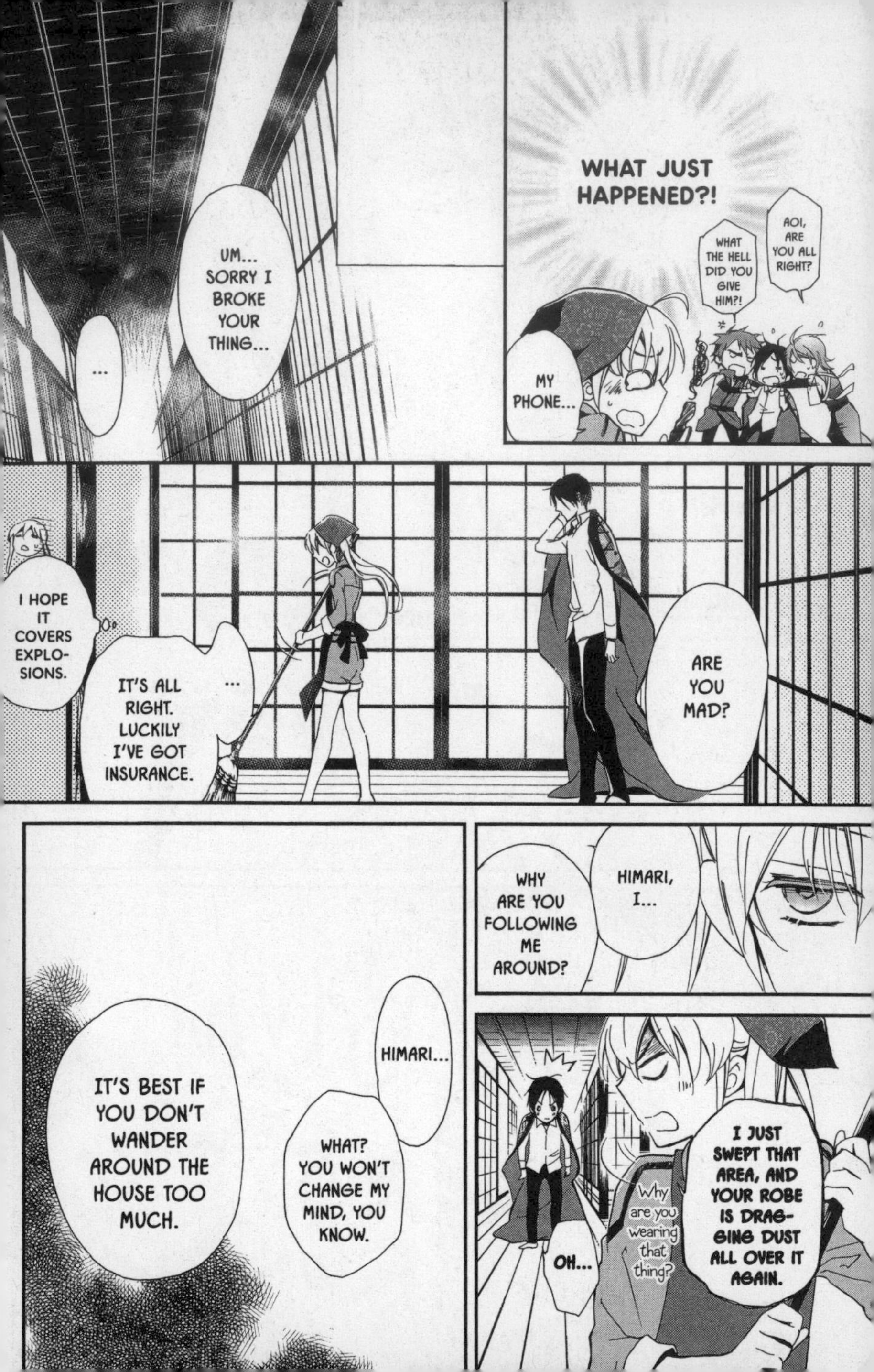
WHAT JUST HAPPENED?!
AOI, ARE YOU ALL RIGHT?
WHAT THE HELL DID YOU GIVE HIM?!
MY PHONE...
UM... SORRY I BROKE YOUR THING...
...
ARE YOU MAD?
...
IT'S ALL RIGHT. LUCKILY I'VE GOT INSURANCE.
I HOPE IT COVERS EXPLOSIONS.
HIMARI, I...
WHY ARE YOU FOLLOWING ME AROUND?
I JUST SWEPT THAT AREA, AND YOUR ROBE IS DRAG-GING DUST ALL OVER IT AGAIN.
Why are you wearing that thing?
OH...
HIMARI...
WHAT? YOU WON'T CHANGE MY MIND, YOU KNOW.
IT'S BEST IF YOU DON'T WANDER AROUND THE HOUSE TOO MUCH.

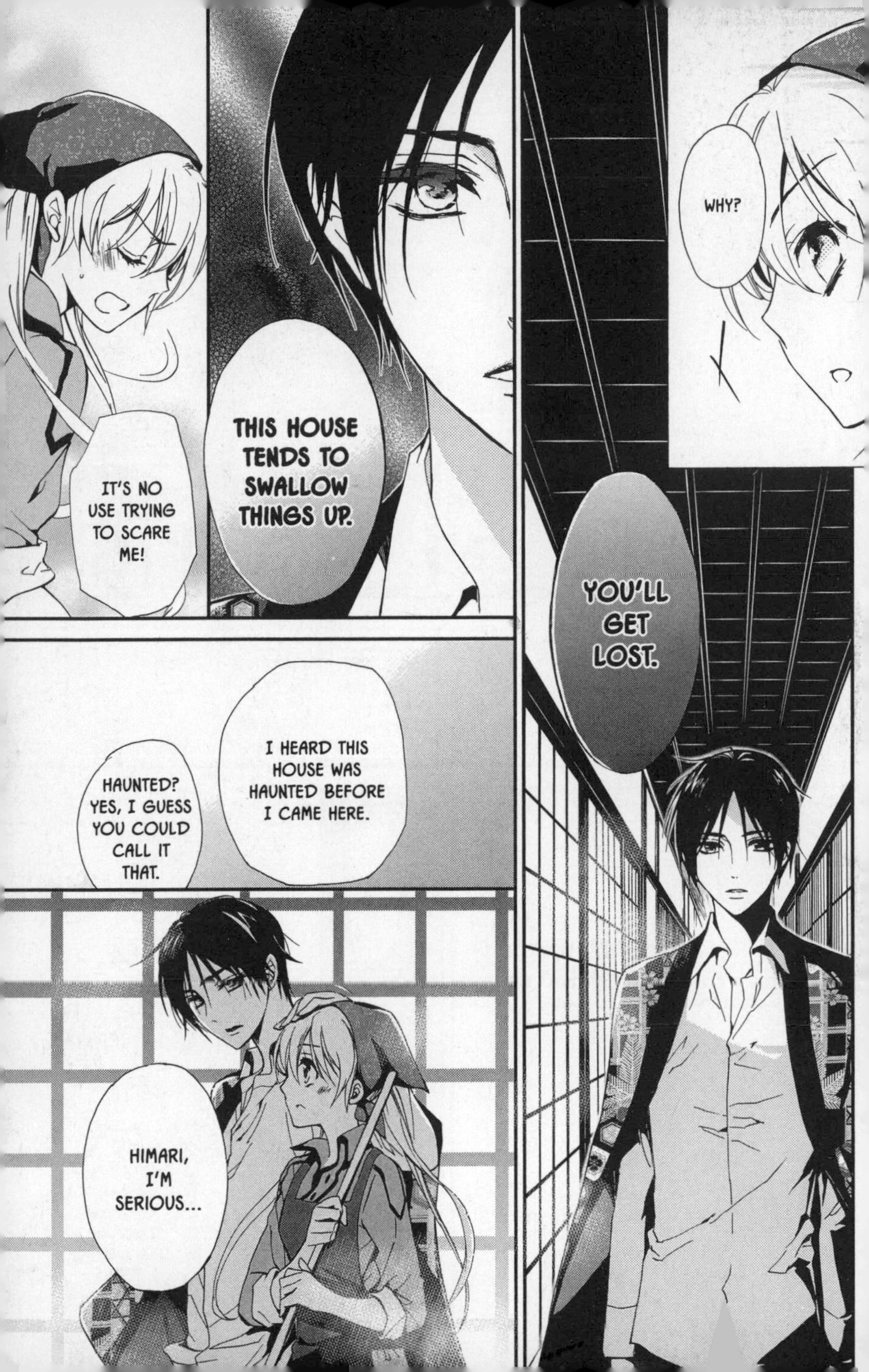
WHY?
YOU'LL GET LOST.
THIS HOUSE TENDS TO SWALLOW THINGS UP.
IT'S NO USE TRYING TO SCARE ME!
I HEARD THIS HOUSE WAS HAUNTED BEFORE I CAME HERE.
HAUNTED? YES, I GUESS YOU COULD CALL IT THAT.
HIMARI, I'M SERIOUS...

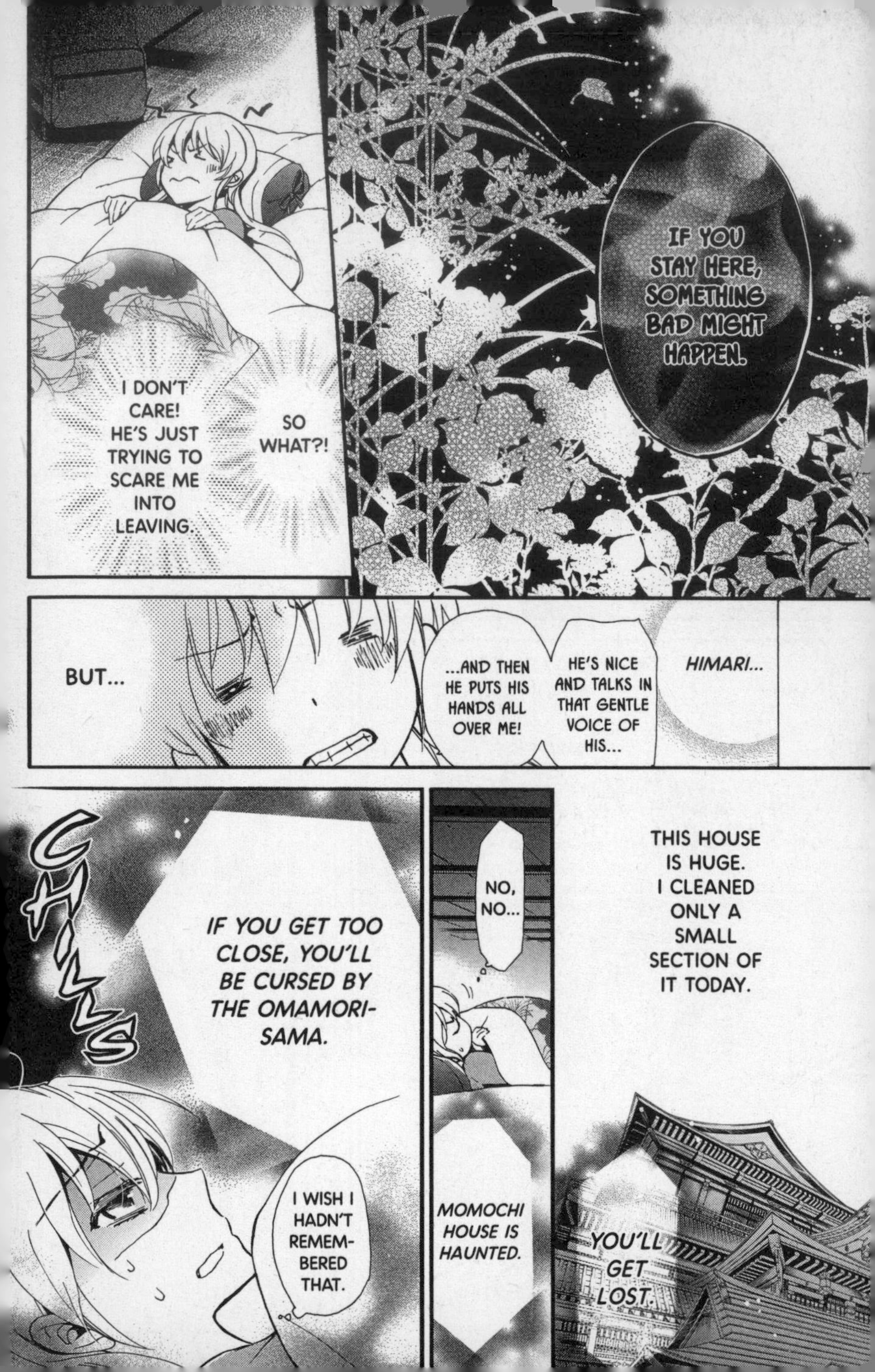
IF YOU STAY HERE, SOMETHING BAD MIGHT HAPPEN.
SO WHAT?!
I DON'T CARE! HE'S JUST TRYING TO SCARE ME INTO LEAVING.
HIMARI...
HE'S NICE AND TALKS IN THAT GENTLE VOICE OF HIS...
...AND THEN HE PUTS HIS HANDS ALL OVER ME!
BUT...
THIS HOUSE IS HUGE. I CLEANED ONLY A SMALL SECTION OF IT TODAY.
YOU'LL GET LOST.
NO, NO...
MOMOCHI HOUSE IS HAUNTED.
IF YOU GET TOO CLOSE, YOU'LL BE CURSED BY THE OMAMORI-SAMA.
CHILLS
I WISH I HADN'T REMEMBERED THAT.

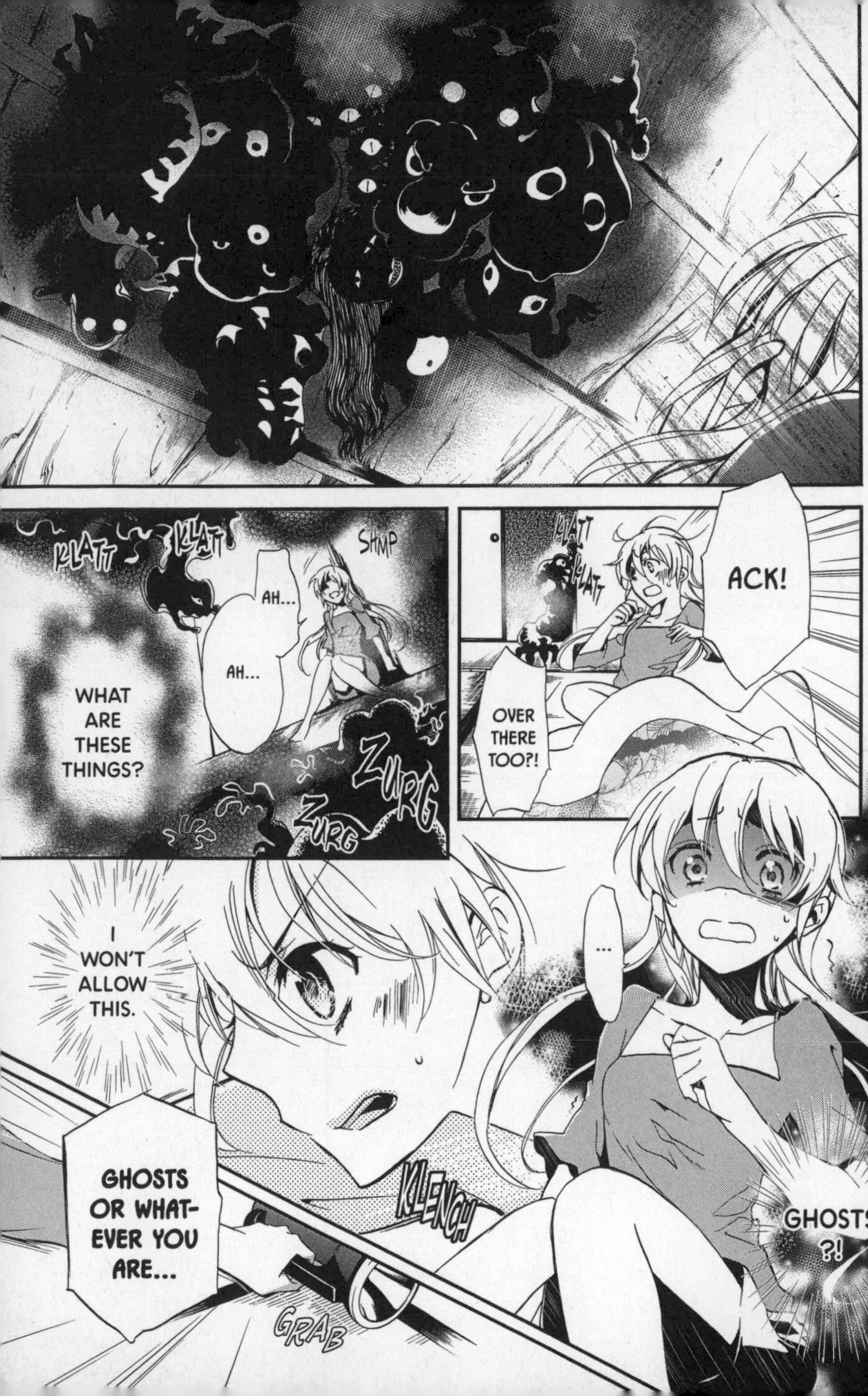
ACK!
KLATT KLATT
OVER THERE TOO?!
SHMP
AH...
AH...
KLATT KLATT
WHAT ARE THESE THINGS?
ZURG
ZURG
...
I WON'T ALLOW THIS.
KLENCH
GHOSTS ?!
GHOSTS OR WHAT-EVER YOU ARE...
GRAB

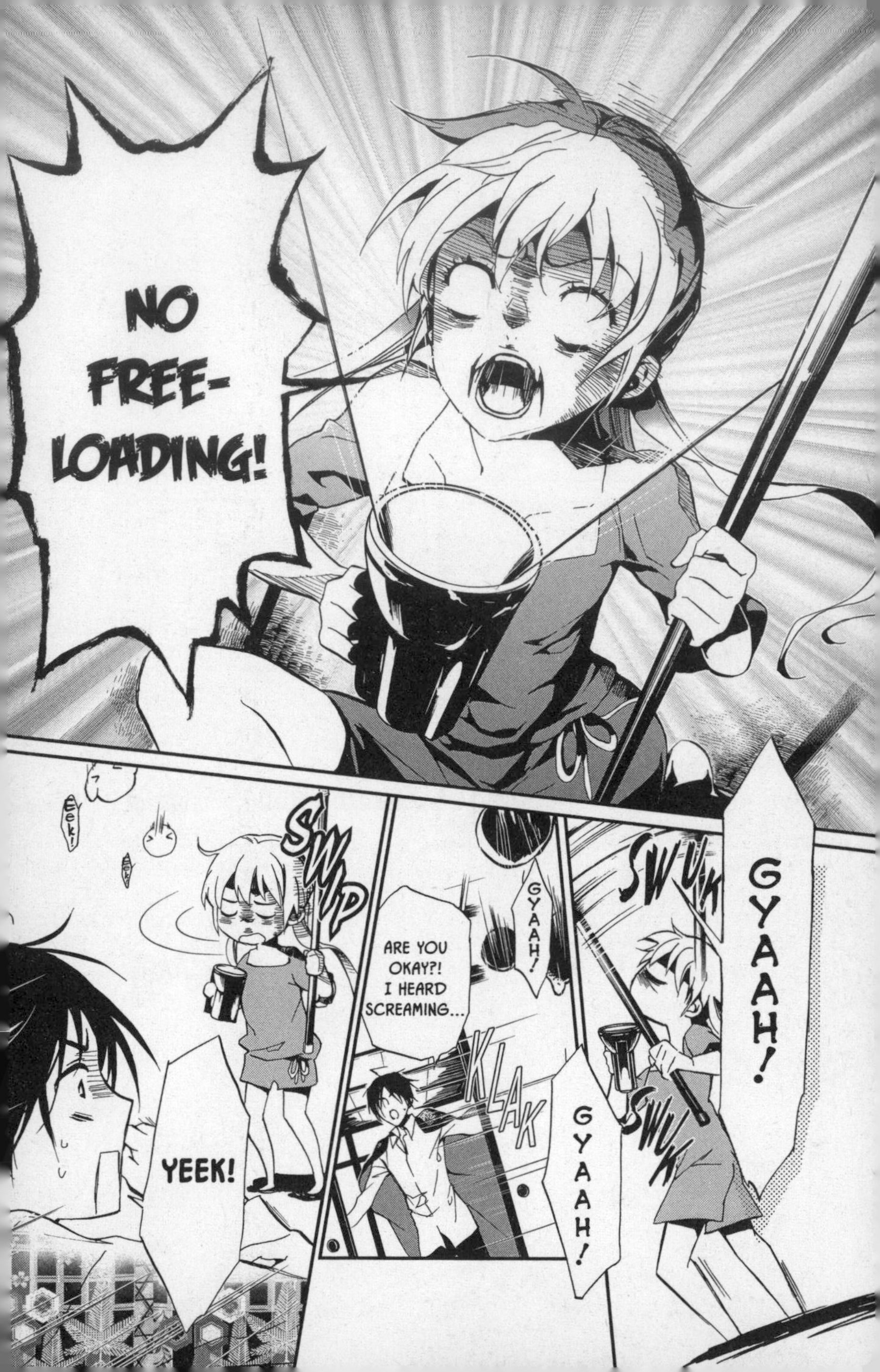
NO FREE-LOADING!
GYAAH!
SWUK
GYAAH!
SWUK
GYAAH!
ARE YOU OKAY?! I HEARD SCREAMING...
KLAK
SWIP
Eek!
Eek!
YEEK!

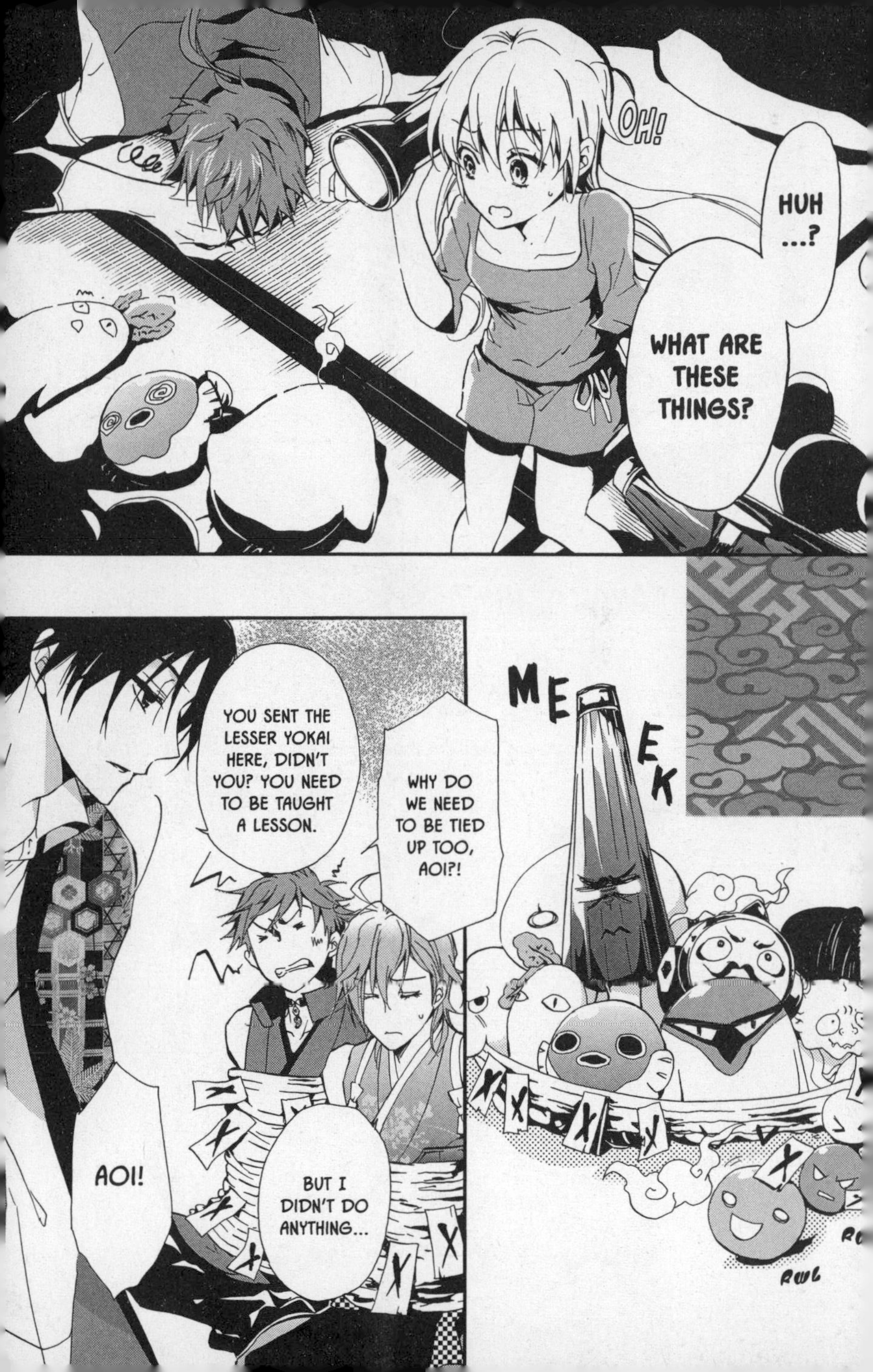
OH!
HUH ...?
WHAT ARE THESE THINGS?
MEEEK
YOU SENT THE LESSER YOKAI HERE, DIDN'T YOU? YOU NEED TO BE TAUGHT A LESSON.
WHY DO WE NEED TO BE TIED UP TOO, AOI?!
AOI!
BUT I DIDN'T DO ANYTHING...

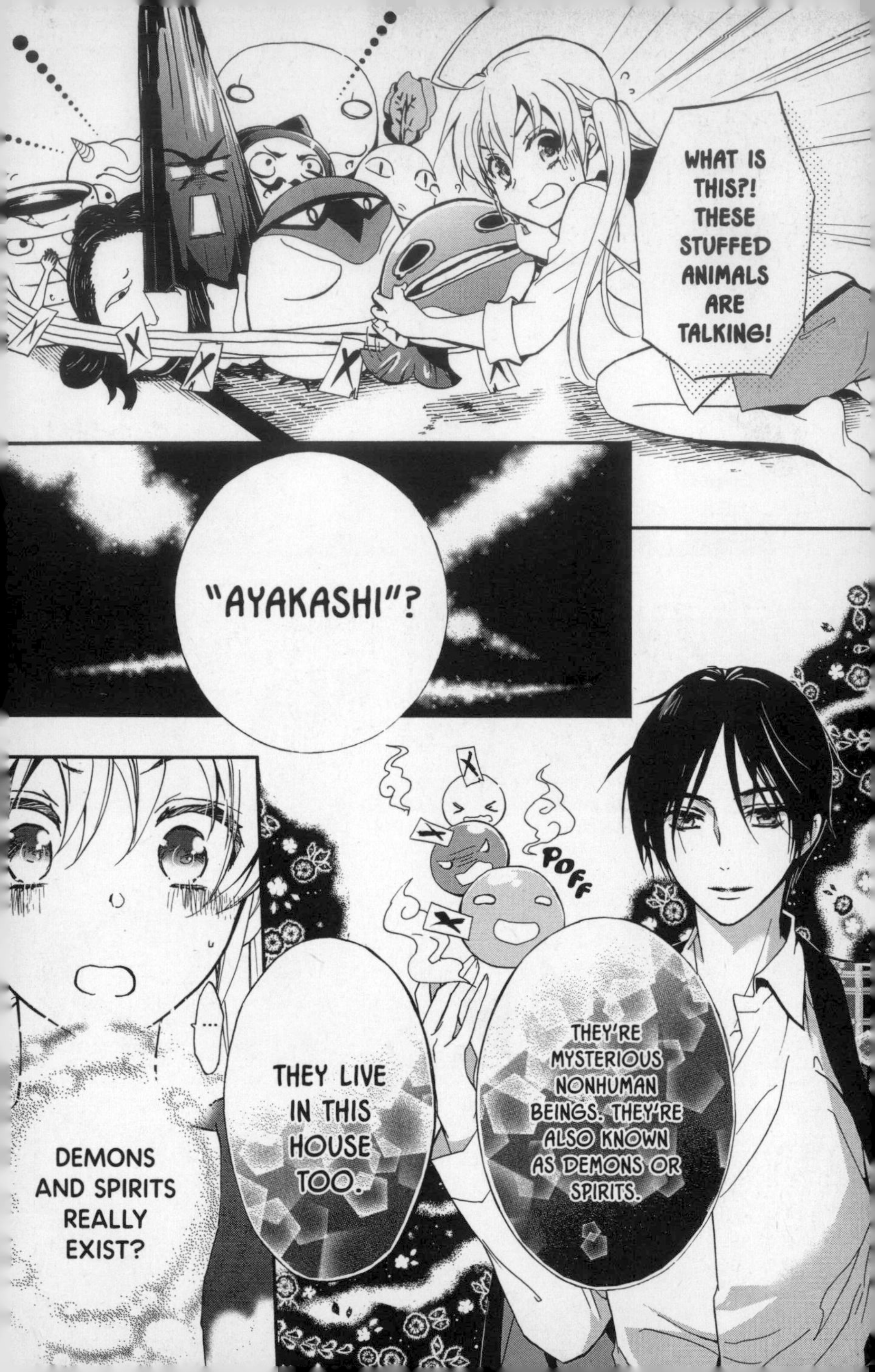
WHAT IS THIS?! THESE STUFFED ANIMALS ARE TALKING!
"AYAKASHI"?
THEY'RE MYSTERIOUS NONHUMAN BEINGS. THEY'RE ALSO KNOWN AS DEMONS OR SPIRITS.
POFF
THEY LIVE IN THIS HOUSE TOO.
...
DEMONS AND SPIRITS REALLY EXIST?

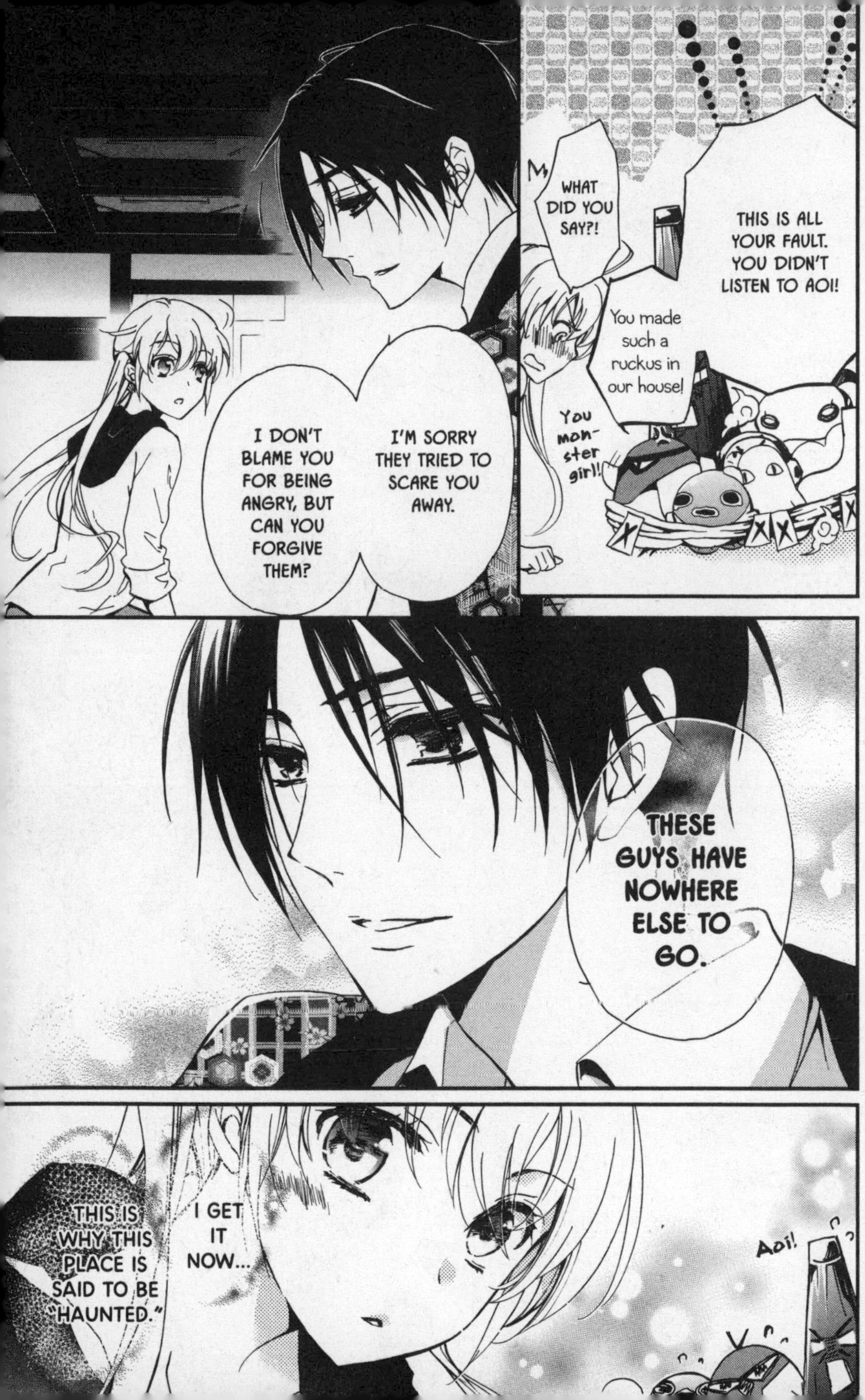
THIS IS ALL YOUR FAULT. YOU DIDN'T LISTEN TO AOI!
You made such a ruckus in our house!
You monster girl!!
M
WHAT DID YOU SAY?!
I'M SORRY THEY TRIED TO SCARE YOU AWAY.
I DON'T BLAME YOU FOR BEING ANGRY, BUT CAN YOU FORGIVE THEM?
THESE GUYS HAVE NOWHERE ELSE TO GO.
Aoi!
I GET IT NOW...
THIS IS WHY THIS PLACE IS SAID TO BE "HAUNTED."

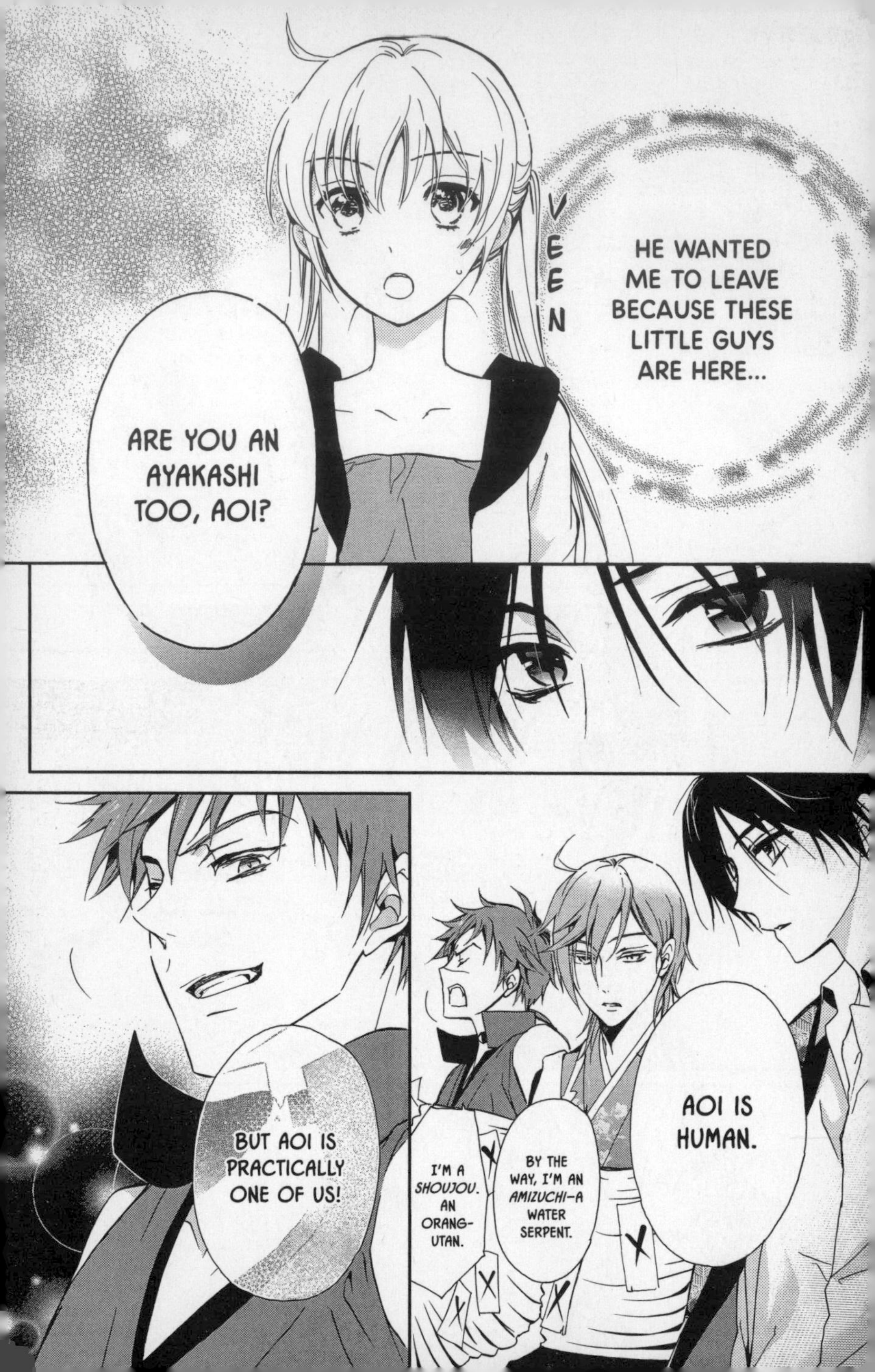
HE WANTED ME TO LEAVE BECAUSE THESE LITTLE GUYS ARE HERE...
VEEN
ARE YOU AN AYAKASHI TOO, AOI?
AOI IS HUMAN.
BY THE WAY, I'M AN *AMIZUCHI*—A WATER SERPENT.
I'M A *SHOUJOU*. AN ORANG-UTAN.
BUT AOI IS PRACTICALLY ONE OF US!

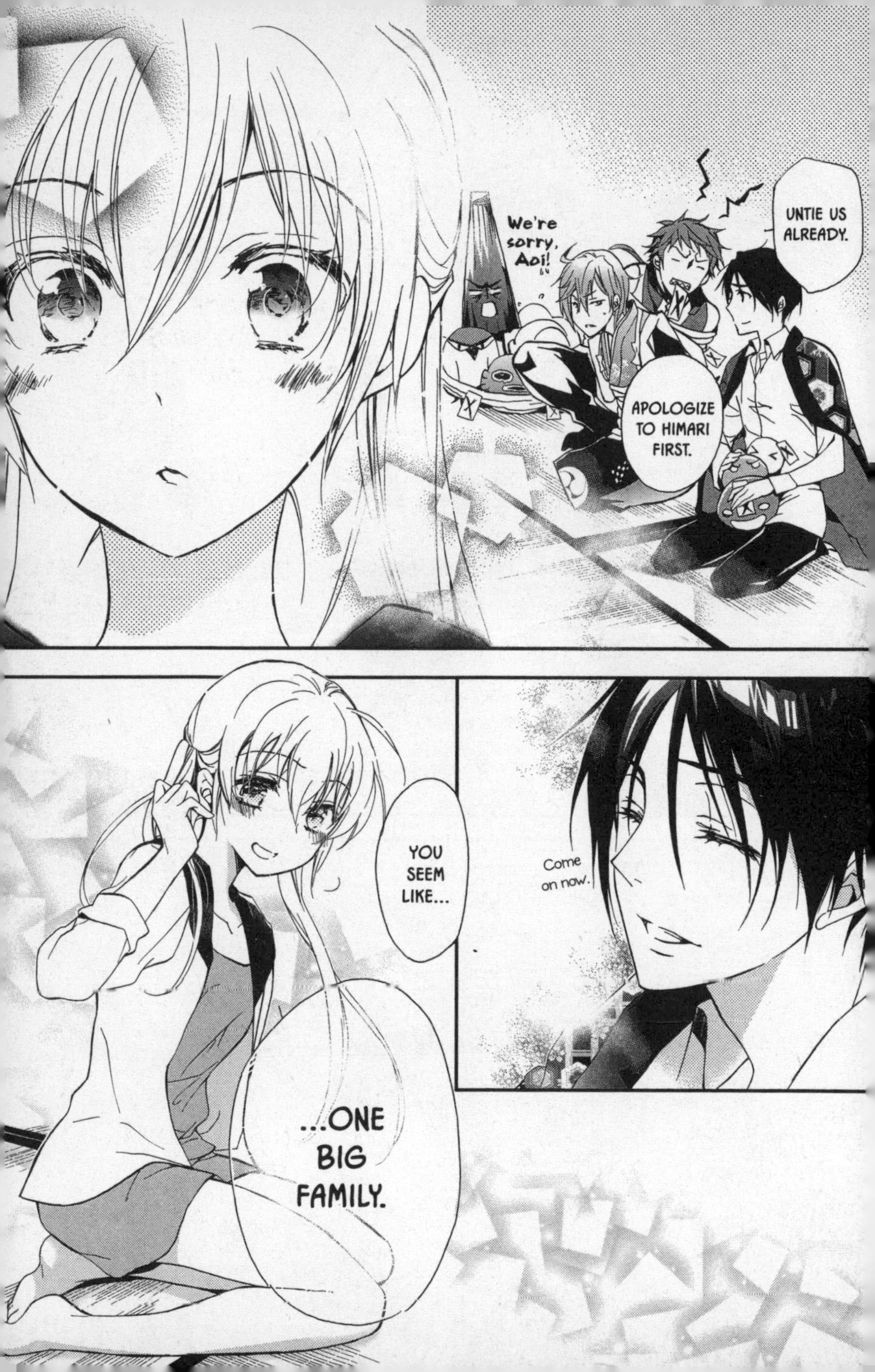
UNTIE US ALREADY.
We're sorry, Aoi!
APOLOGIZE TO HIMARI FIRST.
Come on now.
YOU SEEM LIKE...
...ONE BIG FAMILY.

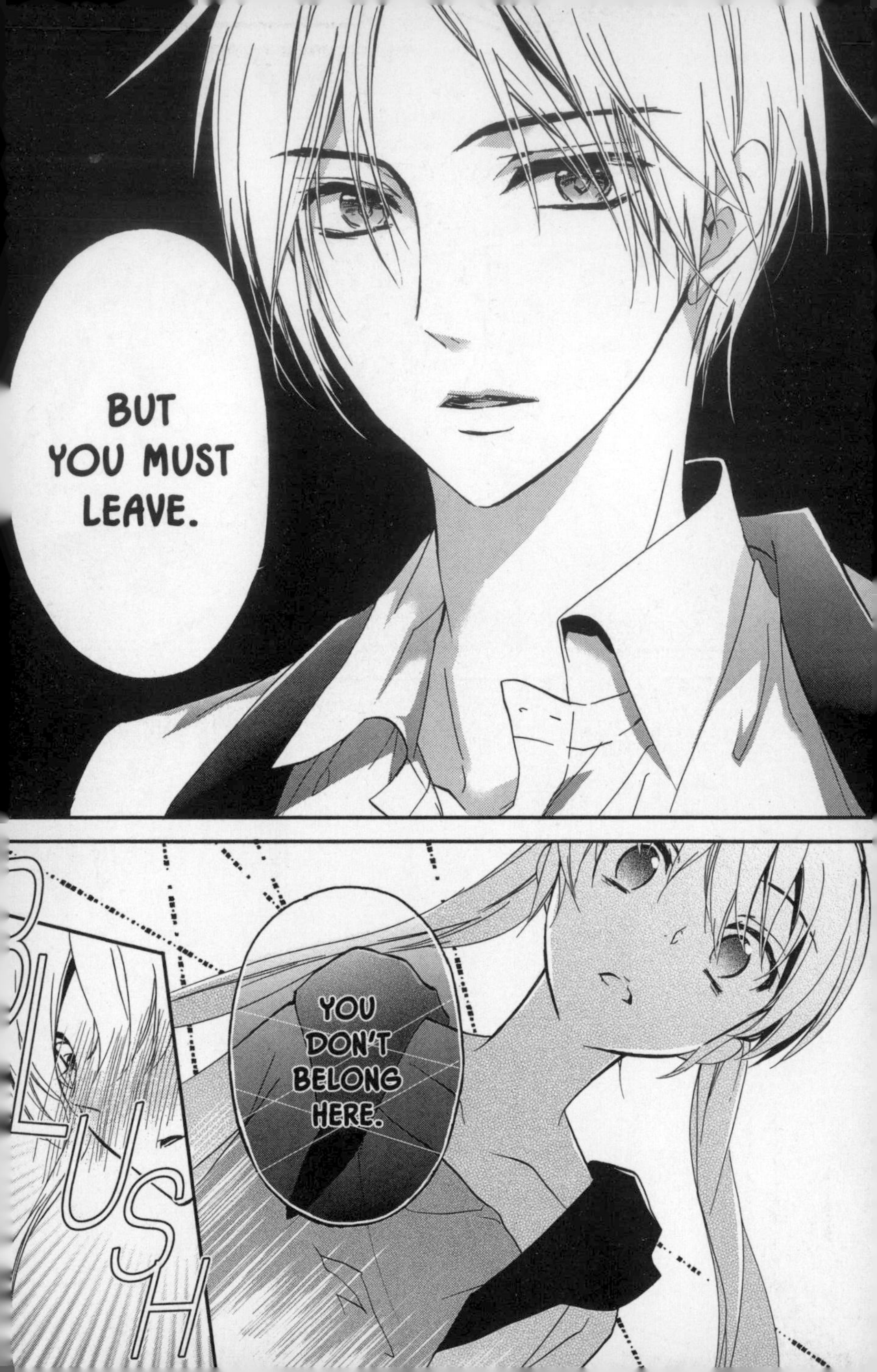
BUT YOU MUST LEAVE.
YOU DON'T BELONG HERE.
BLUSH

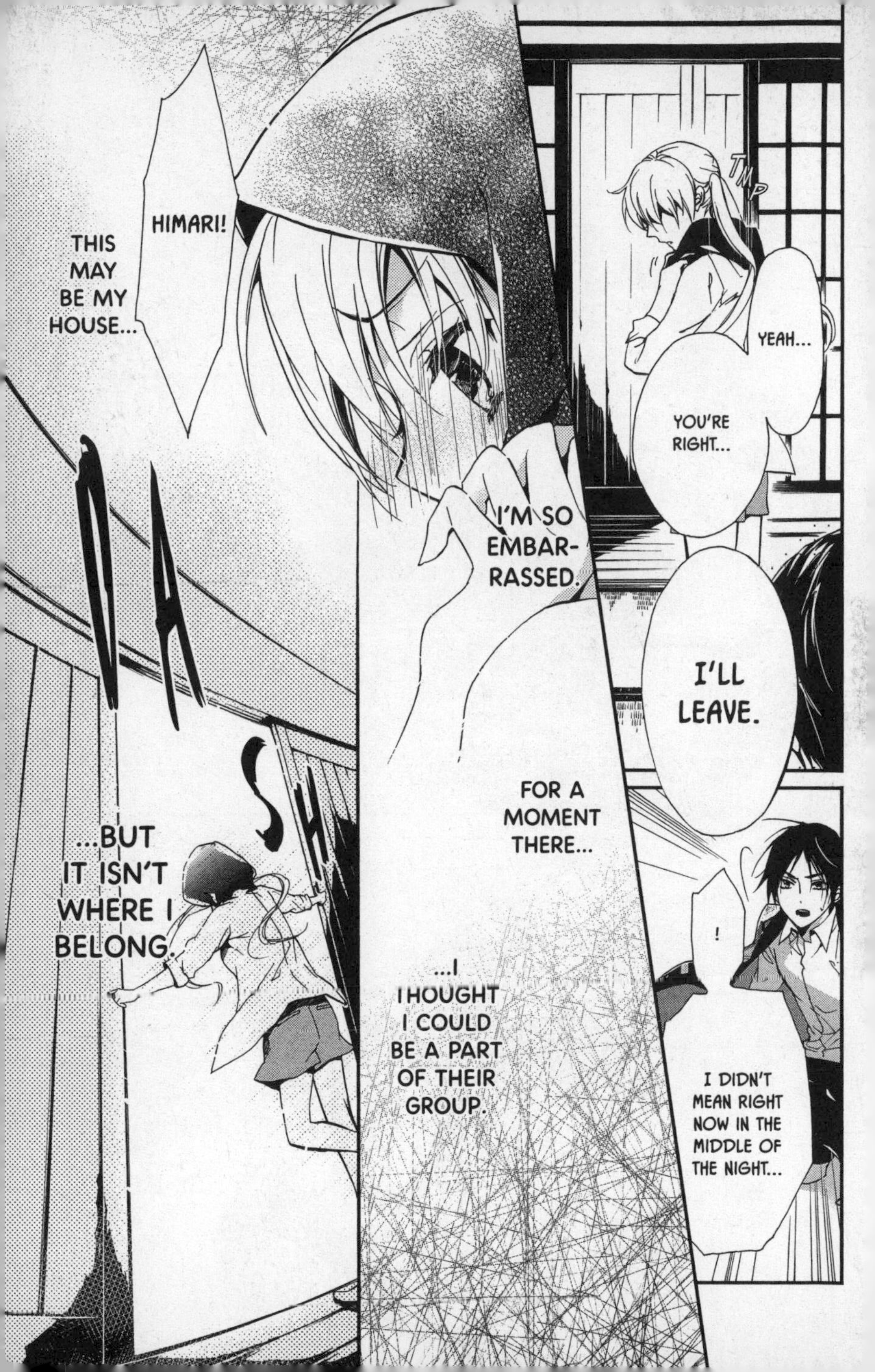
TMP
YEAH...
YOU'RE RIGHT...
I'LL LEAVE.
!
I DIDN'T MEAN RIGHT NOW IN THE MIDDLE OF THE NIGHT...
I'M SO EMBARRASSED.
FOR A MOMENT THERE...
...I THOUGHT I COULD BE A PART OF THEIR GROUP.
HIMARI!
THIS MAY BE MY HOUSE...
DASH
...BUT IT ISN'T WHERE I BELONG.

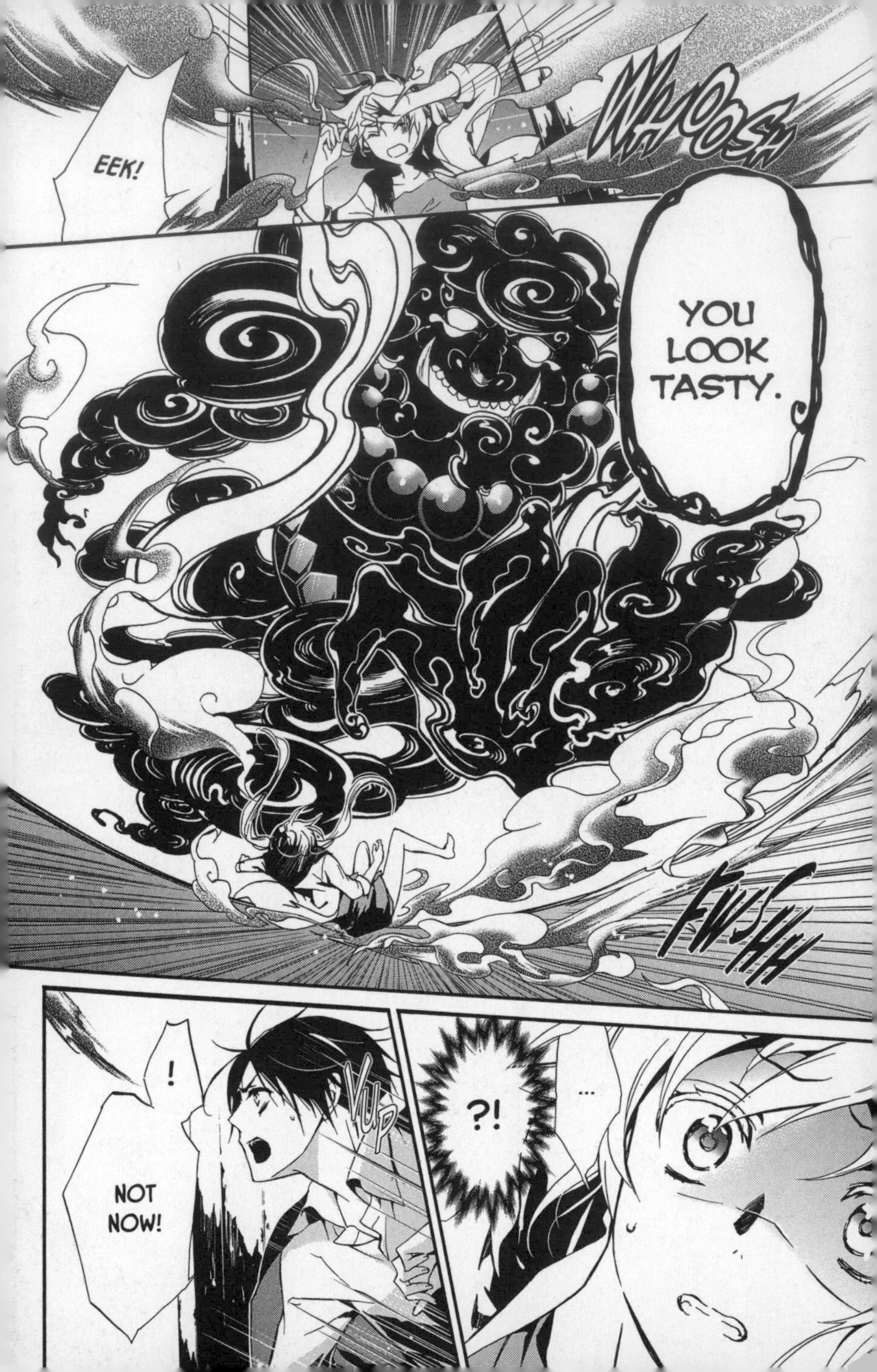
WHOOSH
EEK!
YOU LOOK TASTY.
FWSHH
...
?!
!
VUP
NOT NOW!

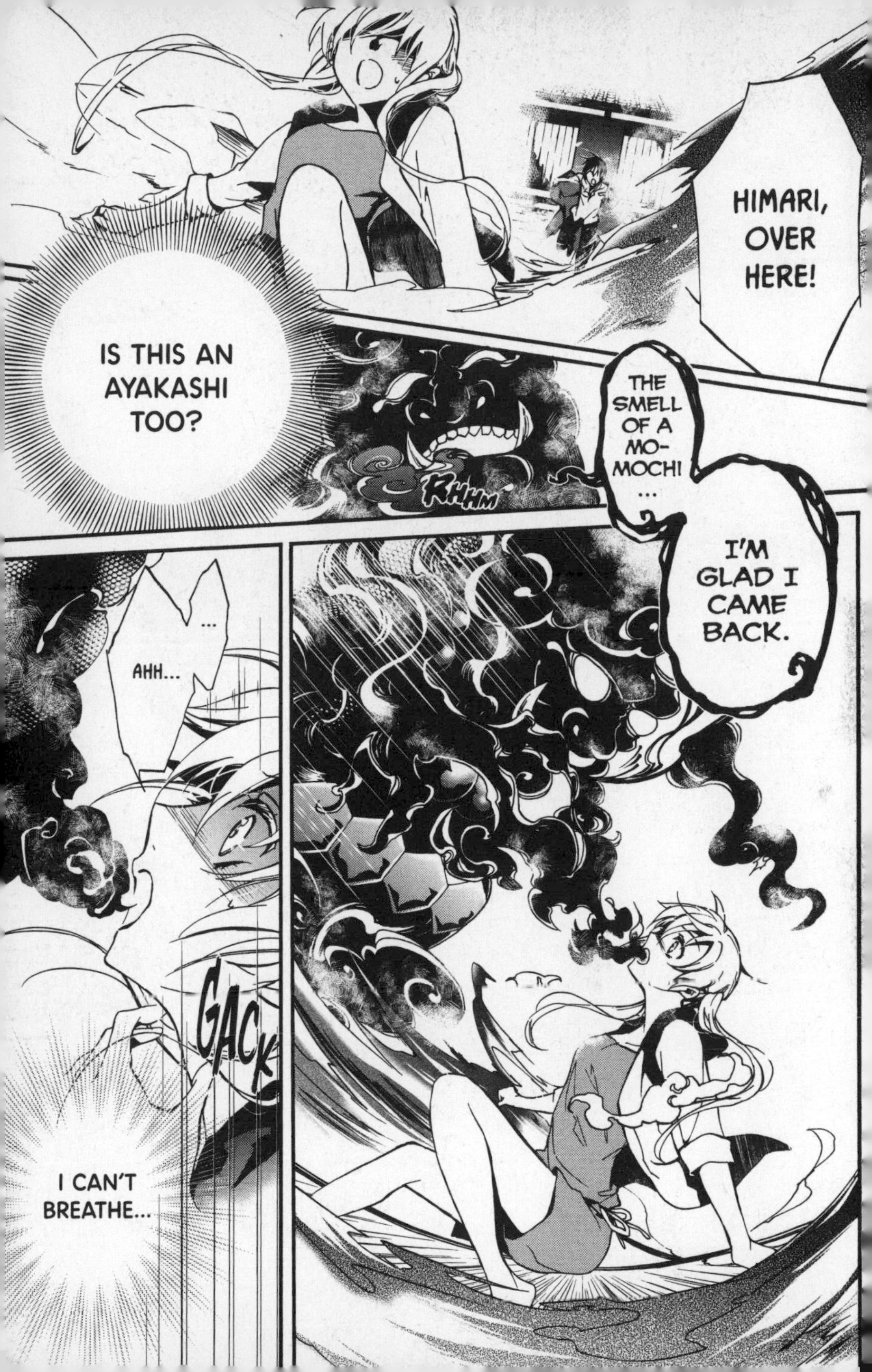
HIMARI, OVER HERE!
THE SMELL OF A MO-MOCHI ...
I'M GLAD I CAME BACK.
RHHM
IS THIS AN AYAKASHI TOO?
... AHH...
GACK
I CAN'T BREATHE...

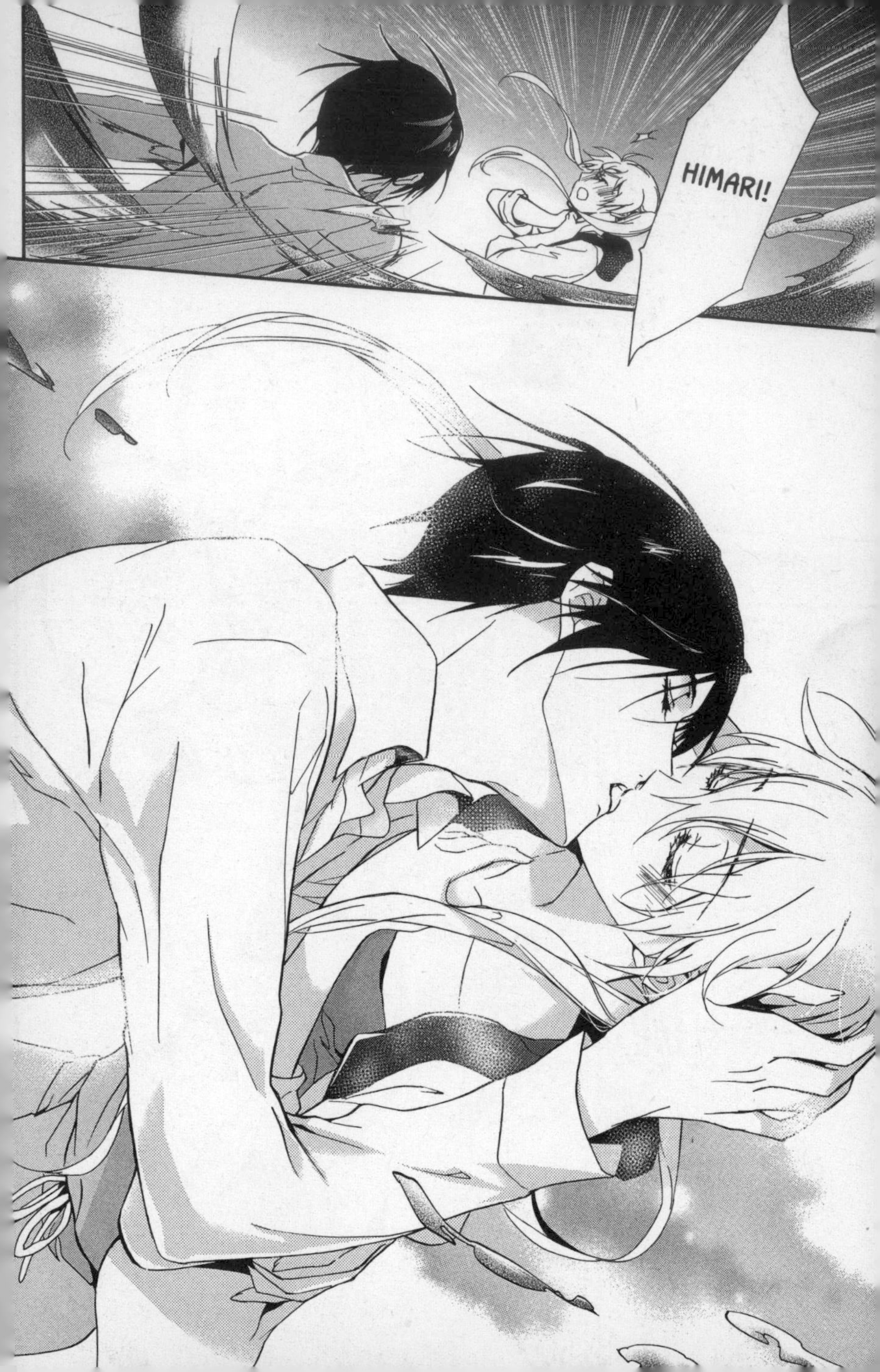
HIMARI!

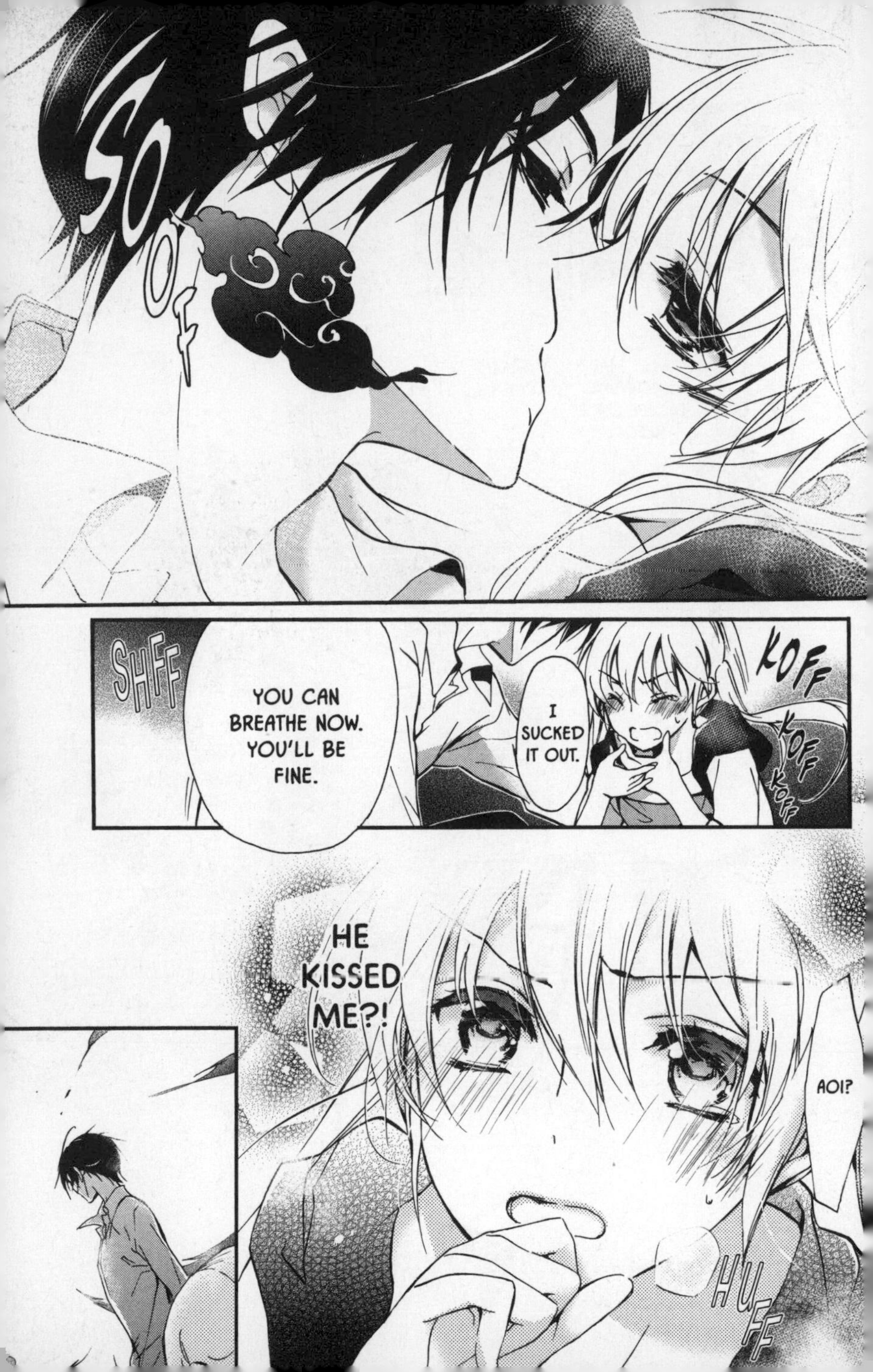
SOOF
KOFF KOFF KOFF
I SUCKED IT OUT.
YOU CAN BREATHE NOW. YOU'LL BE FINE.
SHFF
AOI?
HE KISSED ME?!
HUFF

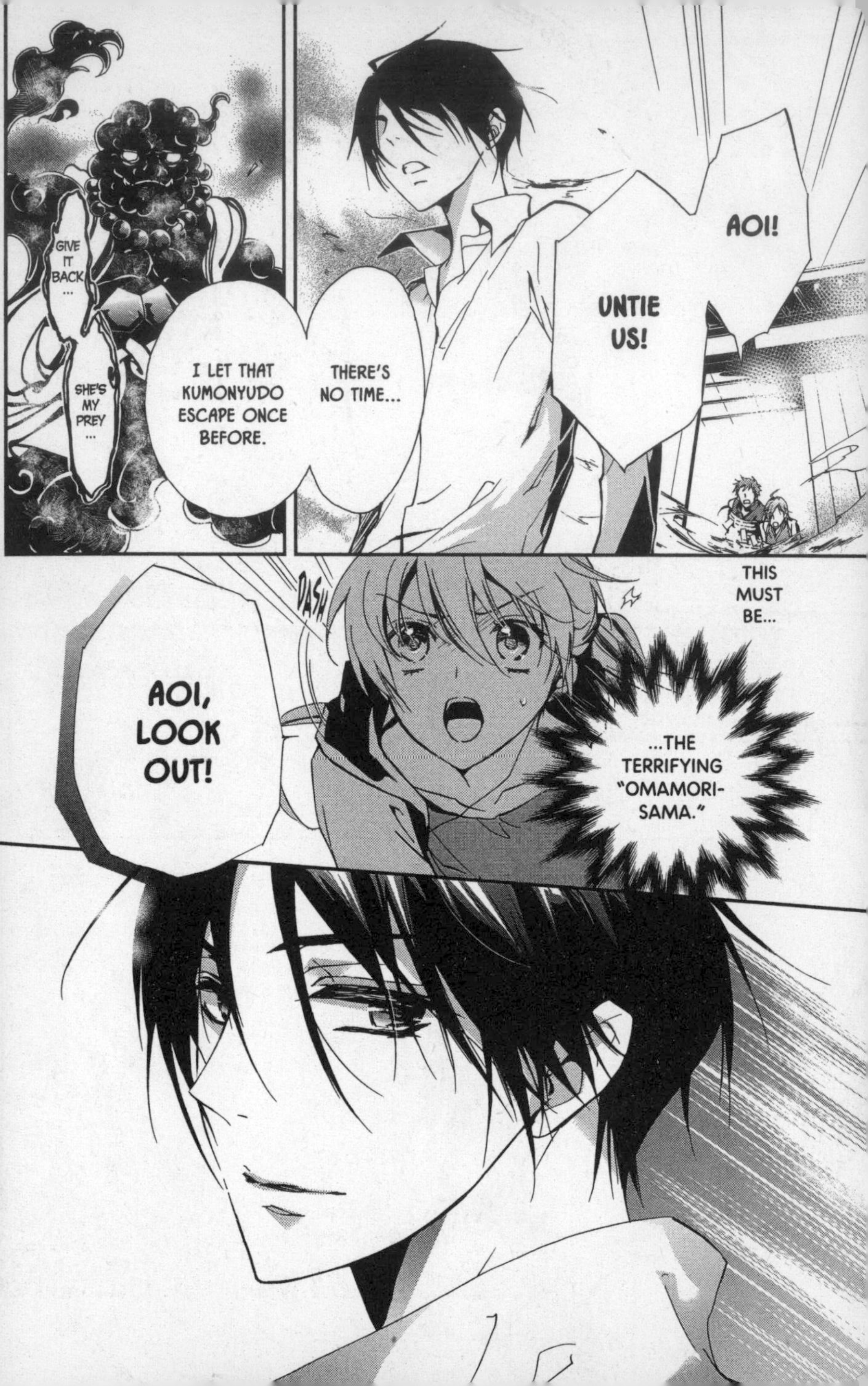
AOI!
UNTIE US!
THERE'S NO TIME...
I LET THAT KUMONYUDO ESCAPE ONCE BEFORE.
GIVE IT BACK...
SHE'S MY PREY...
THIS MUST BE...
DASH
...THE TERRIFYING "OMAMORI-SAMA."
AOI, LOOK OUT!

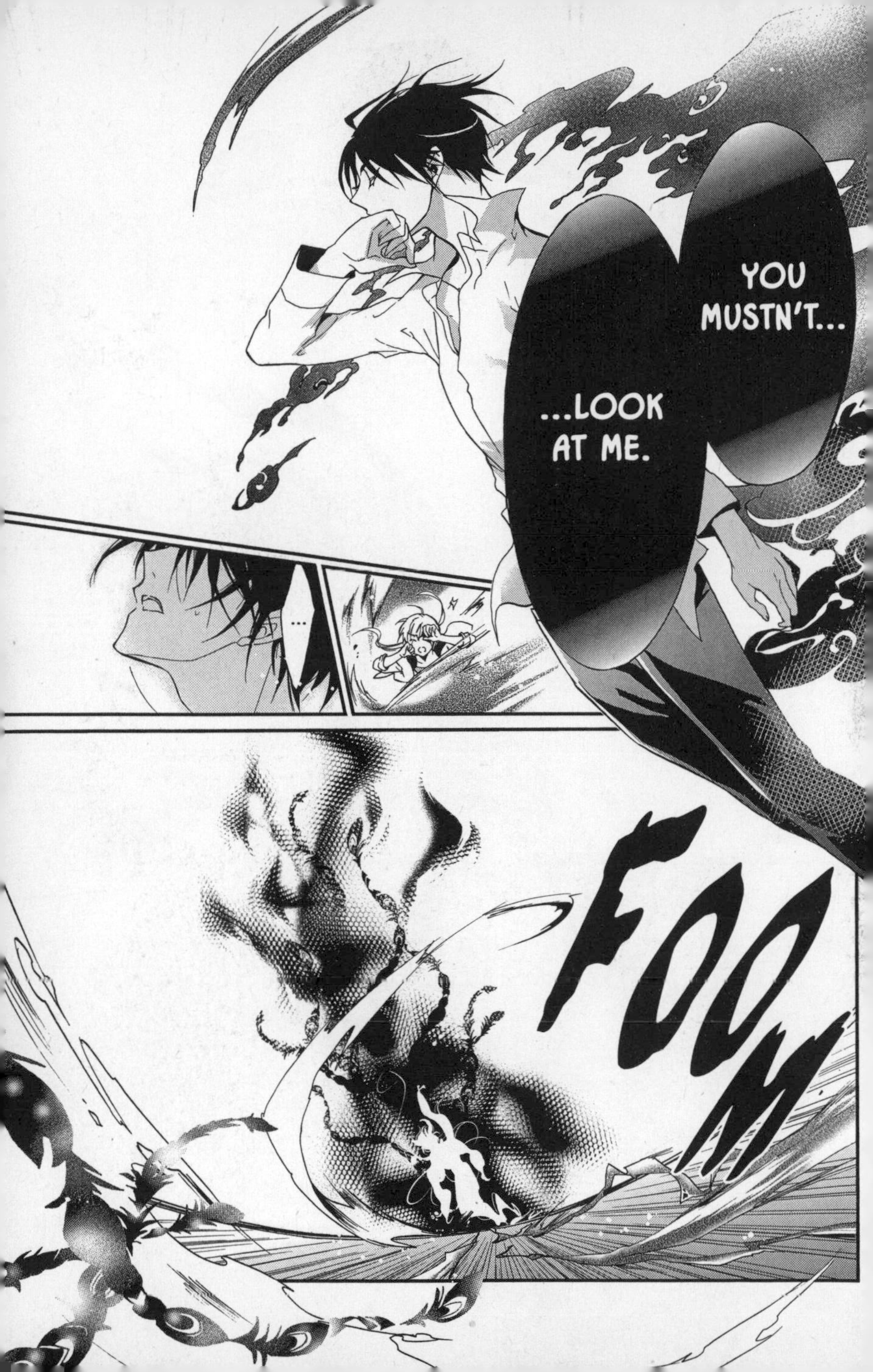
YOU MUSTN'T...
...LOOK AT ME.
...
FOOM

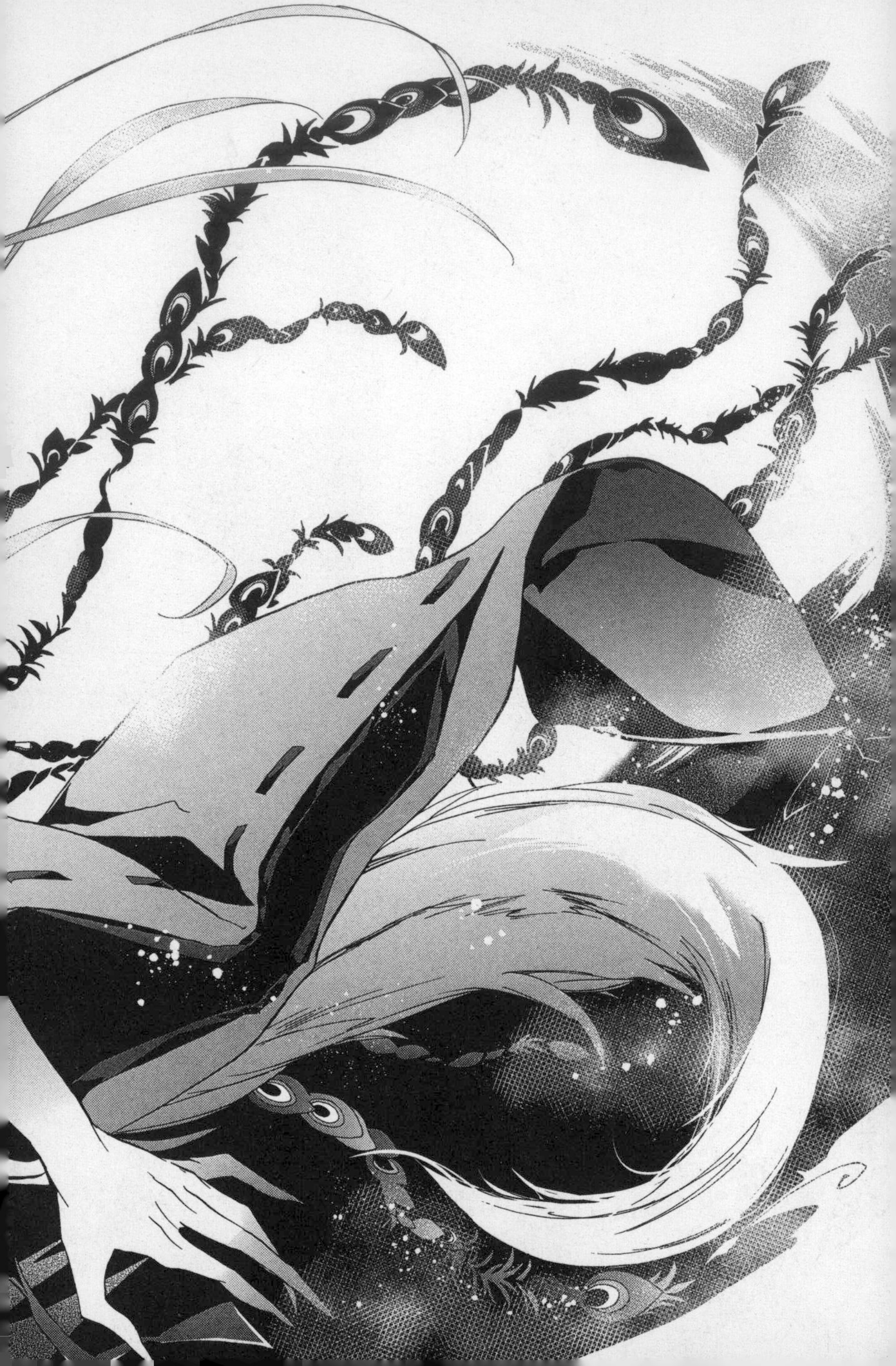

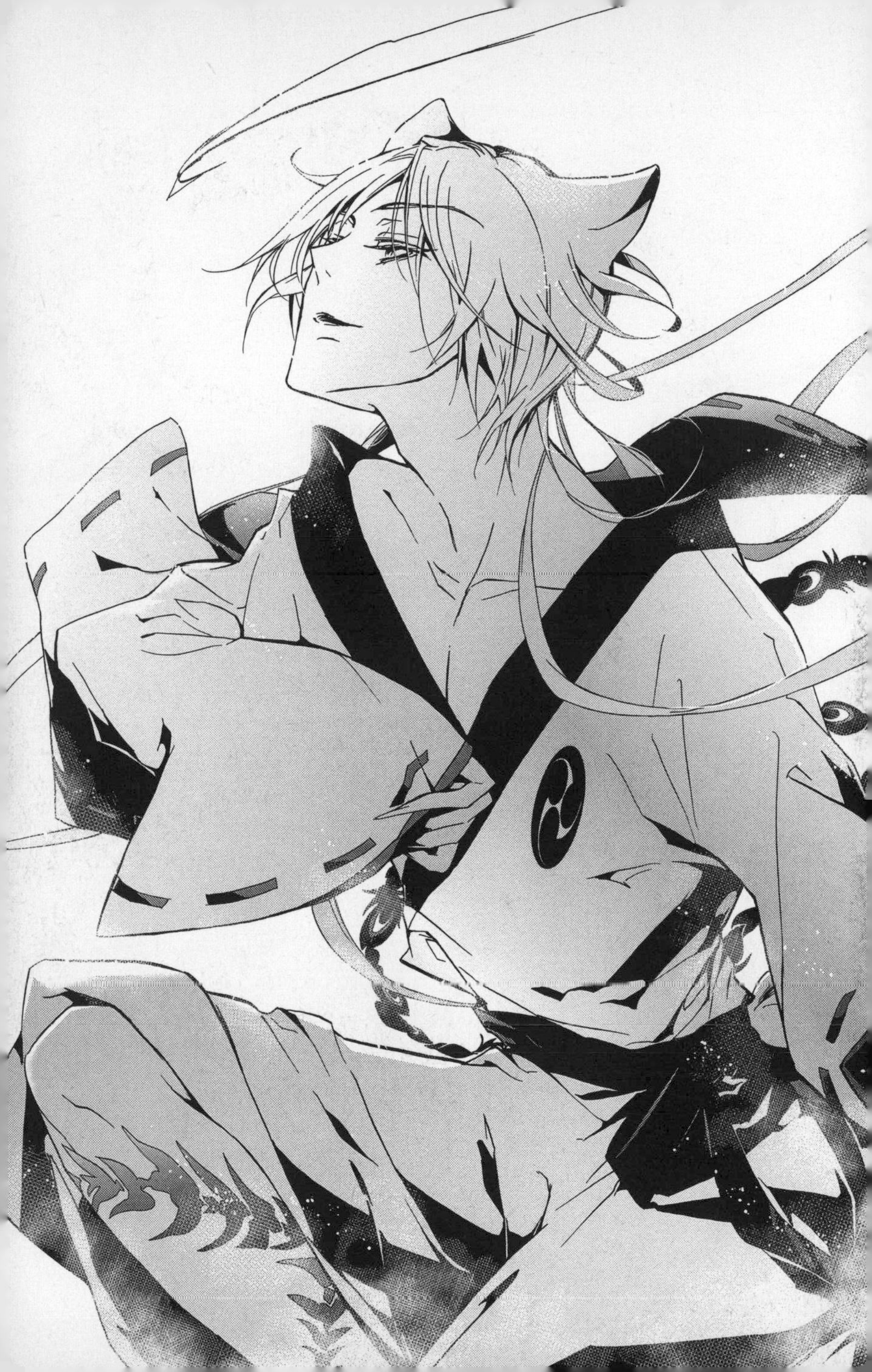

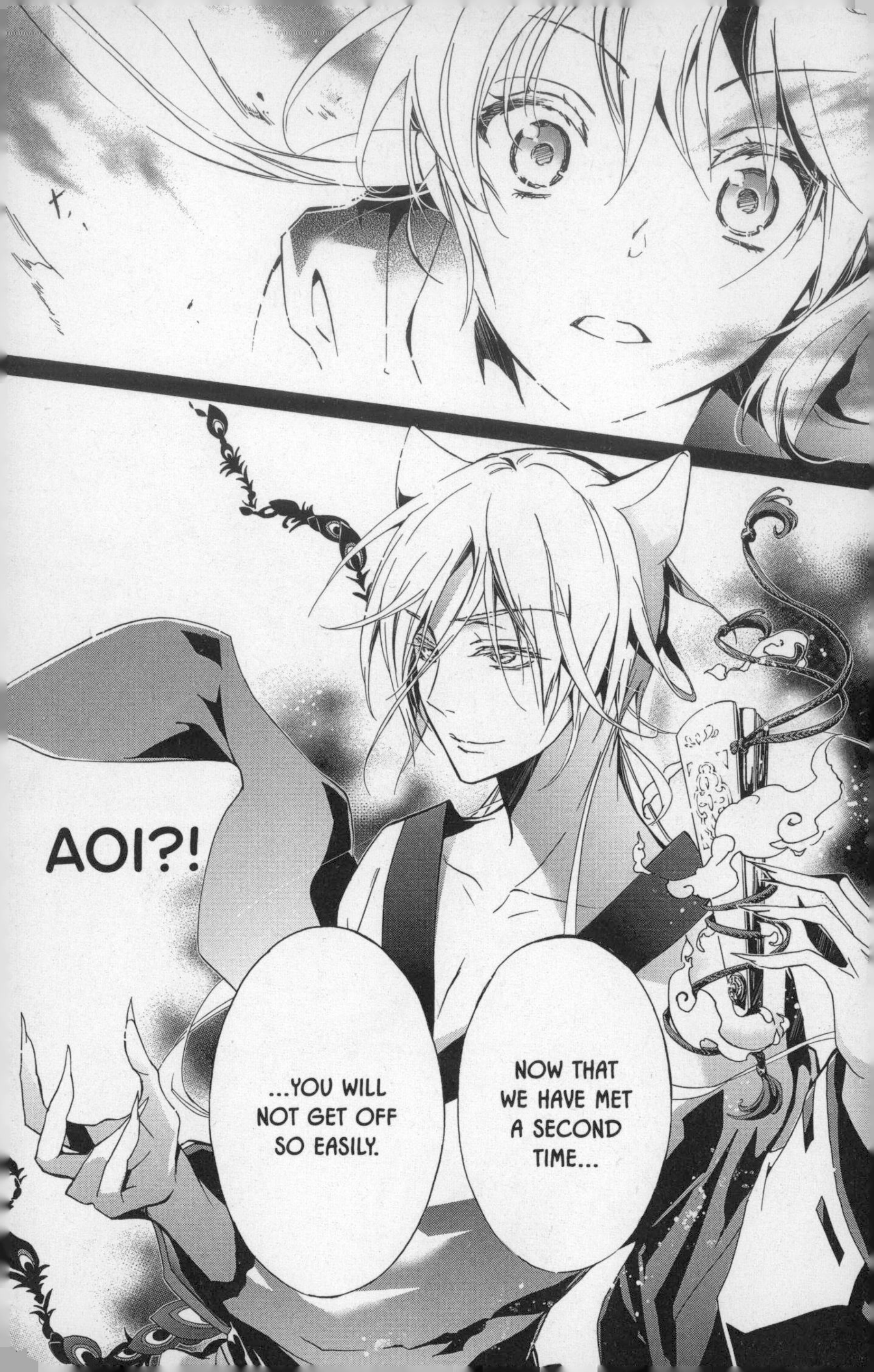
NOW THAT WE HAVE MET A SECOND TIME...
...YOU WILL NOT GET OFF SO EASILY.
AOI?!

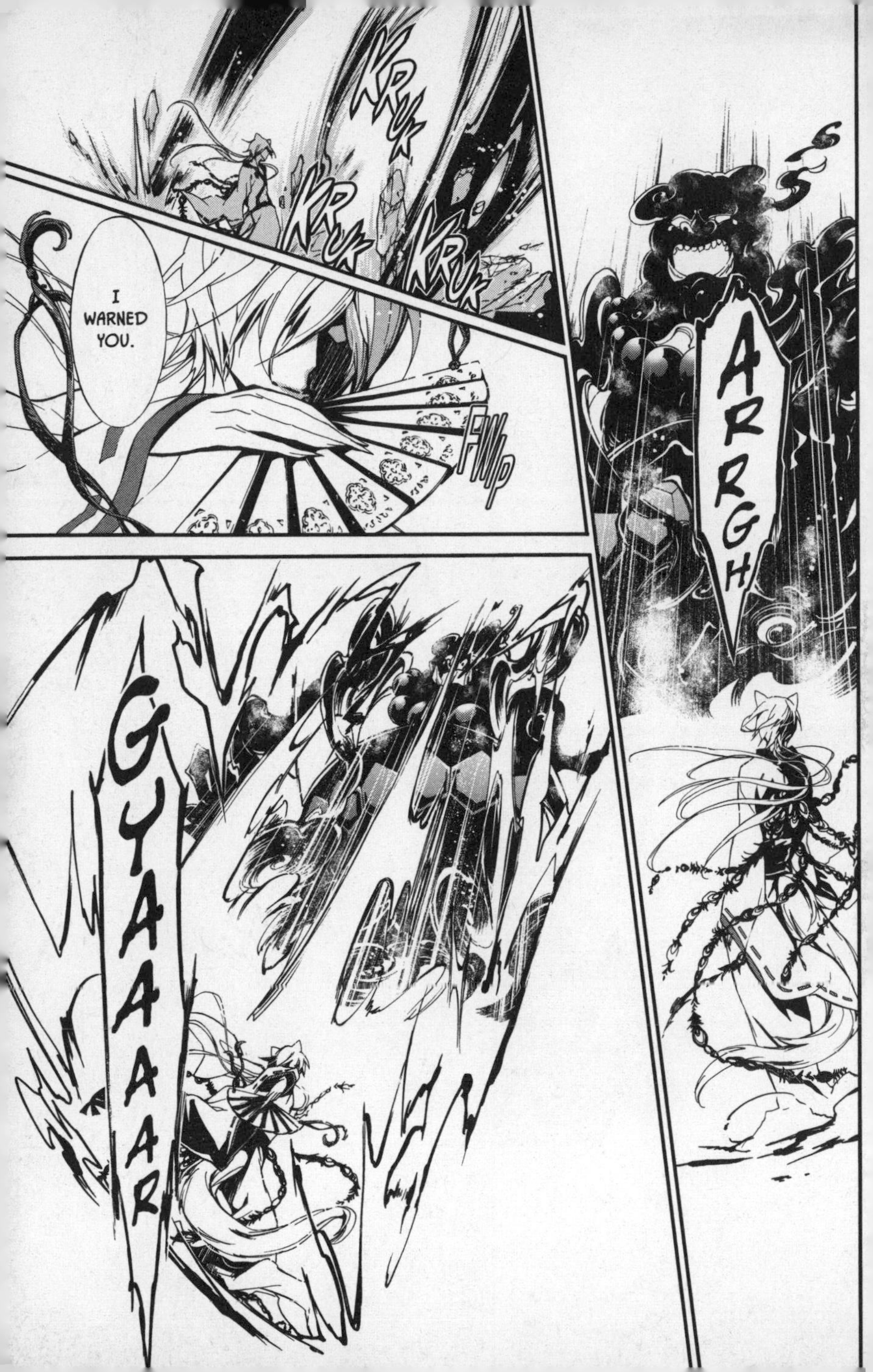
ARRGH
KRUK
KRUK
KRUK
I WARNED YOU.
FWIP
GYAAAAAR

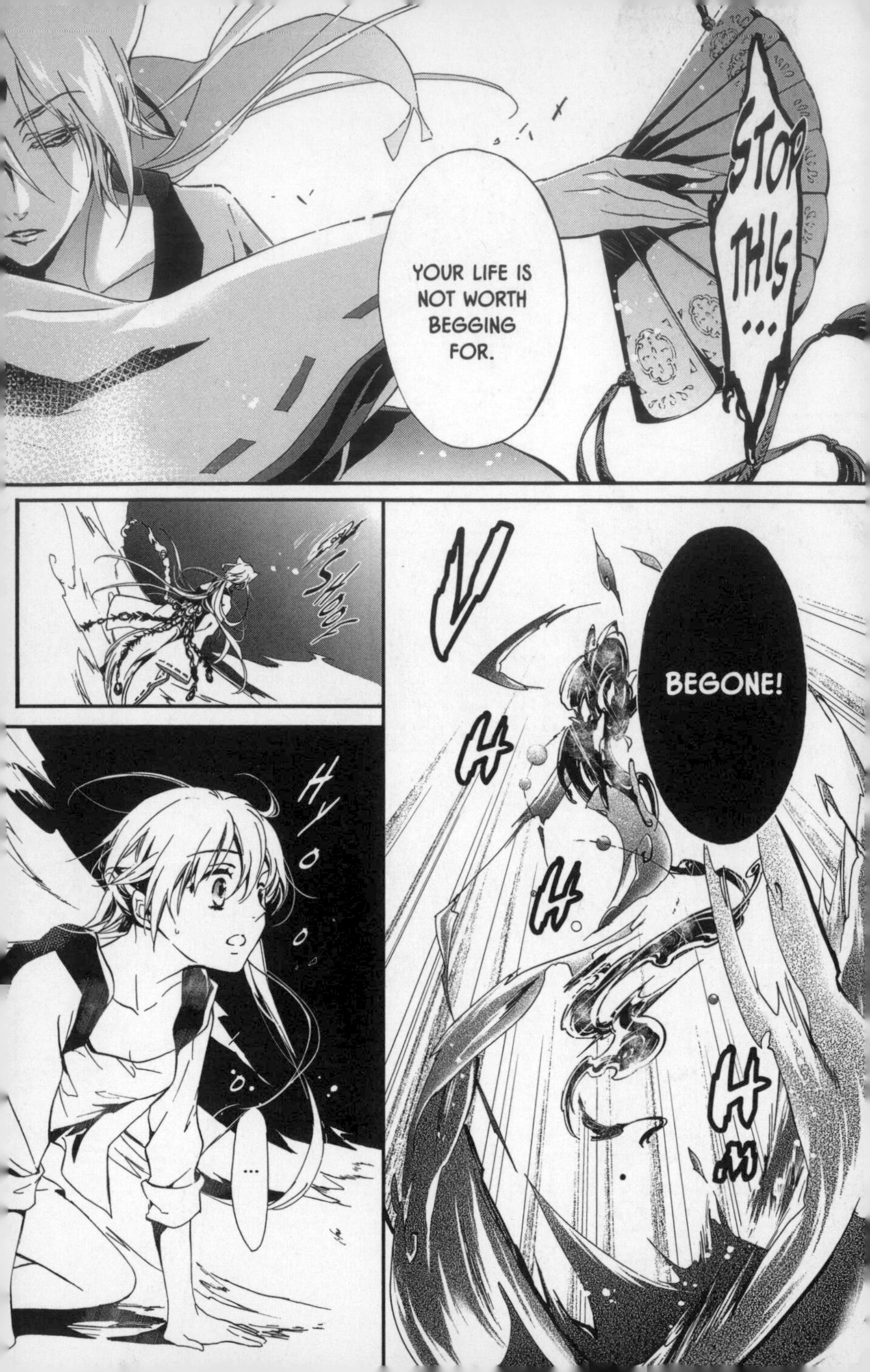
STOP THIS...
YOUR LIFE IS NOT WORTH BEGGING FOR.
BEGONE!
...

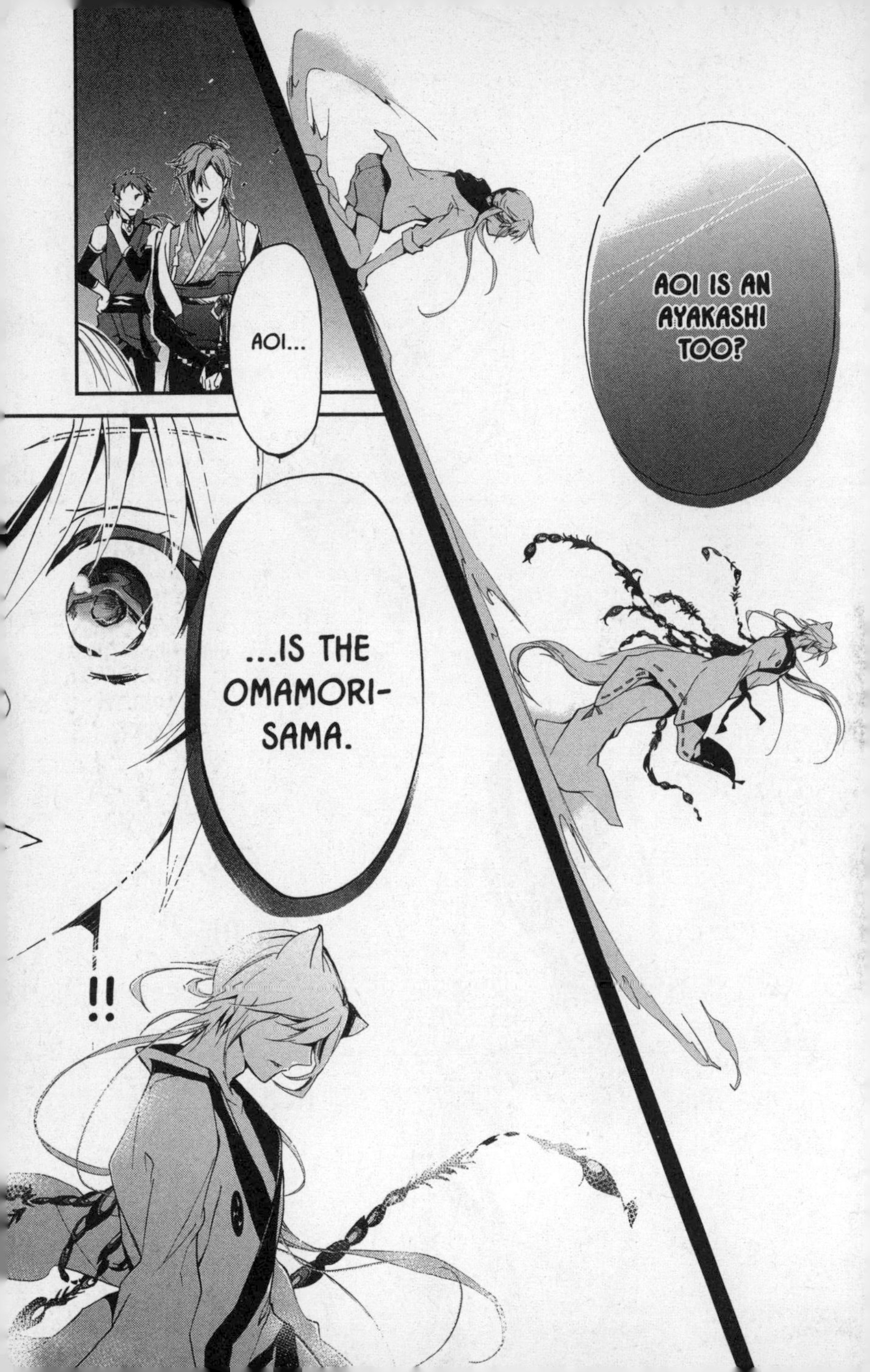
AOI IS AN AYAKASHI TOO?
AOI...
...IS THE OMAMORI-SAMA.
!!

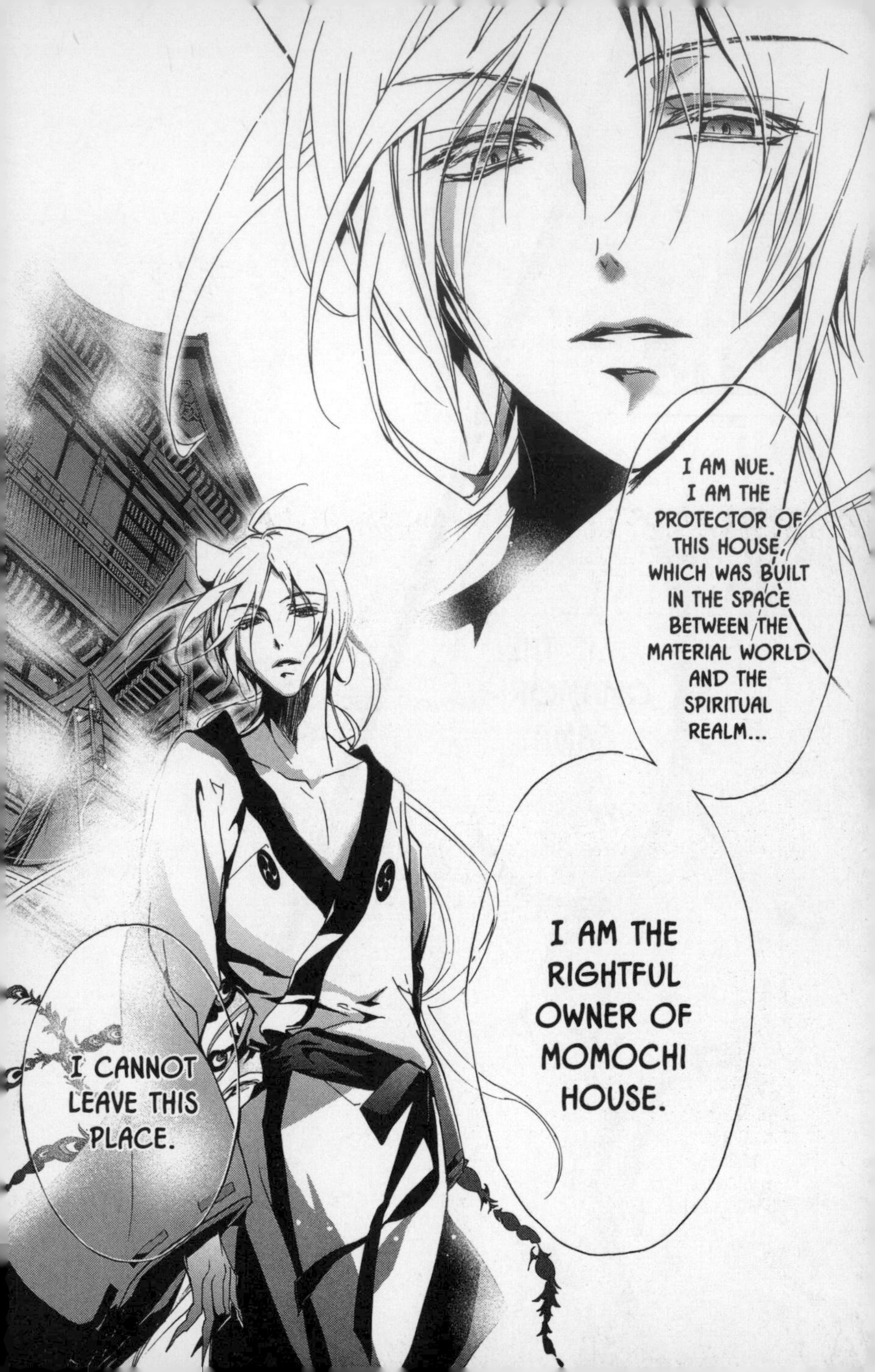
I AM NUE. I AM THE PROTECTOR OF THIS HOUSE, WHICH WAS BUILT IN THE SPACE BETWEEN THE MATERIAL WORLD AND THE SPIRITUAL REALM...
I AM THE RIGHTFUL OWNER OF MOMOCHI HOUSE.
I CANNOT LEAVE THIS PLACE.

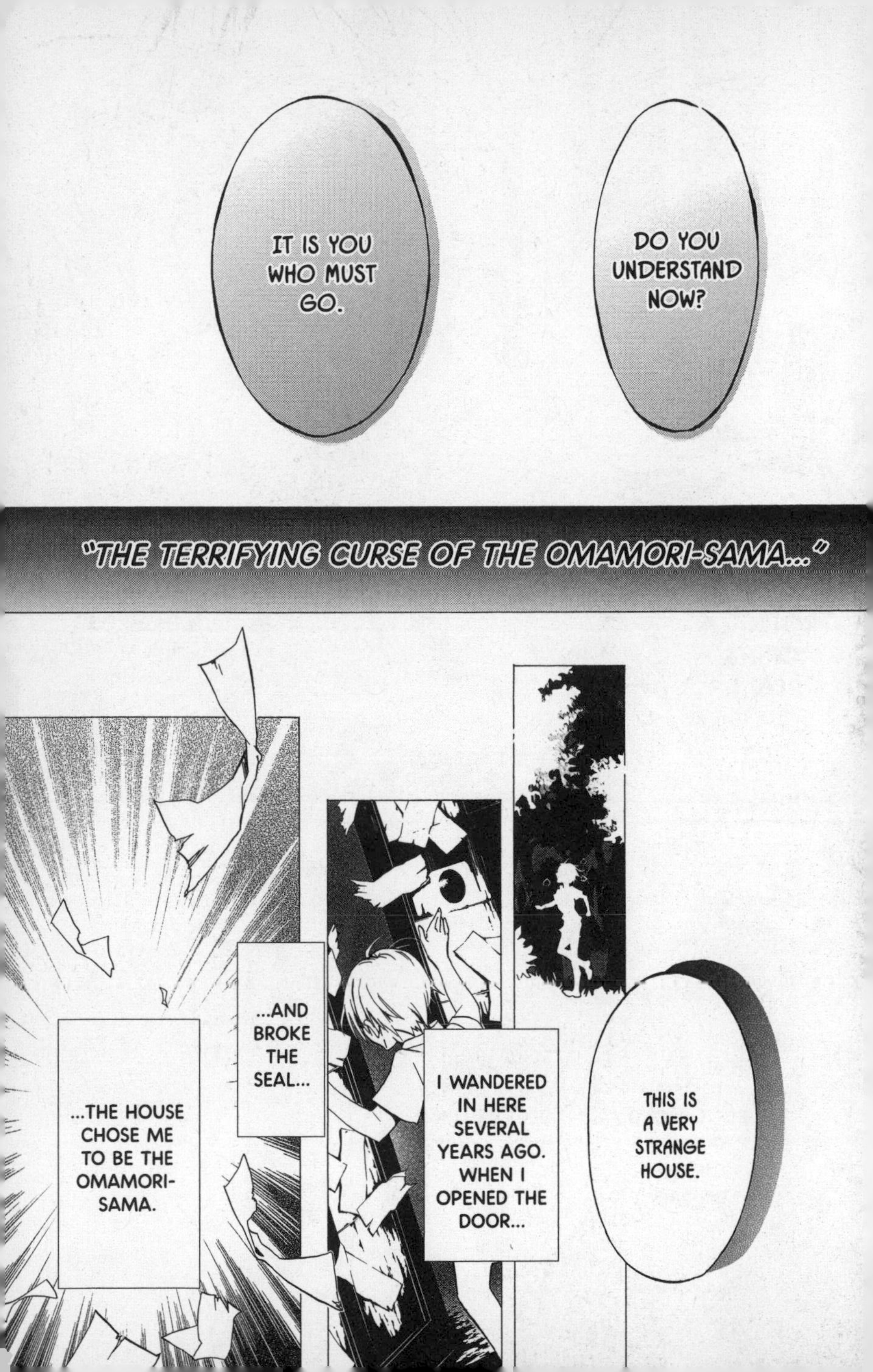
DO YOU UNDERSTAND NOW?
IT IS YOU WHO MUST GO.
"THE TERRIFYING CURSE OF THE OMAMORI-SAMA..."
THIS IS A VERY STRANGE HOUSE.
I WANDERED IN HERE SEVERAL YEARS AGO. WHEN I OPENED THE DOOR...
...AND BROKE THE SEAL...
...THE HOUSE CHOSE ME TO BE THE OMAMORI-SAMA.

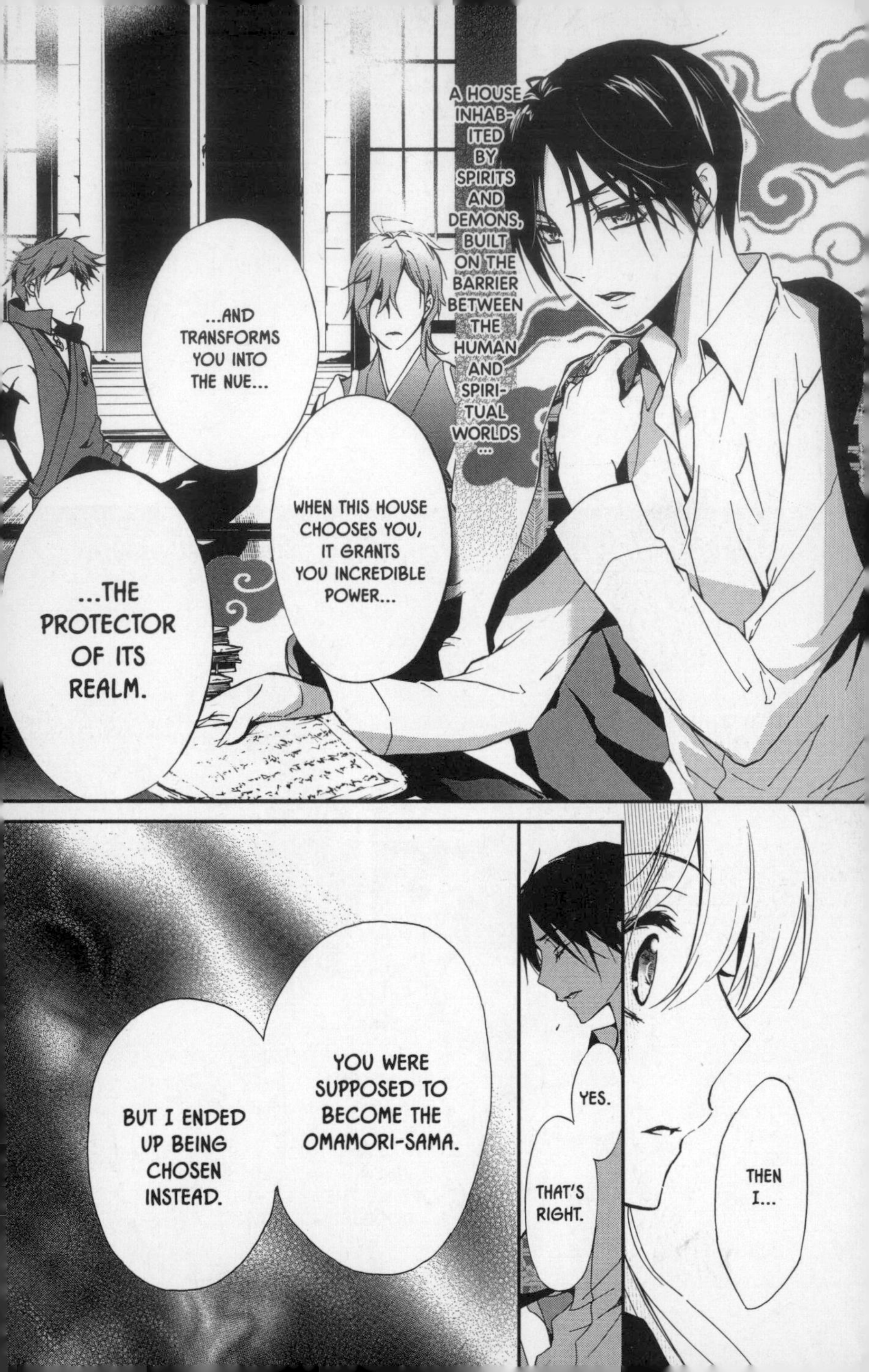
A HOUSE INHABITED BY SPIRITS AND DEMONS, BUILT ON THE BARRIER BETWEEN THE HUMAN AND SPIRITUAL WORLDS...
WHEN THIS HOUSE CHOOSES YOU, IT GRANTS YOU INCREDIBLE POWER...
...AND TRANSFORMS YOU INTO THE NUE...
...THE PROTECTOR OF ITS REALM.
THEN I...
YES.
THAT'S RIGHT.
YOU WERE SUPPOSED TO BECOME THE OMAMORI-SAMA.
BUT I ENDED UP BEING CHOSEN INSTEAD.

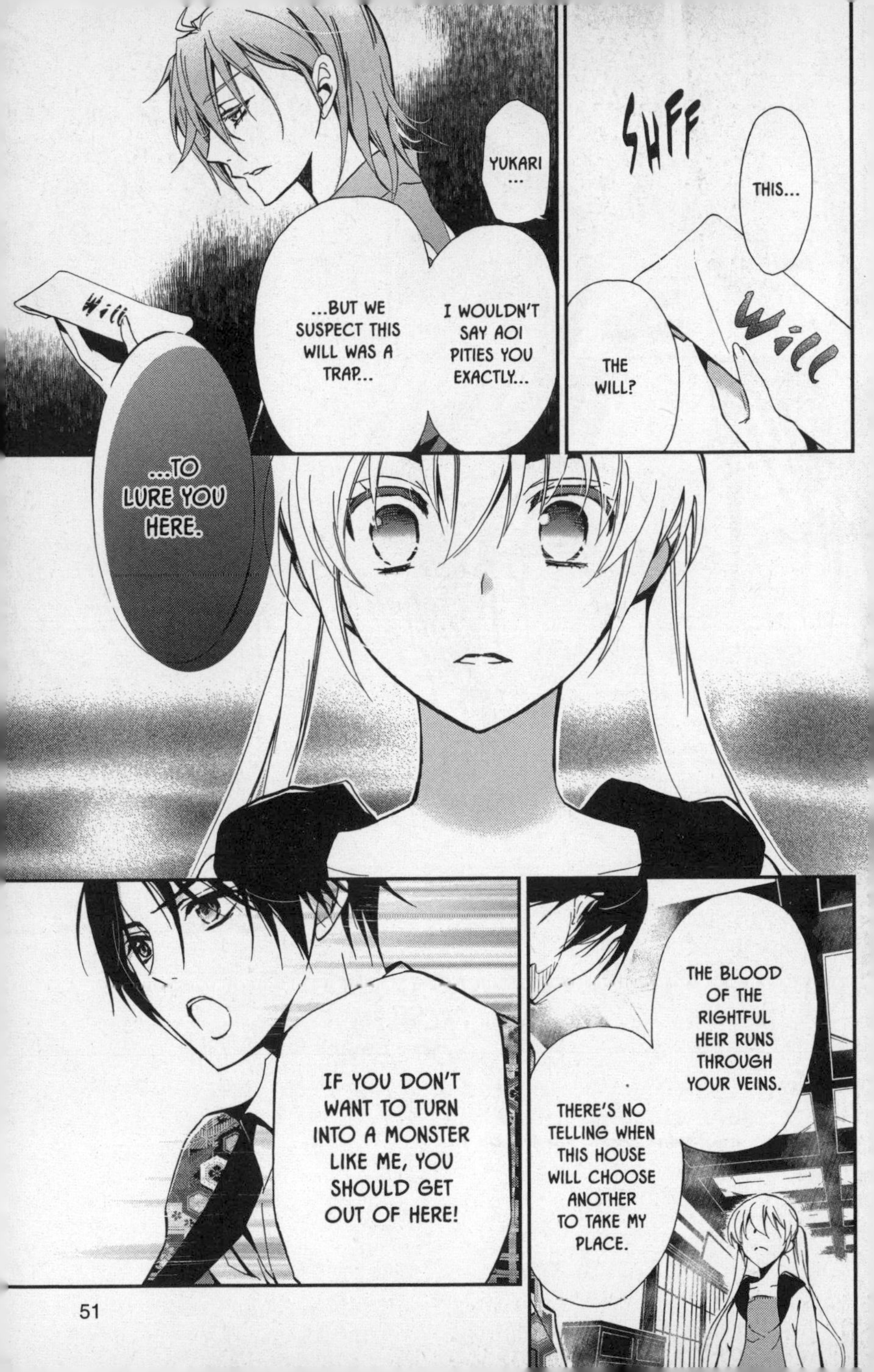
SHFF
THIS...
Will
THE WILL?
YUKARI ...
I WOULDN'T SAY AOI PITIES YOU EXACTLY...
...BUT WE SUSPECT THIS WILL WAS A TRAP...
Will
...TO LURE YOU HERE.
THE BLOOD OF THE RIGHTFUL HEIR RUNS THROUGH YOUR VEINS.
THERE'S NO TELLING WHEN THIS HOUSE WILL CHOOSE ANOTHER TO TAKE MY PLACE.
IF YOU DON'T WANT TO TURN INTO A MONSTER LIKE ME, YOU SHOULD GET OUT OF HERE!

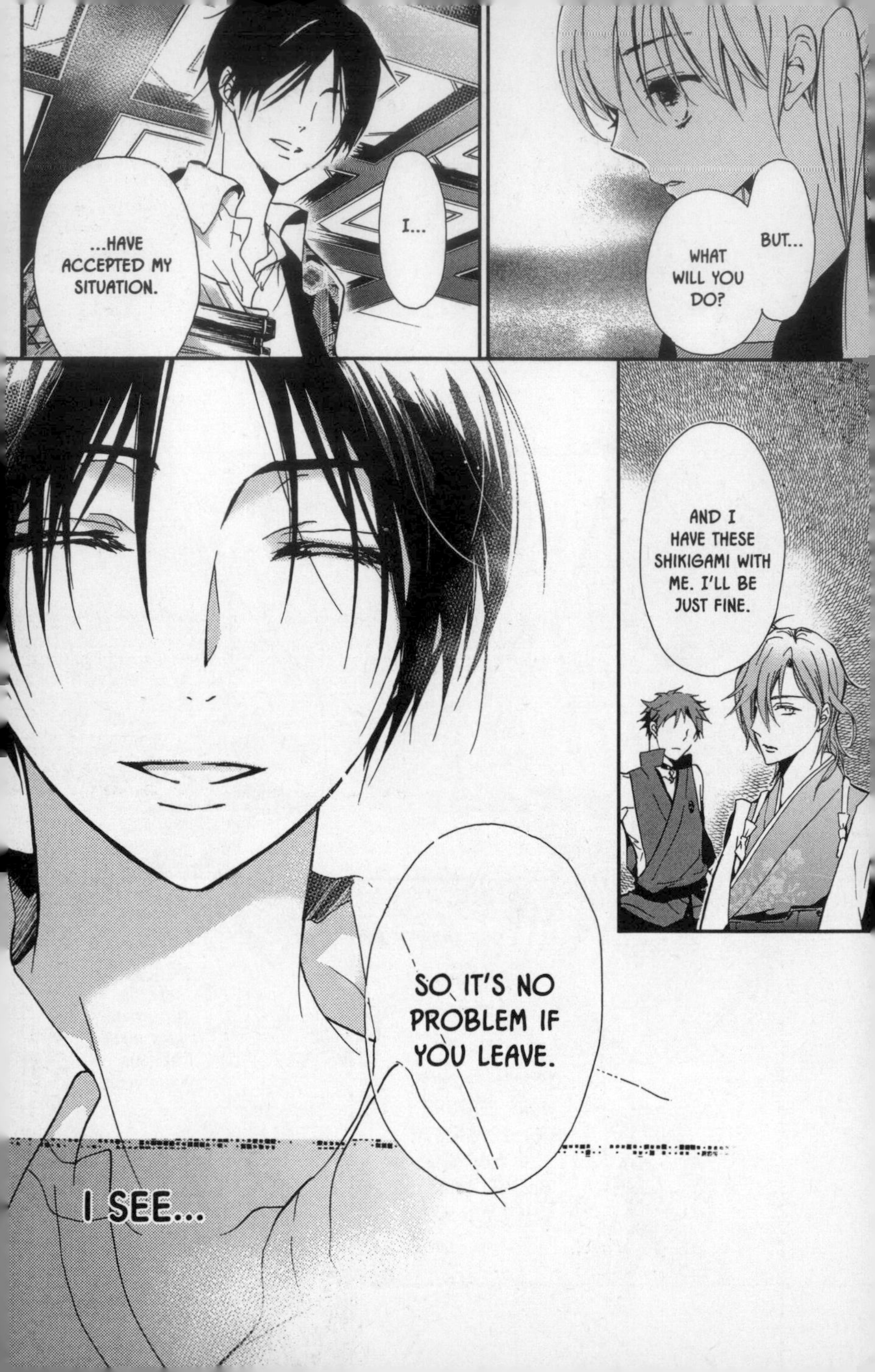
BUT...
WHAT WILL YOU DO?
I...
...HAVE ACCEPTED MY SITUATION.
AND I HAVE THESE SHIKIGAMI WITH ME. I'LL BE JUST FINE.
SO IT'S NO PROBLEM IF YOU LEAVE.
I SEE...

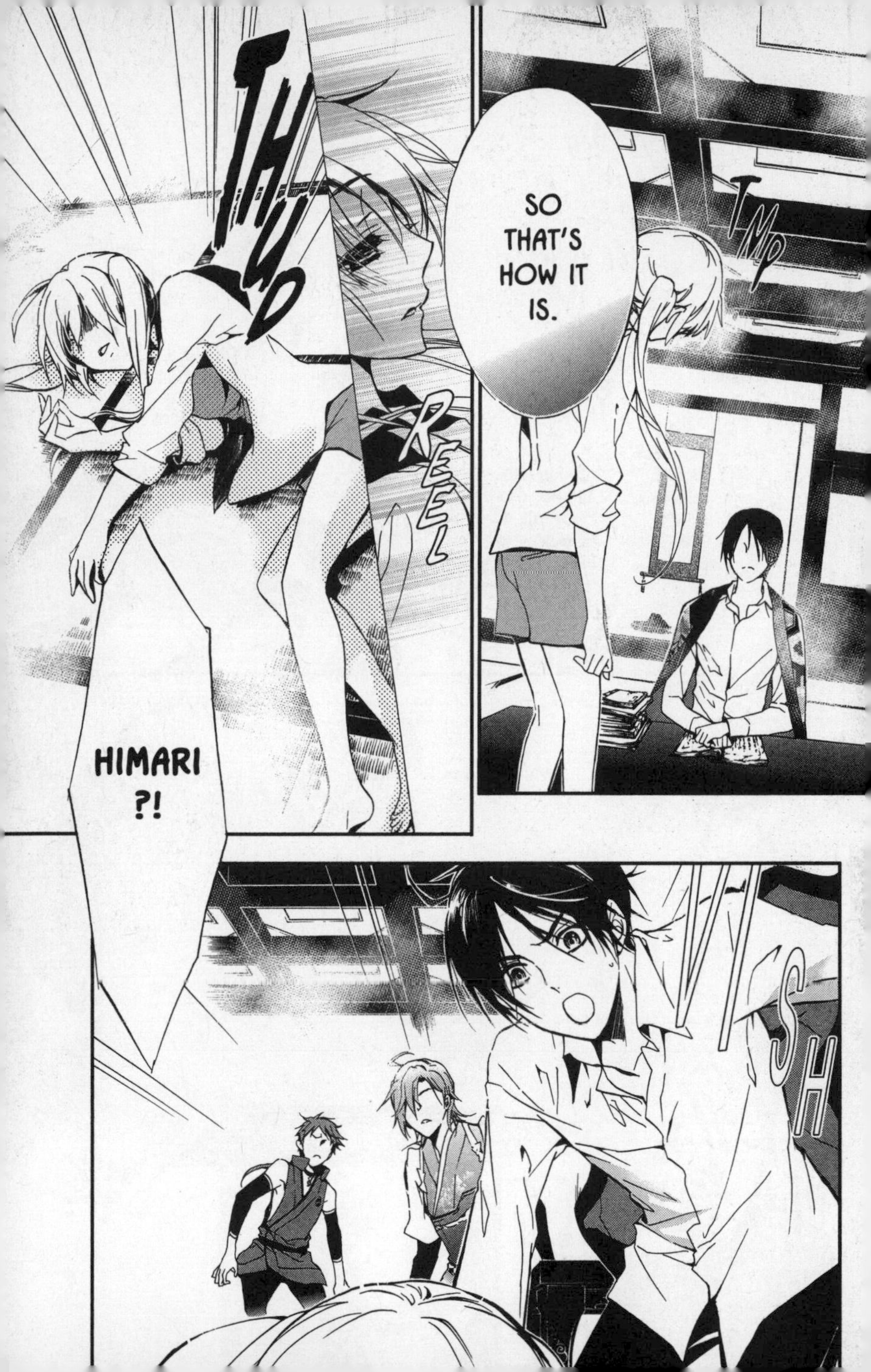
SO THAT'S HOW IT IS.
TMP
REEL
THUD
HIMARI?!
WISH

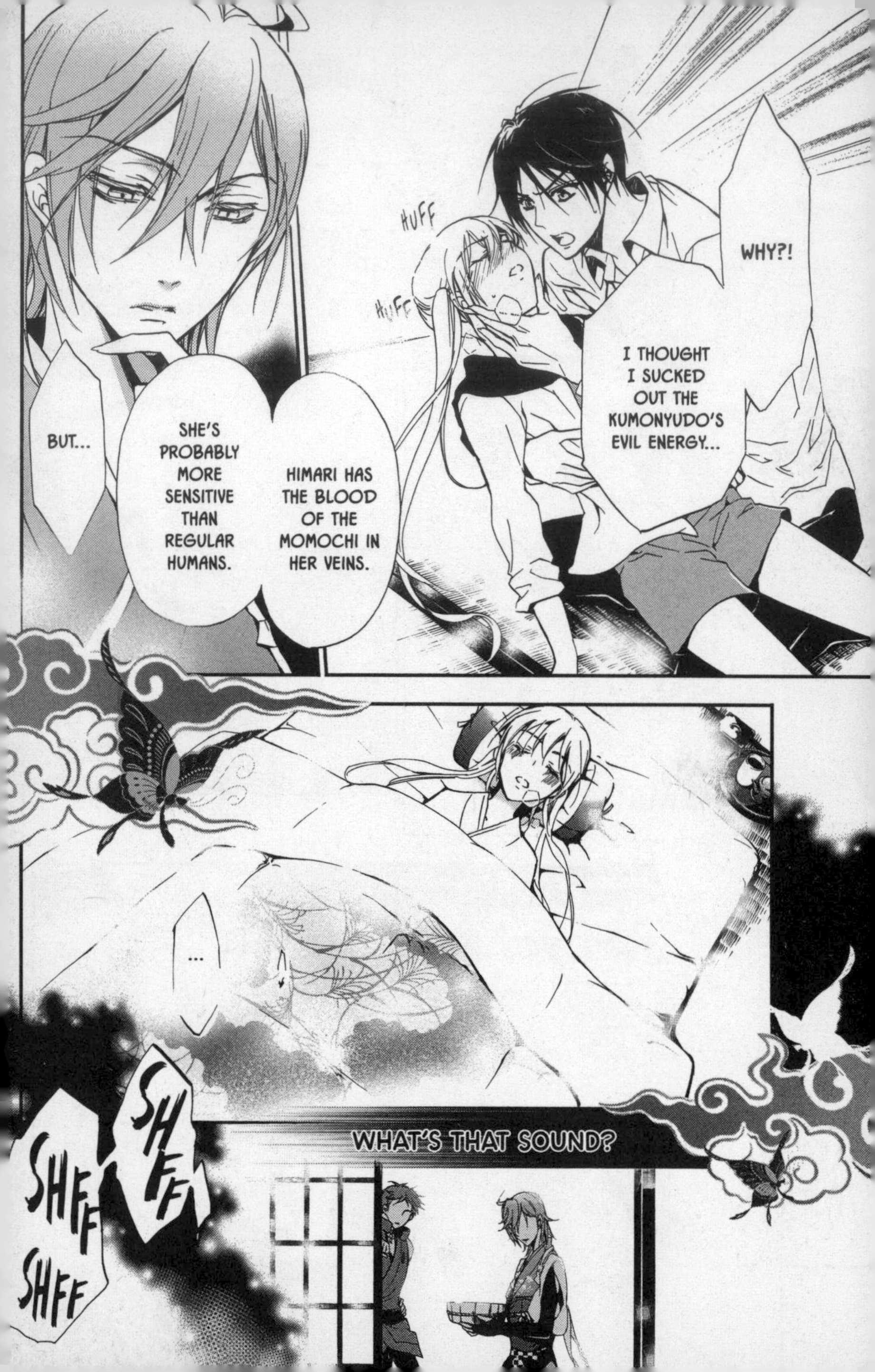
WHY?!
HUFF
HUFF
I THOUGHT I SUCKED OUT THE KUMONYUDO'S EVIL ENERGY...
HIMARI HAS THE BLOOD OF THE MOMOCHI IN HER VEINS.
SHE'S PROBABLY MORE SENSITIVE THAN REGULAR HUMANS.
BUT...
...
WHAT'S THAT SOUND?
SHFF
SHFF
SHFF

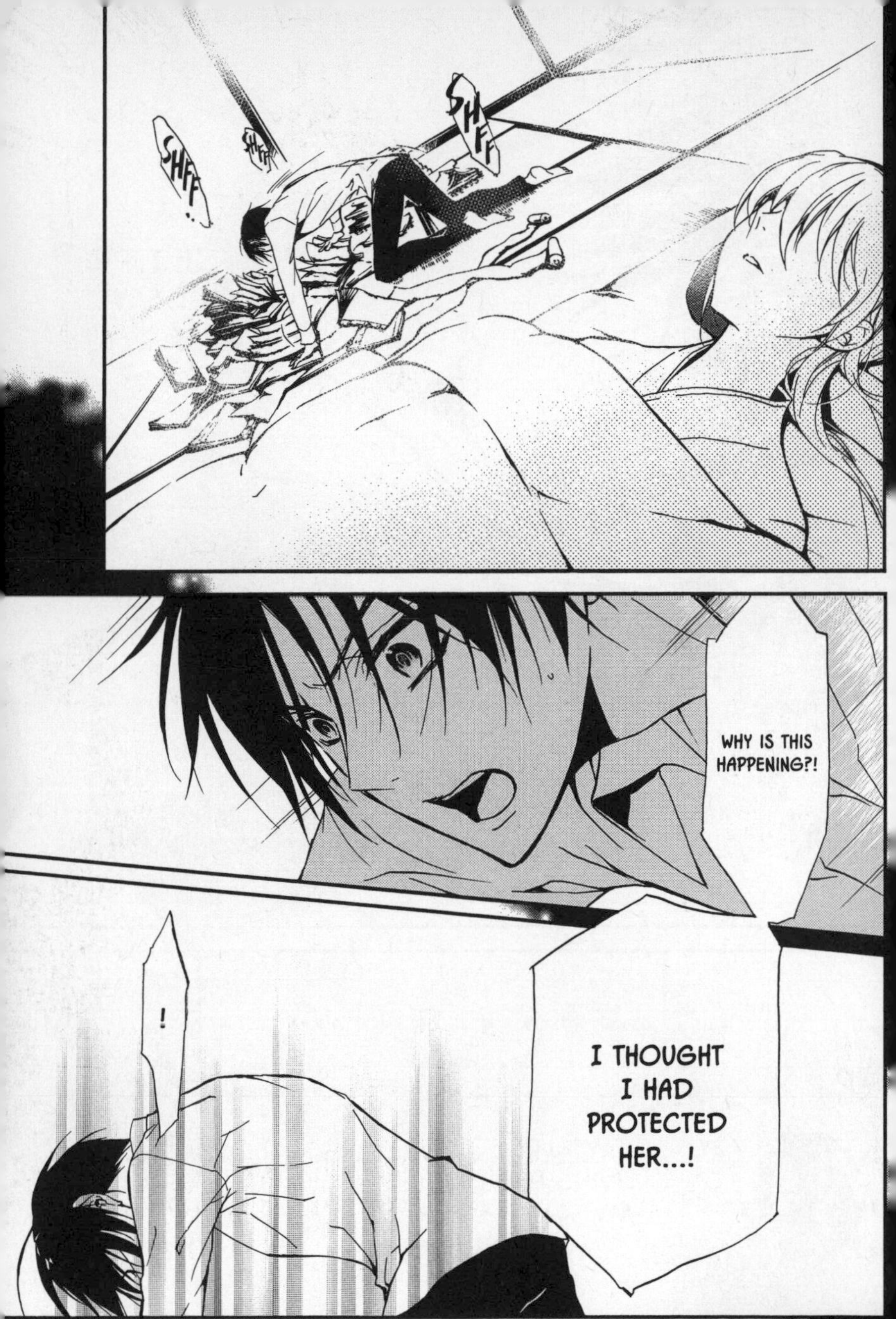
SHFF
SHFF
SHFF
WHY IS THIS HAPPENING?!
!
I THOUGHT I HAD PROTECTED HER...!

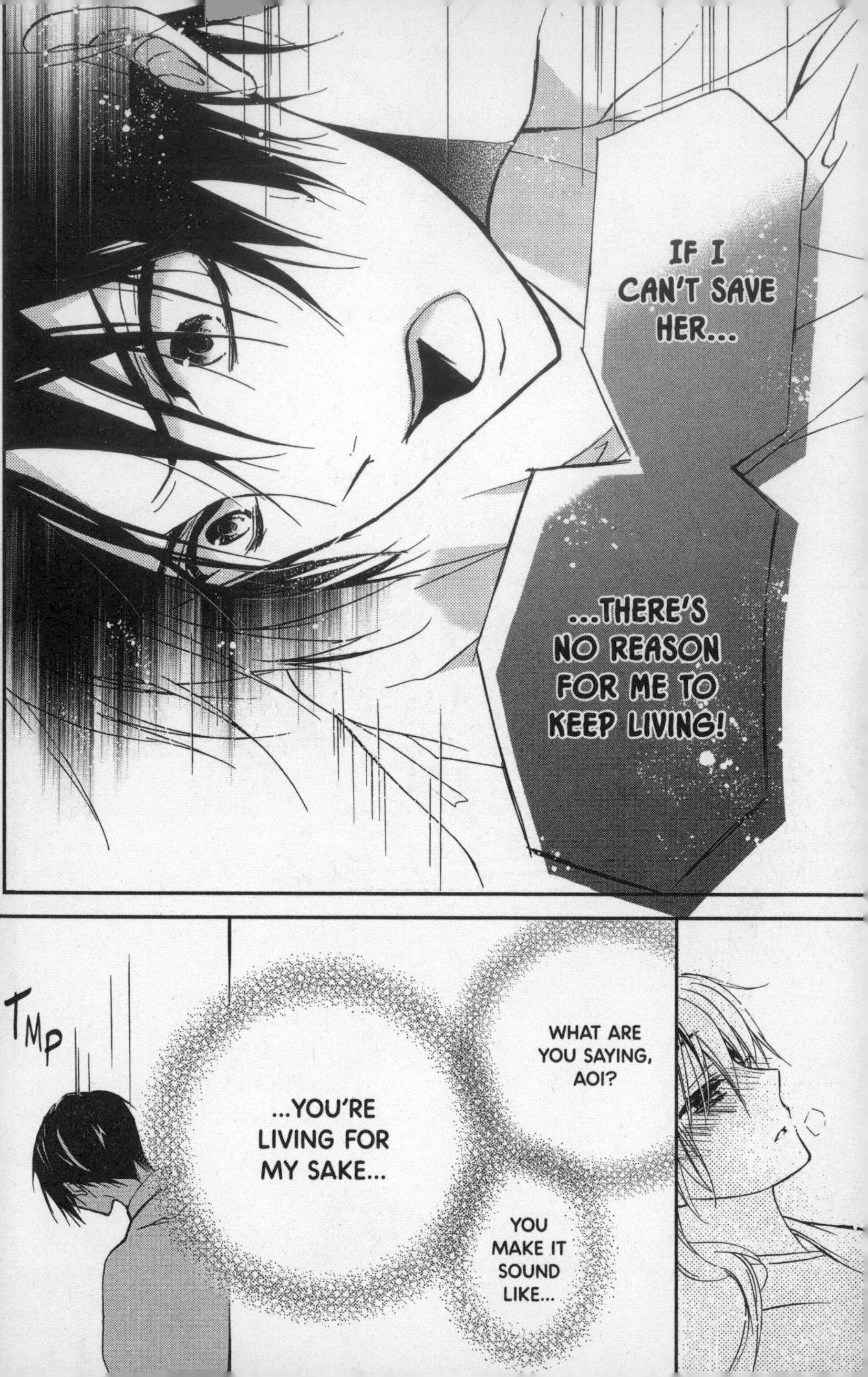
IF I CAN'T SAVE HER...
...THERE'S NO REASON FOR ME TO KEEP LIVING!
WHAT ARE YOU SAYING, AOI?
YOU MAKE IT SOUND LIKE...
...YOU'RE LIVING FOR MY SAKE...
TMP

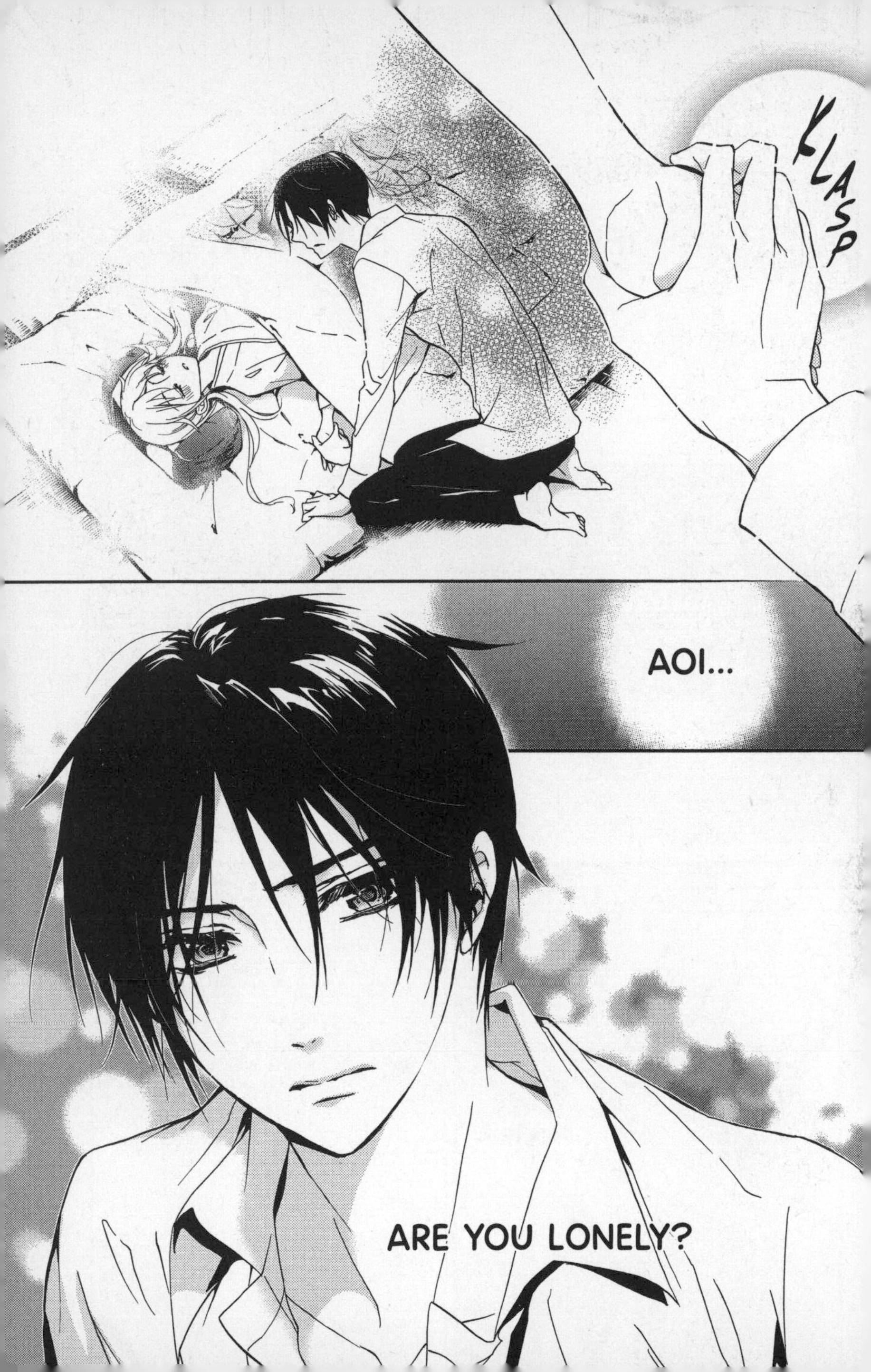
KLASP
AOI...
ARE YOU LONELY?

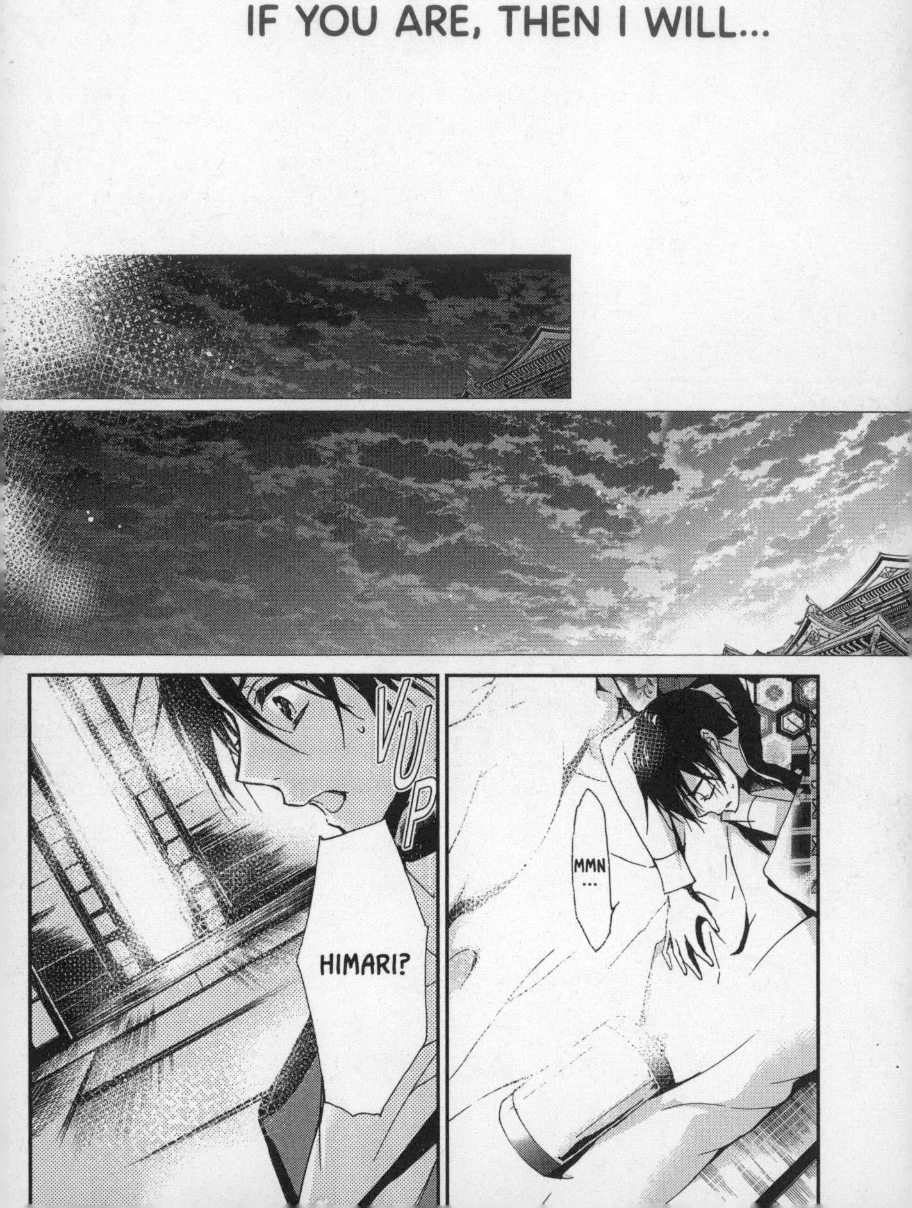
IF YOU ARE, THEN I WILL...
MMN...
VUP
HIMARI?

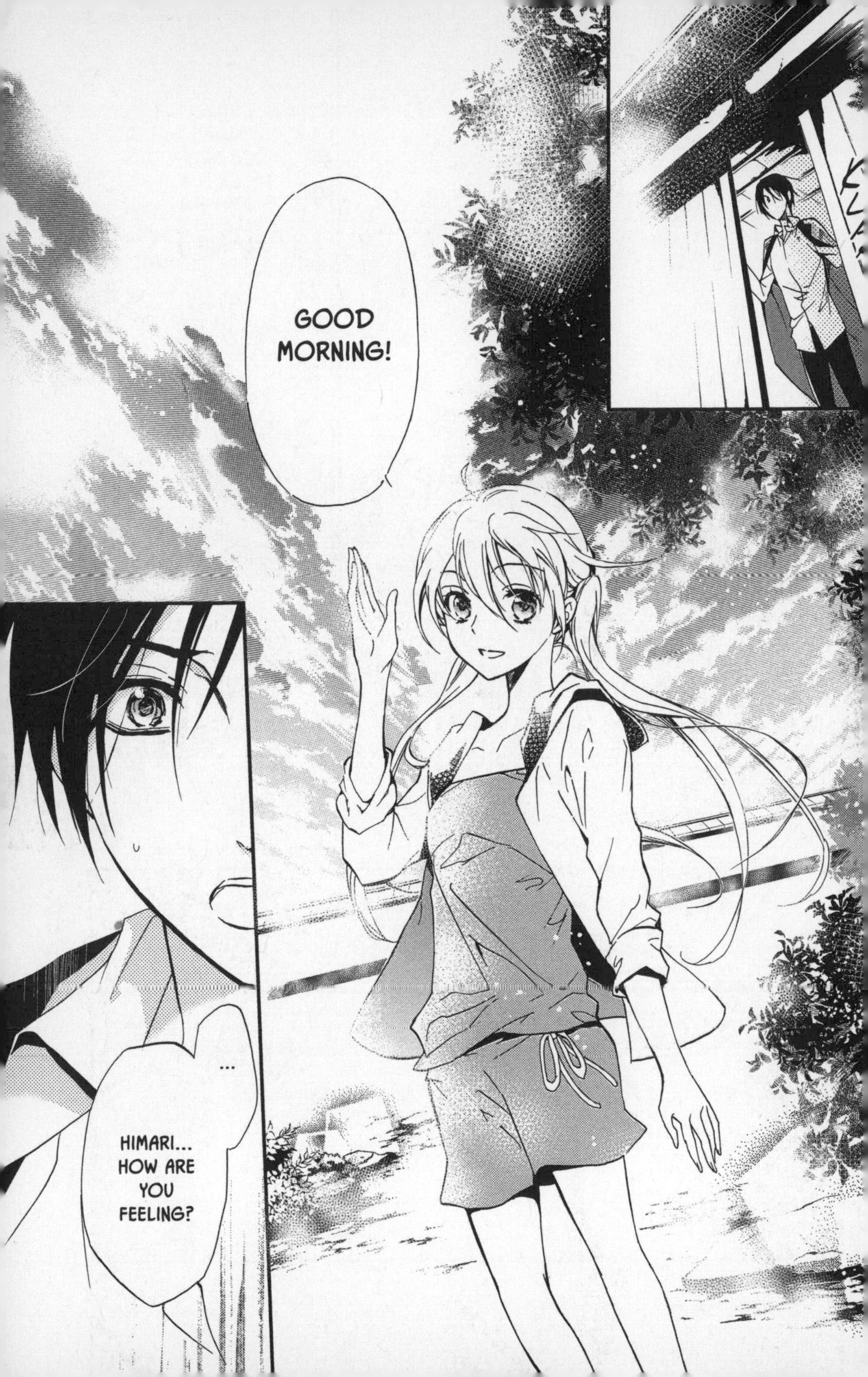
GOOD MORNING!
...
HIMARI... HOW ARE YOU FEELING?

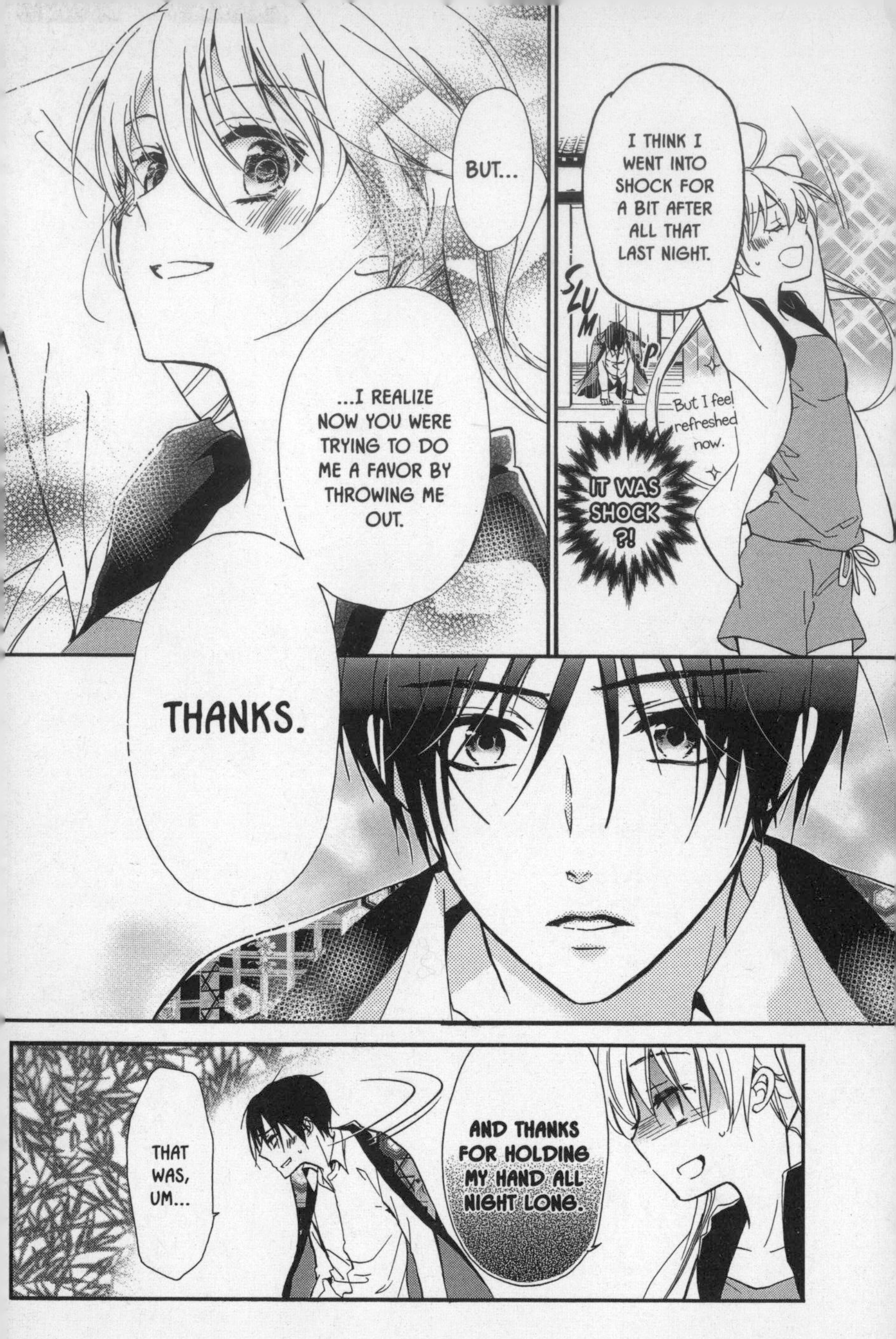
I THINK I WENT INTO SHOCK FOR A BIT AFTER ALL THAT LAST NIGHT.
SLUMP
But I feel refreshed now.
IT WAS SHOCK?!
BUT...
...I REALIZE NOW YOU WERE TRYING TO DO ME A FAVOR BY THROWING ME OUT.
THANKS.
AND THANKS FOR HOLDING MY HAND ALL NIGHT LONG.
THAT WAS, UM...

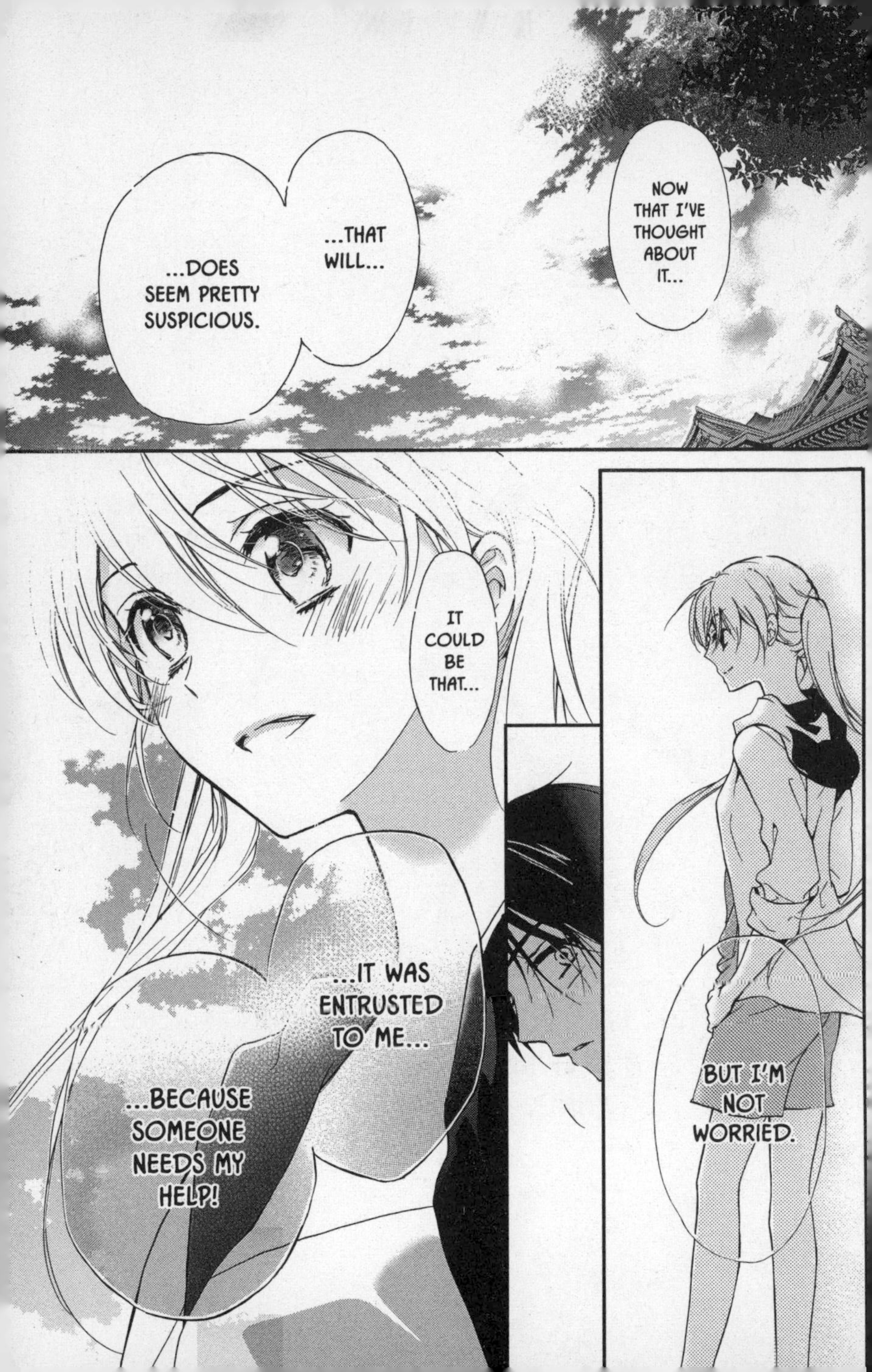
NOW THAT I'VE THOUGHT ABOUT IT...
...THAT WILL...
...DOES SEEM PRETTY SUSPICIOUS.
BUT I'M NOT WORRIED.
IT COULD BE THAT...
...IT WAS ENTRUSTED TO ME...
...BECAUSE SOMEONE NEEDS MY HELP!

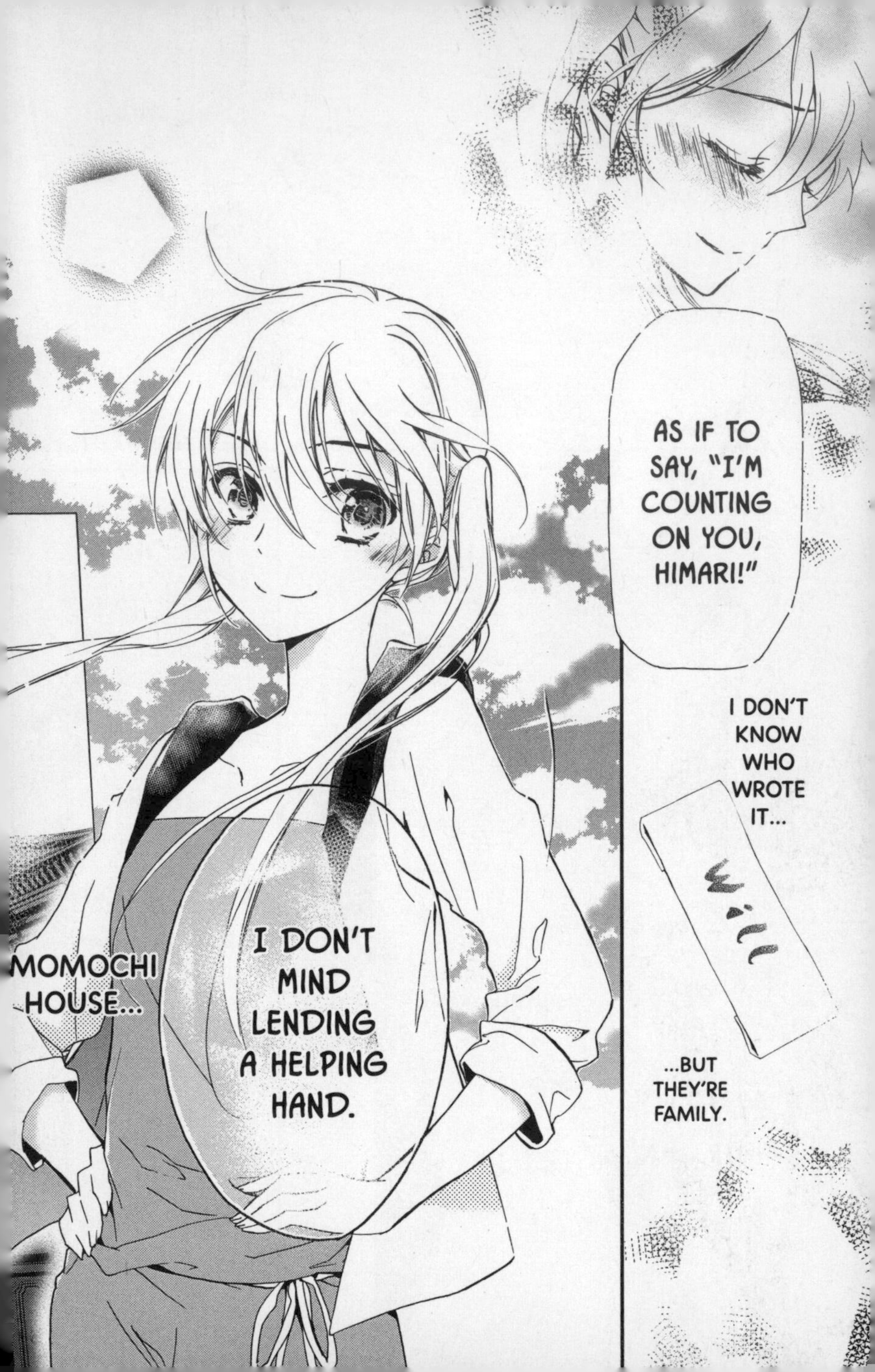
AS IF TO SAY, "I'M COUNTING ON YOU, HIMARI!"
I DON'T KNOW WHO WROTE IT...
will
...BUT THEY'RE FAMILY.
I DON'T MIND LENDING A HELPING HAND.
MOMOCHI HOUSE...

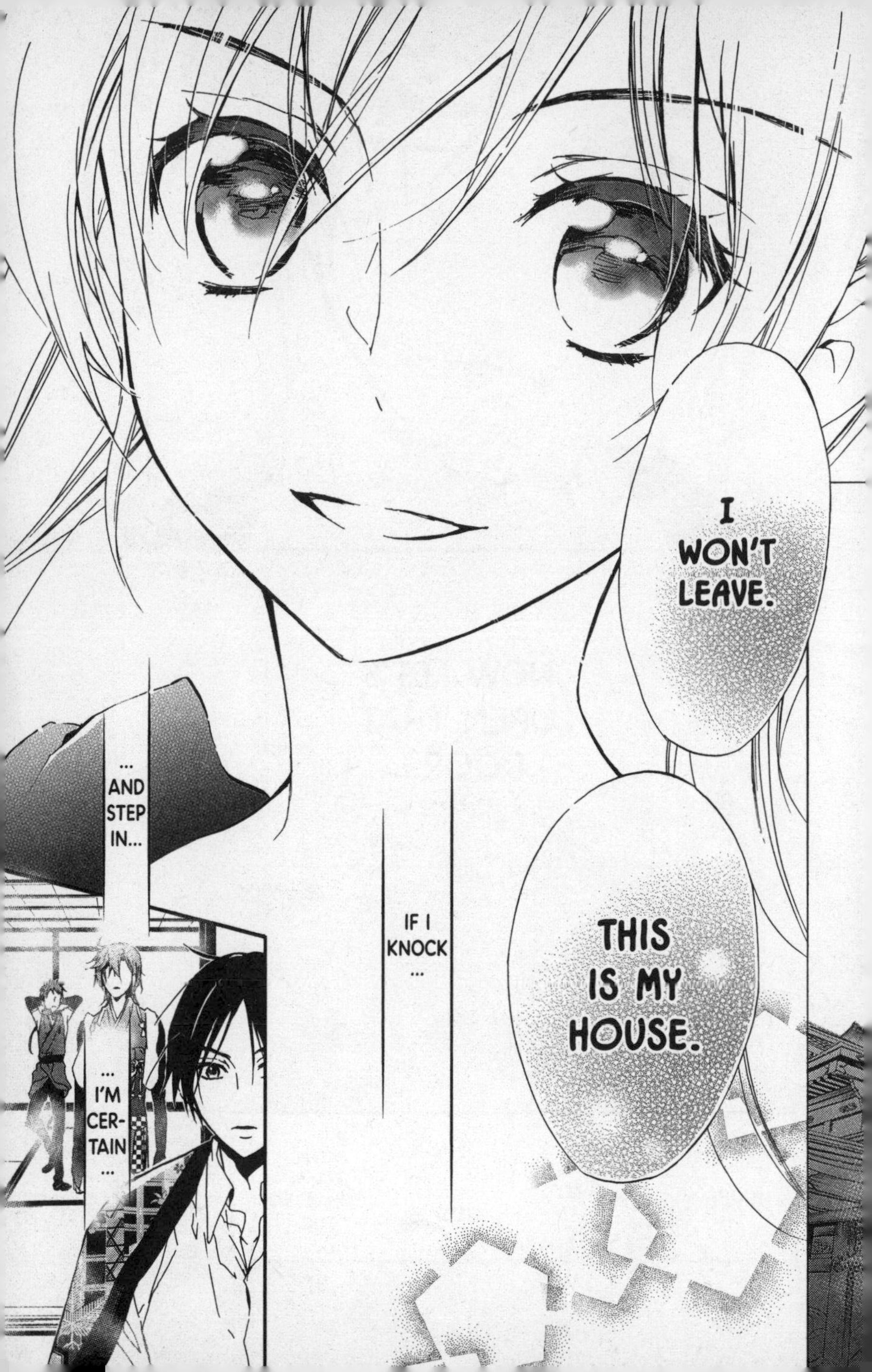
I WON'T LEAVE.
THIS IS MY HOUSE.
IF I KNOCK...
...AND STEP IN...
...I'M CER-TAIN...

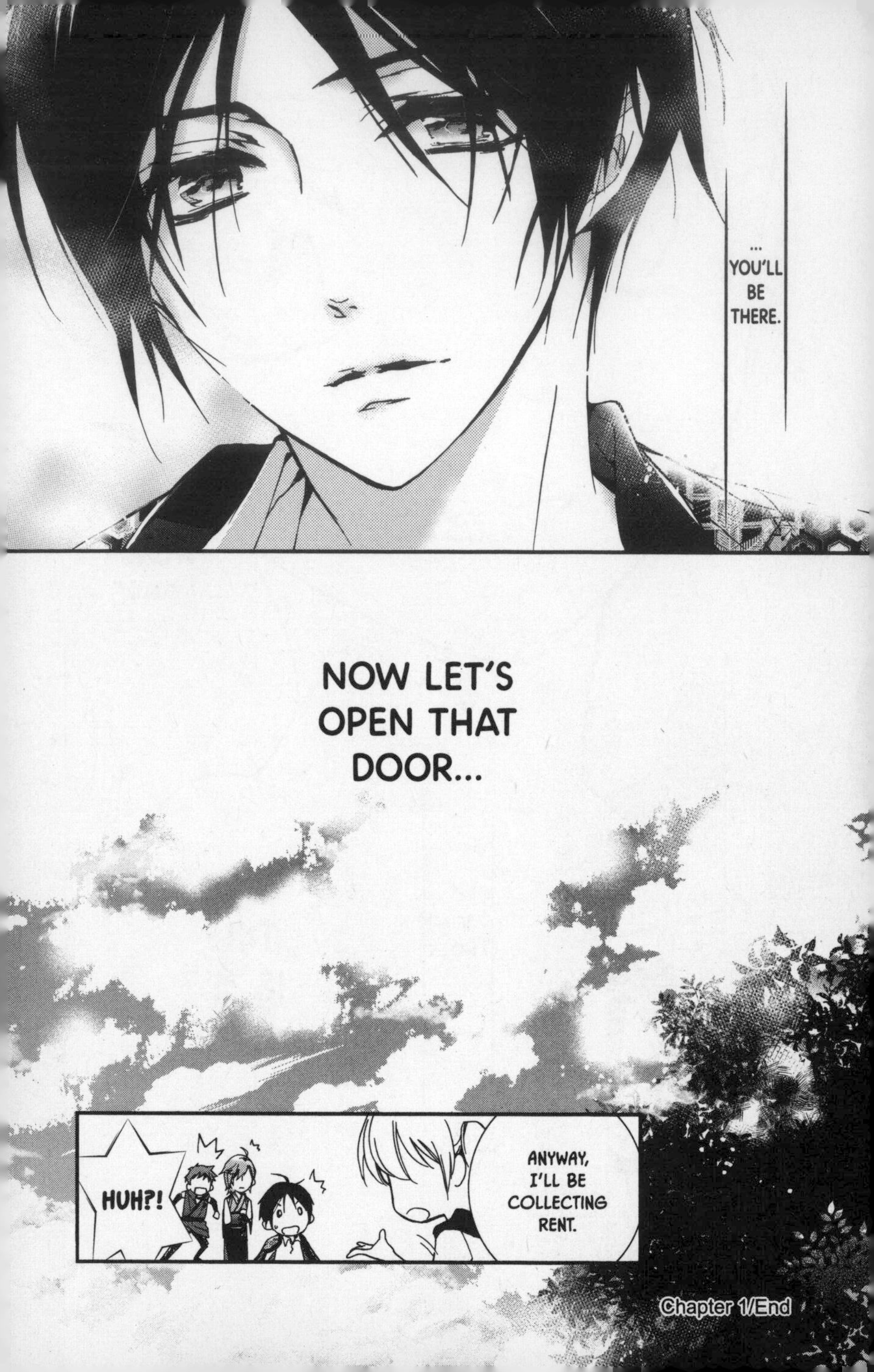

... YOU'LL BE THERE.
NOW LET'S OPEN THAT DOOR...
ANYWAY, I'LL BE COLLECTING RENT.
HUH?!
Chapter 1/End

The
DEMON
PRINCE
of MOMOCHI
HOUSE

The
DEMON
PRINCE
of MOMOCHI
HOUSE

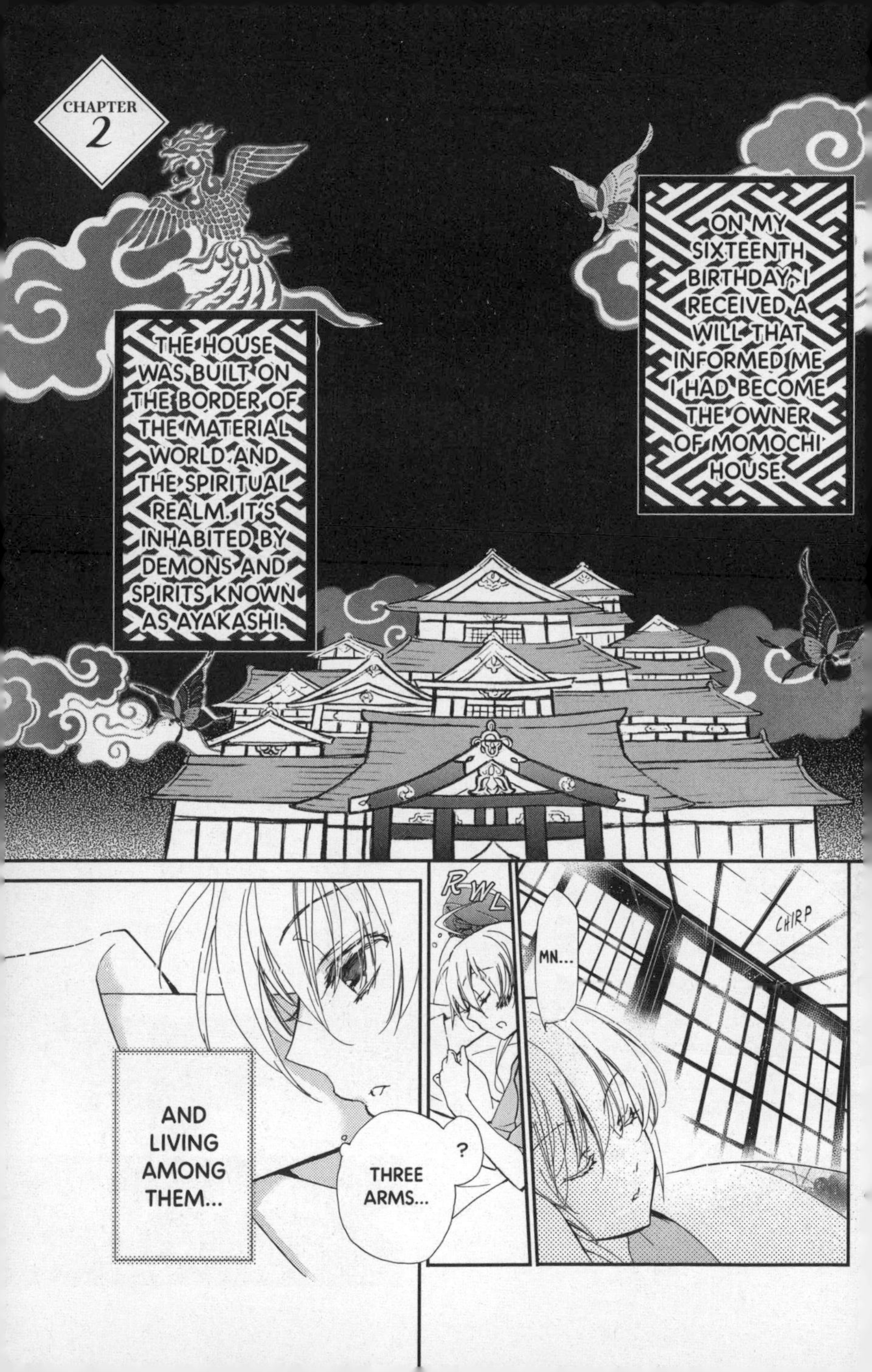
CHAPTER 2
ON MY SIXTEENTH BIRTHDAY, I RECEIVED A WILL THAT INFORMED ME I HAD BECOME THE OWNER OF MOMOCHI HOUSE.
THE HOUSE WAS BUILT ON THE BORDER OF THE MATERIAL WORLD AND THE SPIRITUAL REALM. IT'S INHABITED BY DEMONS AND SPIRITS KNOWN AS AYAKASHI.
CHIRP
MN...
RWL
?
THREE ARMS...
AND LIVING AMONG THEM...

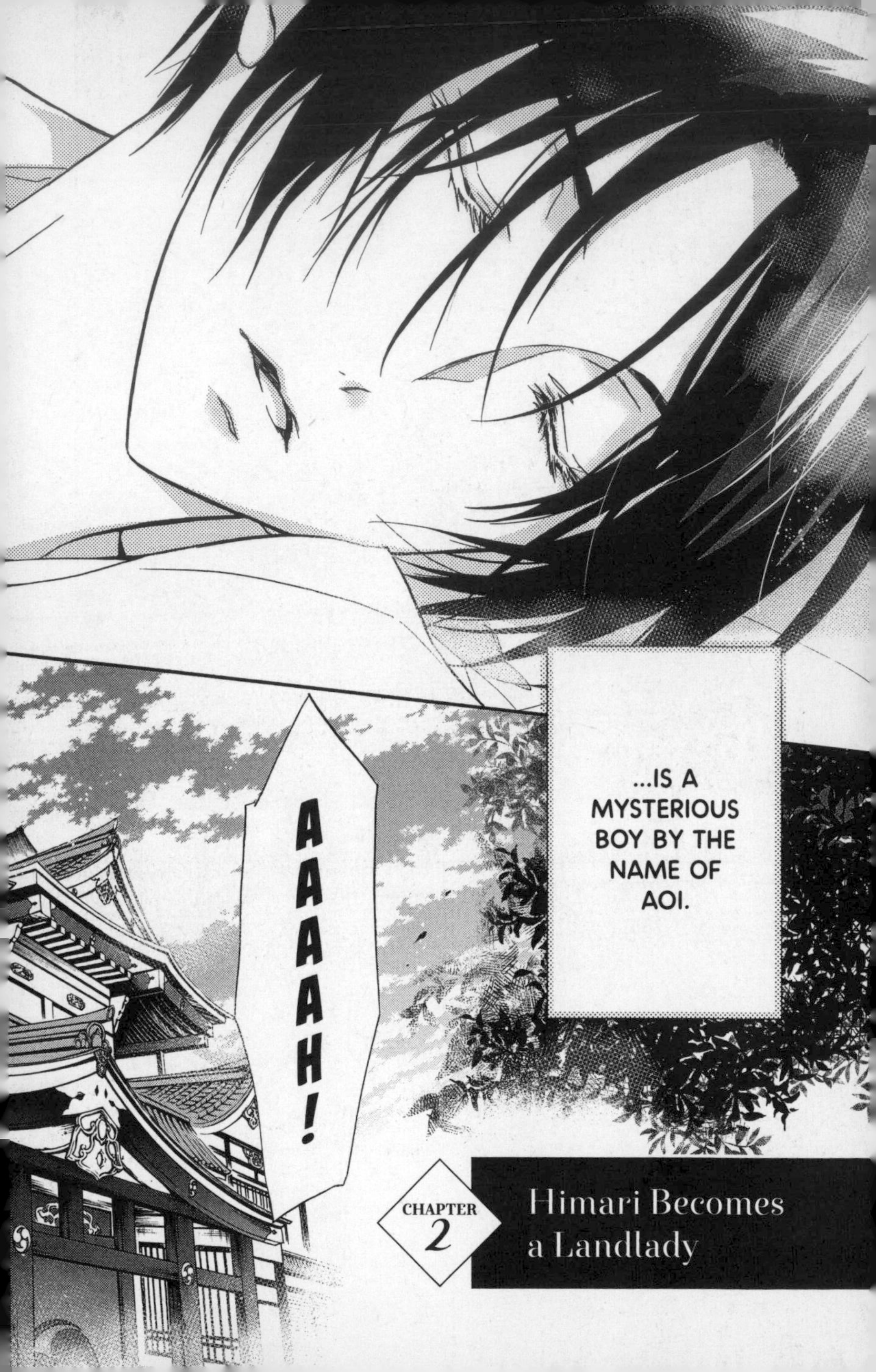
...IS A MYSTERIOUS BOY BY THE NAME OF AOI.
AAAAAH!
CHAPTER 2
Himari Becomes a Landlady

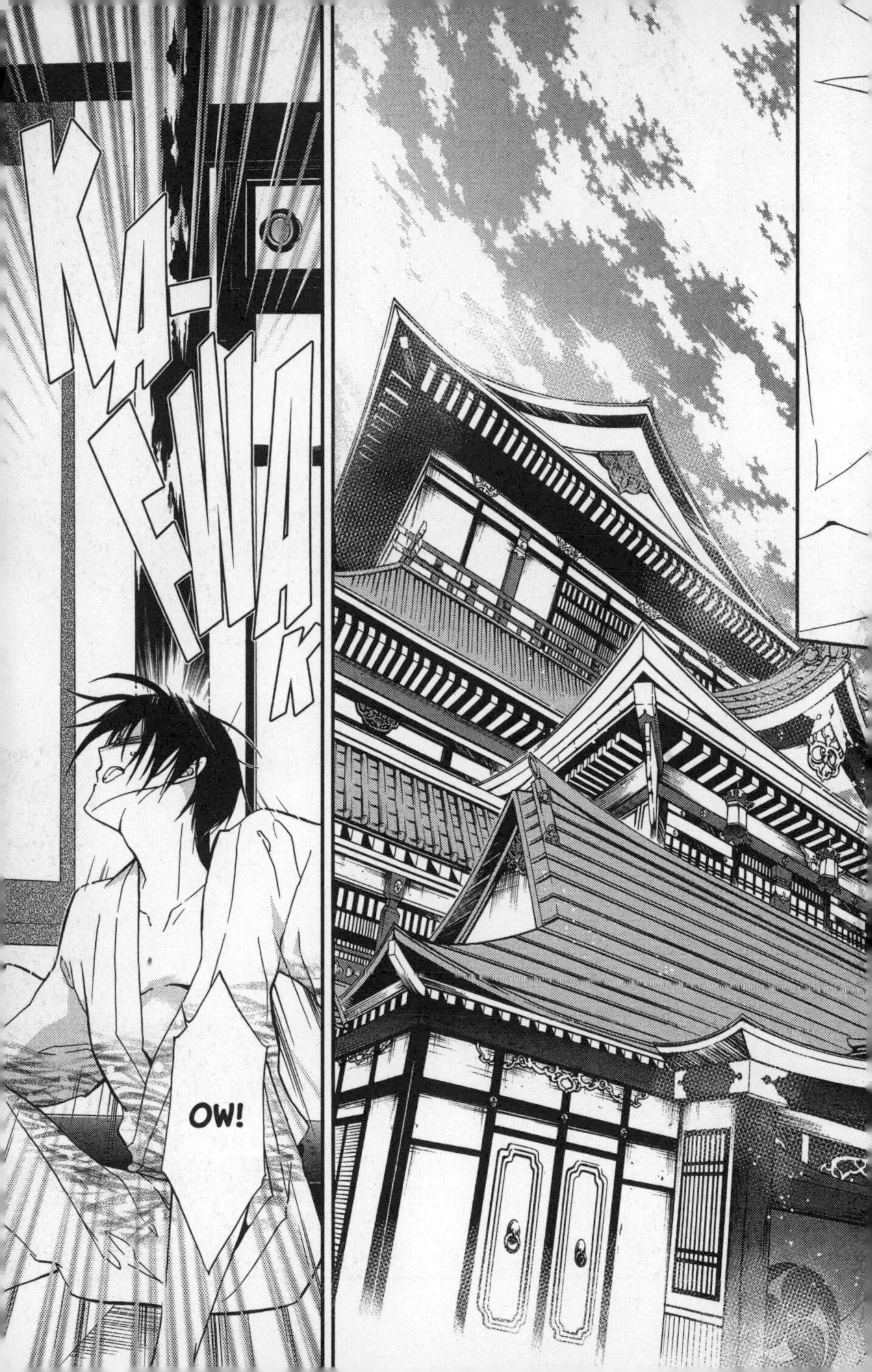
OW!

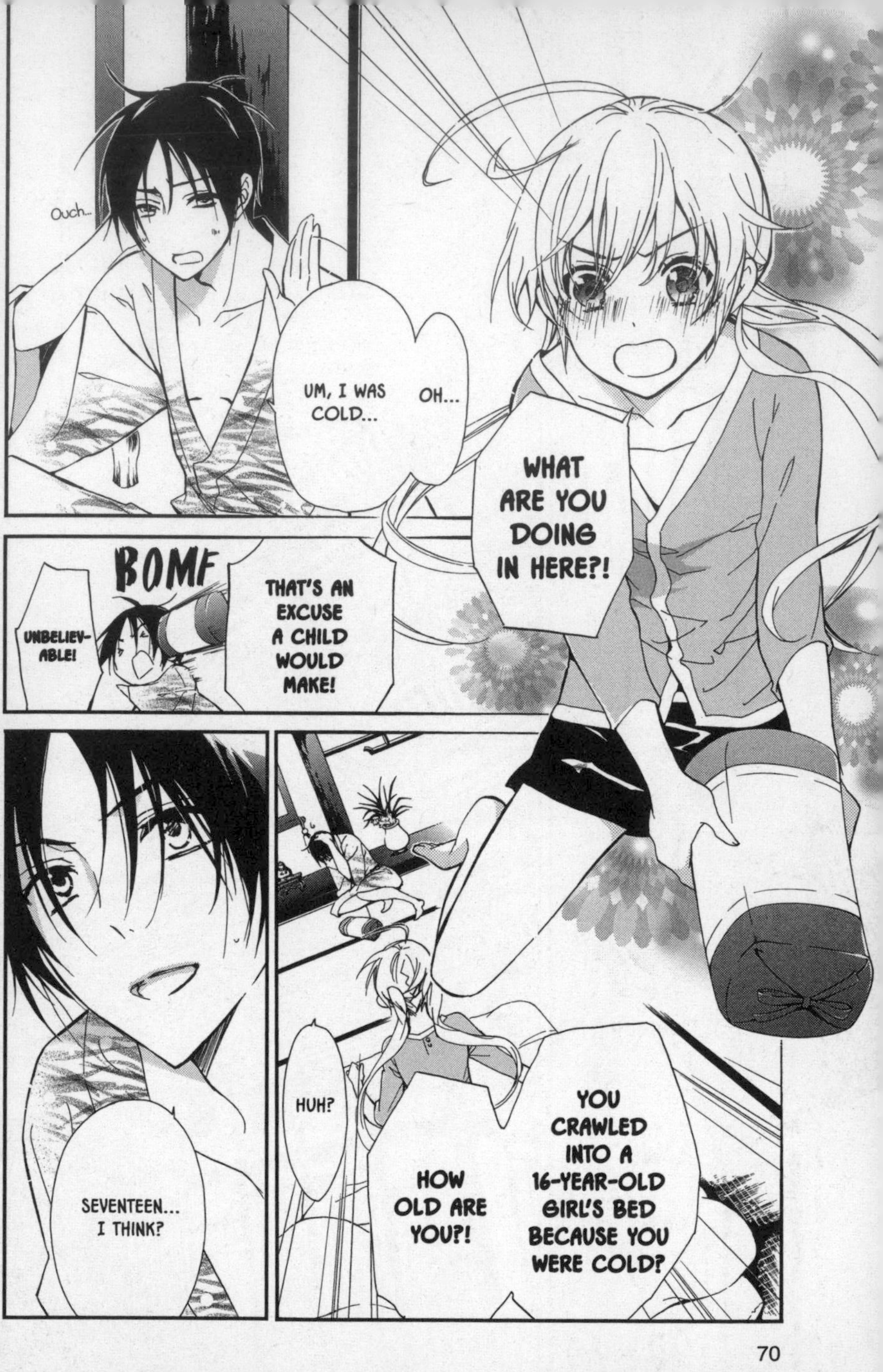
WHAT ARE YOU DOING IN HERE?!
OH...
UM, I WAS COLD...
Ouch...
THAT'S AN EXCUSE A CHILD WOULD MAKE!
BOMF
UNBELIEV-ABLE!
YOU CRAWLED INTO A 16-YEAR-OLD GIRL'S BED BECAUSE YOU WERE COLD?
HOW OLD ARE YOU?!
HUH?
SEVENTEEN... I THINK?

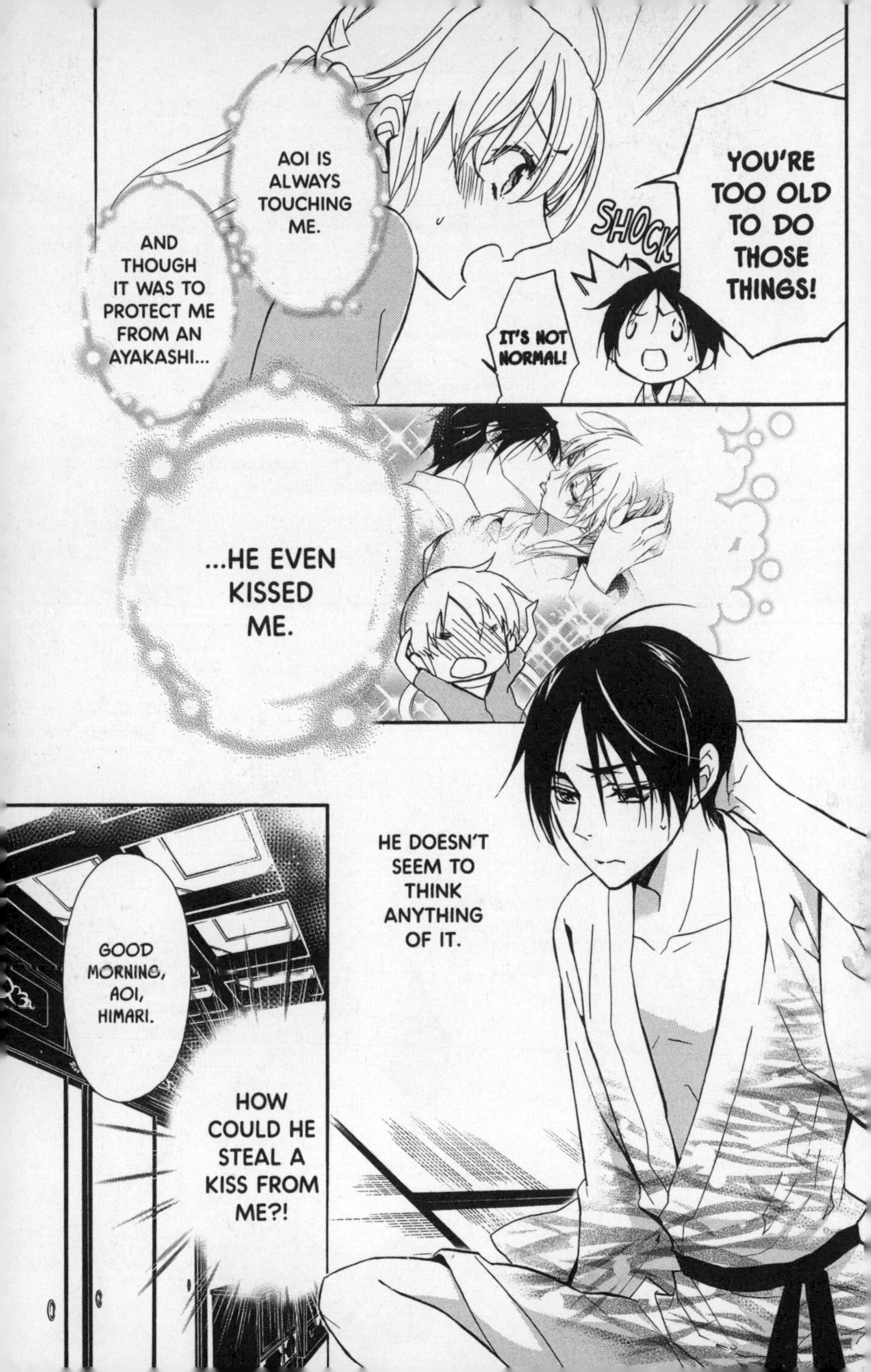
YOU'RE TOO OLD TO DO THOSE THINGS!
SHOCK
IT'S NOT NORMAL!
AOI IS ALWAYS TOUCHING ME.
AND THOUGH IT WAS TO PROTECT ME FROM AN AYAKASHI...
...HE EVEN KISSED ME.
HE DOESN'T SEEM TO THINK ANYTHING OF IT.
GOOD MORNING, AOI, HIMARI.
HOW COULD HE STEAL A KISS FROM ME?!

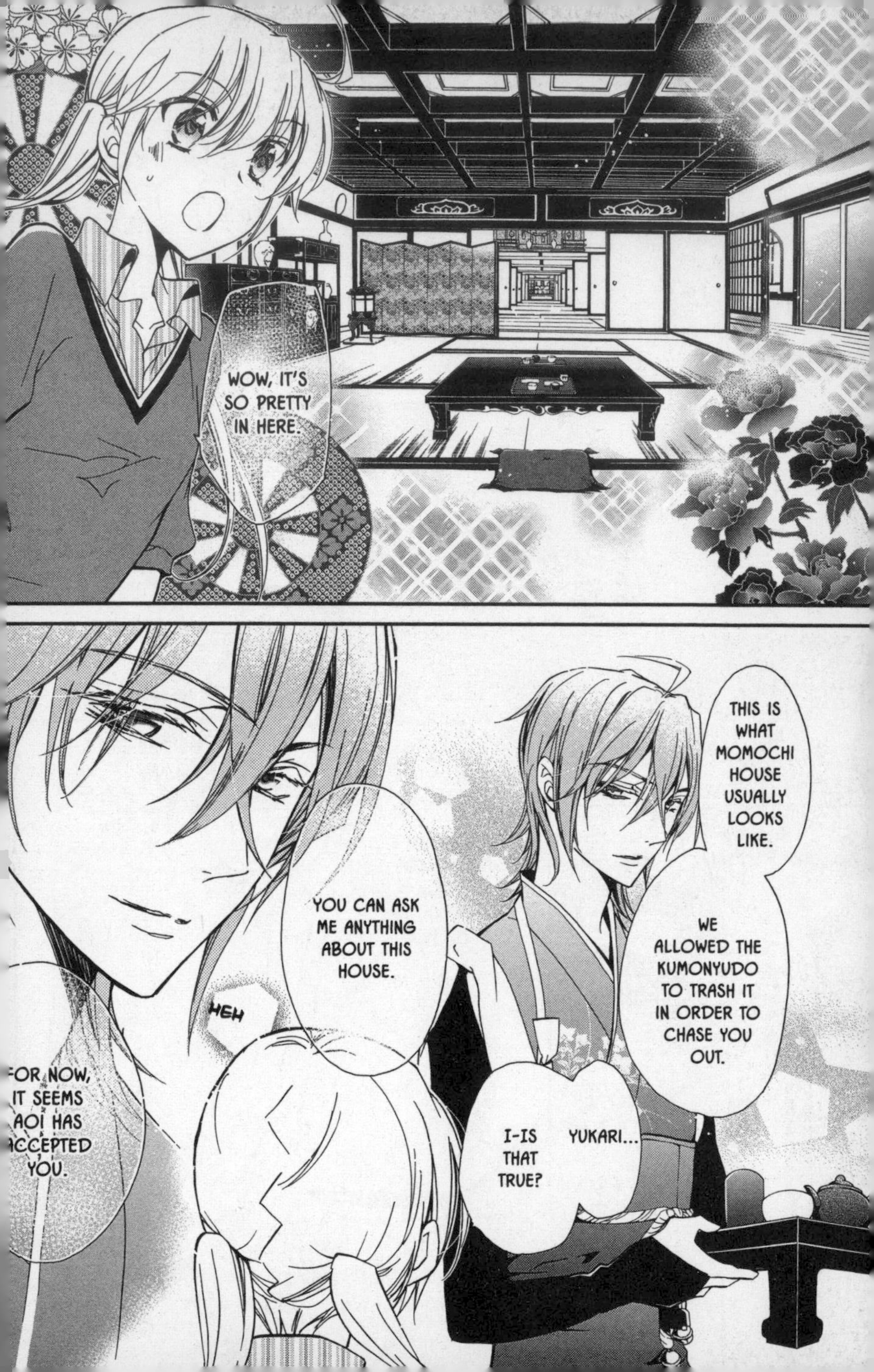
WOW, IT'S SO PRETTY IN HERE.
THIS IS WHAT MOMOCHI HOUSE USUALLY LOOKS LIKE.
WE ALLOWED THE KUMONYUDO TO TRASH IT IN ORDER TO CHASE YOU OUT.
YOU CAN ASK ME ANYTHING ABOUT THIS HOUSE.
YUKARI...
I-IS THAT TRUE?
HEH
FOR NOW, IT SEEMS AOI HAS ACCEPTED YOU.

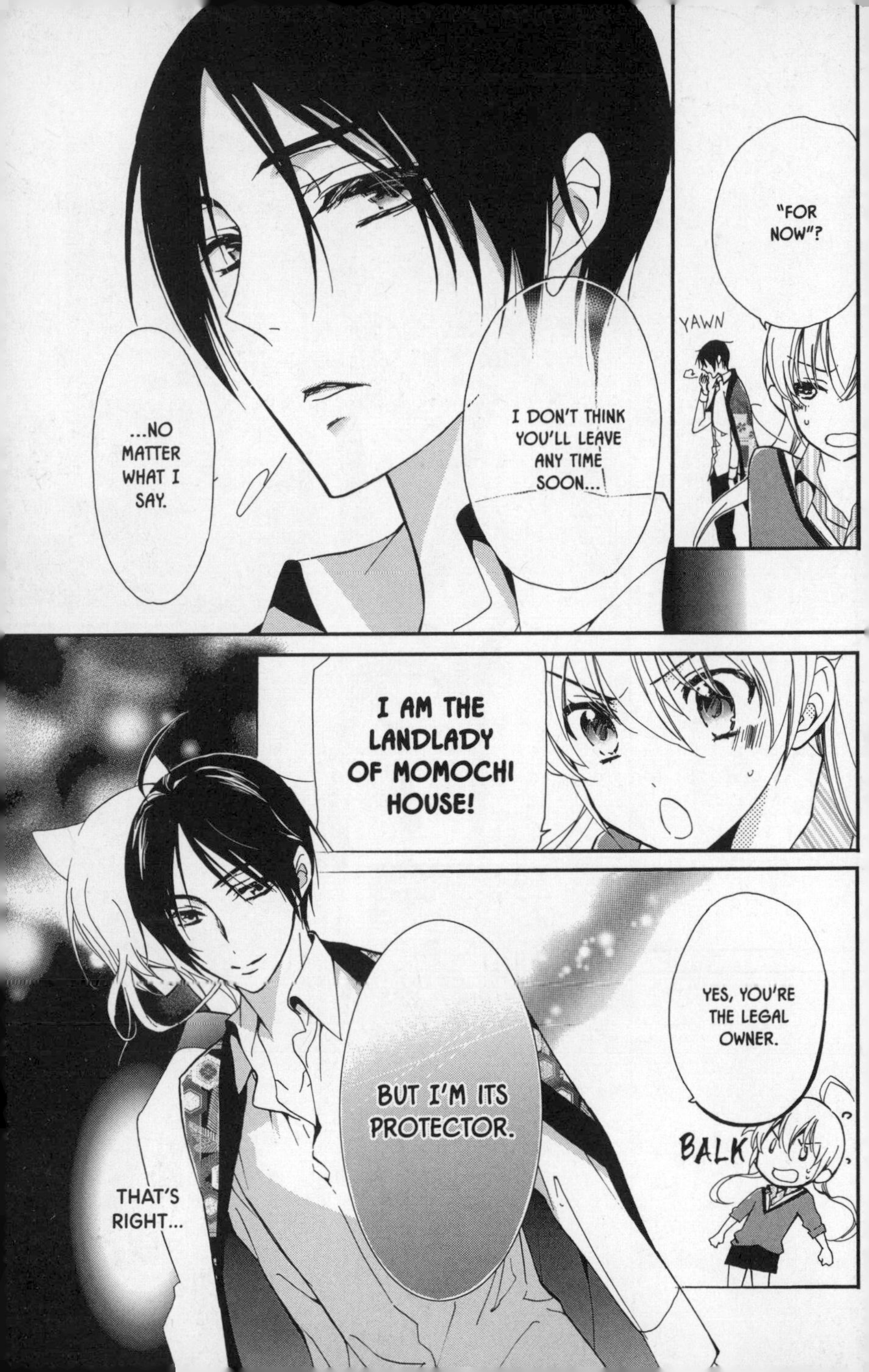
"FOR NOW"?
YAWN
I DON'T THINK YOU'LL LEAVE ANY TIME SOON...
...NO MATTER WHAT I SAY.
I AM THE LANDLADY OF MOMOCHI HOUSE!
YES, YOU'RE THE LEGAL OWNER.
BALK
BUT I'M ITS PROTECTOR.
THAT'S RIGHT...

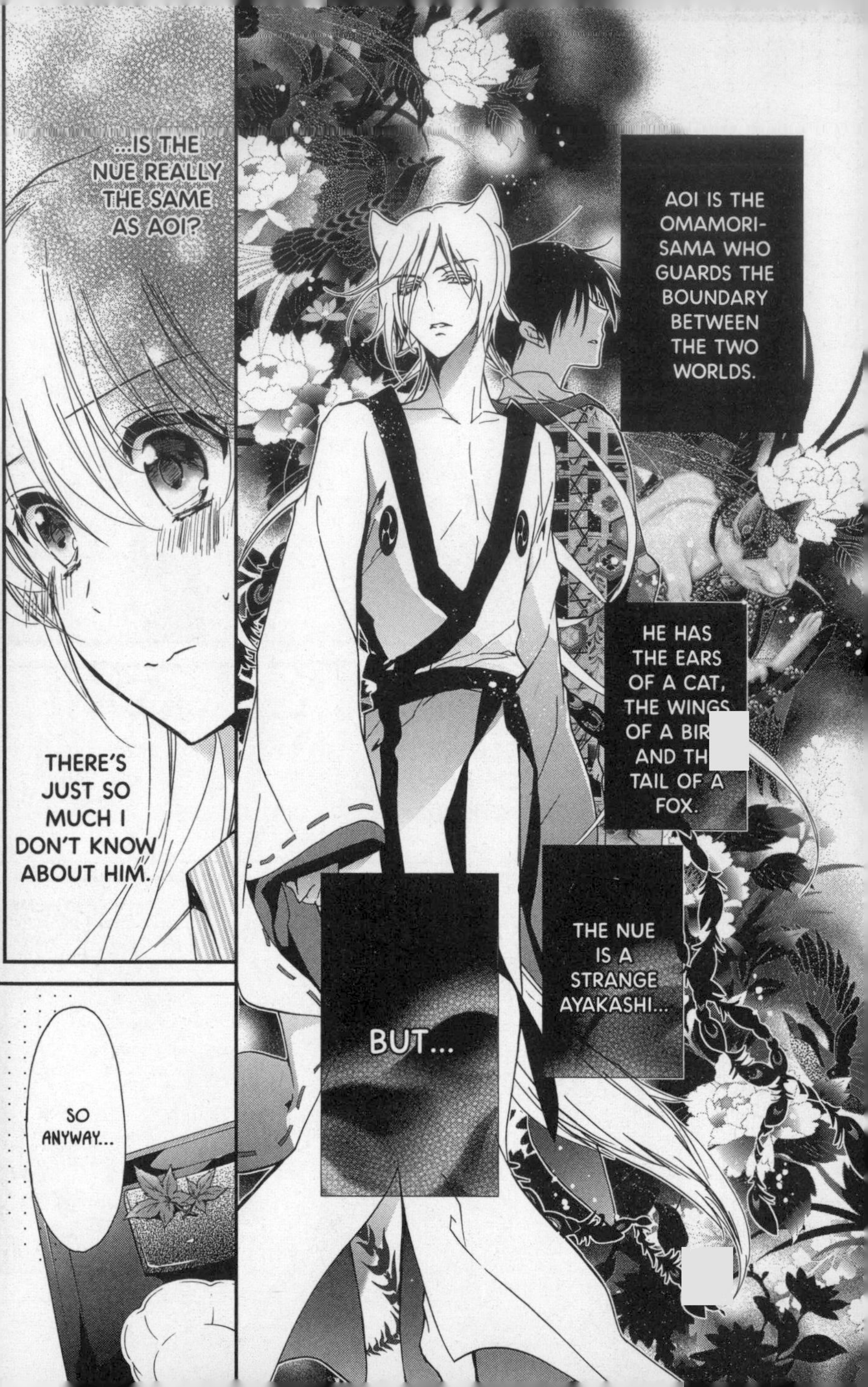
AOI IS THE OMAMORI-SAMA WHO GUARDS THE BOUNDARY BETWEEN THE TWO WORLDS.
HE HAS THE EARS OF A CAT, THE WINGS OF A BIR AND TH TAIL OF A FOX.
THE NUE IS A STRANGE AYAKASHI...
BUT...
...IS THE NUE REALLY THE SAME AS AOI?
THERE'S JUST SO MUCH I DON'T KNOW ABOUT HIM.
SO ANYWAY...

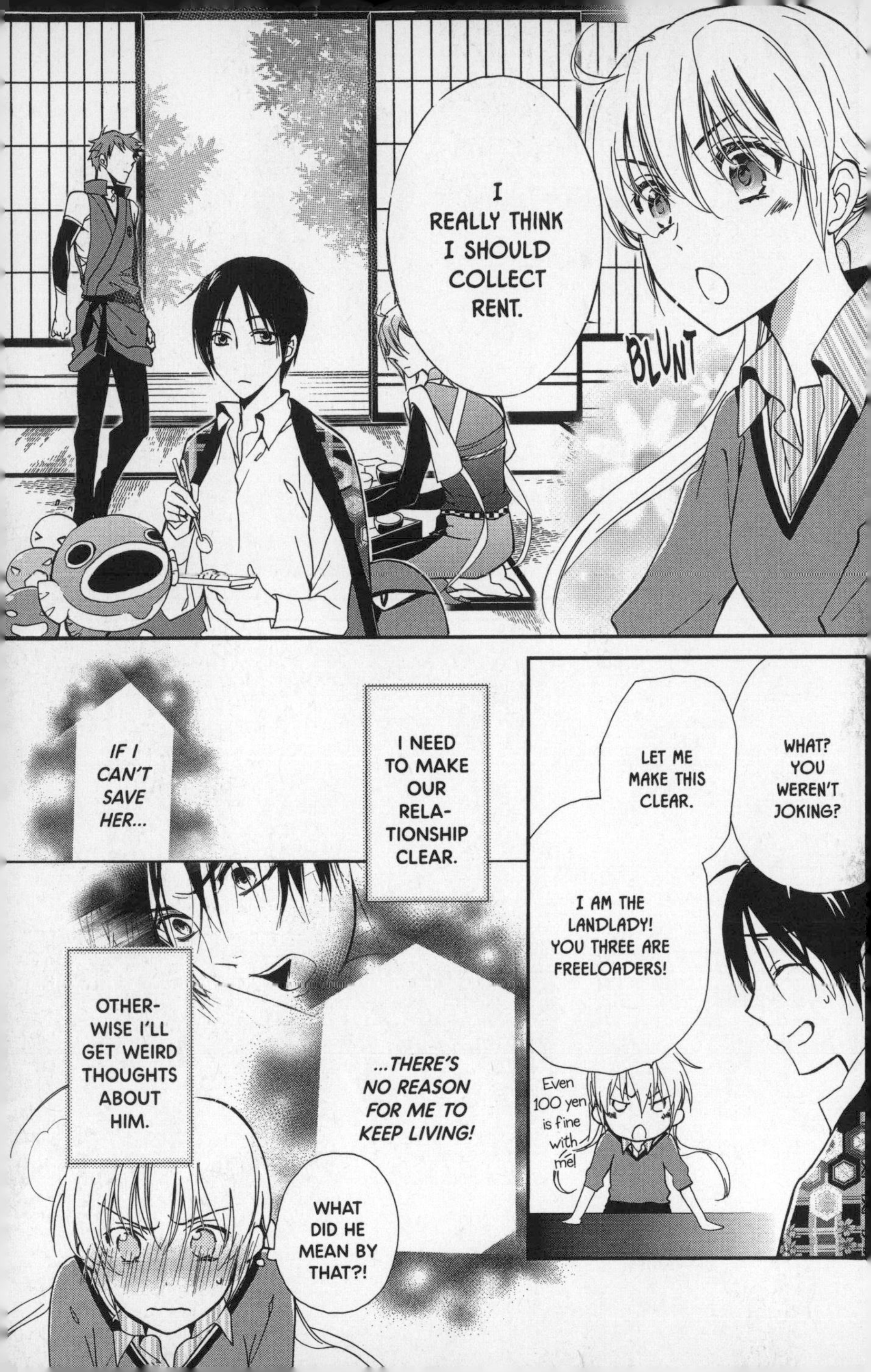
I REALLY THINK I SHOULD COLLECT RENT.
BLUNT
WHAT? YOU WEREN'T JOKING?
LET ME MAKE THIS CLEAR.
I AM THE LANDLADY! YOU THREE ARE FREELOADERS!
Even 100 yen is fine with me!
I NEED TO MAKE OUR RELA-TIONSHIP CLEAR.
IF I CAN'T SAVE HER...
...THERE'S NO REASON FOR ME TO KEEP LIVING!
OTHER-WISE I'LL GET WEIRD THOUGHTS ABOUT HIM.
WHAT DID HE MEAN BY THAT?!

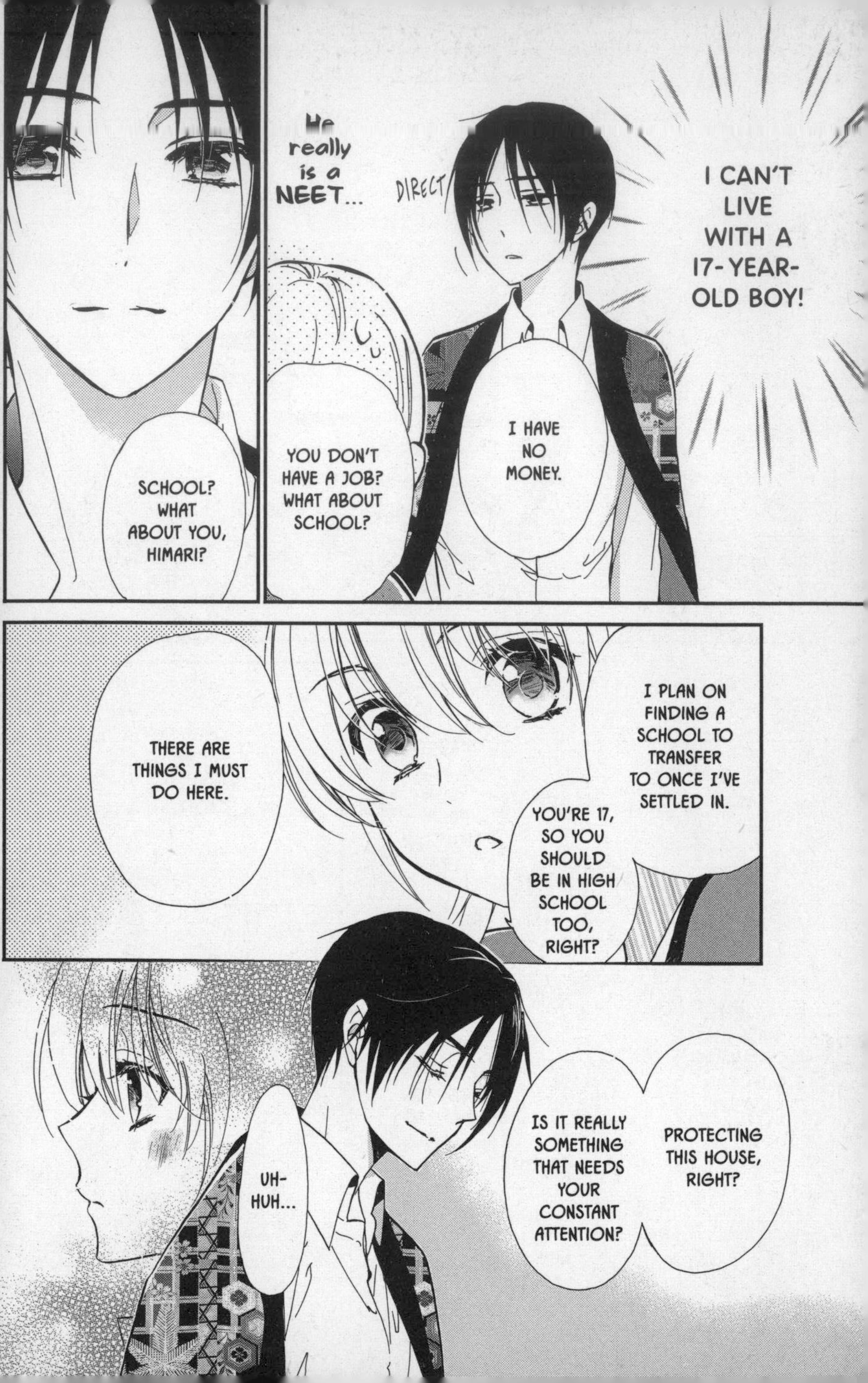
I CAN'T LIVE WITH A 17-YEAR-OLD BOY!
DIRECT
He really is a NEET...
I HAVE NO MONEY.
YOU DON'T HAVE A JOB? WHAT ABOUT SCHOOL?
SCHOOL? WHAT ABOUT YOU, HIMARI?
I PLAN ON FINDING A SCHOOL TO TRANSFER TO ONCE I'VE SETTLED IN.
YOU'RE 17, SO YOU SHOULD BE IN HIGH SCHOOL TOO, RIGHT?
THERE ARE THINGS I MUST DO HERE.
PROTECTING THIS HOUSE, RIGHT?
IS IT REALLY SOMETHING THAT NEEDS YOUR CONSTANT ATTENTION?
UH-HUH...

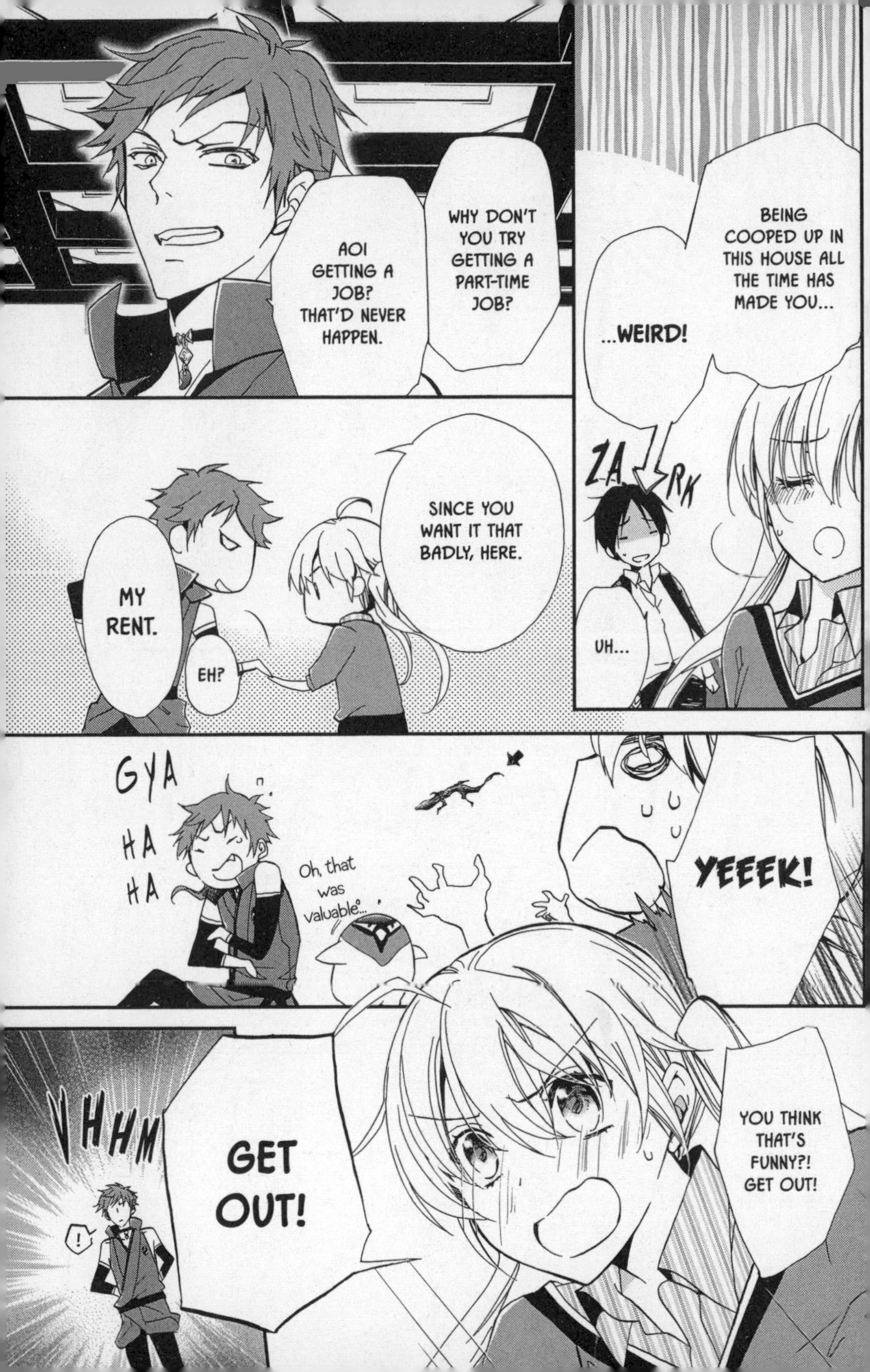
BEING COOPED UP IN THIS HOUSE ALL THE TIME HAS MADE YOU...
...WEIRD!
ZARK
UH...
WHY DON'T YOU TRY GETTING A PART-TIME JOB?
AOI GETTING A JOB? THAT'D NEVER HAPPEN.
SINCE YOU WANT IT THAT BADLY, HERE.
MY RENT.
EH?
YEEEK!
Oh, that was valuable...
GYA HA HA
YOU THINK THAT'S FUNNY?! GET OUT!
GET OUT!
VHHM
!

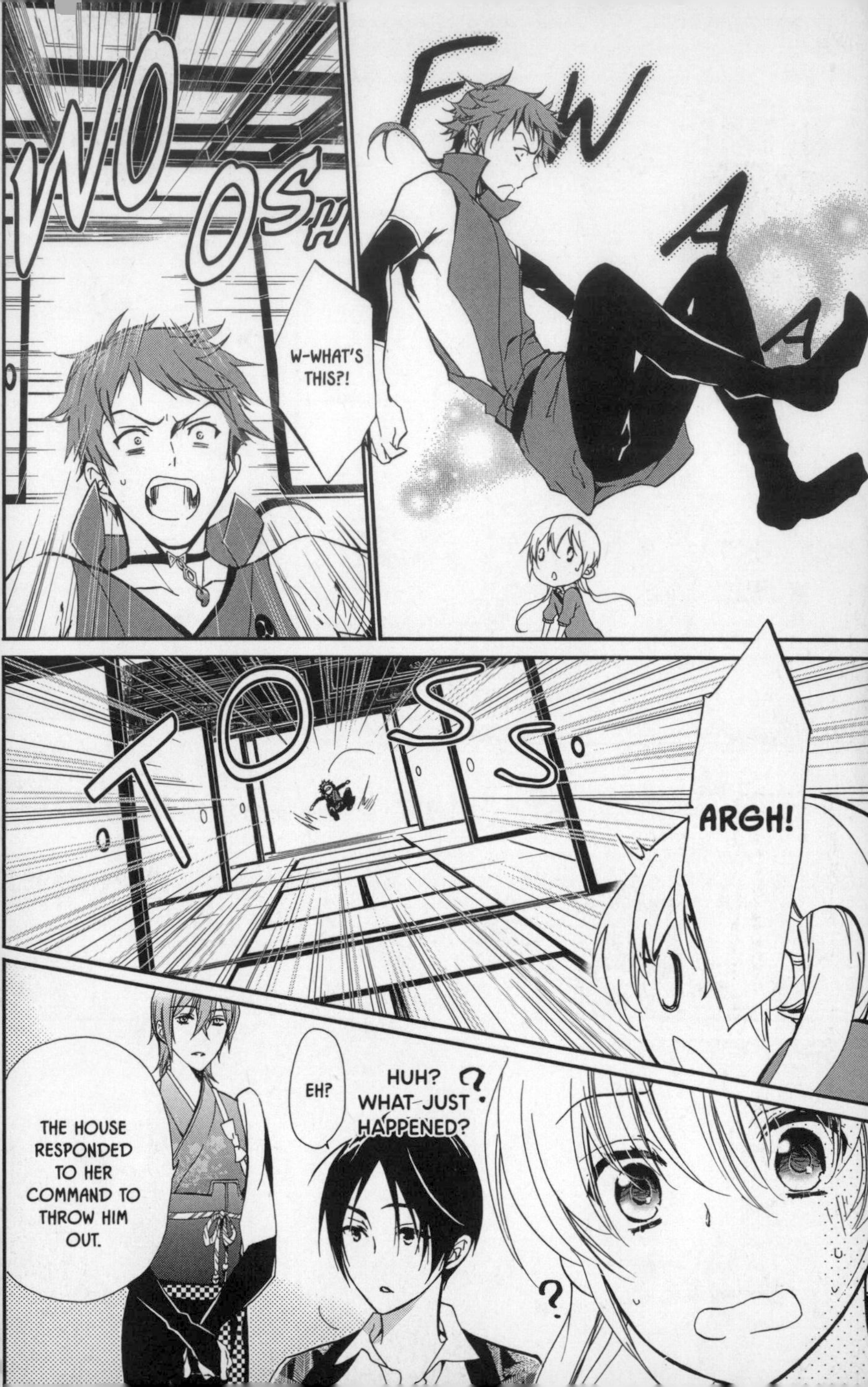

FWAAA
WOOSH
W-WHAT'S THIS?!
ARGH!
TOSS
HUH? WHAT JUST HAPPENED?
EH?
THE HOUSE RESPONDED TO HER COMMAND TO THROW HIM OUT.

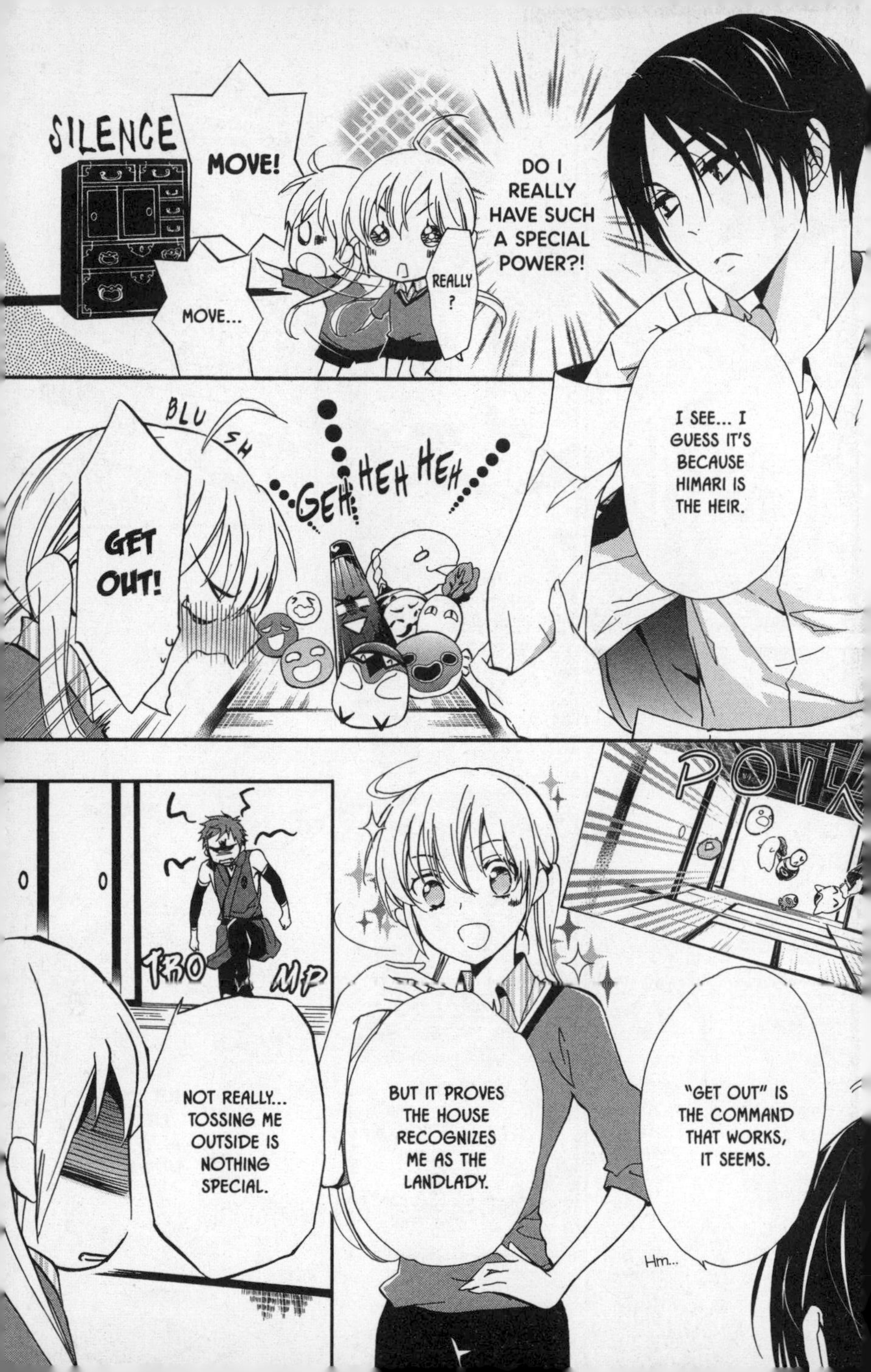
DO I REALLY HAVE SUCH A SPECIAL POWER?!
REALLY?
MOVE!
MOVE...
SILENCE
I SEE... I GUESS IT'S BECAUSE HIMARI IS THE HEIR.
GEH HEH HEH
BLUSH
GET OUT!
POIK
"GET OUT" IS THE COMMAND THAT WORKS, IT SEEMS.
Hm...
BUT IT PROVES THE HOUSE RECOGNIZES ME AS THE LANDLADY.
TROMP
NOT REALLY... TOSSING ME OUTSIDE IS NOTHING SPECIAL.

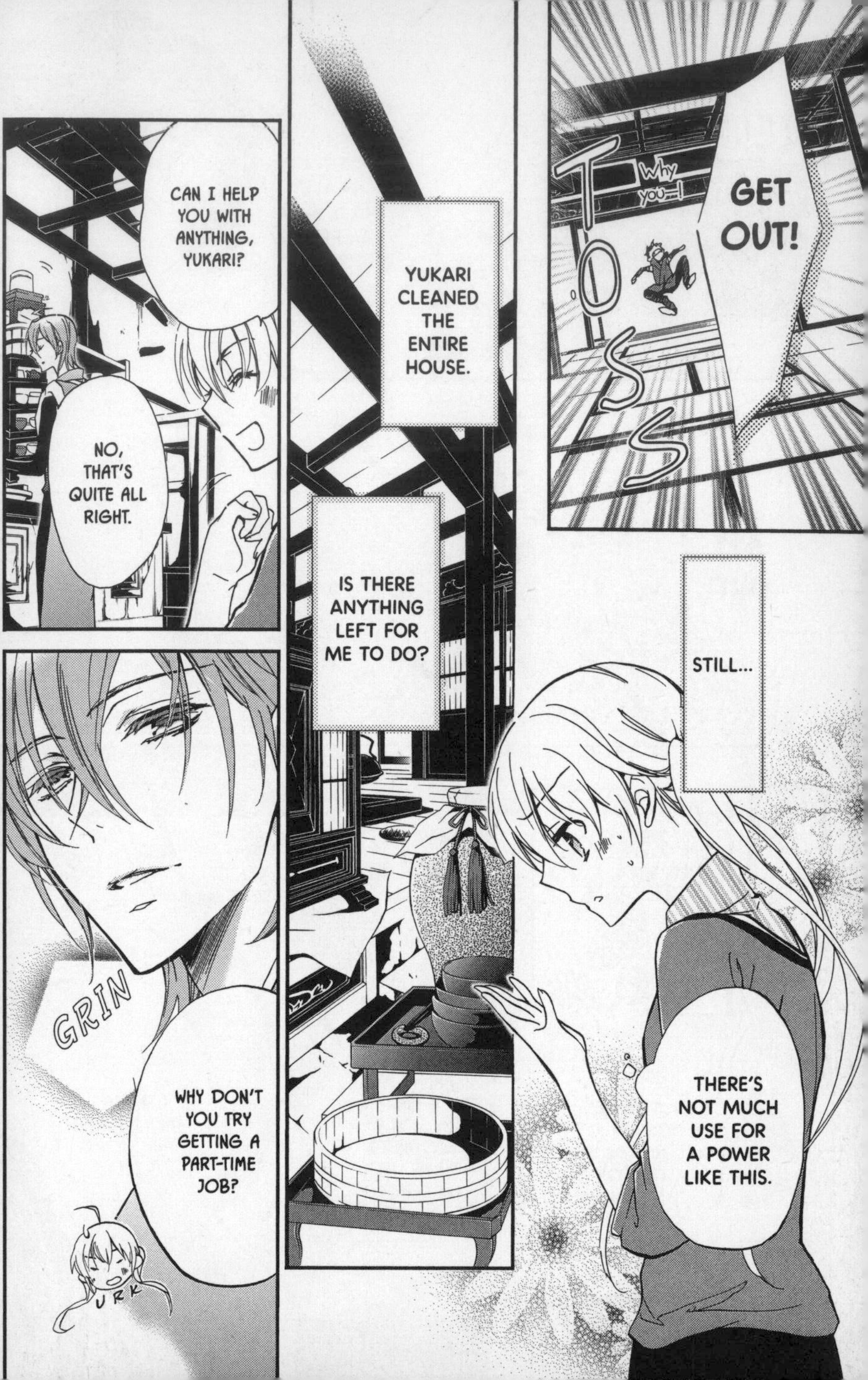
GET OUT!
why you—!
TOSS
STILL...
THERE'S NOT MUCH USE FOR A POWER LIKE THIS.
YUKARI CLEANED THE ENTIRE HOUSE.
IS THERE ANYTHING LEFT FOR ME TO DO?
CAN I HELP YOU WITH ANYTHING, YUKARI?
NO, THAT'S QUITE ALL RIGHT.
GRIN
WHY DON'T YOU TRY GETTING A PART-TIME JOB?
URK

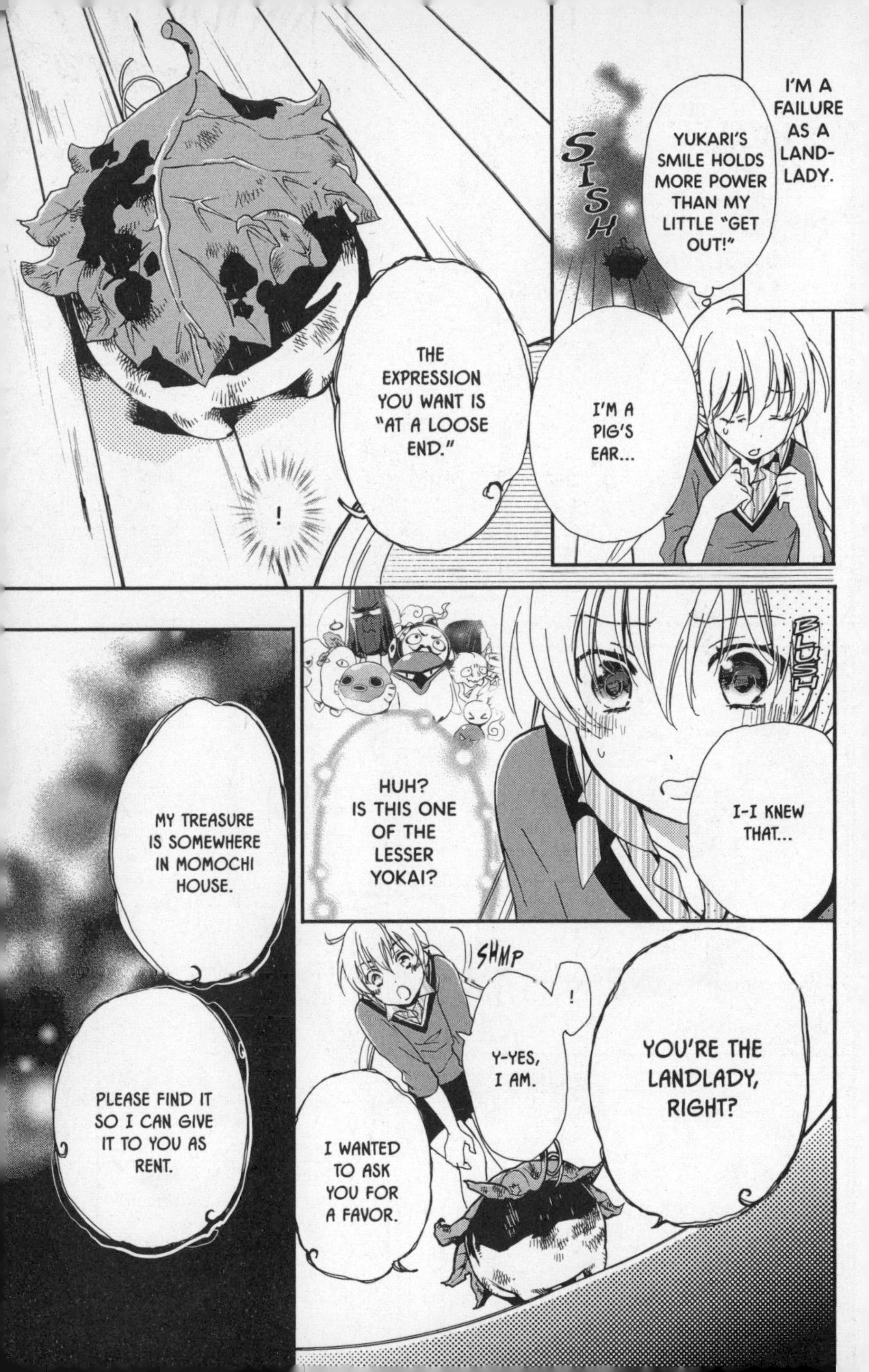
I'M A FAILURE AS A LANDLADY.
YUKARI'S SMILE HOLDS MORE POWER THAN MY LITTLE "GET OUT!"
SISH
I'M A PIG'S EAR...
THE EXPRESSION YOU WANT IS "AT A LOOSE END."
!
BLUSH
I-I KNEW THAT...
HUH? IS THIS ONE OF THE LESSER YOKAI?
YOU'RE THE LANDLADY, RIGHT?
SHMP
!
Y-YES, I AM.
I WANTED TO ASK YOU FOR A FAVOR.
MY TREASURE IS SOMEWHERE IN MOMOCHI HOUSE.
PLEASE FIND IT SO I CAN GIVE IT TO YOU AS RENT.

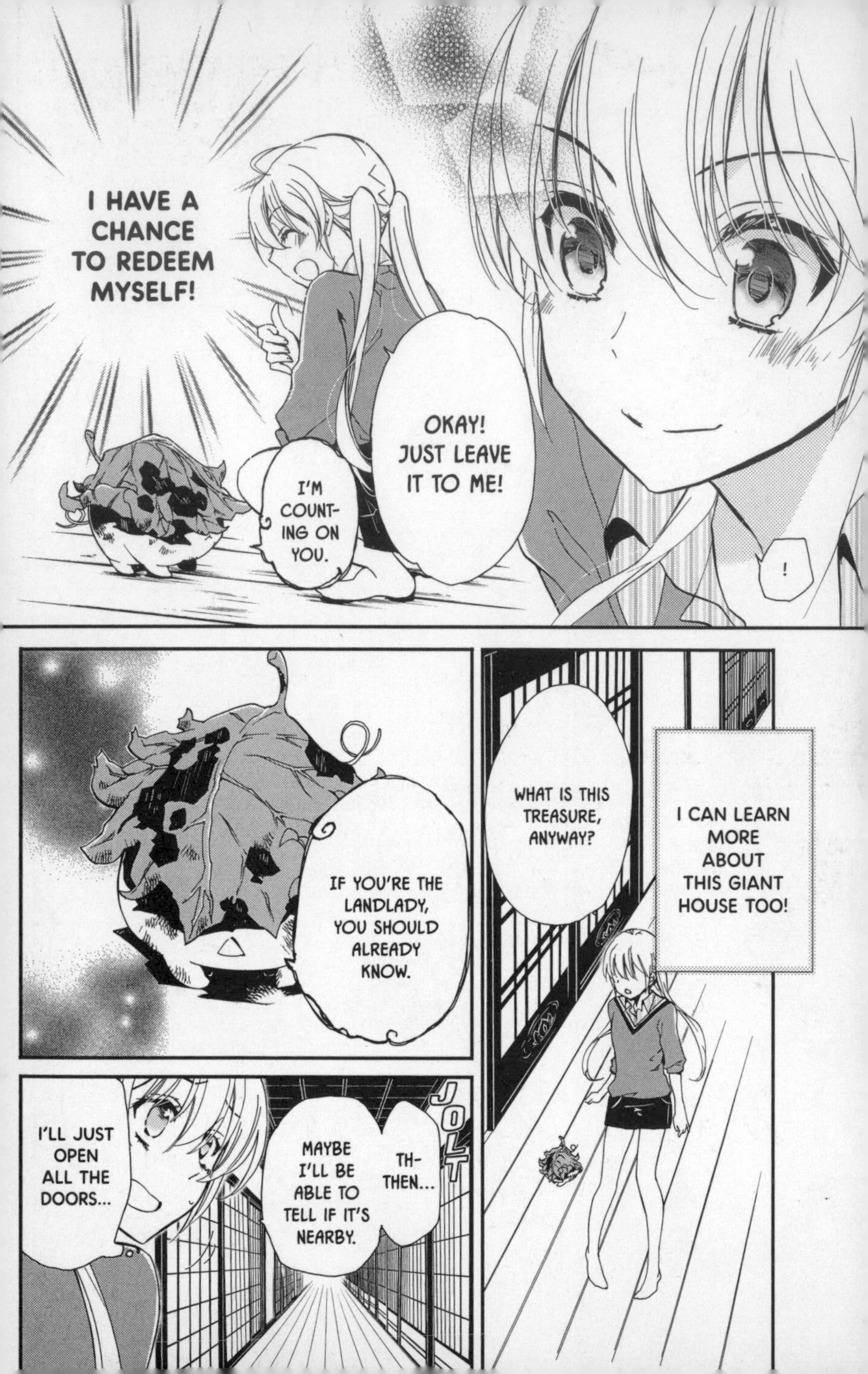
!
OKAY! JUST LEAVE IT TO ME!
I'M COUNTING ON YOU.
I HAVE A CHANCE TO REDEEM MYSELF!
I CAN LEARN MORE ABOUT THIS GIANT HOUSE TOO!
WHAT IS THIS TREASURE, ANYWAY?
IF YOU'RE THE LANDLADY, YOU SHOULD ALREADY KNOW.
JOLT
TH-THEN...
MAYBE I'LL BE ABLE TO TELL IF IT'S NEARBY.
I'LL JUST OPEN ALL THE DOORS...

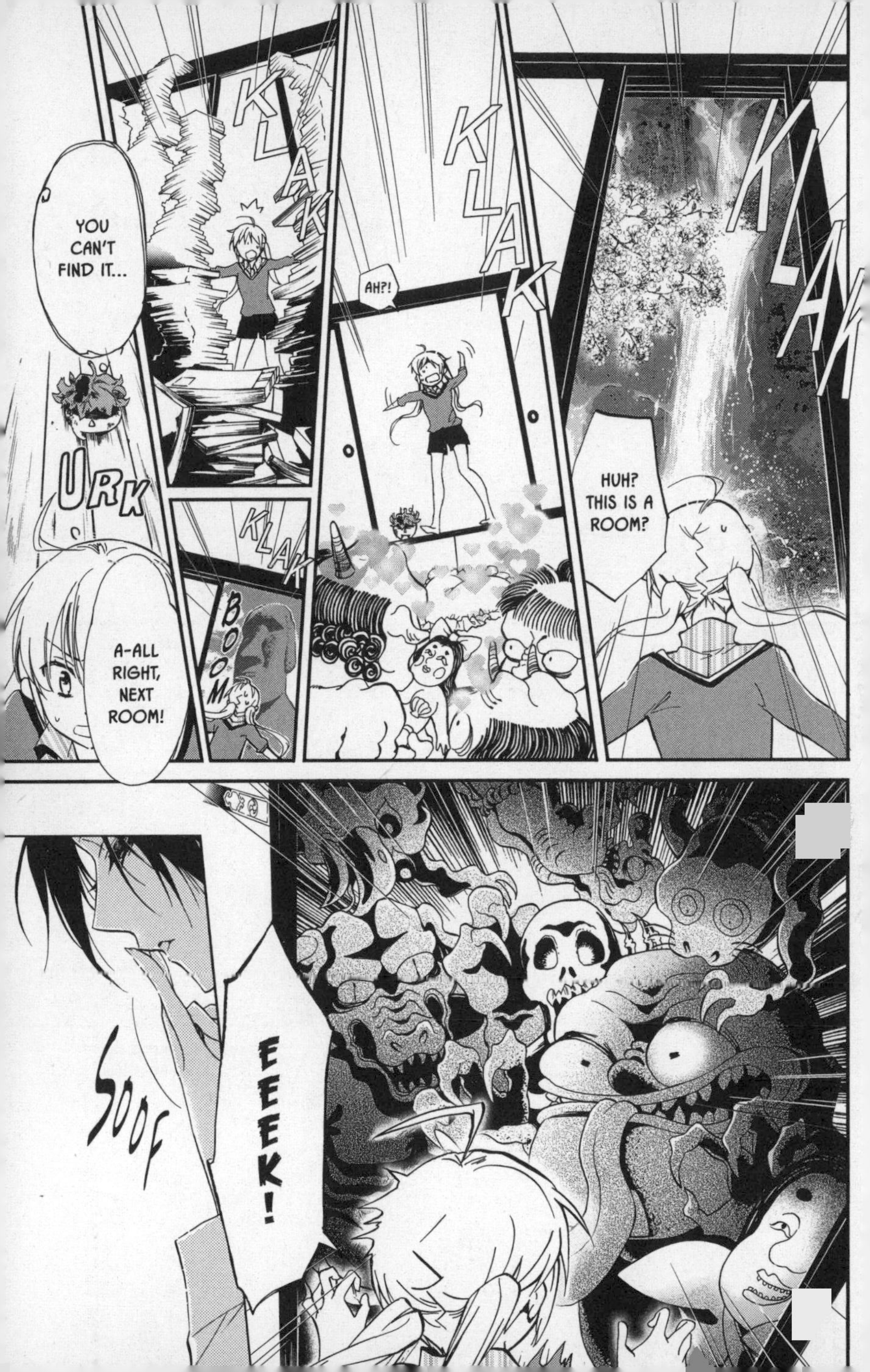
KLAK
HUH? THIS IS A ROOM?
KLAK
AH?!
KLAK
KLAK
BOOM
YOU CAN'T FIND IT...
URK
A-ALL RIGHT, NEXT ROOM!
EEEEK!
SOOF

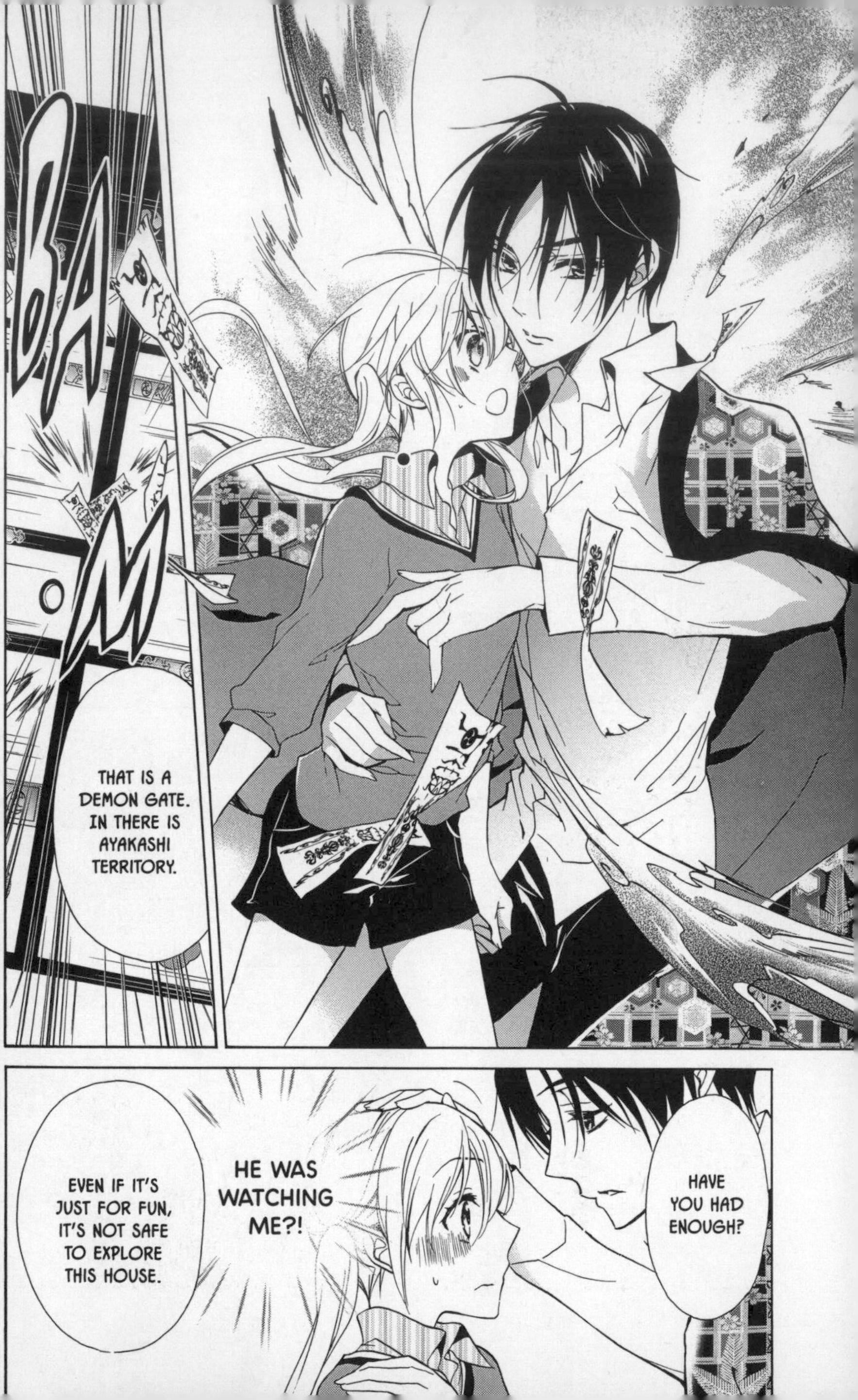
BAM
THAT IS A DEMON GATE. IN THERE IS AYAKASHI TERRITORY.
HAVE YOU HAD ENOUGH?
HE WAS WATCHING ME?!
EVEN IF IT'S JUST FOR FUN, IT'S NOT SAFE TO EXPLORE THIS HOUSE.

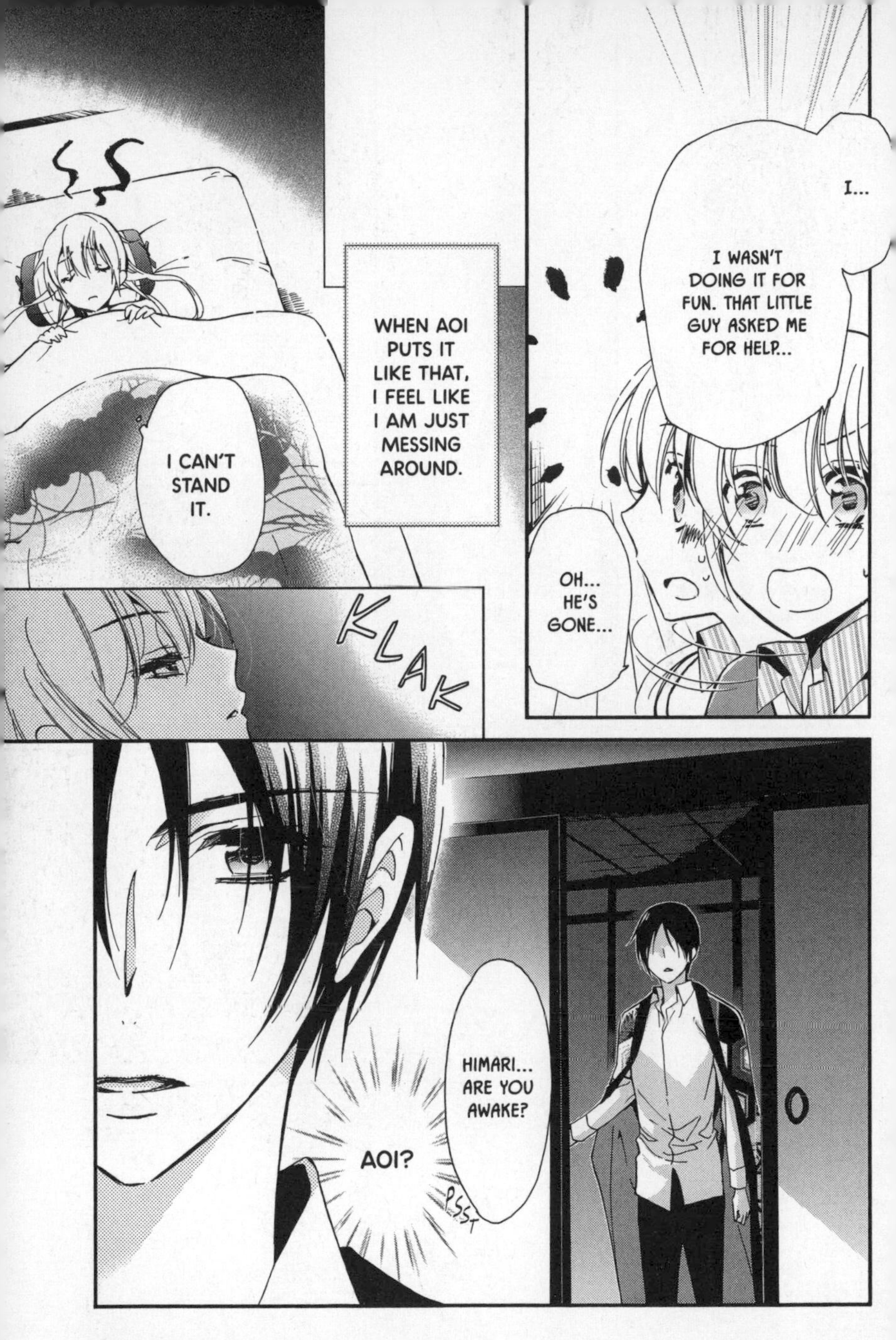
I...
I WASN'T DOING IT FOR FUN. THAT LITTLE GUY ASKED ME FOR HELP...
OH... HE'S GONE...
WHEN AOI PUTS IT LIKE THAT, I FEEL LIKE I AM JUST MESSING AROUND.
I CAN'T STAND IT.
KLAK
HIMARI... ARE YOU AWAKE?
AOI?
PSST

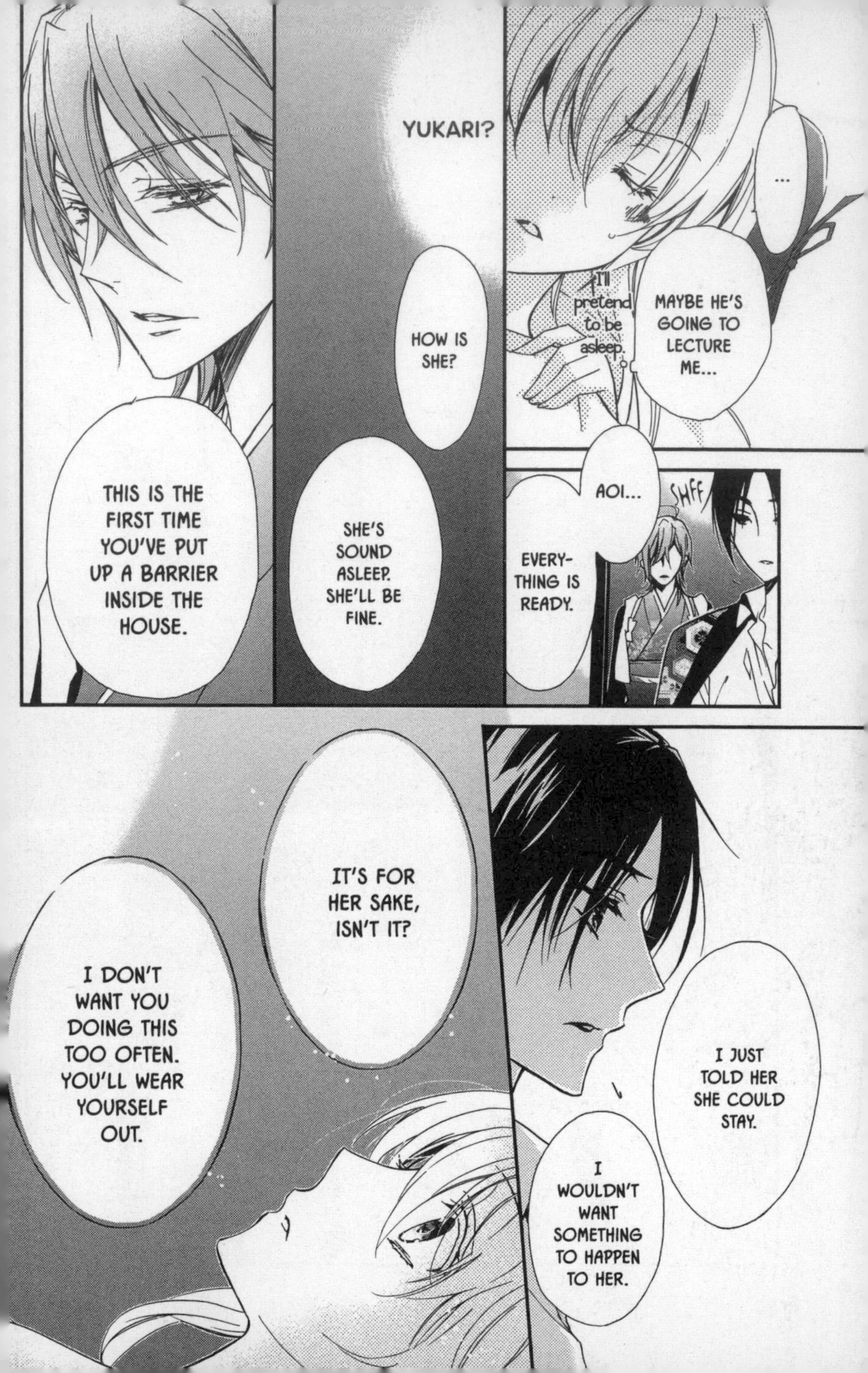
...
MAYBE HE'S GOING TO LECTURE ME...
I'll pretend to be asleep.
SHFF
AOI...
EVERYTHING IS READY.
YUKARI?
HOW IS SHE?
SHE'S SOUND ASLEEP. SHE'LL BE FINE.
THIS IS THE FIRST TIME YOU'VE PUT UP A BARRIER INSIDE THE HOUSE.
I JUST TOLD HER SHE COULD STAY.
I WOULDN'T WANT SOMETHING TO HAPPEN TO HER.
IT'S FOR HER SAKE, ISN'T IT?
I DON'T WANT YOU DOING THIS TOO OFTEN. YOU'LL WEAR YOURSELF OUT.

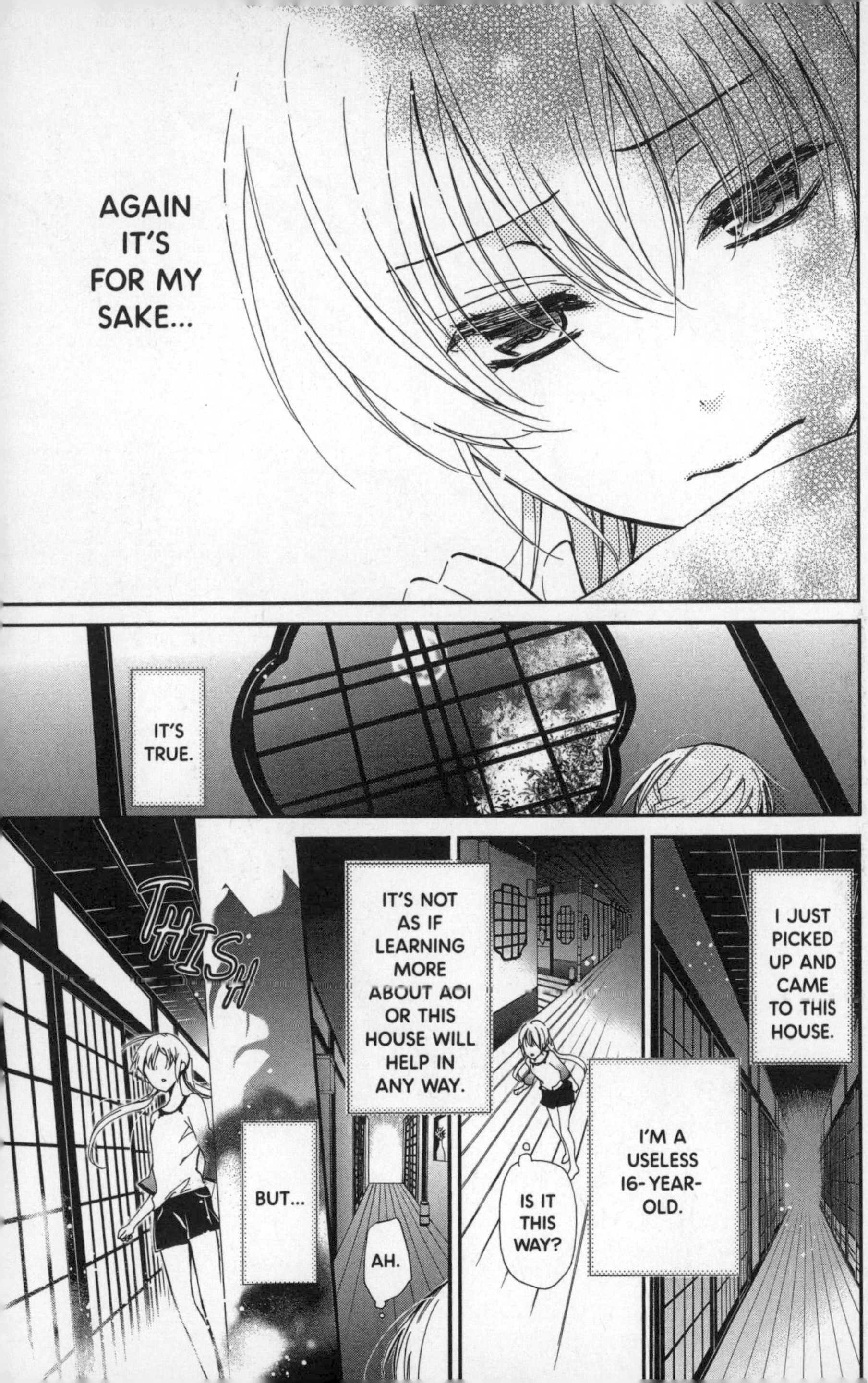
AGAIN IT'S FOR MY SAKE...
IT'S TRUE.
I JUST PICKED UP AND CAME TO THIS HOUSE.
I'M A USELESS 16-YEAR-OLD.
IS IT THIS WAY?
IT'S NOT AS IF LEARNING MORE ABOUT AOI OR THIS HOUSE WILL HELP IN ANY WAY.
AH.
THISH
BUT...

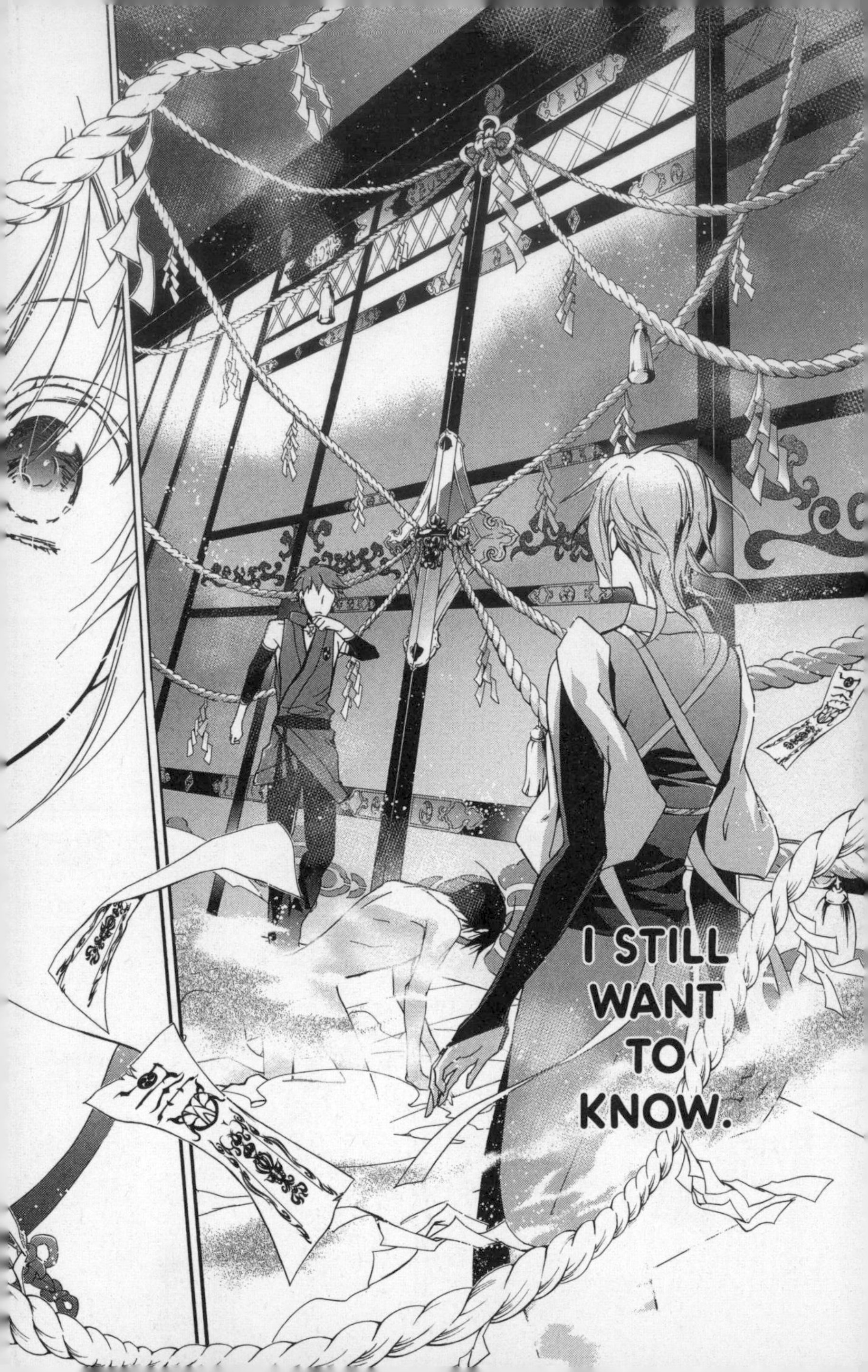
I STILL WANT TO KNOW.

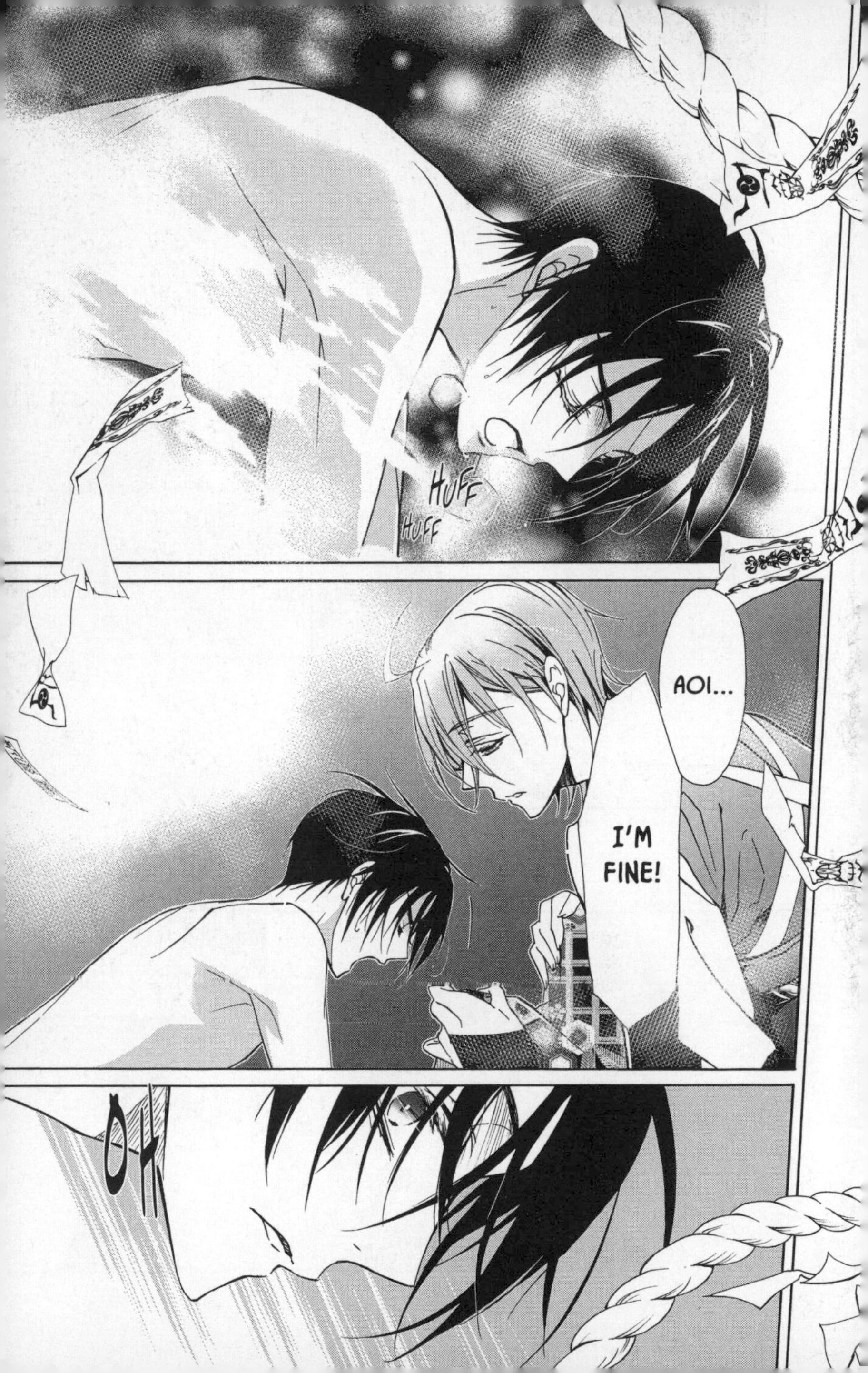
HUFF
HUFF
AOI...
I'M FINE!
OH

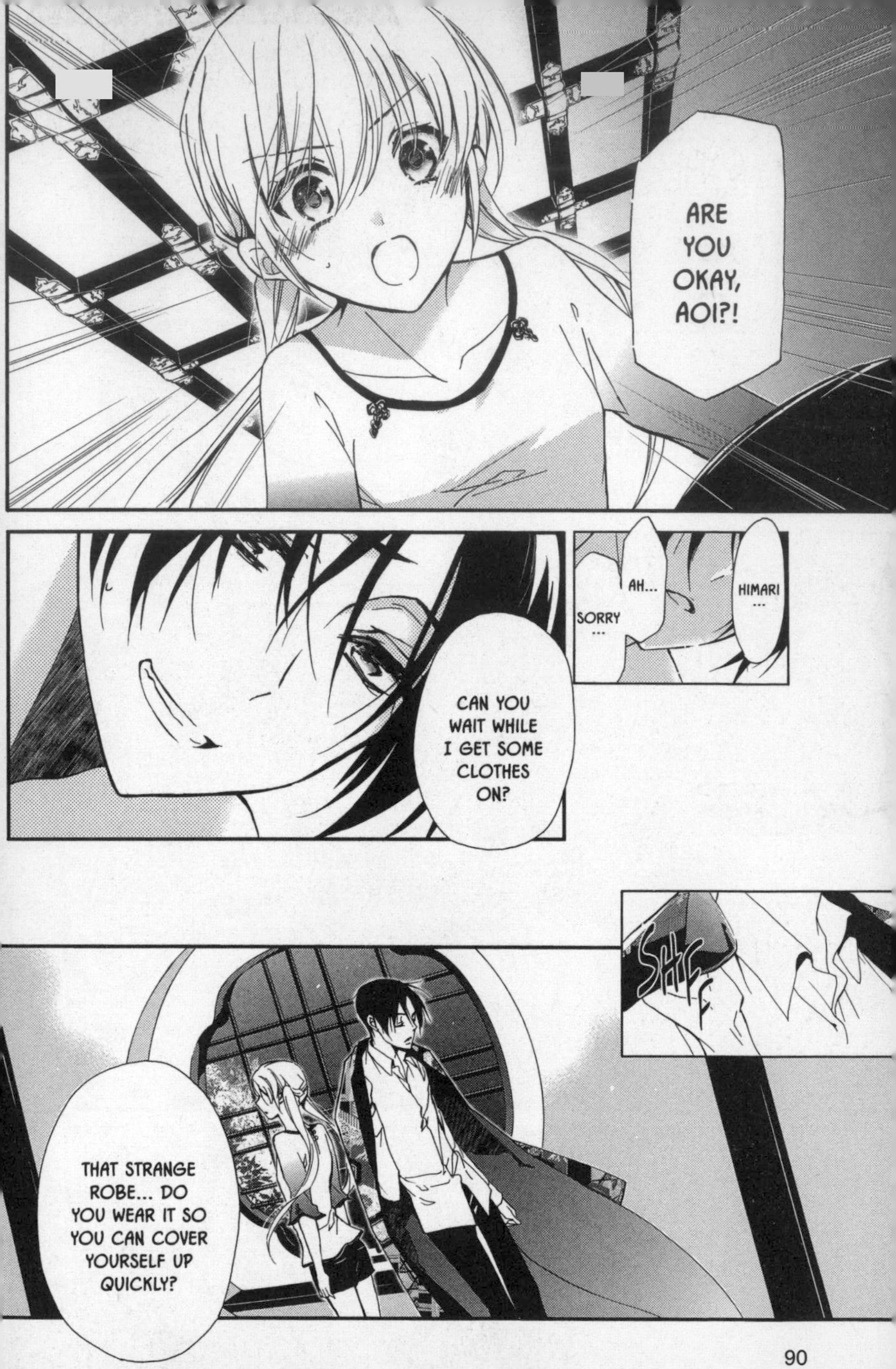
ARE YOU OKAY, AOI?!
HIMARI ...
AH...
SORRY ...
CAN YOU WAIT WHILE I GET SOME CLOTHES ON?
THAT STRANGE ROBE... DO YOU WEAR IT SO YOU CAN COVER YOURSELF UP QUICKLY?

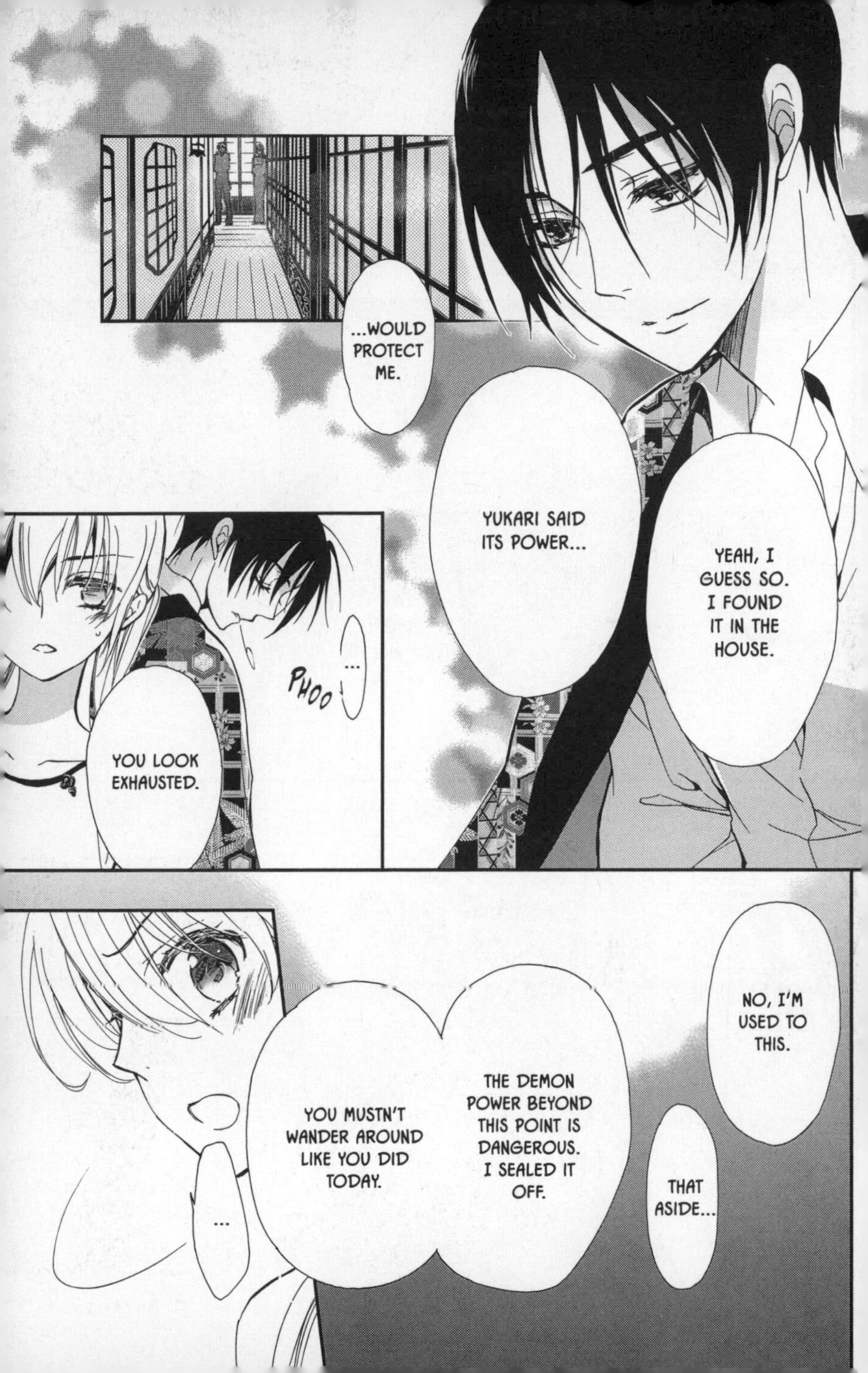
YUKARI SAID ITS POWER...
...WOULD PROTECT ME.
YEAH, I GUESS SO. I FOUND IT IN THE HOUSE.
...
PHOO
YOU LOOK EXHAUSTED.
NO, I'M USED TO THIS.
THAT ASIDE...
THE DEMON POWER BEYOND THIS POINT IS DANGEROUS. I SEALED IT OFF.
YOU MUSTN'T WANDER AROUND LIKE YOU DID TODAY.
...

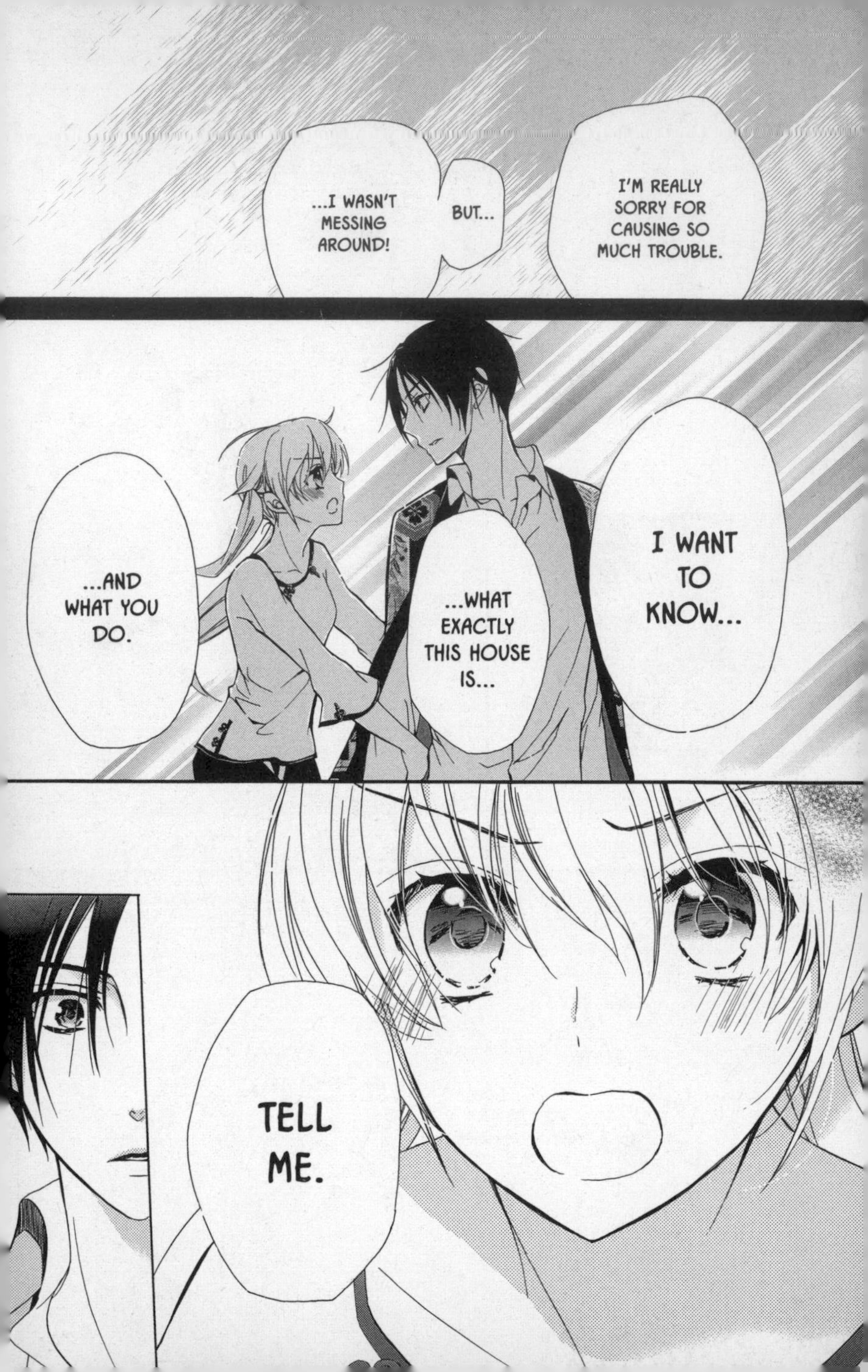
I'M REALLY SORRY FOR CAUSING SO MUCH TROUBLE.
BUT...
...I WASN'T MESSING AROUND!
I WANT TO KNOW...
...WHAT EXACTLY THIS HOUSE IS...
...AND WHAT YOU DO.
TELL ME.

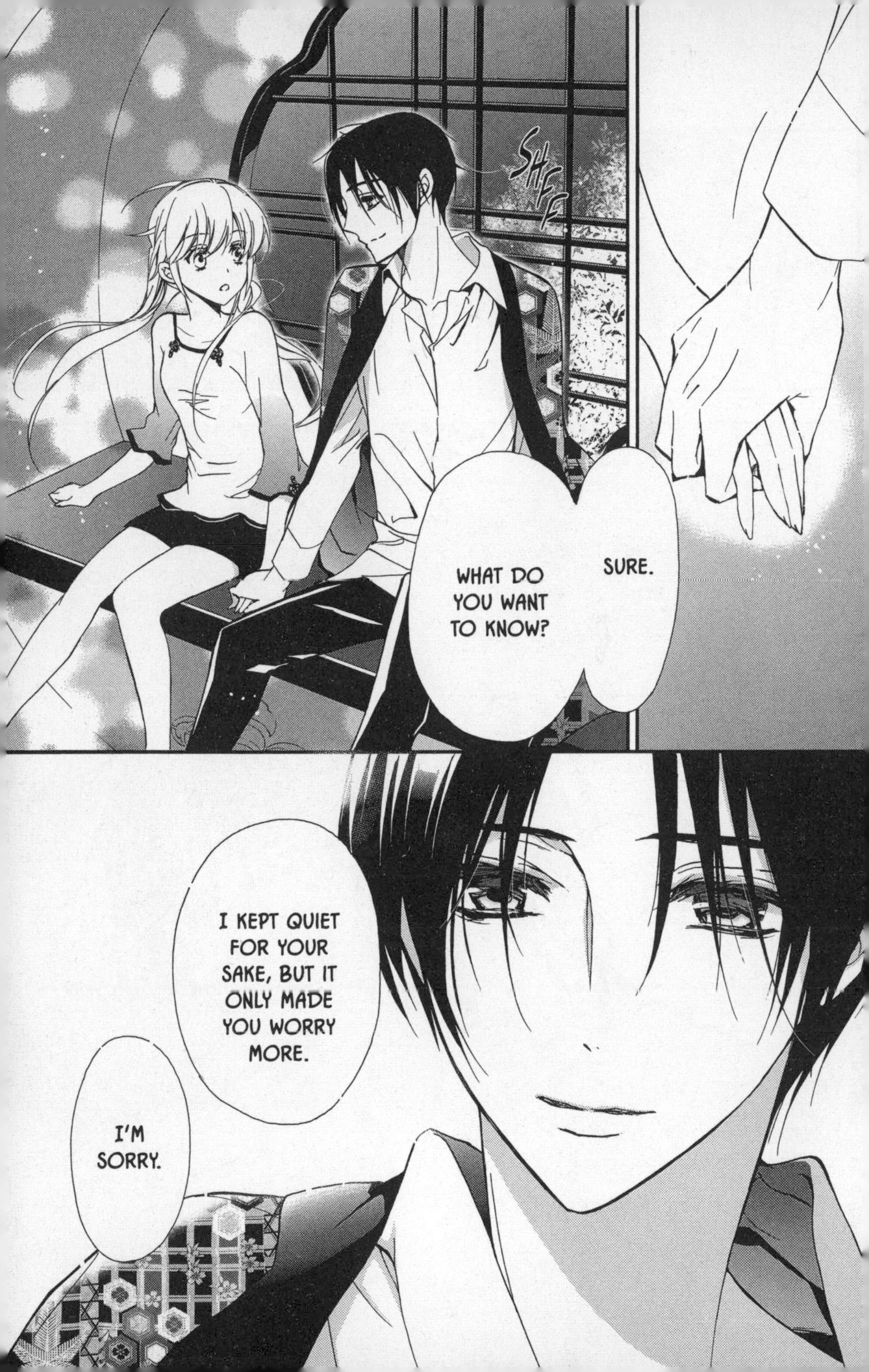
SHFF
SURE.
WHAT DO YOU WANT TO KNOW?
I KEPT QUIET FOR YOUR SAKE, BUT IT ONLY MADE YOU WORRY MORE.
I'M SORRY.

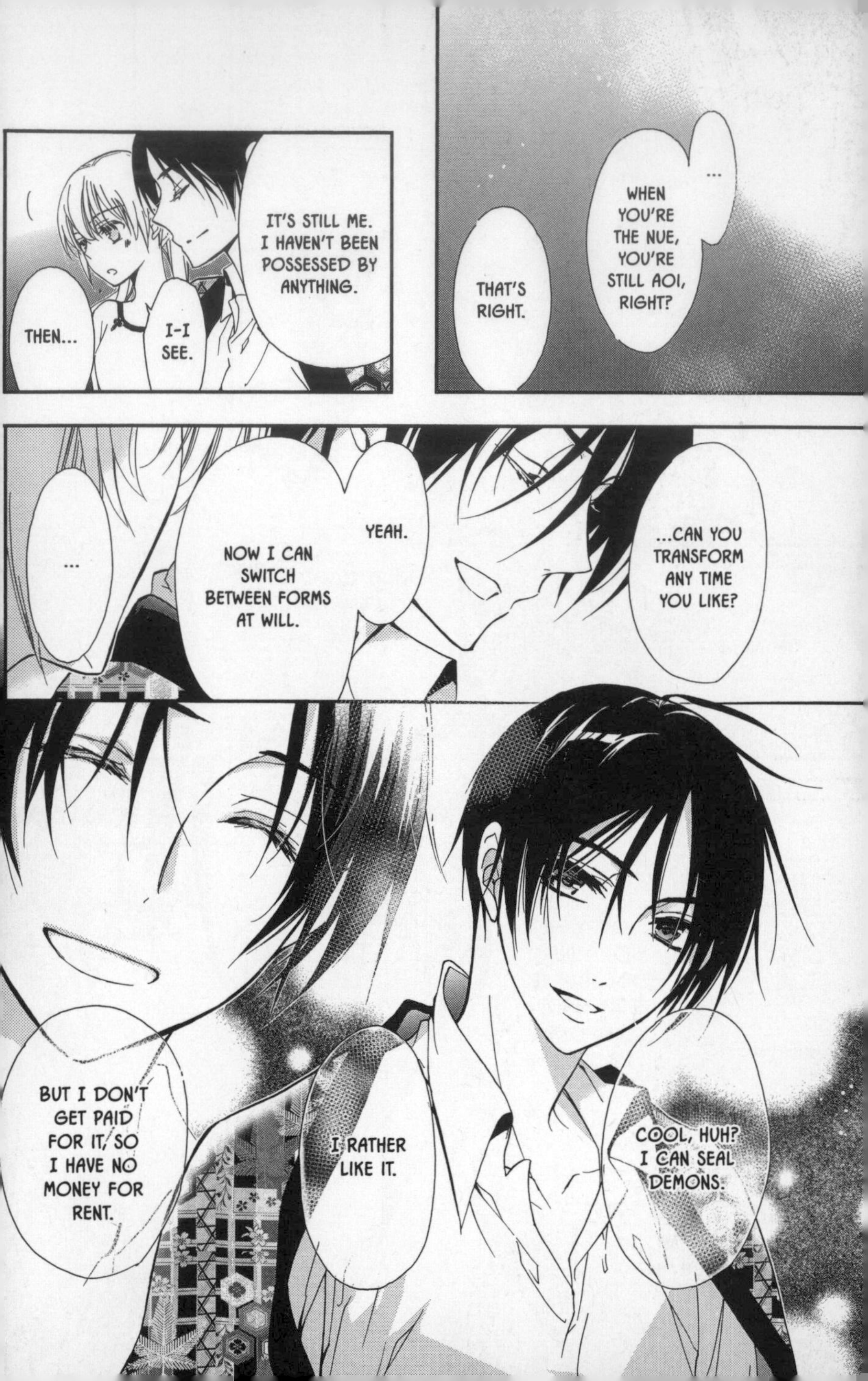
...
WHEN YOU'RE THE NUE, YOU'RE STILL AOI, RIGHT?
THAT'S RIGHT.
IT'S STILL ME. I HAVEN'T BEEN POSSESSED BY ANYTHING.
I-I SEE.
THEN...
...CAN YOU TRANSFORM ANY TIME YOU LIKE?
YEAH.
NOW I CAN SWITCH BETWEEN FORMS AT WILL.
...
COOL, HUH? I CAN SEAL DEMONS.
I RATHER LIKE IT.
BUT I DON'T GET PAID FOR IT, SO I HAVE NO MONEY FOR RENT.

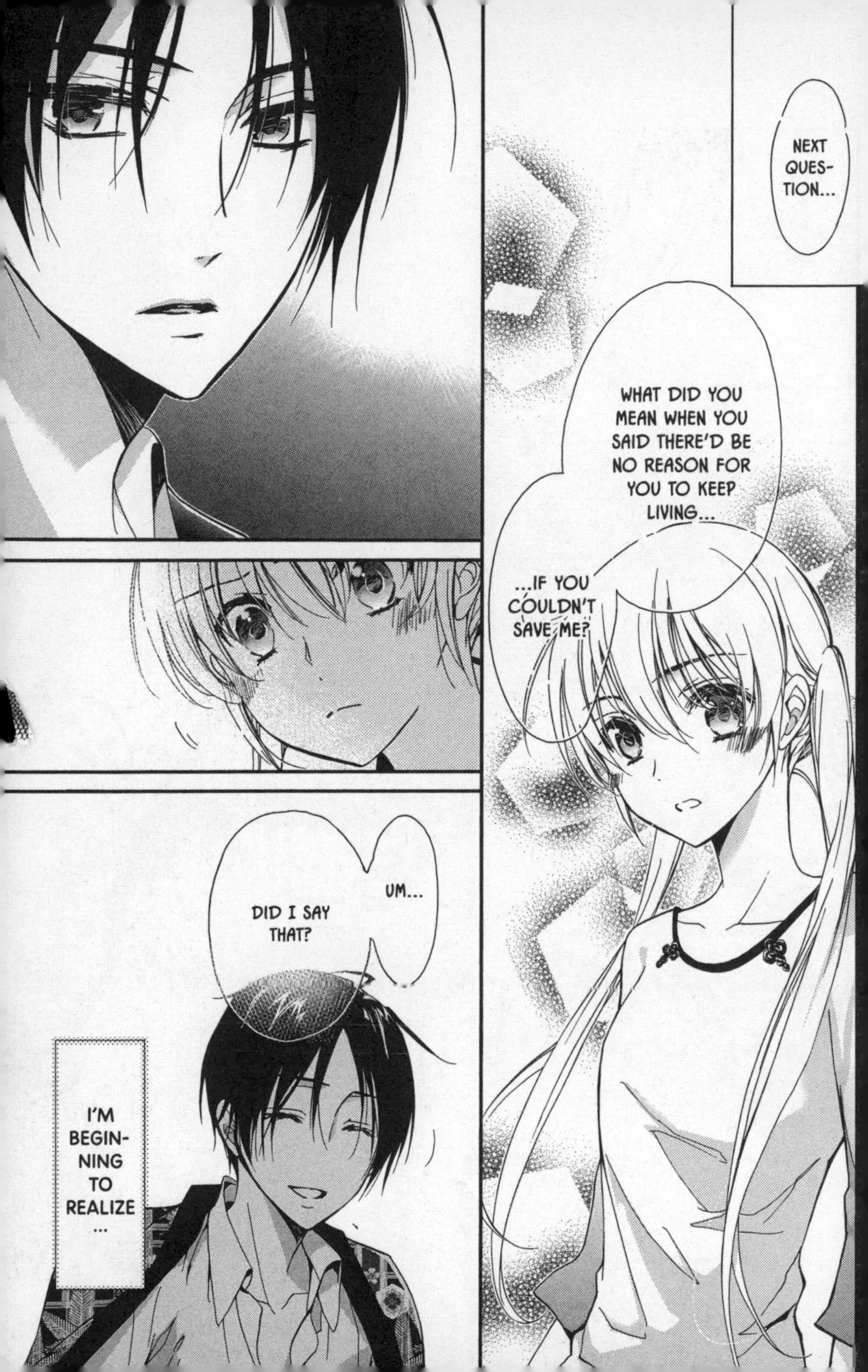
NEXT QUES-TION...
WHAT DID YOU MEAN WHEN YOU SAID THERE'D BE NO REASON FOR YOU TO KEEP LIVING...
...IF YOU COULDN'T SAVE ME?
UM...
DID I SAY THAT?
I'M BEGIN-NING TO REALIZE...

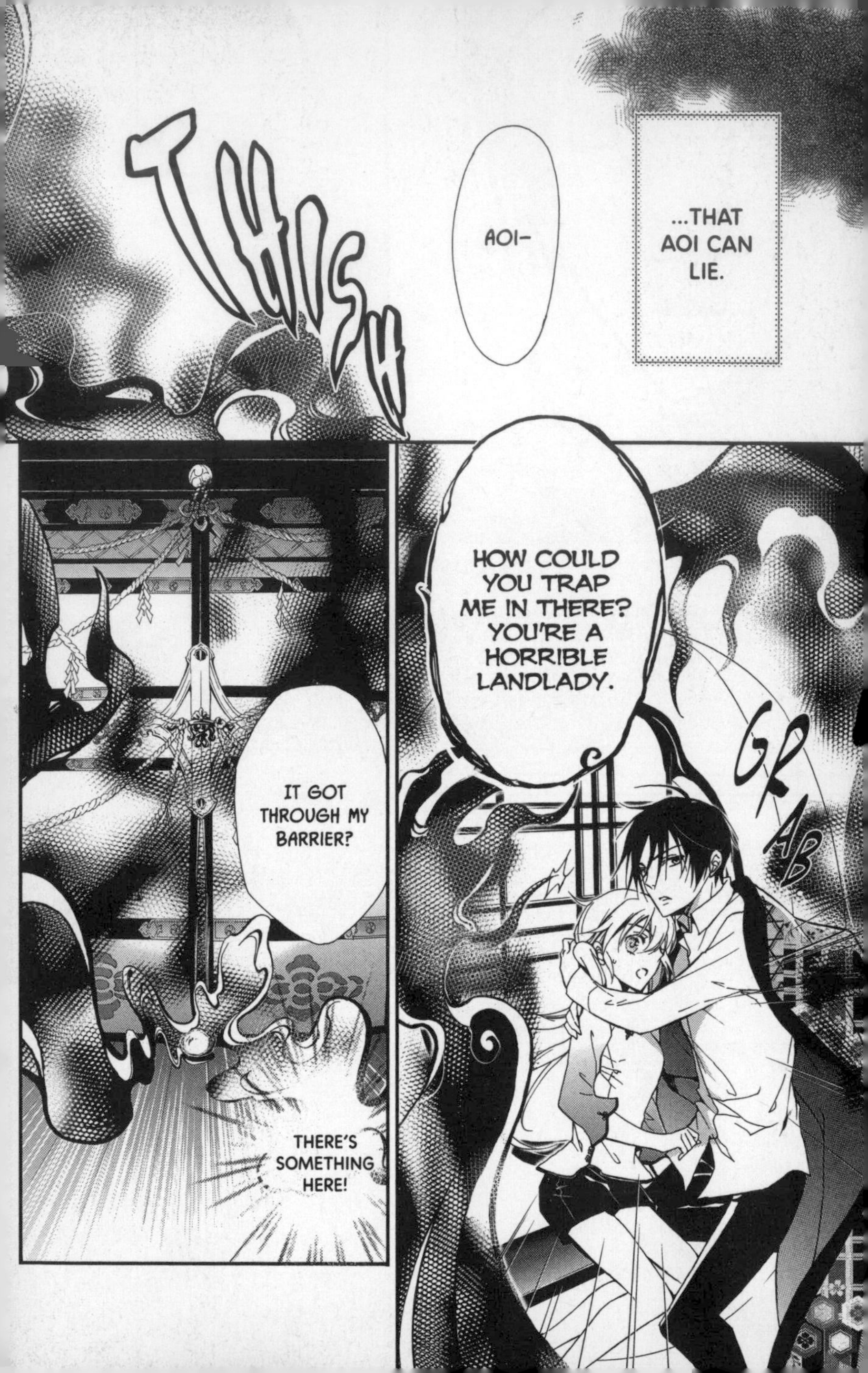
...THAT AOI CAN LIE.
AOI–
HOW COULD YOU TRAP ME IN THERE? YOU'RE A HORRIBLE LANDLADY.
GRAB
IT GOT THROUGH MY BARRIER?
THERE'S SOMETHING HERE!

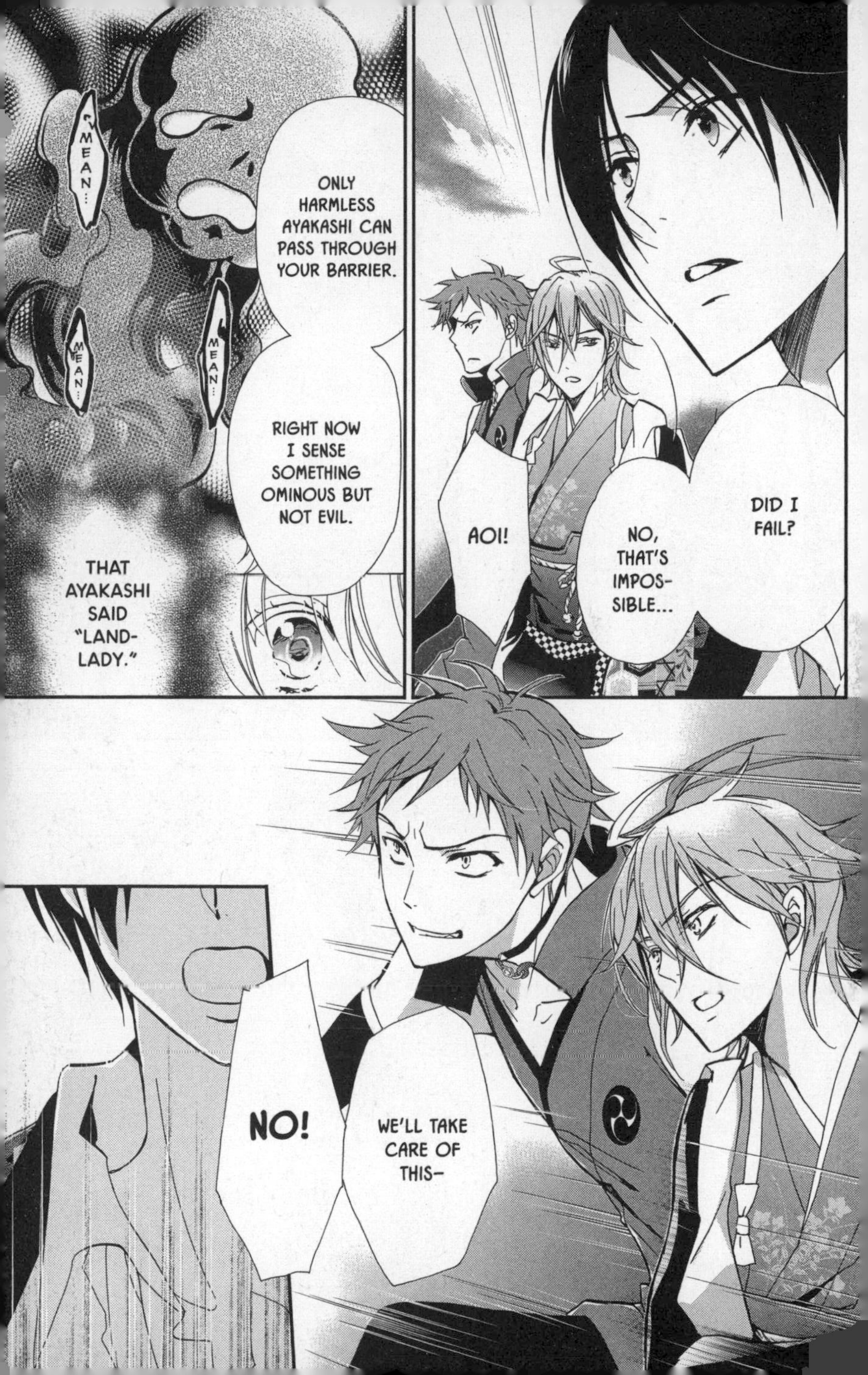
DID I FAIL?
NO, THAT'S IMPOSSIBLE...
AOI!
ONLY HARMLESS AYAKASHI CAN PASS THROUGH YOUR BARRIER.
RIGHT NOW I SENSE SOMETHING OMINOUS BUT NOT EVIL.
MEAN...
MEAN...
MEAN...
THAT AYAKASHI SAID "LAND-LADY."
WE'LL TAKE CARE OF THIS–
NO!

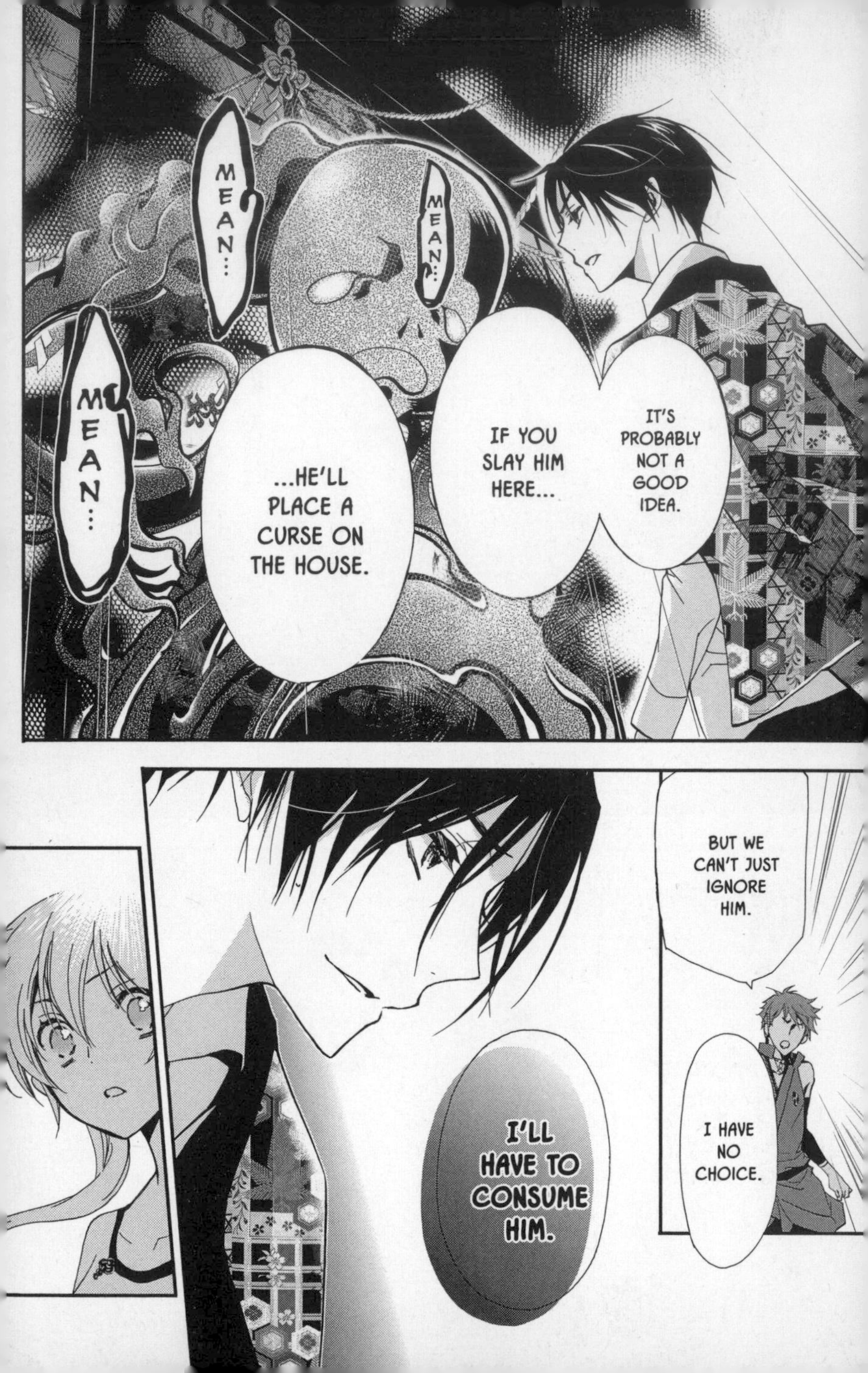
MEAN...
MEAN...
MEAN...
IT'S PROBABLY NOT A GOOD IDEA.
IF YOU SLAY HIM HERE...
...HE'LL PLACE A CURSE ON THE HOUSE.
BUT WE CAN'T JUST IGNORE HIM.
I HAVE NO CHOICE.
I'LL HAVE TO CONSUME HIM.

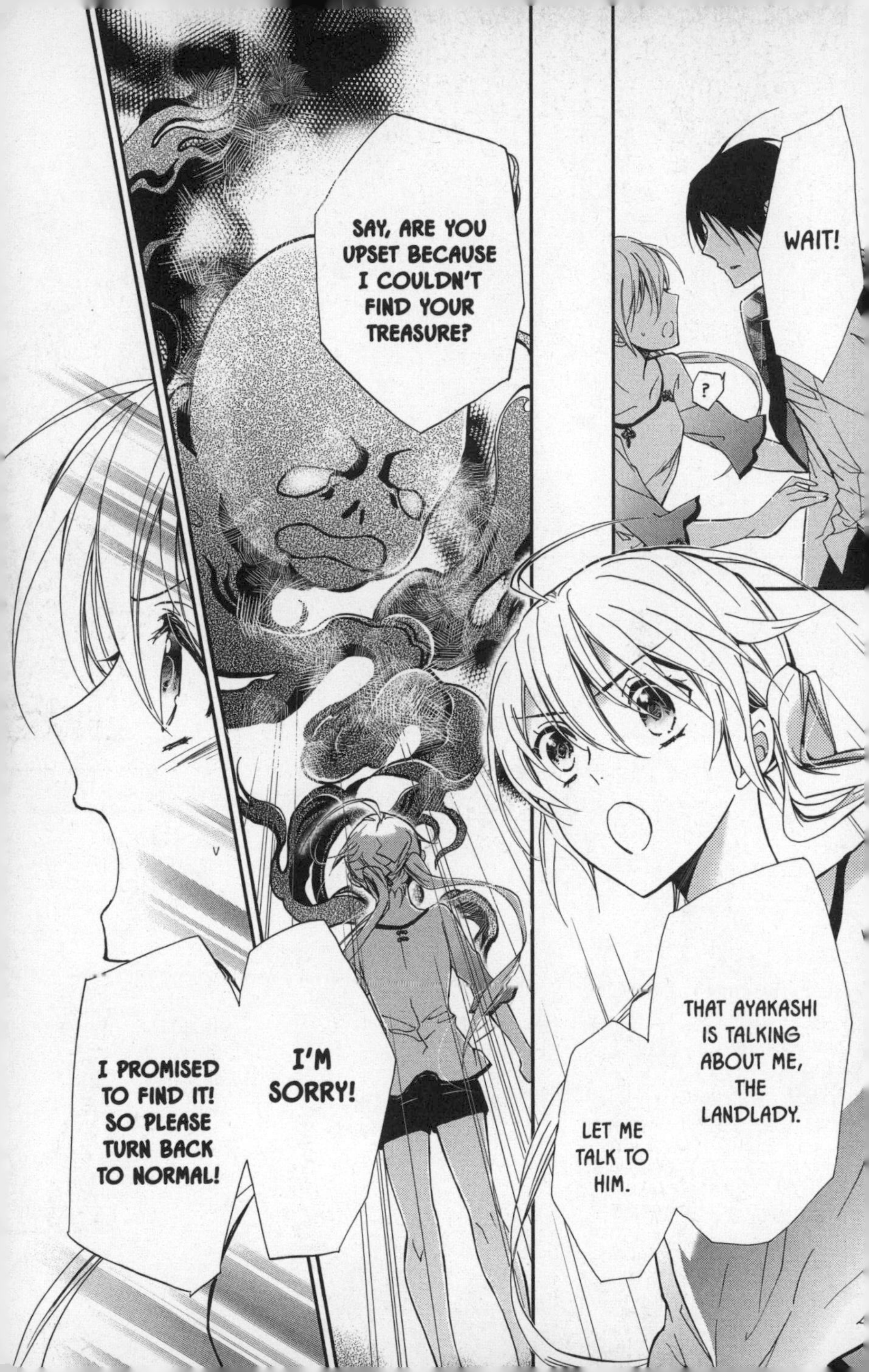
WAIT!
?
THAT AYAKASHI IS TALKING ABOUT ME, THE LANDLADY.
LET ME TALK TO HIM.
SAY, ARE YOU UPSET BECAUSE I COULDN'T FIND YOUR TREASURE?
I'M SORRY!
I PROMISED TO FIND IT! SO PLEASE TURN BACK TO NORMAL!

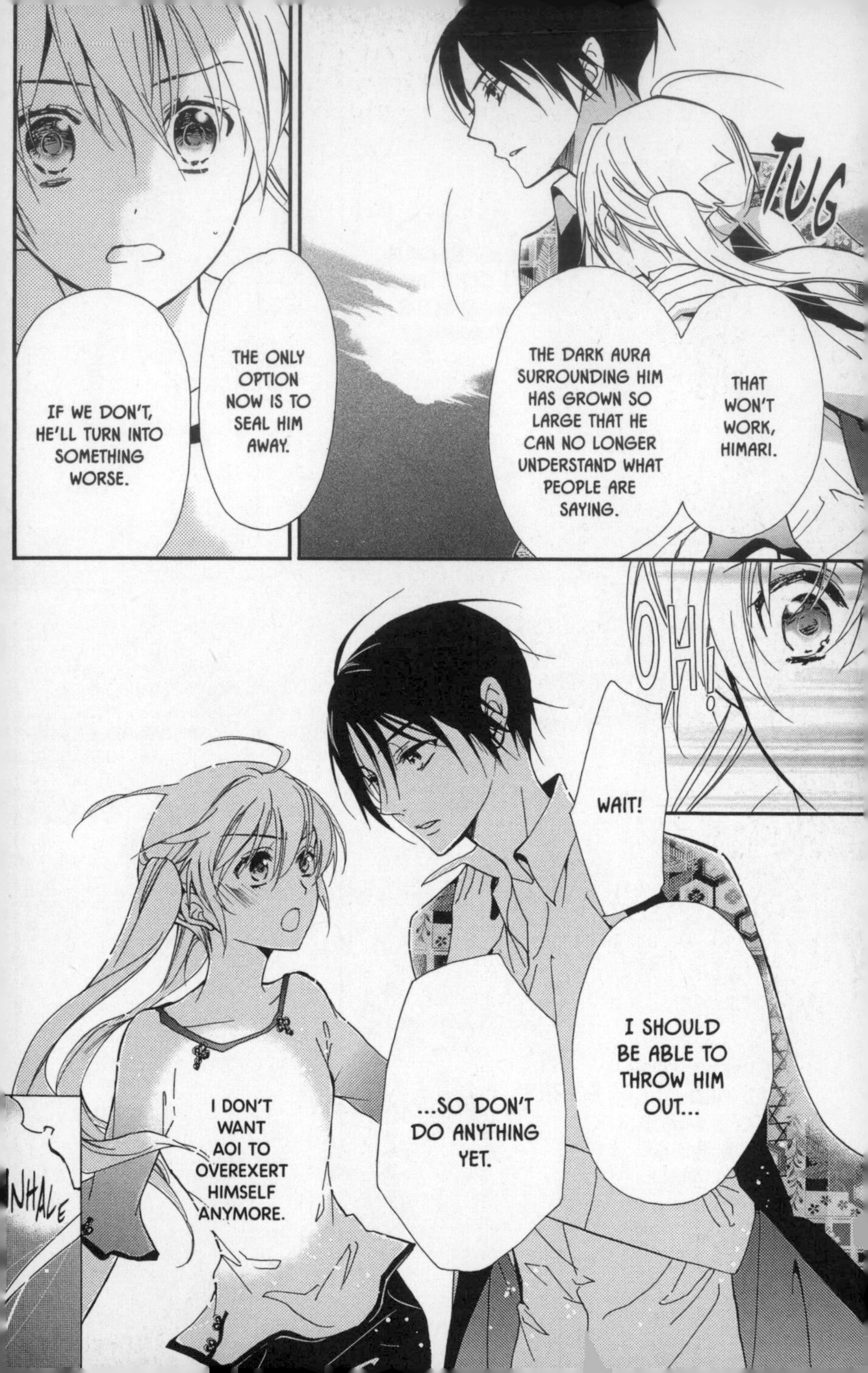
TUG
THAT WON'T WORK, HIMARI.
THE DARK AURA SURROUNDING HIM HAS GROWN SO LARGE THAT HE CAN NO LONGER UNDERSTAND WHAT PEOPLE ARE SAYING.
THE ONLY OPTION NOW IS TO SEAL HIM AWAY.
IF WE DON'T, HE'LL TURN INTO SOMETHING WORSE.
OH!
WAIT!
I SHOULD BE ABLE TO THROW HIM OUT...
...SO DON'T DO ANYTHING YET.
NHALE
I DON'T WANT AOI TO OVEREXERT HIMSELF ANYMORE.

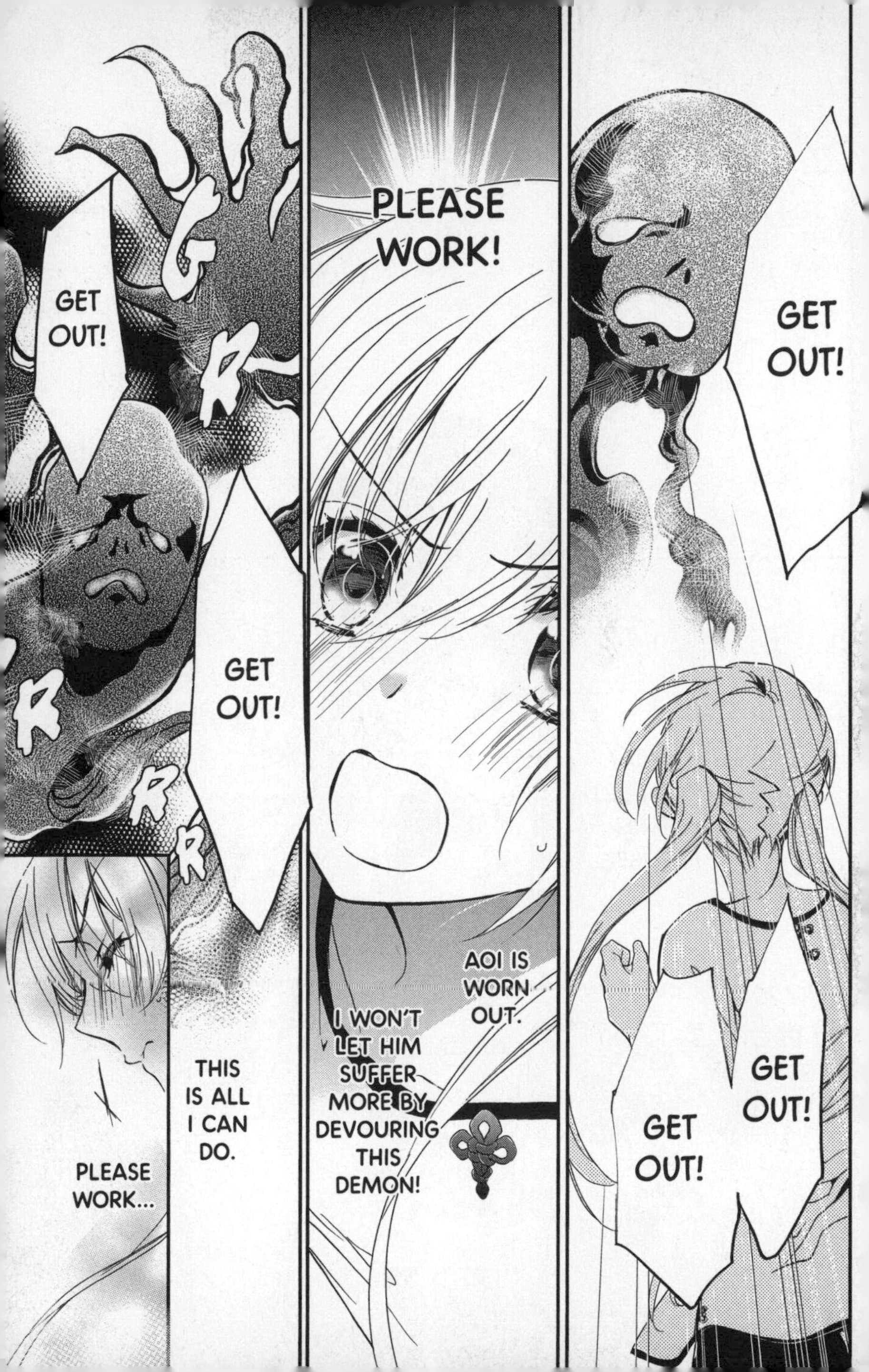
GET OUT!
GET OUT!
GET OUT!
GET OUT!
PLEASE WORK!
AOI IS WORN OUT.
I WON'T LET HIM SUFFER MORE BY DEVOURING THIS DEMON!
GET OUT!
GET OUT!
GRRRR
THIS IS ALL I CAN DO.
PLEASE WORK...

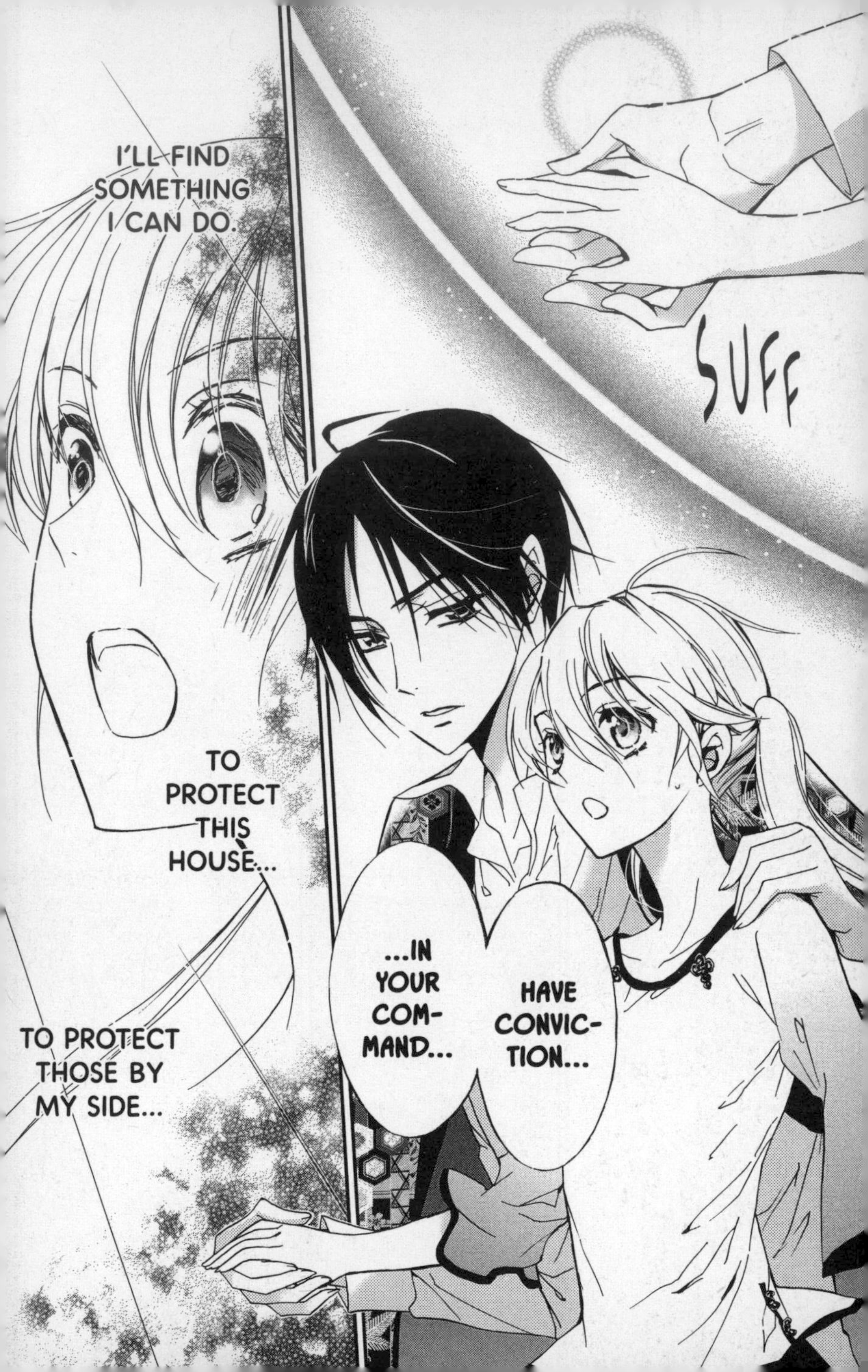
SUFF
HAVE CONVIC- TION...
...IN YOUR COM- MAND...
I'LL FIND SOMETHING I CAN DO.
TO PROTECT THIS HOUSE...
TO PROTECT THOSE BY MY SIDE...

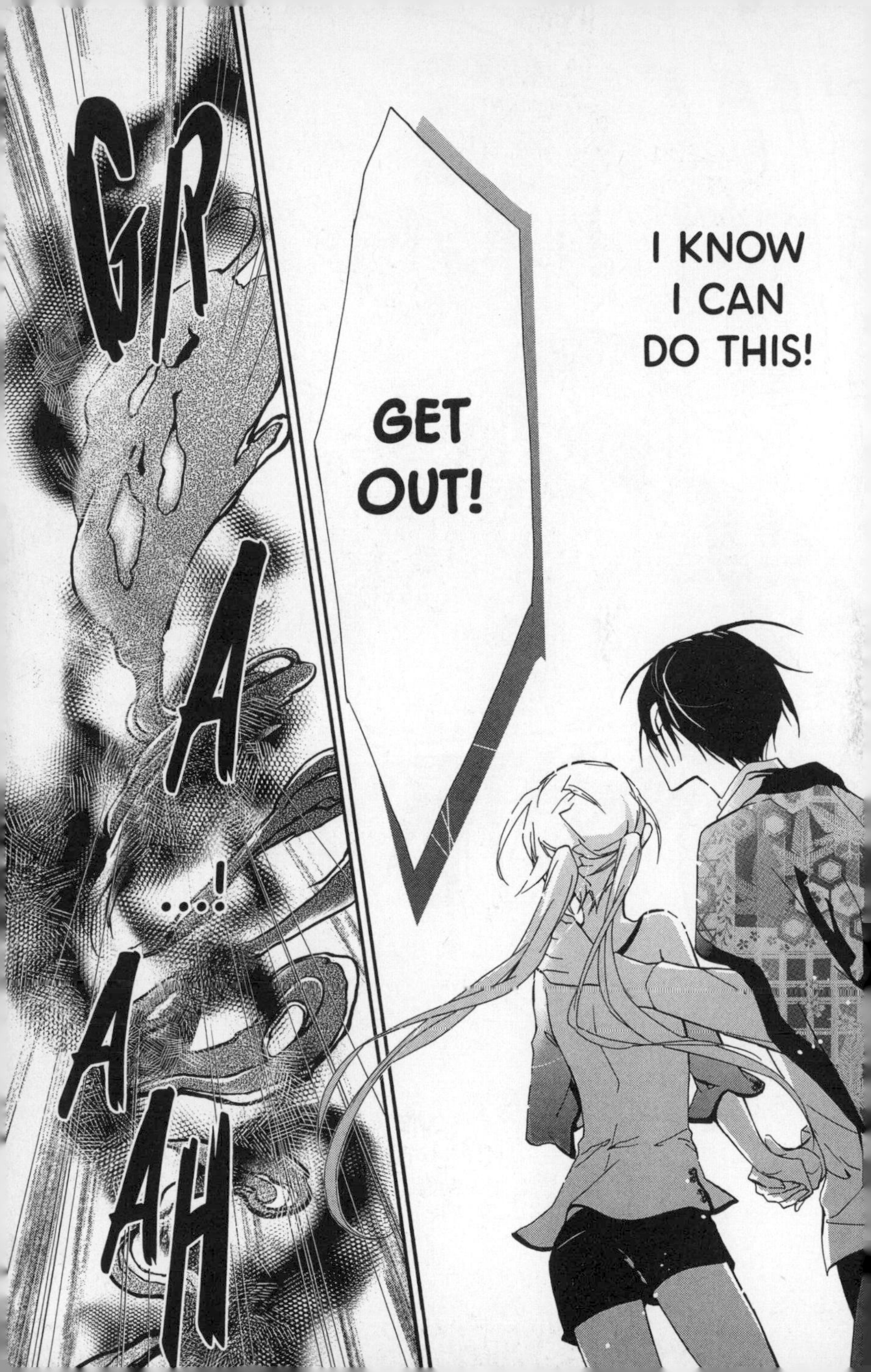
I KNOW I CAN DO THIS!
GET OUT!
GRAAAH
...!

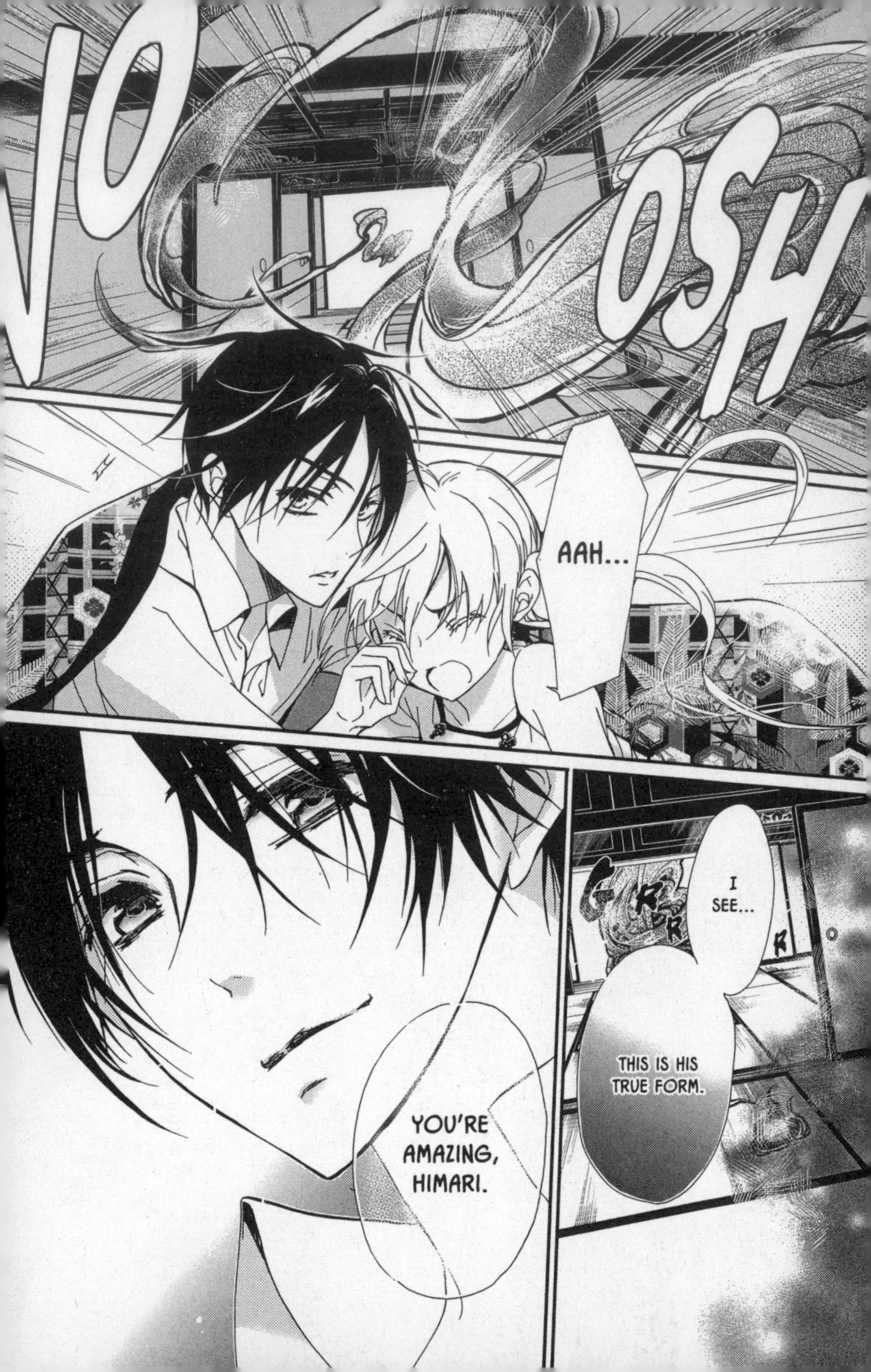
OSH
AAH...
I SEE...
GRRR
THIS IS HIS TRUE FORM.
YOU'RE AMAZING, HIMARI.

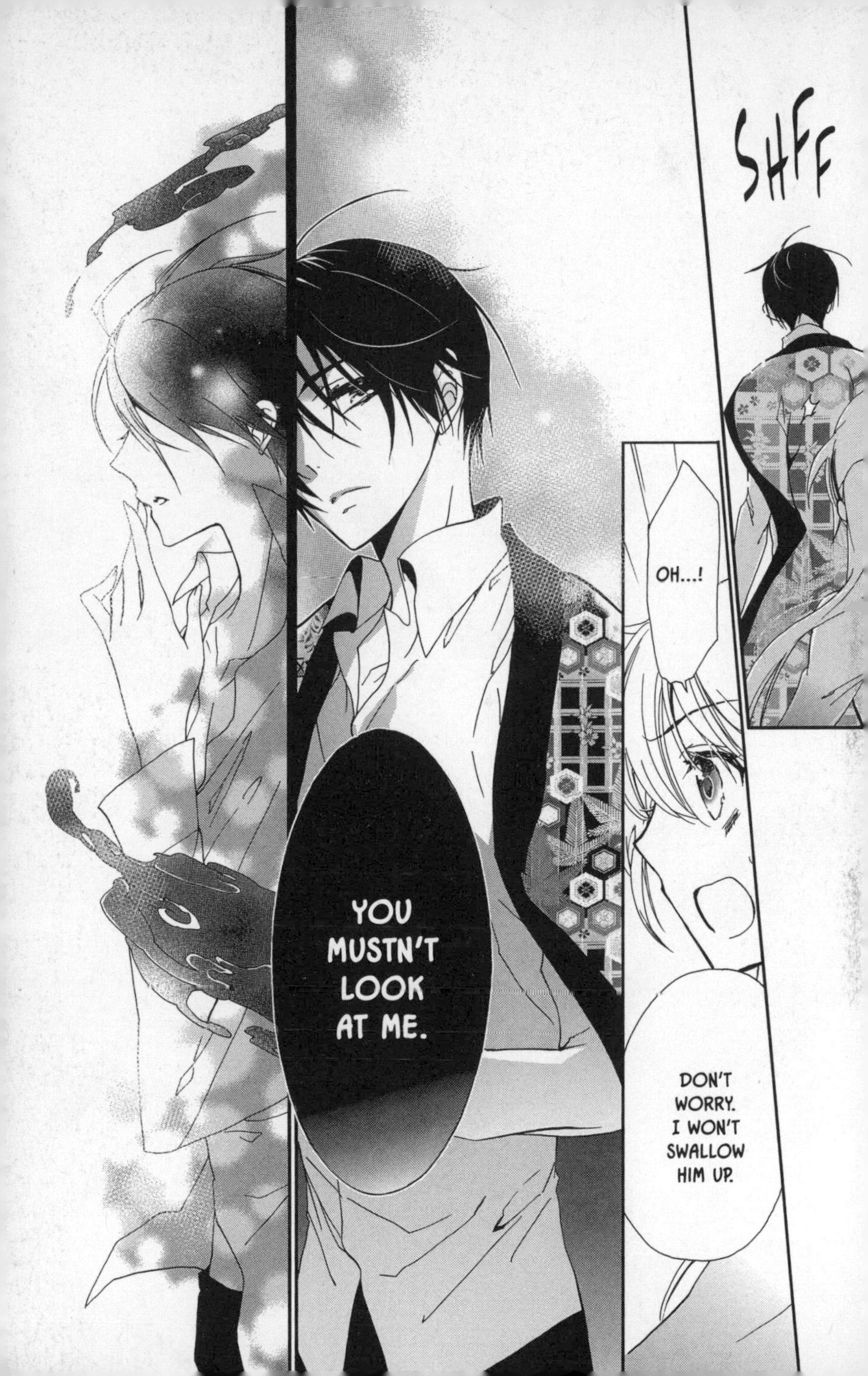
SHFF
OH...!
DON'T WORRY. I WON'T SWALLOW HIM UP.
YOU MUSTN'T LOOK AT ME.

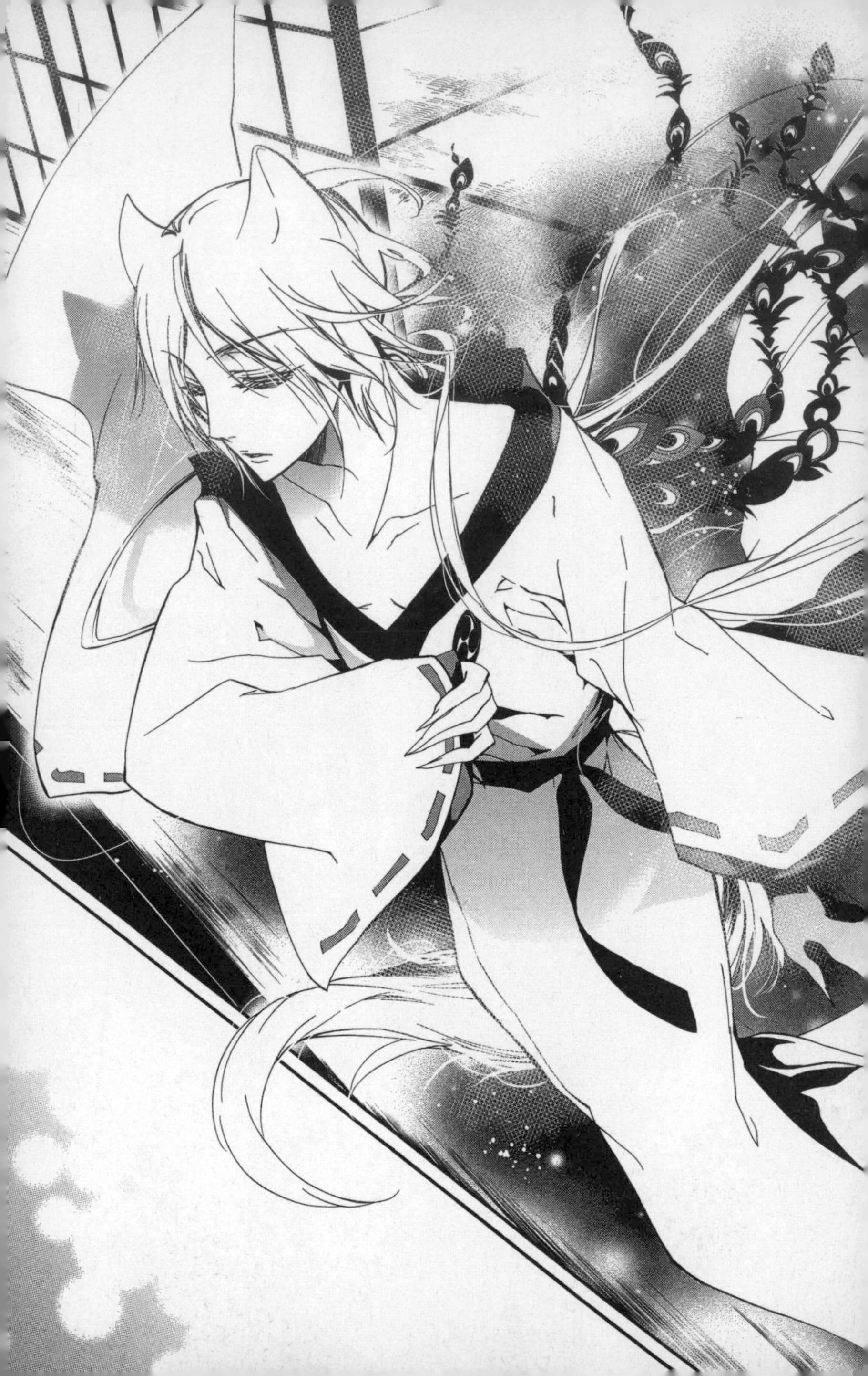

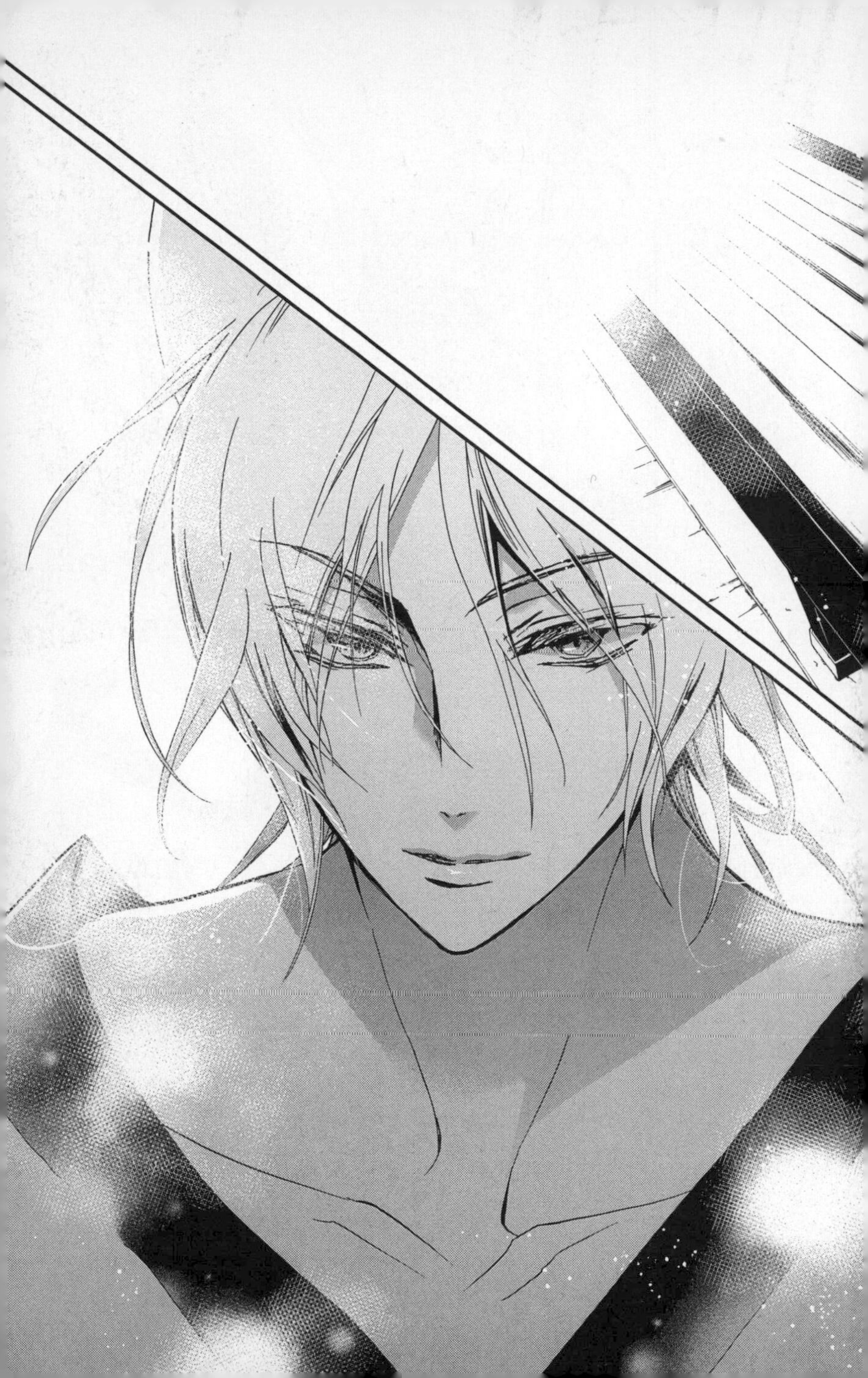

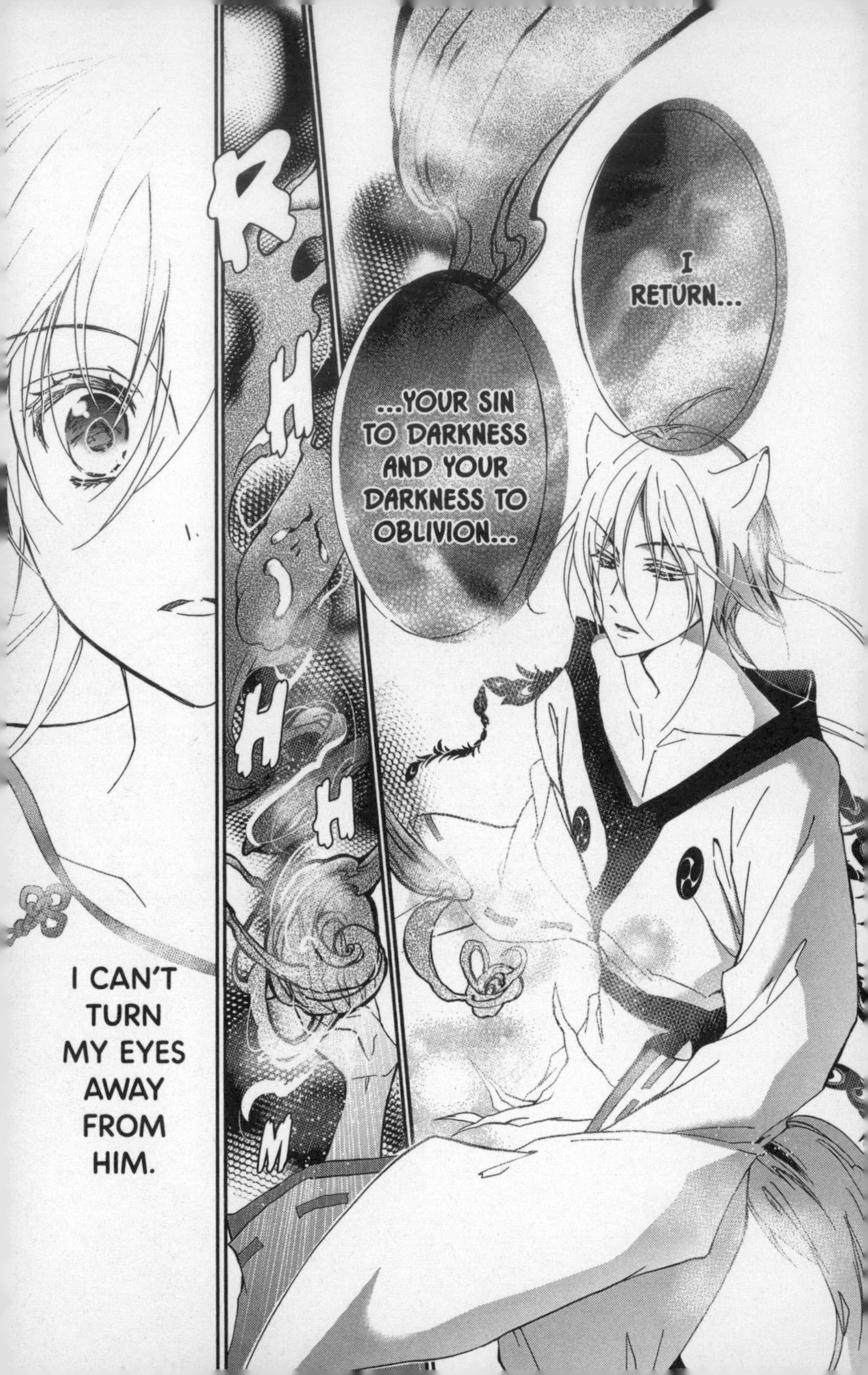
I RETURN...
...YOUR SIN TO DARKNESS AND YOUR DARKNESS TO OBLIVION...
RHHHM
I CAN'T TURN MY EYES AWAY FROM HIM.

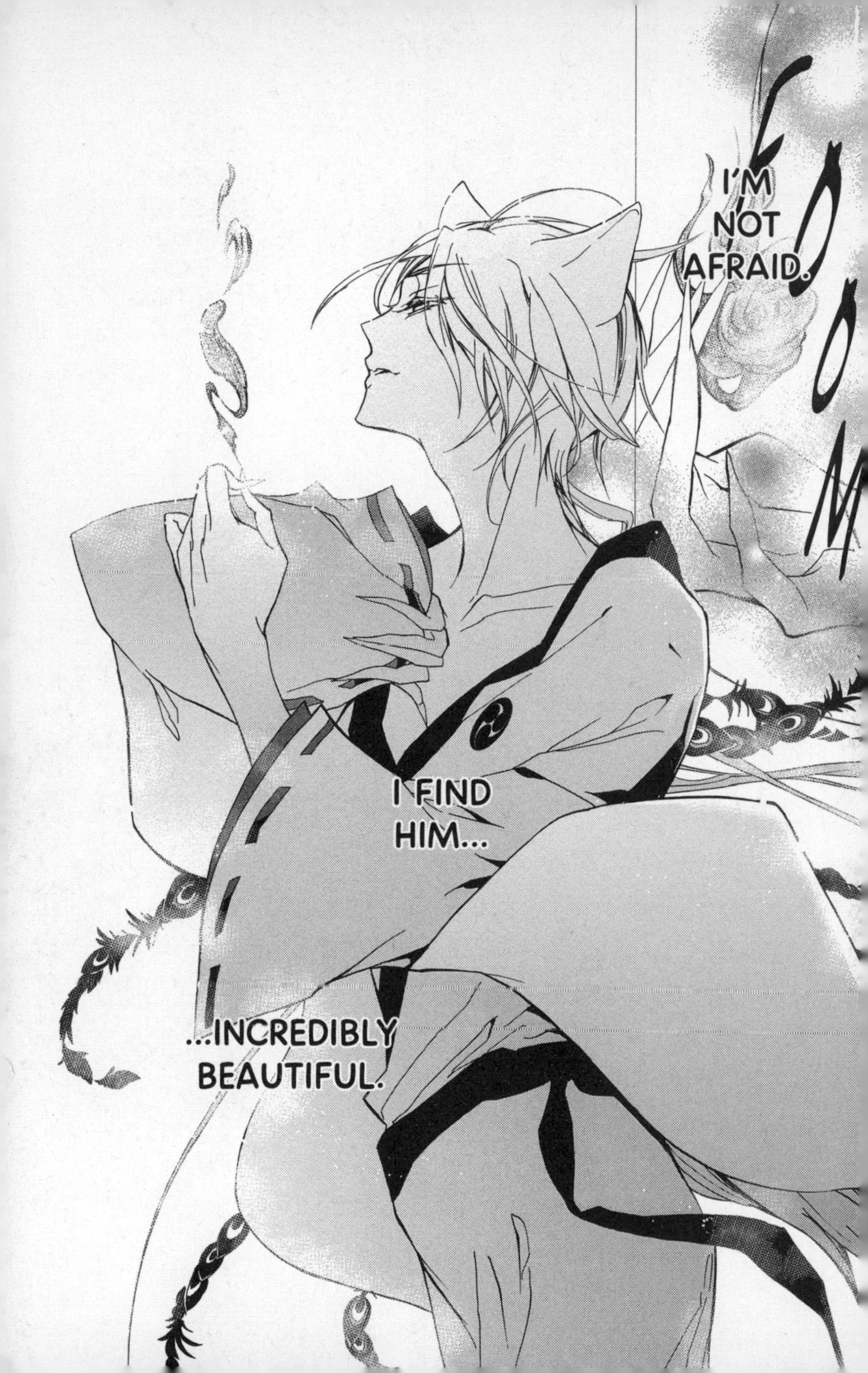
I'M NOT AFRAID.
I FIND HIM...
...INCREDIBLY BEAUTIFUL.

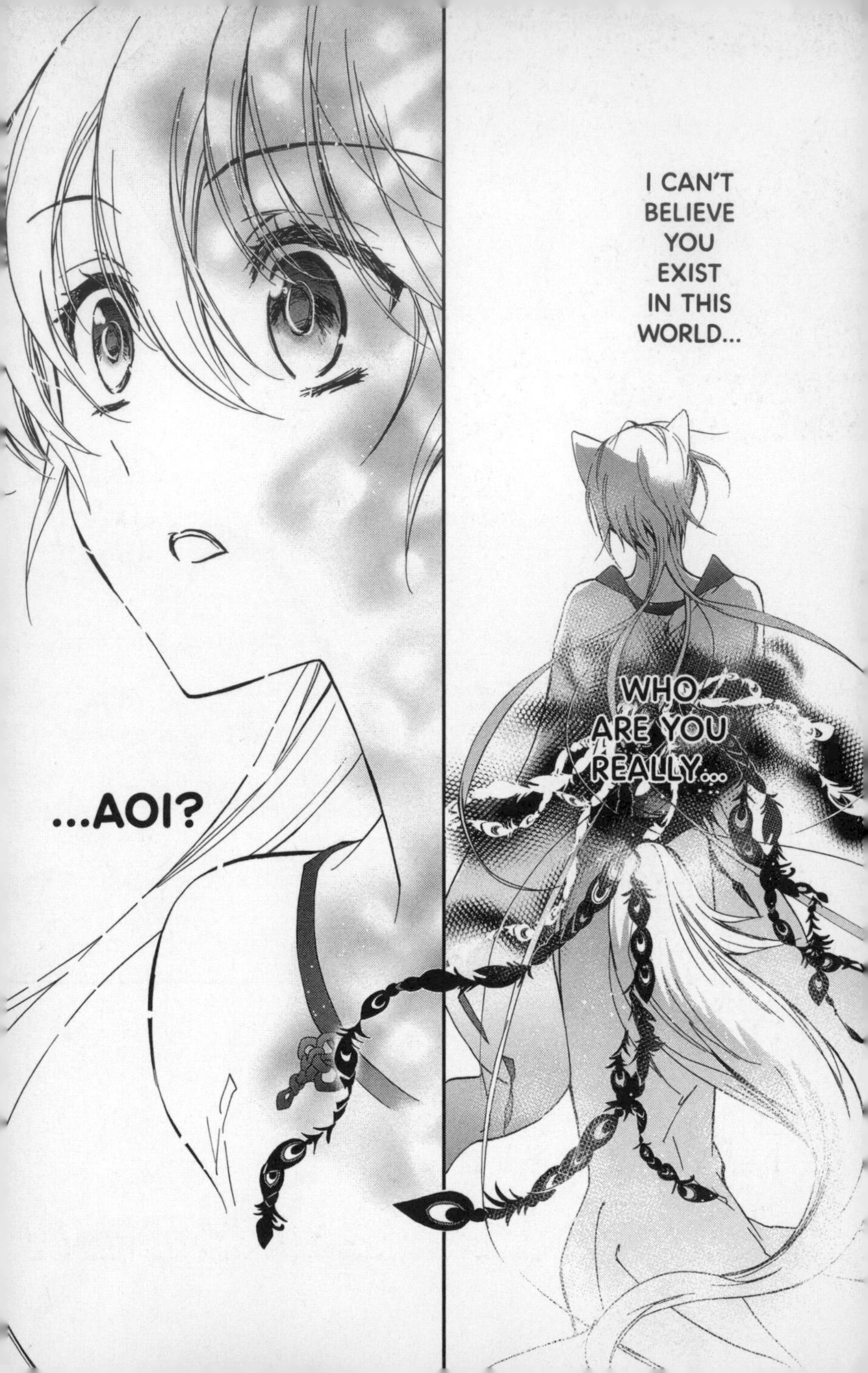
I CAN'T BELIEVE YOU EXIST IN THIS WORLD...
WHO ARE YOU REALLY...
...AOI?

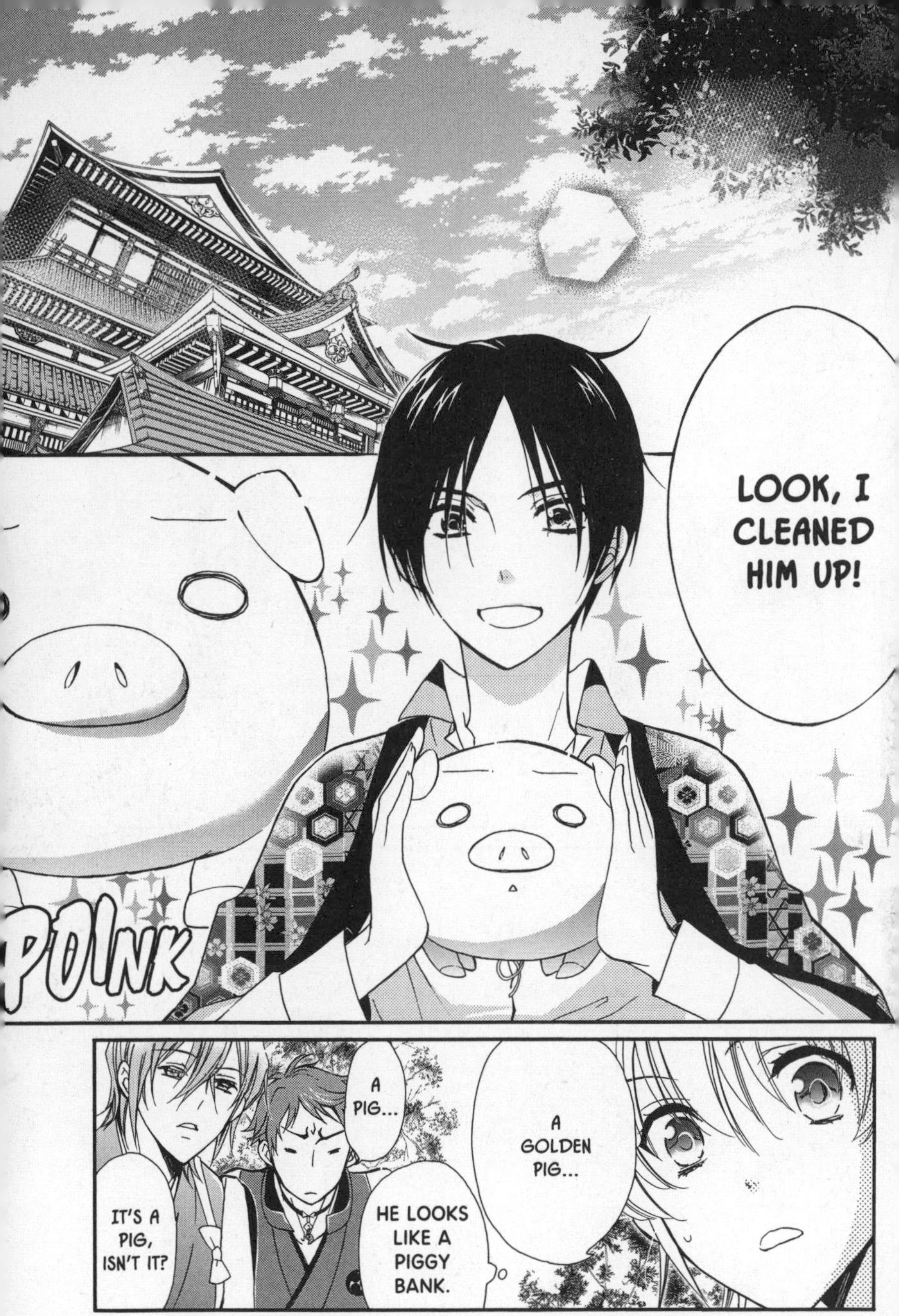
LOOK, I CLEANED HIM UP!
POINK
A GOLDEN PIG...
A PIG...
HE LOOKS LIKE A PIGGY BANK.
IT'S A PIG, ISN'T IT?

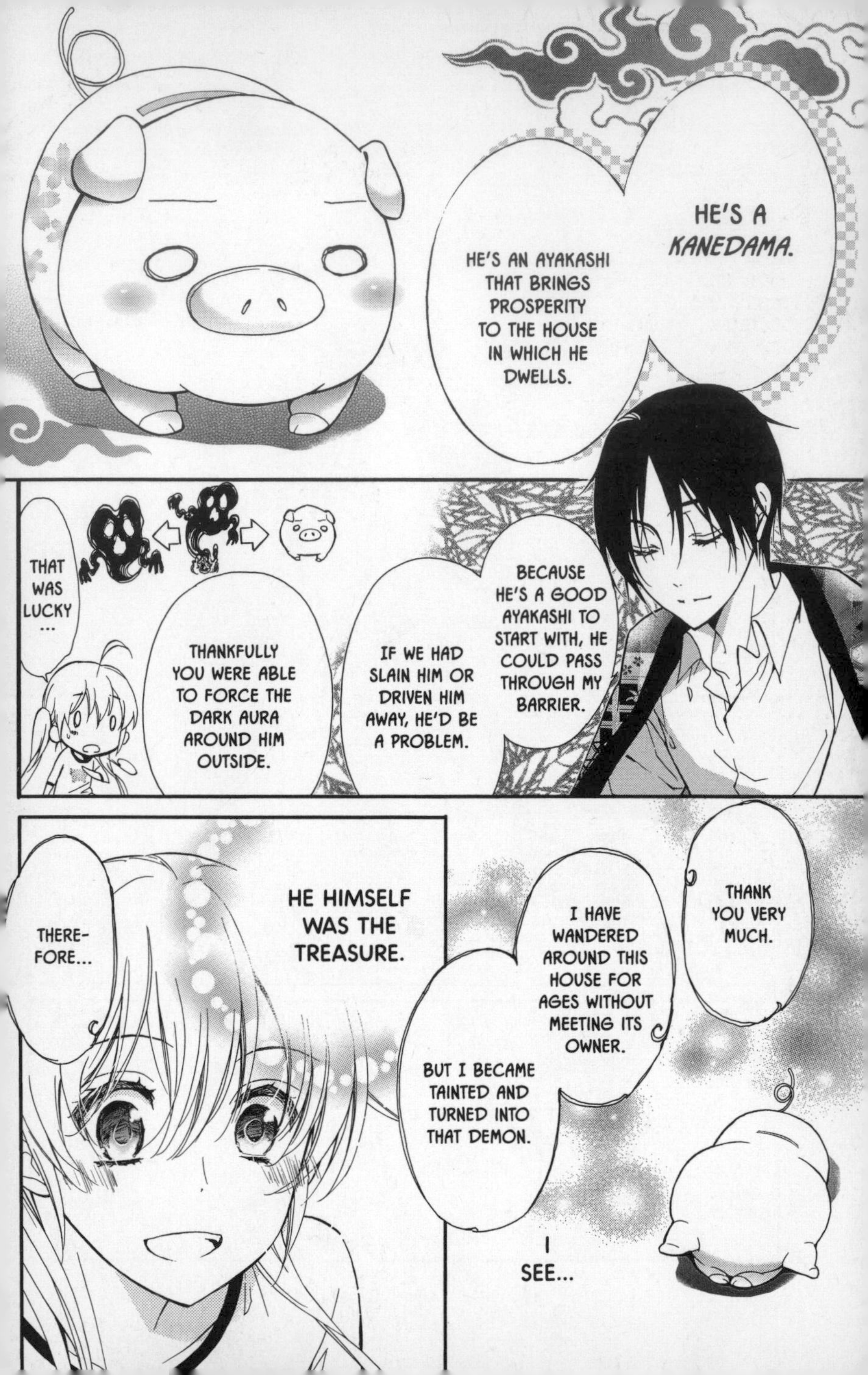
HE'S A *KANEDAMA.*
HE'S AN AYAKASHI THAT BRINGS PROSPERITY TO THE HOUSE IN WHICH HE DWELLS.
BECAUSE HE'S A GOOD AYAKASHI TO START WITH, HE COULD PASS THROUGH MY BARRIER.
IF WE HAD SLAIN HIM OR DRIVEN HIM AWAY, HE'D BE A PROBLEM.
THANKFULLY YOU WERE ABLE TO FORCE THE DARK AURA AROUND HIM OUTSIDE.
THAT WAS LUCKY...
THANK YOU VERY MUCH.
I HAVE WANDERED AROUND THIS HOUSE FOR AGES WITHOUT MEETING ITS OWNER.
BUT I BECAME TAINTED AND TURNED INTO THAT DEMON.
I SEE...
HE HIMSELF WAS THE TREASURE.
THERE-FORE...

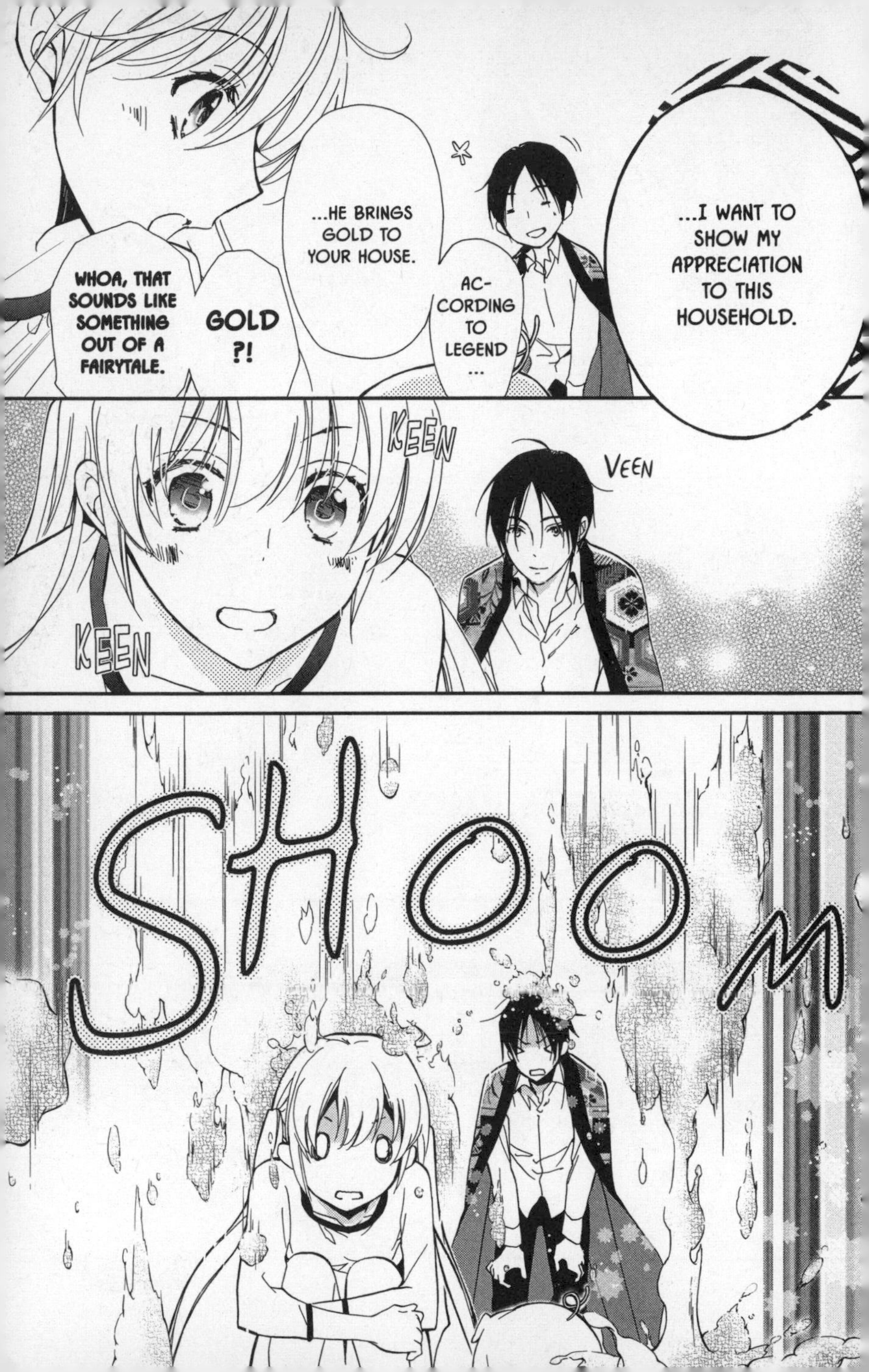
...I WANT TO SHOW MY APPRECIATION TO THIS HOUSEHOLD.
AC-CORDING TO LEGEND...
...HE BRINGS GOLD TO YOUR HOUSE.
GOLD?!
WHOA, THAT SOUNDS LIKE SOMETHING OUT OF A FAIRYTALE.
VEEN
KEEN
KEEN
SHOOM

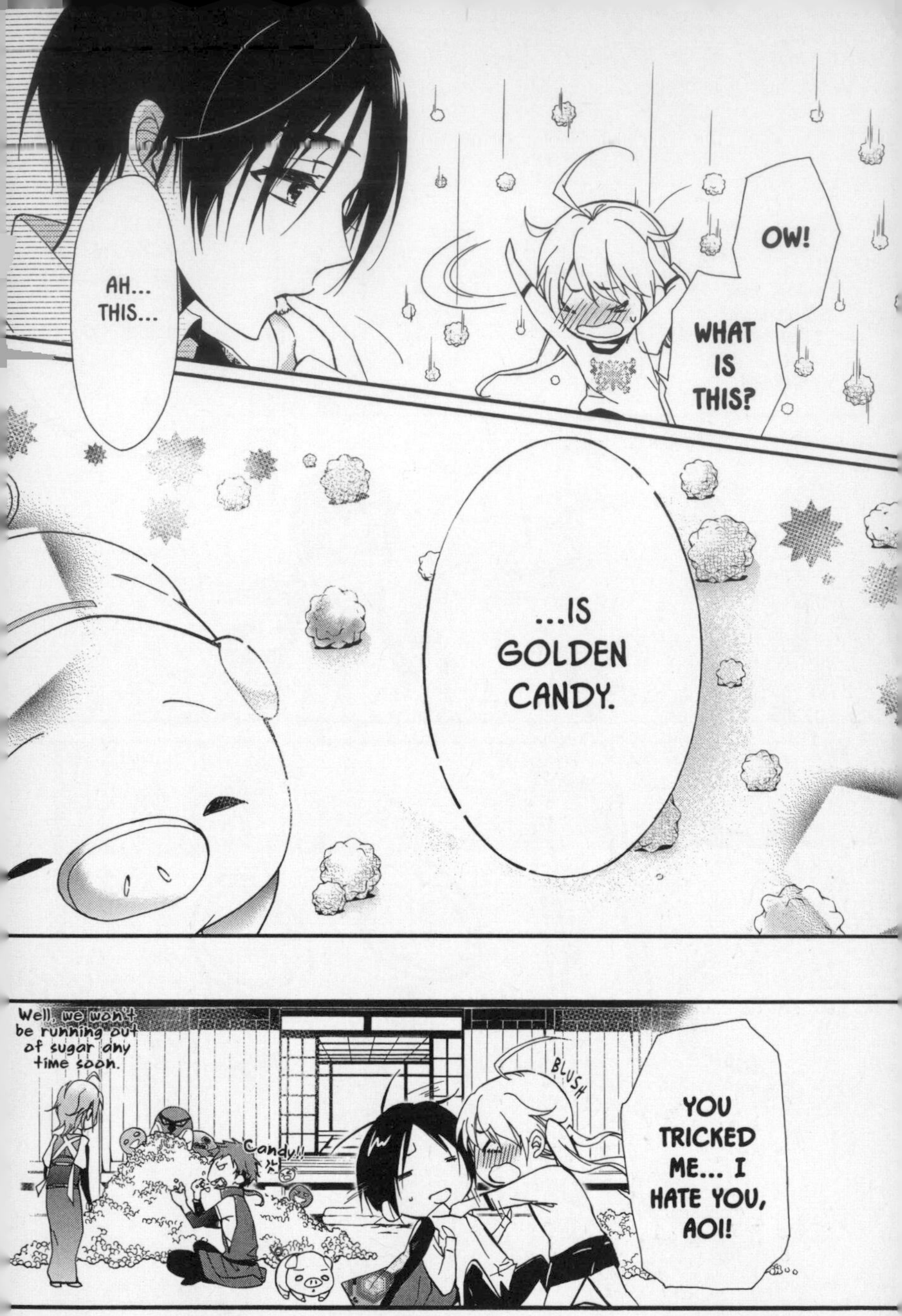
OW!
WHAT IS THIS?
AH... THIS...
...IS GOLDEN CANDY.
YOU TRICKED ME... I HATE YOU, AOI!
BLUSH
Candy!!
Well, we won't be running out of sugar any time soon.

Chapter 2/End

The
DEMON
PRINCE
of MOMOCHI
HOUSE

the
DEMON
PRINCE
of MOMOCHI
HOUSE

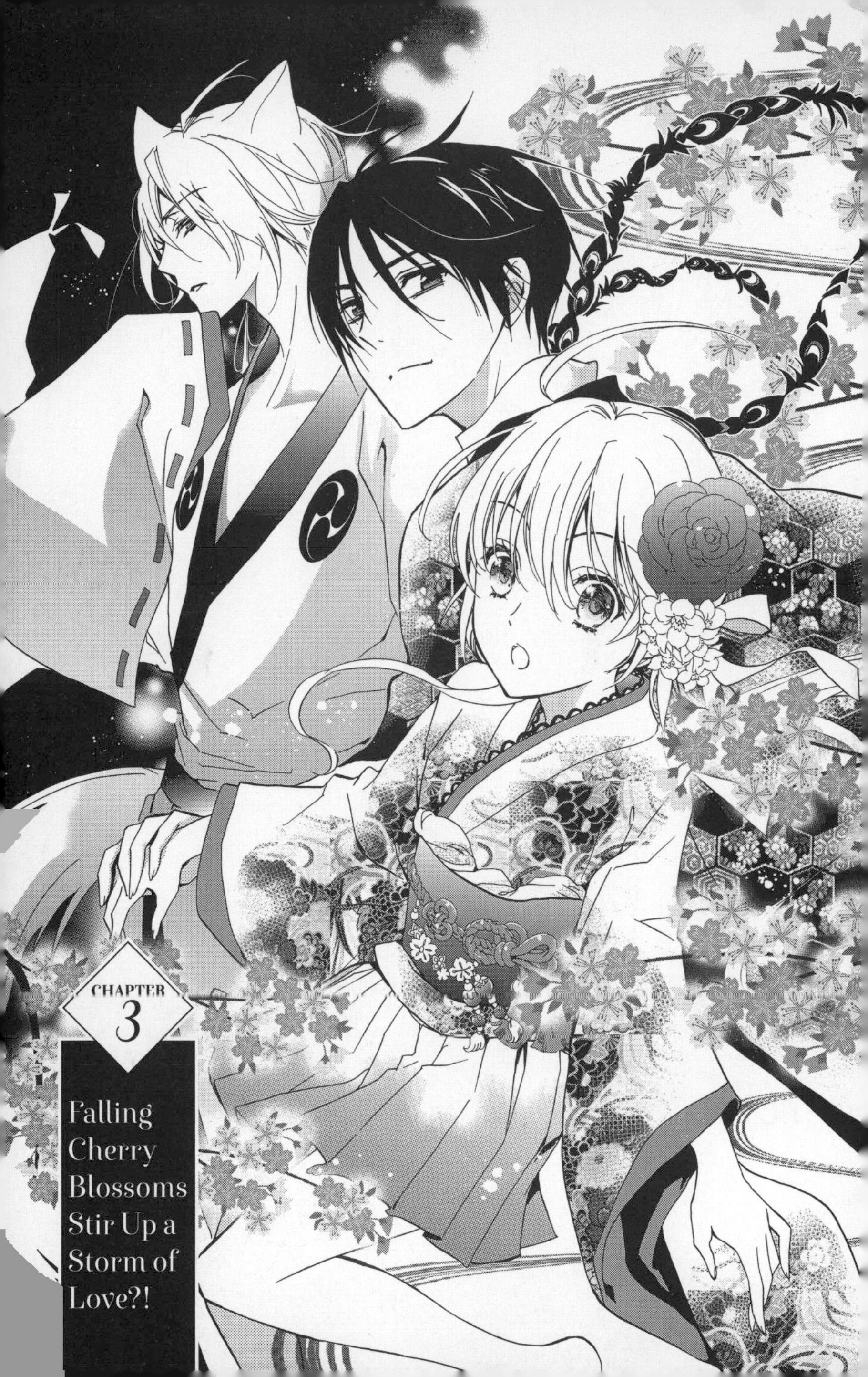
CHAPTER
3
Falling Cherry Blossoms Stir Up a Storm of Love?!

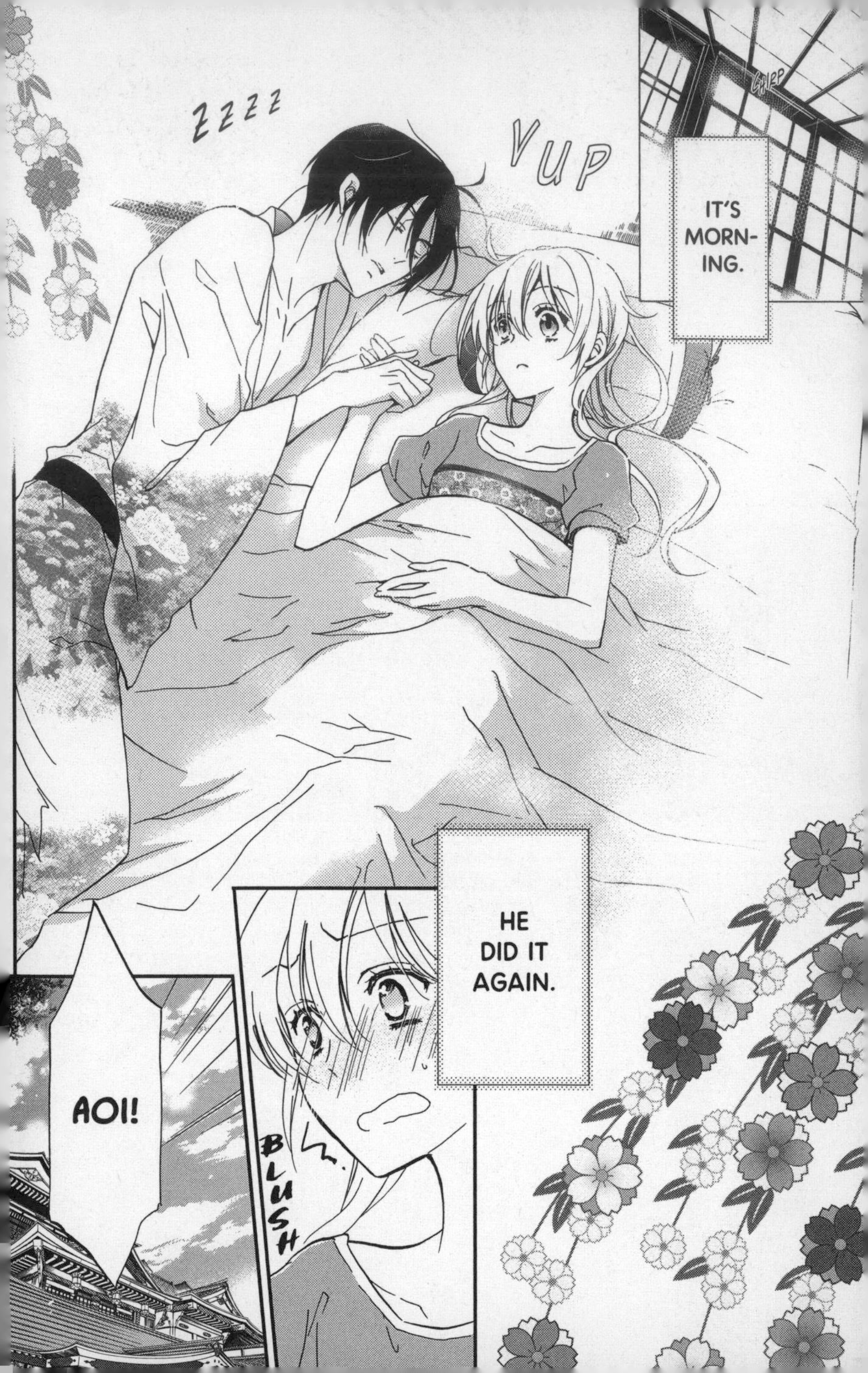
CHIRP
IT'S MORNING.
VUP
ZZZZ
HE DID IT AGAIN.
BLUSH
AOI!

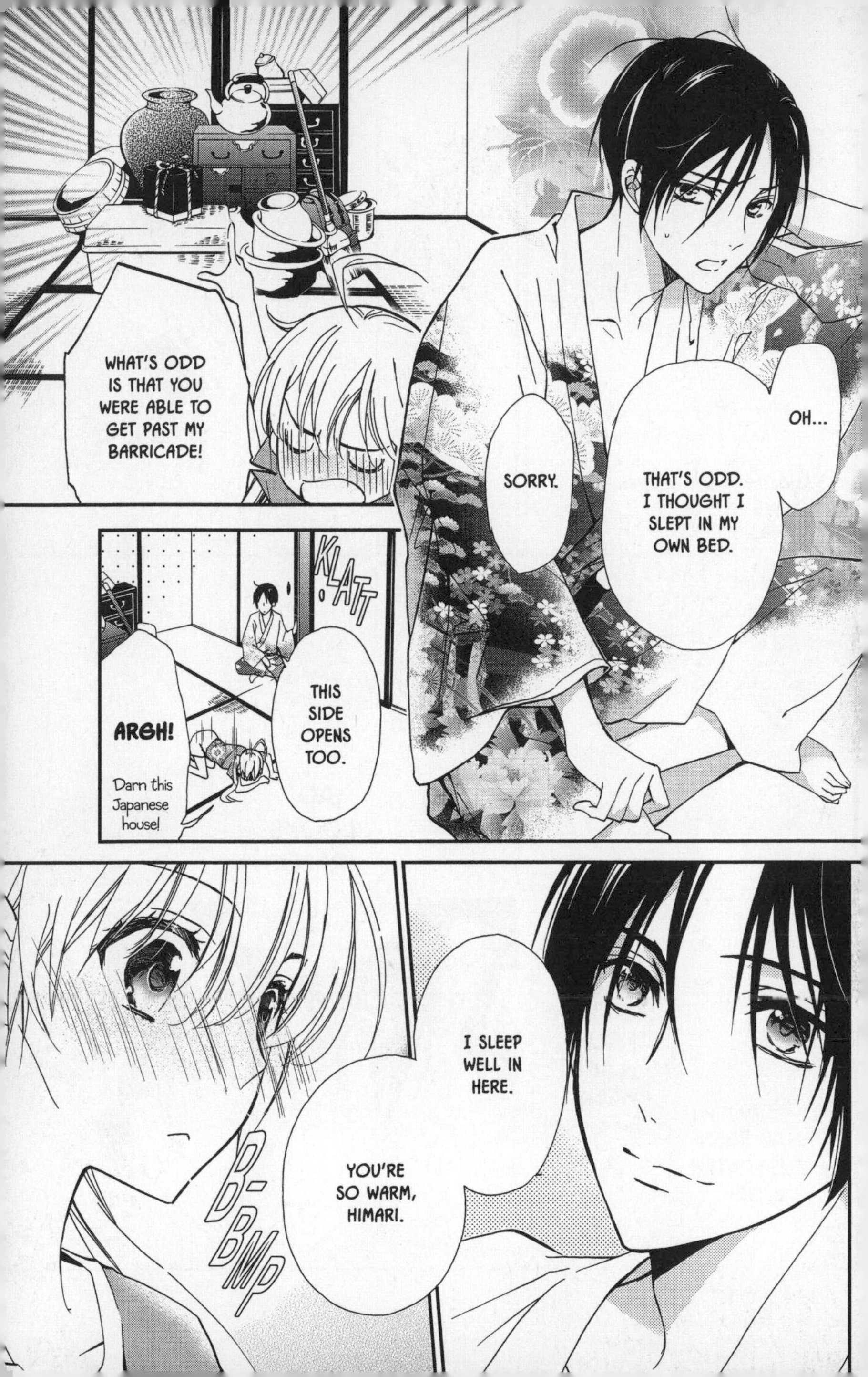
OH...
THAT'S ODD. I THOUGHT I SLEPT IN MY OWN BED.
SORRY.
WHAT'S ODD IS THAT YOU WERE ABLE TO GET PAST MY BARRICADE!
KLATT
THIS SIDE OPENS TOO.
ARGH!
Darn this Japanese house!
I SLEEP WELL IN HERE.
YOU'RE SO WARM, HIMARI.
B-BMP

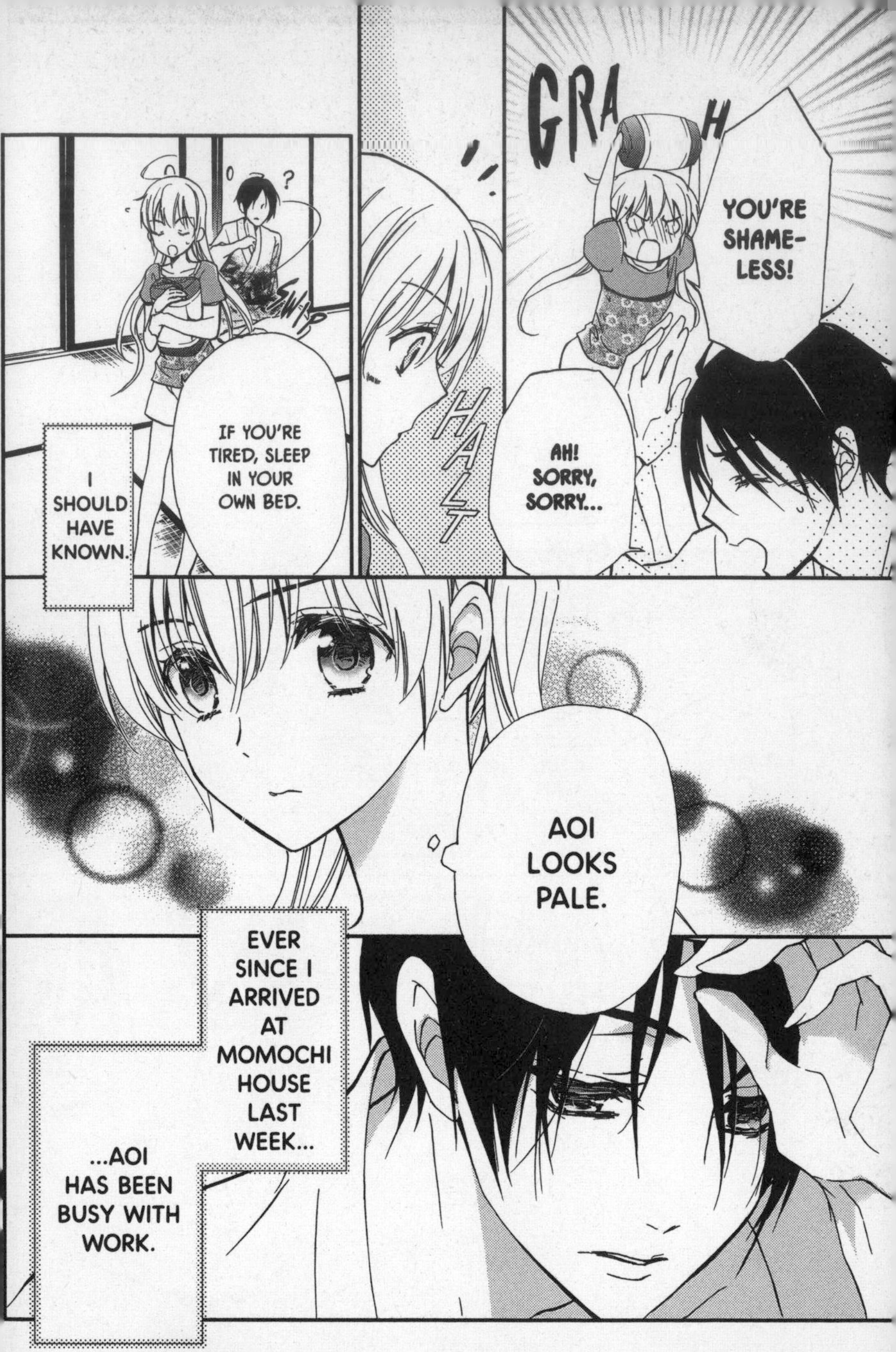
GRAH
YOU'RE SHAME-LESS!
AH! SORRY, SORRY...
HALT
?
SWIP
IF YOU'RE TIRED, SLEEP IN YOUR OWN BED.
I SHOULD HAVE KNOWN.
AOI LOOKS PALE.
EVER SINCE I ARRIVED AT MOMOCHI HOUSE LAST WEEK...
...AOI HAS BEEN BUSY WITH WORK.

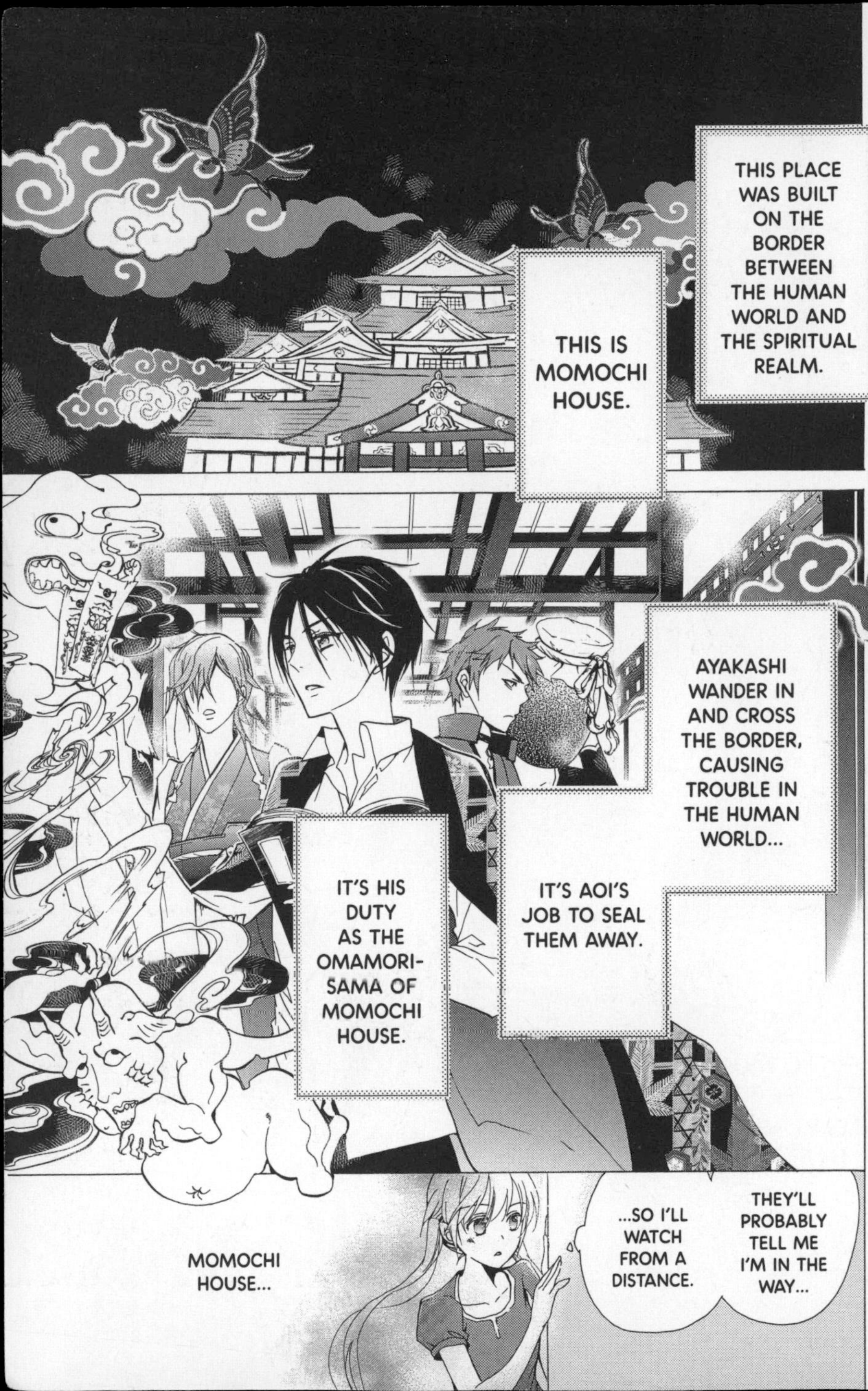
THIS PLACE WAS BUILT ON THE BORDER BETWEEN THE HUMAN WORLD AND THE SPIRITUAL REALM.
THIS IS MOMOCHI HOUSE.
AYAKASHI WANDER IN AND CROSS THE BORDER, CAUSING TROUBLE IN THE HUMAN WORLD...
IT'S AOI'S JOB TO SEAL THEM AWAY.
IT'S HIS DUTY AS THE OMAMORI-SAMA OF MOMOCHI HOUSE.
THEY'LL PROBABLY TELL ME I'M IN THE WAY...
...SO I'LL WATCH FROM A DISTANCE.
MOMOCHI HOUSE...

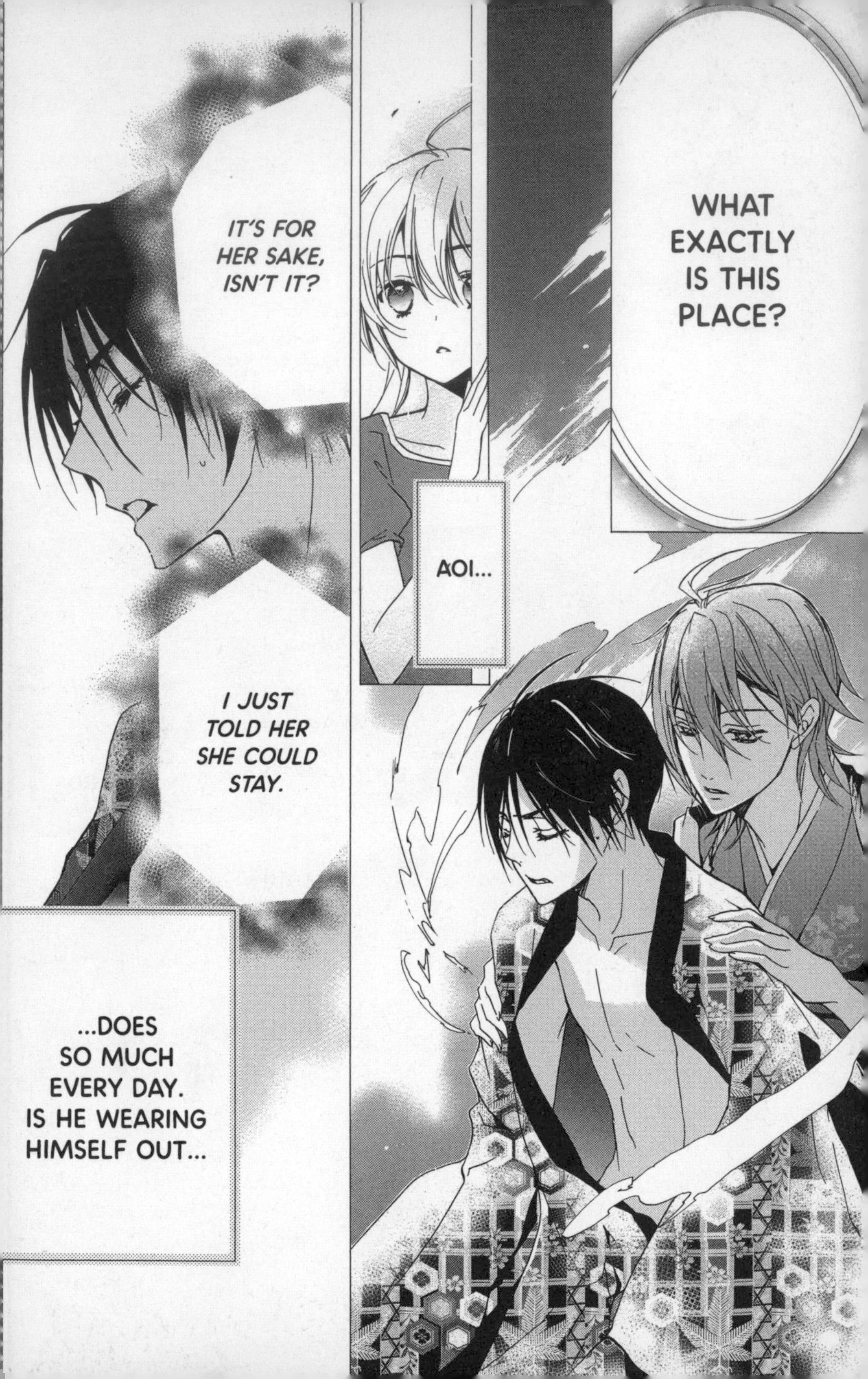
WHAT EXACTLY IS THIS PLACE?
AOI...
IT'S FOR HER SAKE, ISN'T IT?
I JUST TOLD HER SHE COULD STAY.
...DOES SO MUCH EVERY DAY. IS HE WEARING HIMSELF OUT...

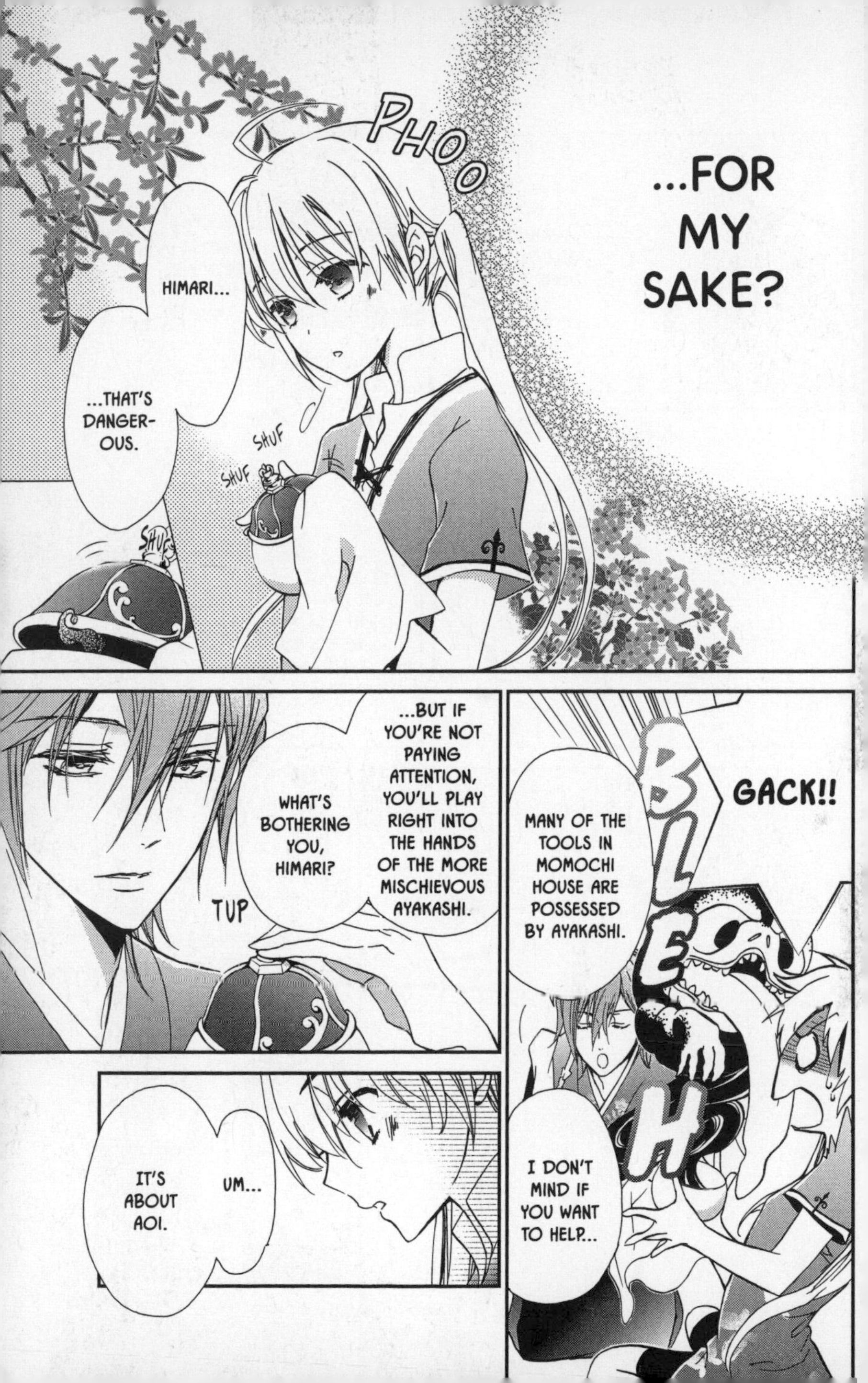
PHOO
...FOR MY SAKE?
HIMARI...
...THAT'S DANGER-OUS.
SHUF
SHUF
SHUF
GACK!!
BLEH
MANY OF THE TOOLS IN MOMOCHI HOUSE ARE POSSESSED BY AYAKASHI.
I DON'T MIND IF YOU WANT TO HELP...
...BUT IF YOU'RE NOT PAYING ATTENTION, YOU'LL PLAY RIGHT INTO THE HANDS OF THE MORE MISCHIEVOUS AYAKASHI.
WHAT'S BOTHERING YOU, HIMARI?
TUP
UM...
IT'S ABOUT AOI.

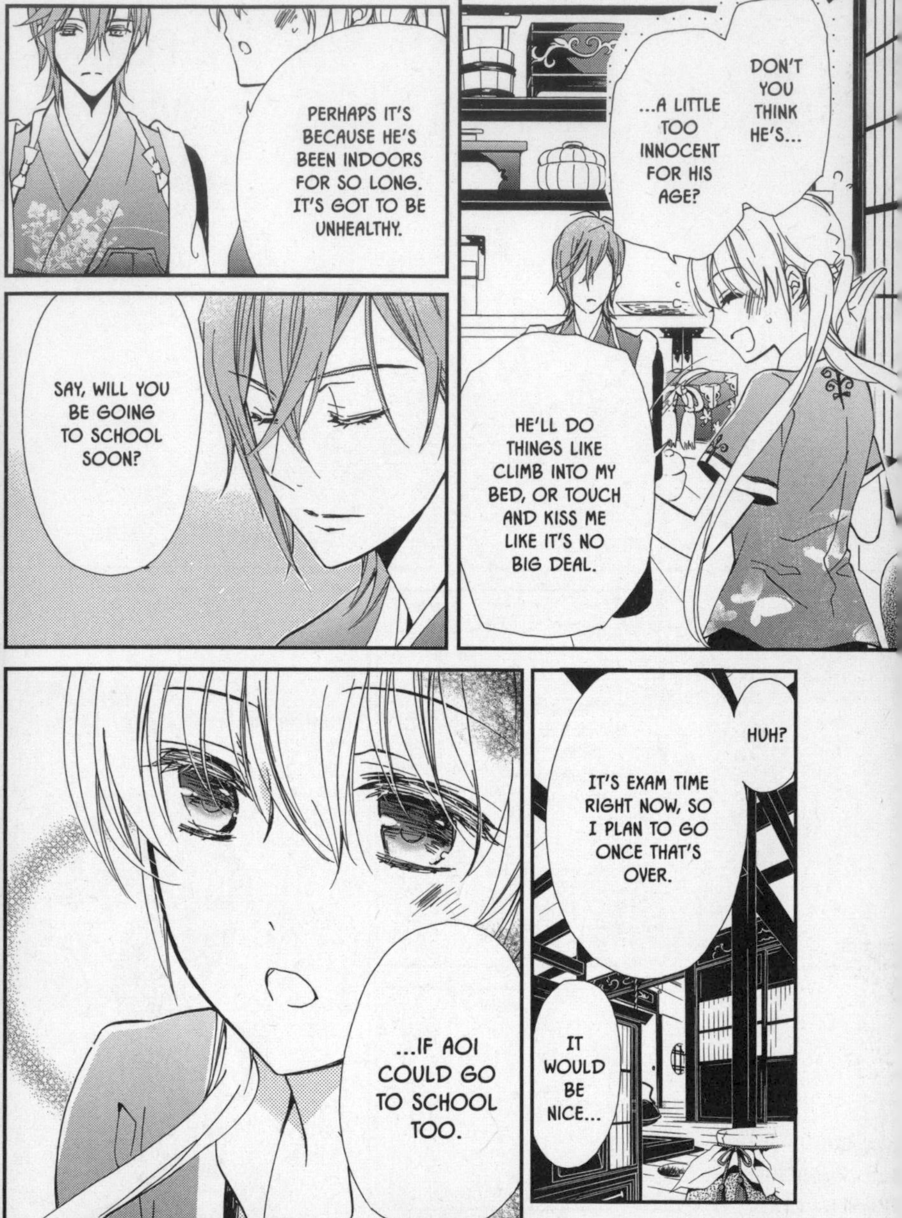
DON'T YOU THINK HE'S...
...A LITTLE TOO INNOCENT FOR HIS AGE?
HE'LL DO THINGS LIKE CLIMB INTO MY BED, OR TOUCH AND KISS ME LIKE IT'S NO BIG DEAL.
PERHAPS IT'S BECAUSE HE'S BEEN INDOORS FOR SO LONG. IT'S GOT TO BE UNHEALTHY.
SAY, WILL YOU BE GOING TO SCHOOL SOON?
HUH?
IT'S EXAM TIME RIGHT NOW, SO I PLAN TO GO ONCE THAT'S OVER.
IT WOULD BE NICE...
...IF AOI COULD GO TO SCHOOL TOO.

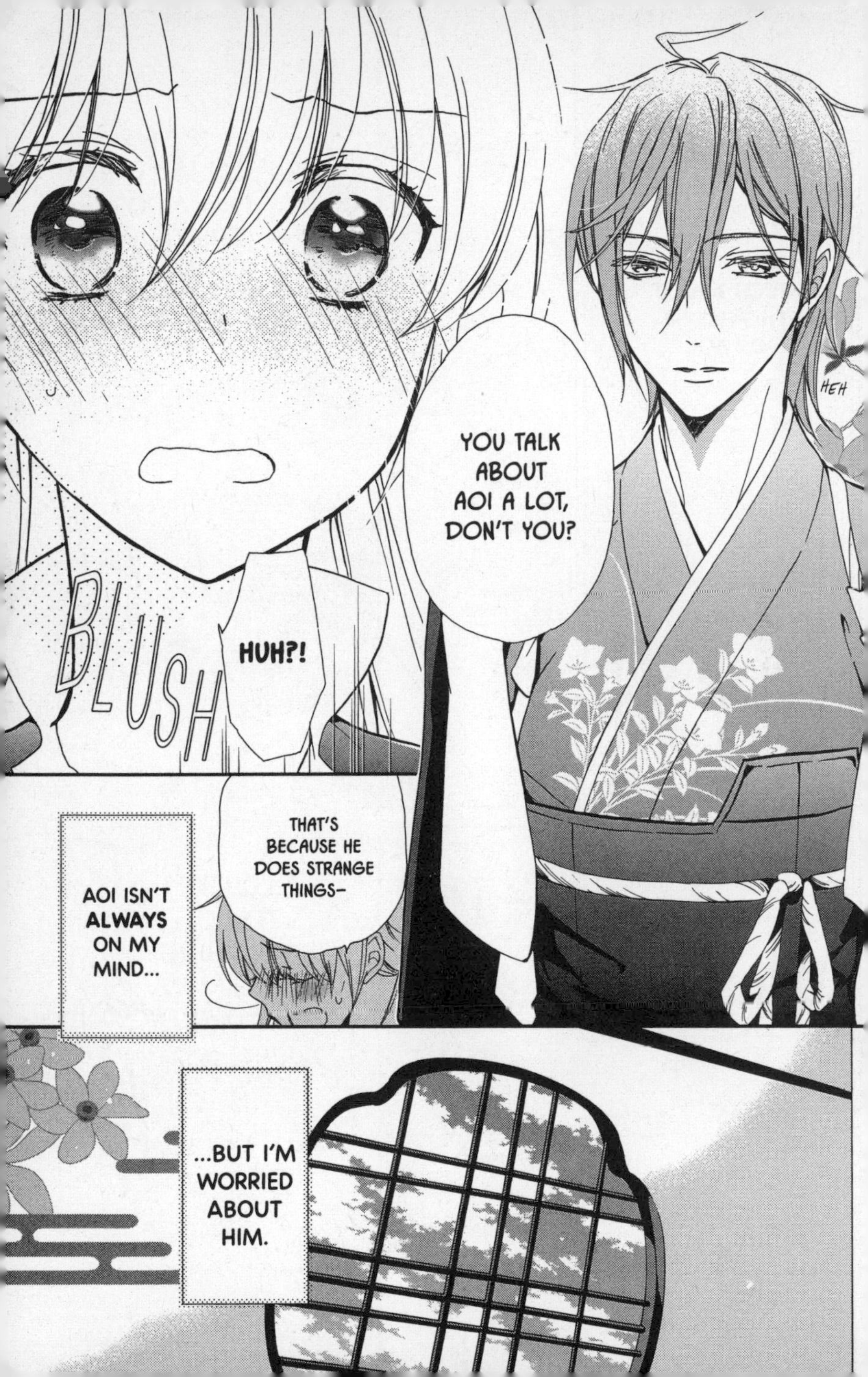
HEH
YOU TALK ABOUT AOI A LOT, DON'T YOU?
HUH?!
BLUSH
THAT'S BECAUSE HE DOES STRANGE THINGS–
AOI ISN'T **ALWAYS** ON MY MIND...
...BUT I'M WORRIED ABOUT HIM.

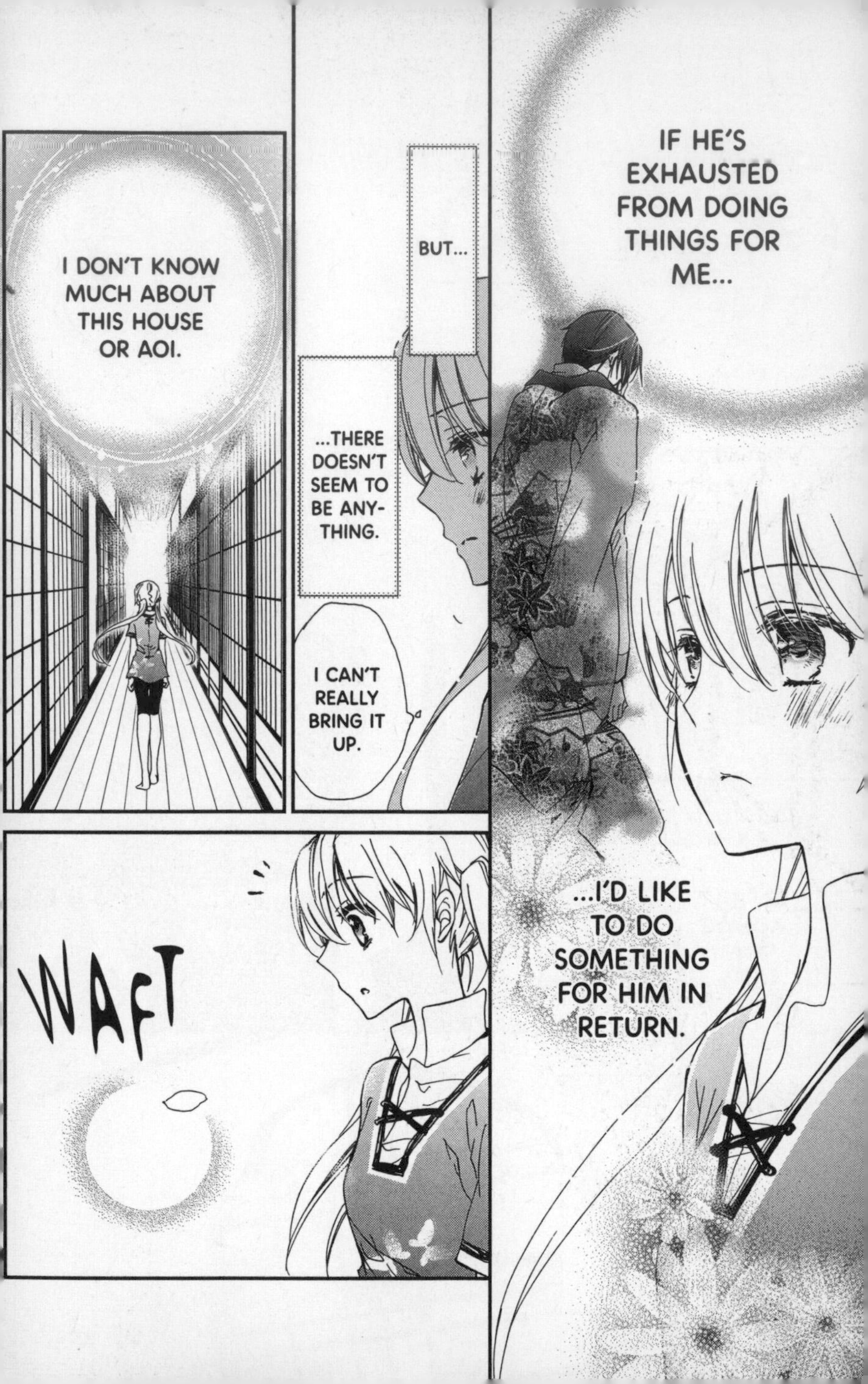
IF HE'S EXHAUSTED FROM DOING THINGS FOR ME...
...I'D LIKE TO DO SOMETHING FOR HIM IN RETURN.
BUT...
...THERE DOESN'T SEEM TO BE ANY-THING.
I CAN'T REALLY BRING IT UP.
I DON'T KNOW MUCH ABOUT THIS HOUSE OR AOI.
WAFT

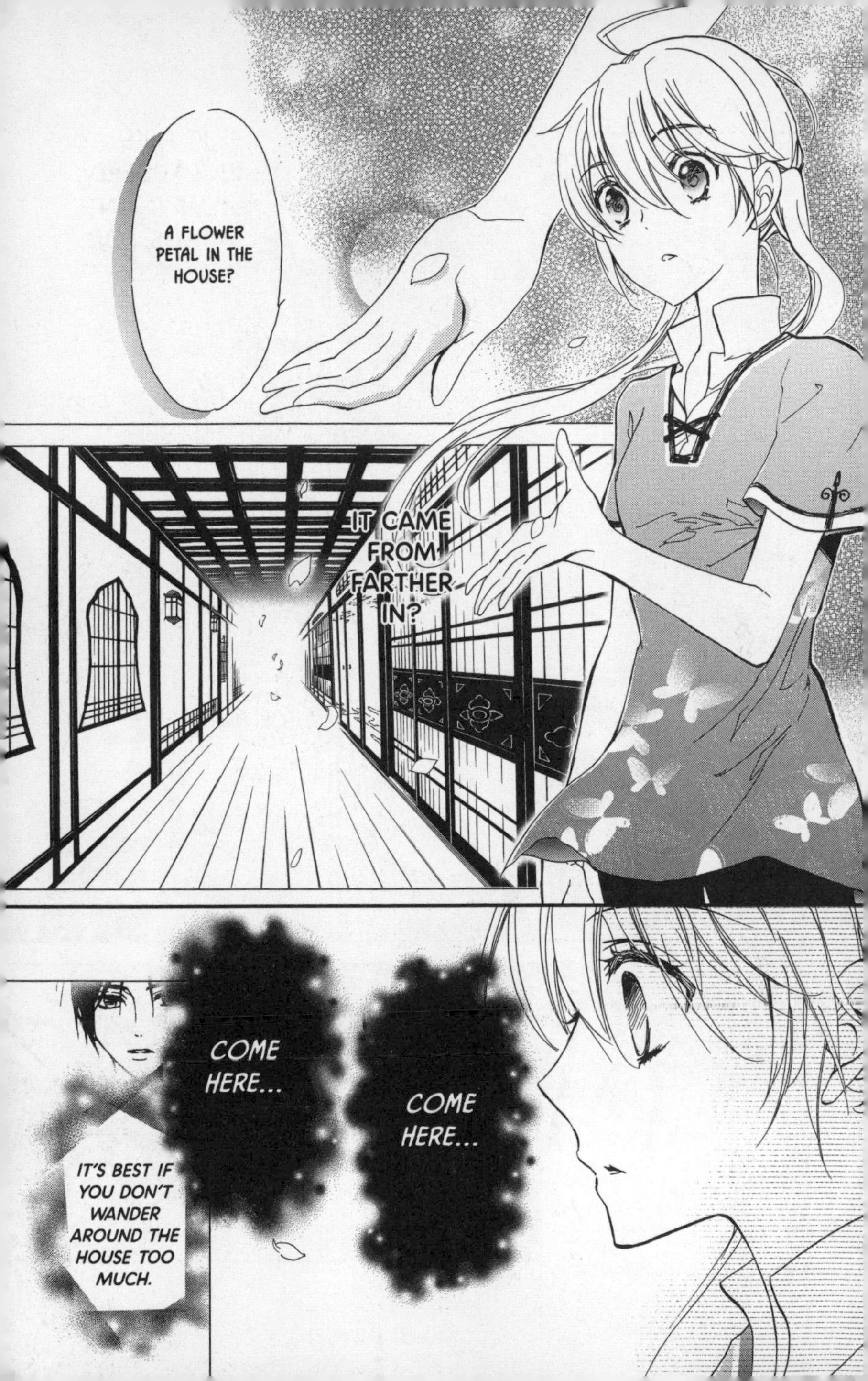
A FLOWER PETAL IN THE HOUSE?
IT CAME FROM FARTHER IN?
COME HERE...
COME HERE...
IT'S BEST IF YOU DON'T WANDER AROUND THE HOUSE TOO MUCH.

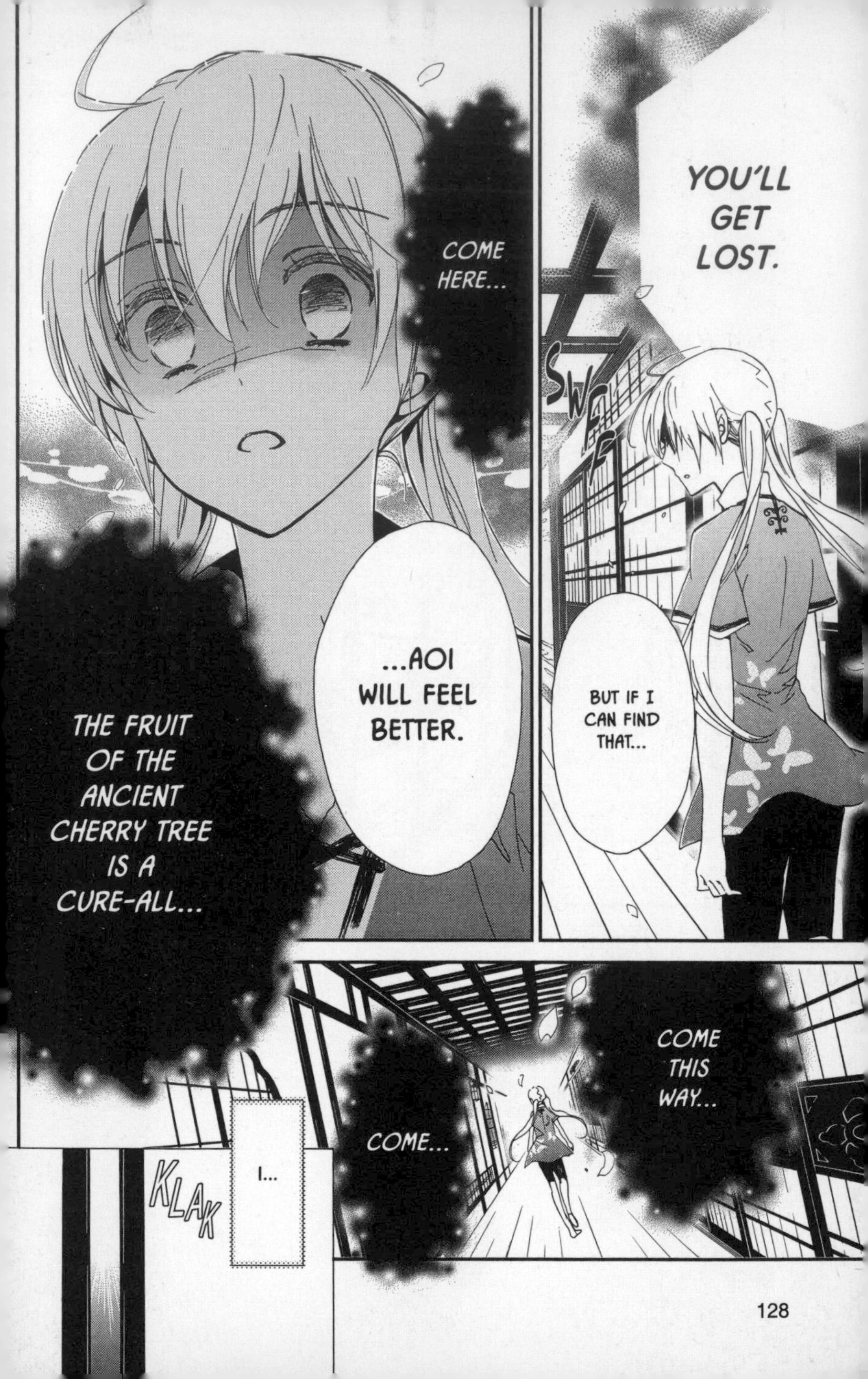

YOU'LL GET LOST.
SWFF
BUT IF I CAN FIND THAT...
COME HERE...
THE FRUIT OF THE ANCIENT CHERRY TREE IS A CURE-ALL...
...AOI WILL FEEL BETTER.
COME THIS WAY...
COME...
KLAK
I...

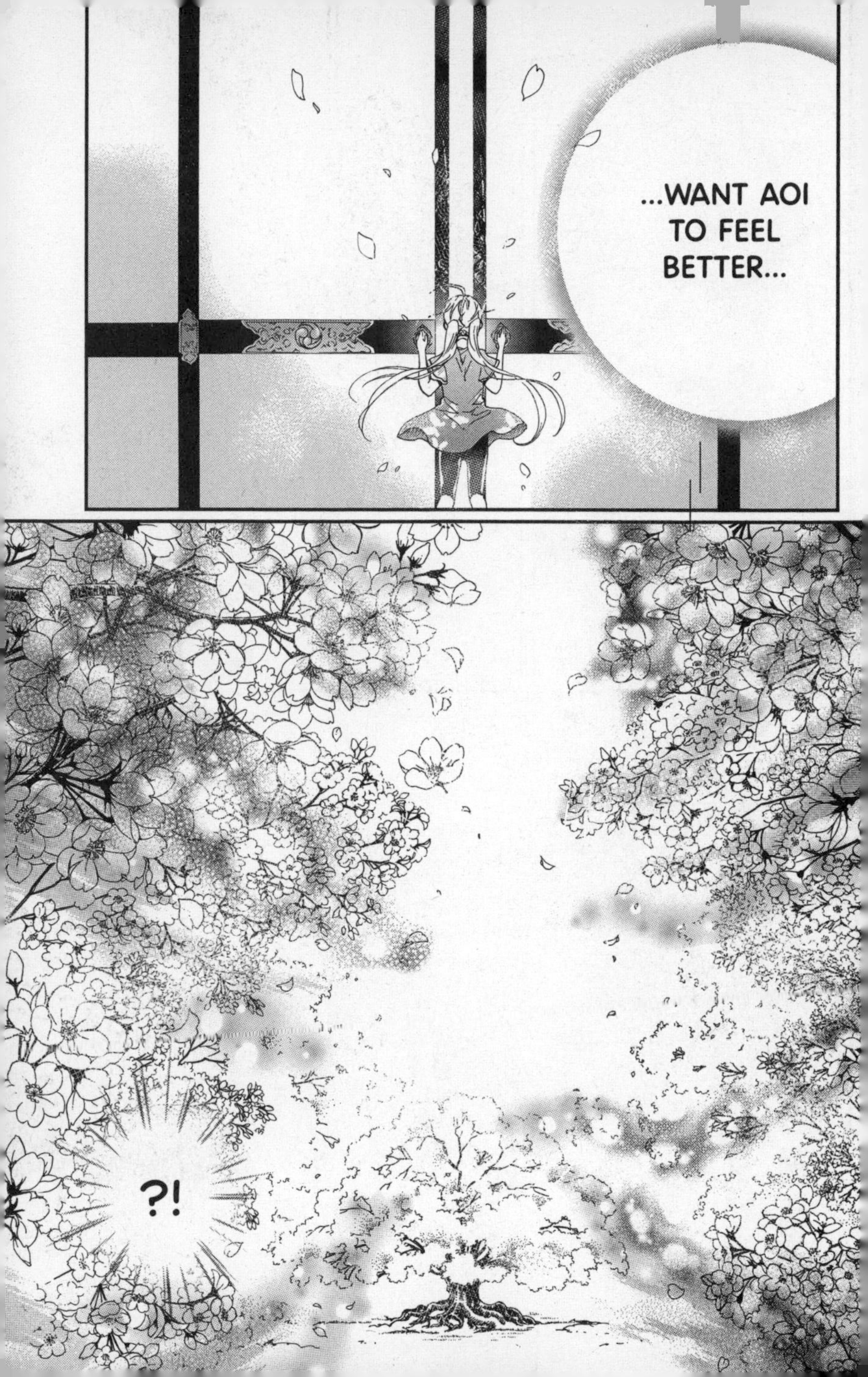
...WANT AOI
TO FEEL
BETTER...
?!

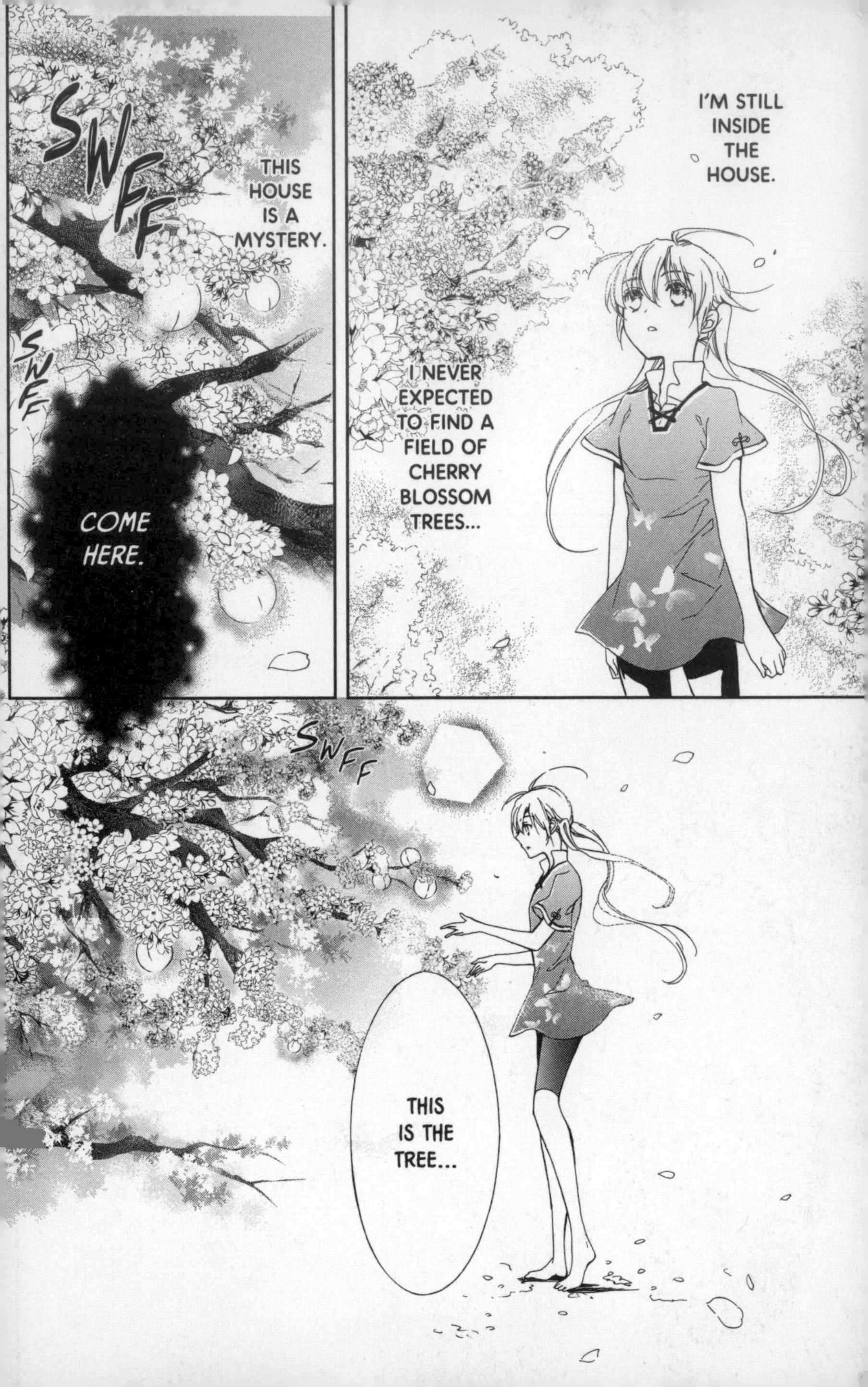
I'M STILL INSIDE THE HOUSE.
I NEVER EXPECTED TO FIND A FIELD OF CHERRY BLOSSOM TREES...
SWFF
THIS HOUSE IS A MYSTERY.
SWFF
COME HERE.
SWFF
THIS IS THE TREE...

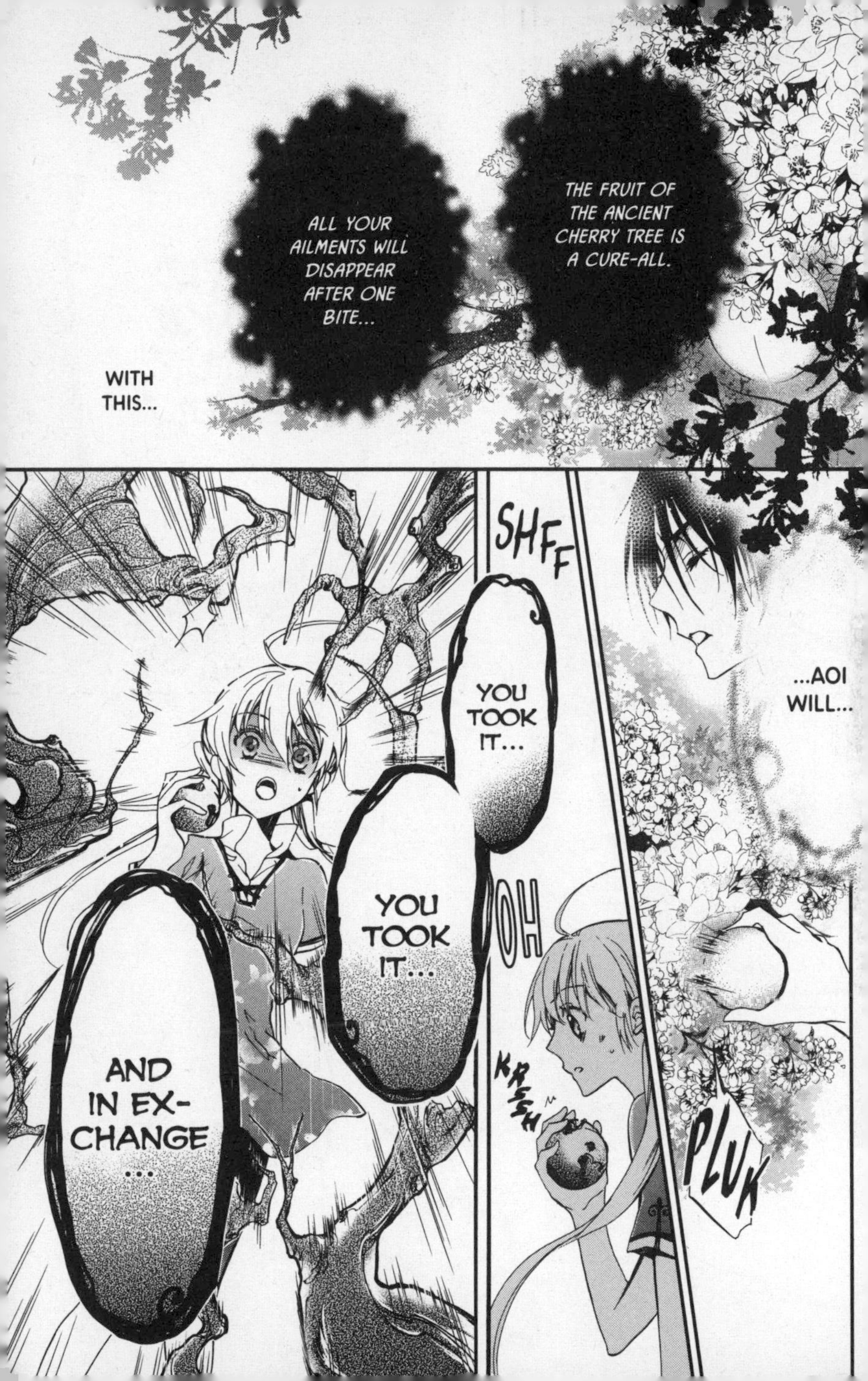
THE FRUIT OF THE ANCIENT CHERRY TREE IS A CURE-ALL.
ALL YOUR AILMENTS WILL DISAPPEAR AFTER ONE BITE...
WITH THIS...
...AOI WILL...
PLUK
KRSSH
SHFF
OH
YOU TOOK IT...
YOU TOOK IT...
AND IN EX-CHANGE ...

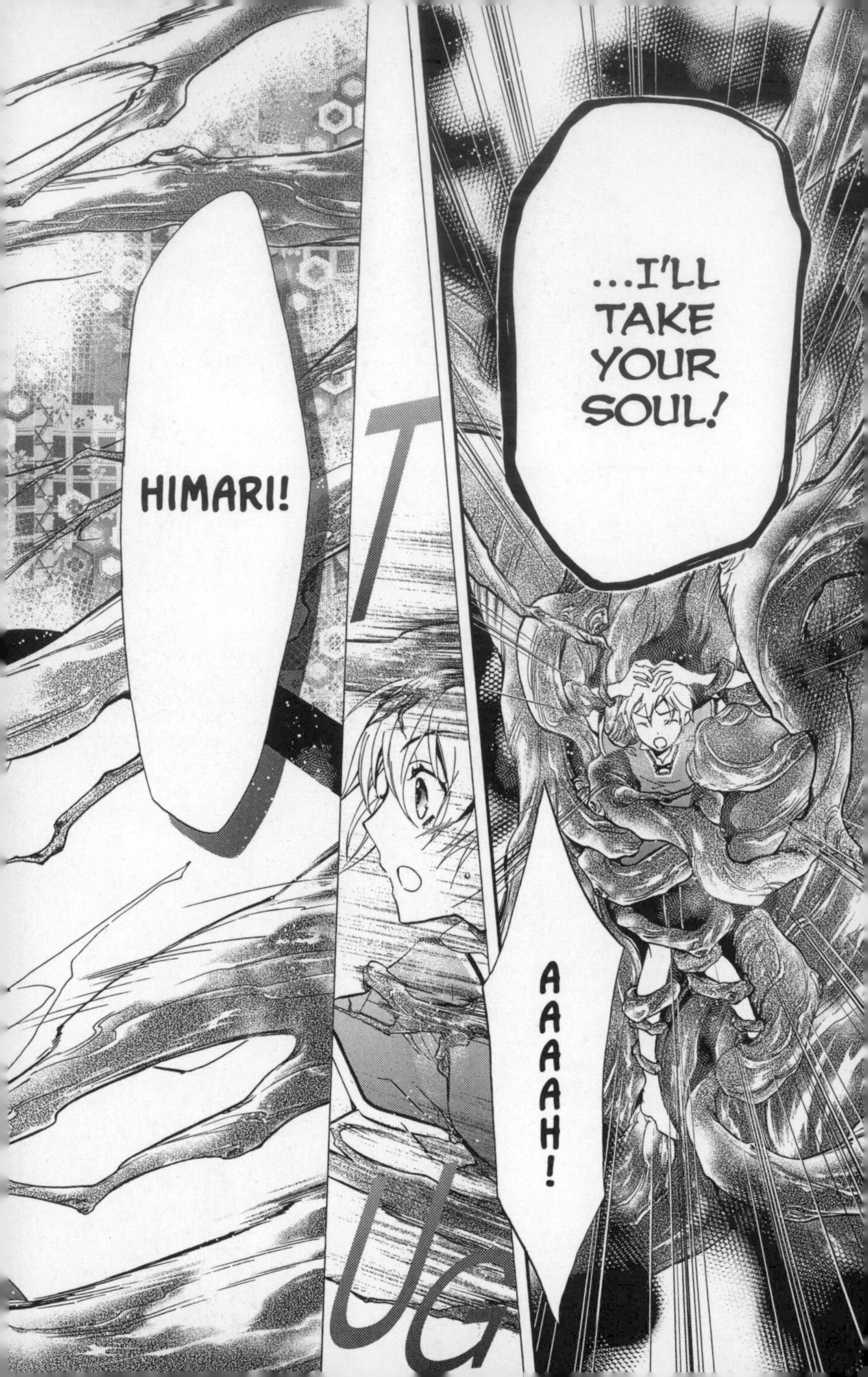
...I'LL TAKE YOUR SOUL!
AAAAAH!
T
UG
HIMARI!

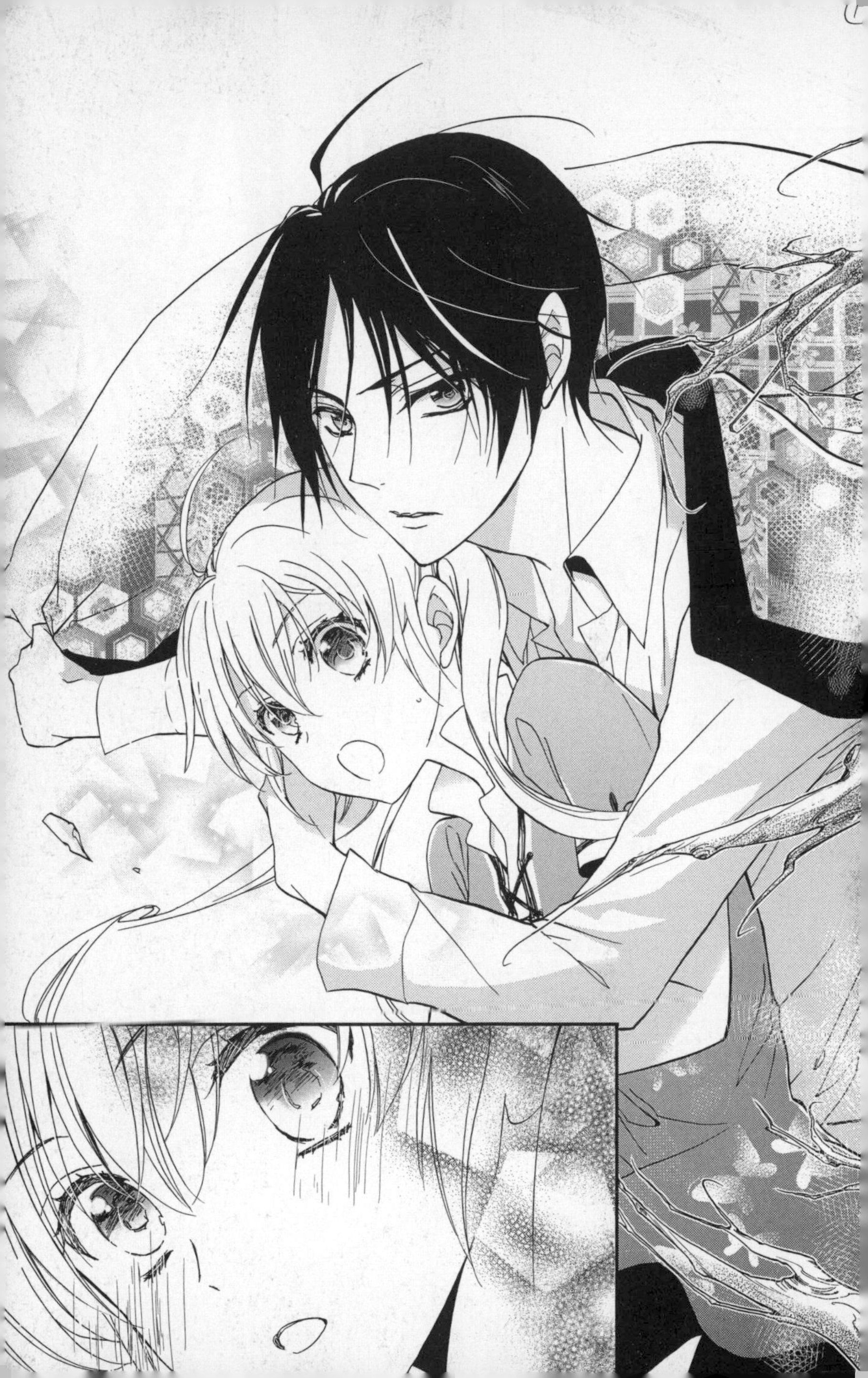

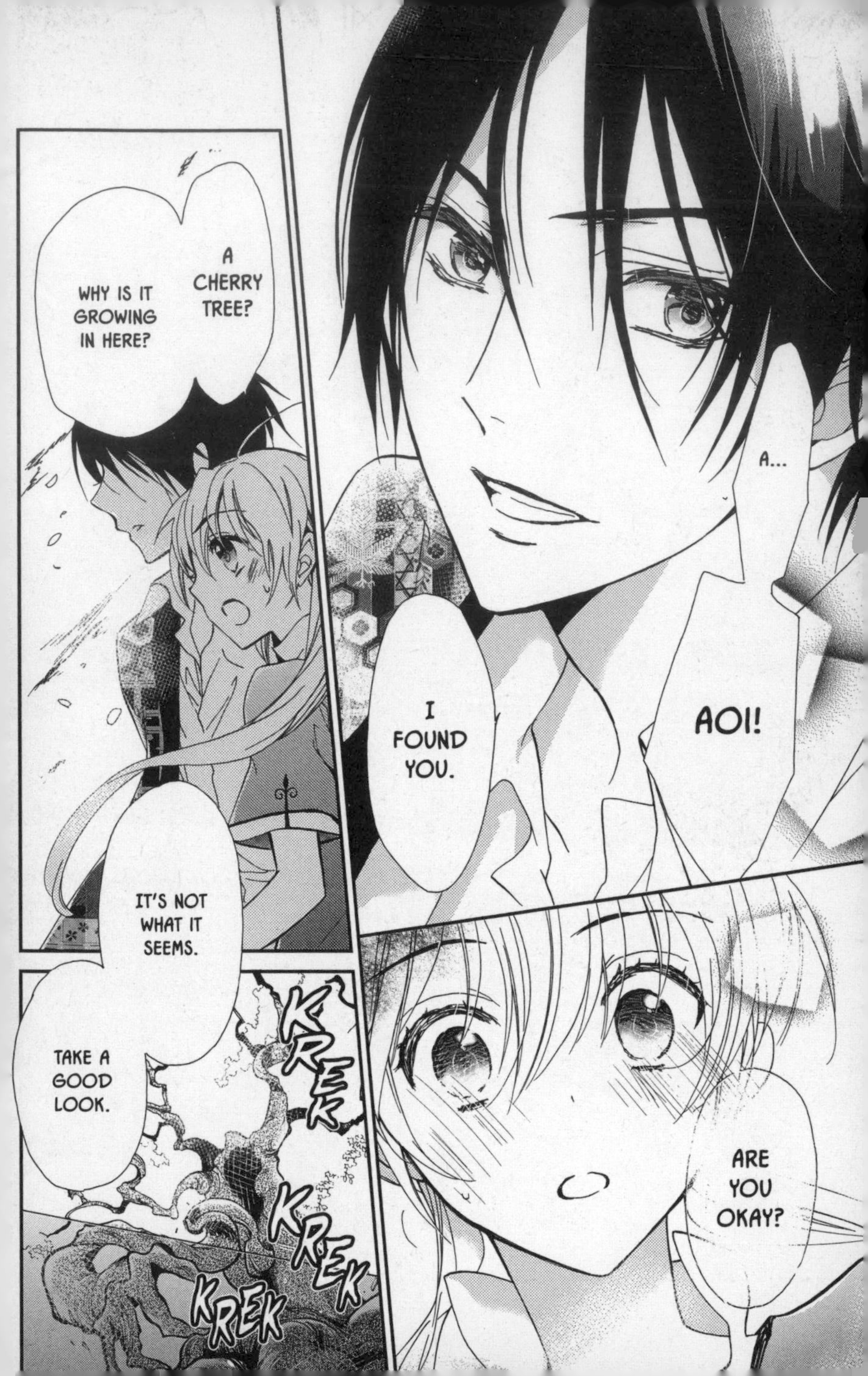
A...
AOI!
I FOUND YOU.
A CHERRY TREE?
WHY IS IT GROWING IN HERE?
IT'S NOT WHAT IT SEEMS.
ARE YOU OKAY?
TAKE A GOOD LOOK.
KREK
KREK
KREK

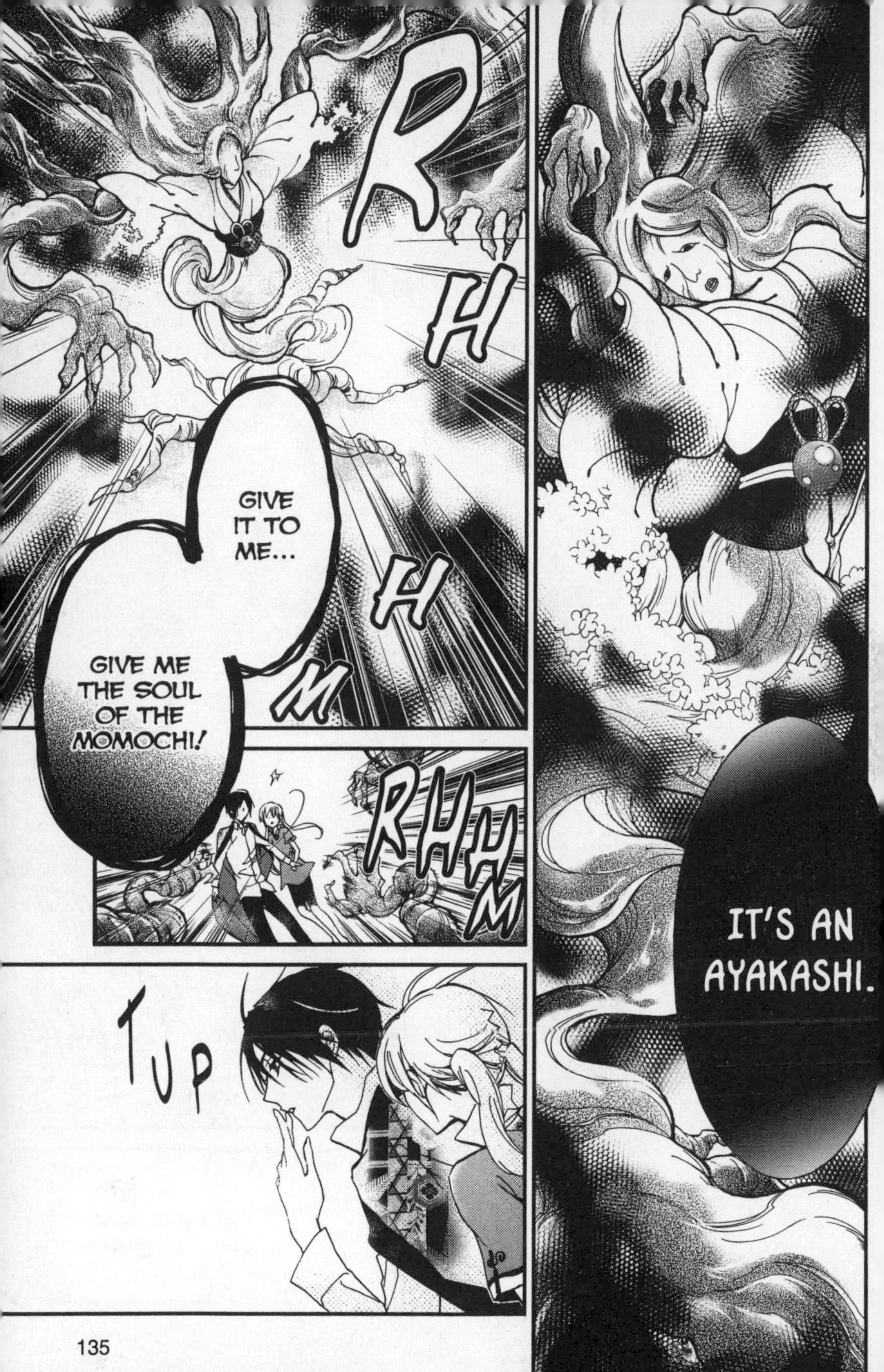

IT'S AN AYAKASHI.
RHHM
GIVE IT TO ME...
GIVE ME THE SOUL OF THE MOMOCHI!
RHHM
TUP

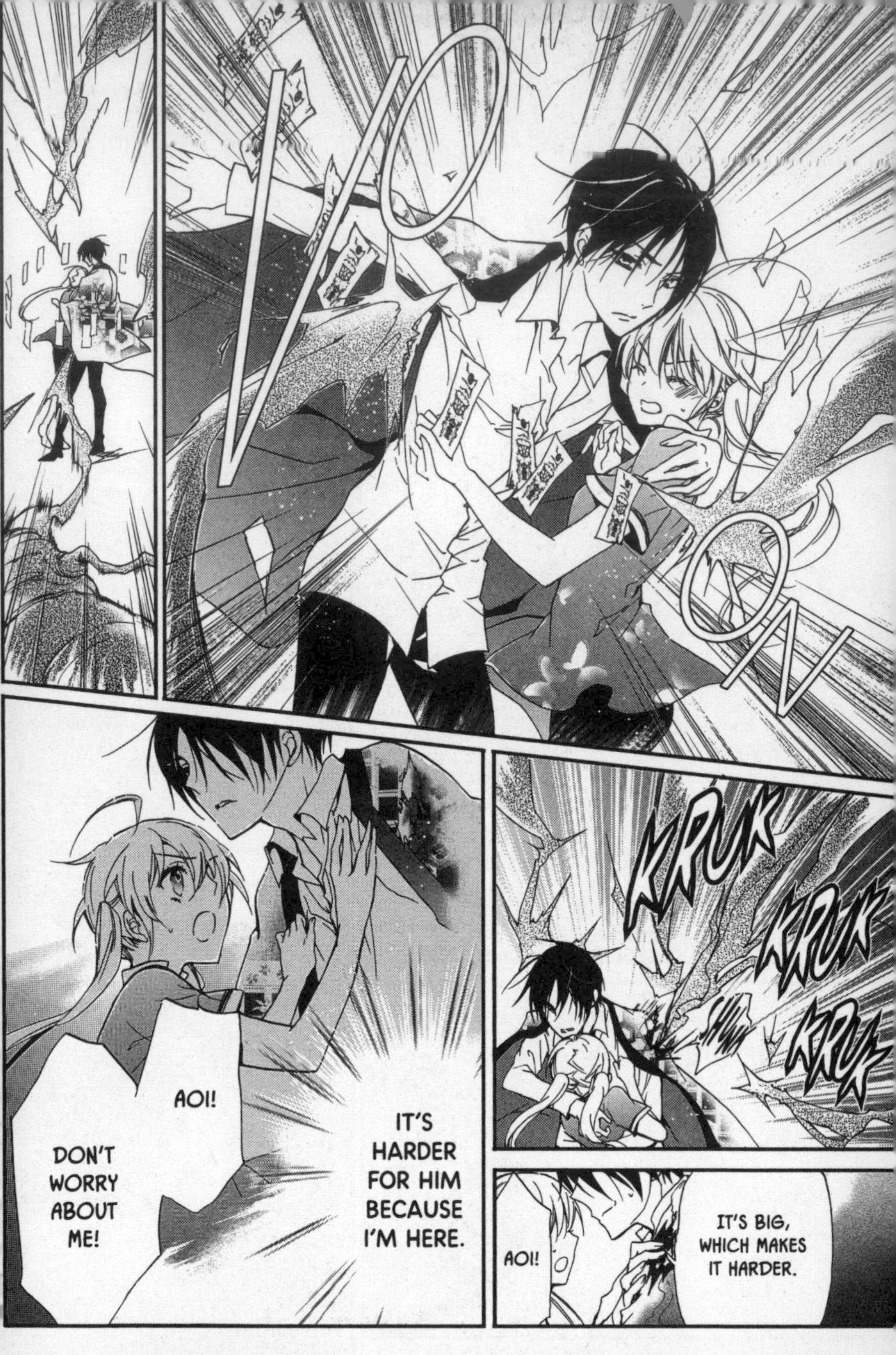
KRUK
KRUK
KRUK
IT'S BIG, WHICH MAKES IT HARDER.
AOI!
IT'S HARDER FOR HIM BECAUSE I'M HERE.
AOI!
DON'T WORRY ABOUT ME!

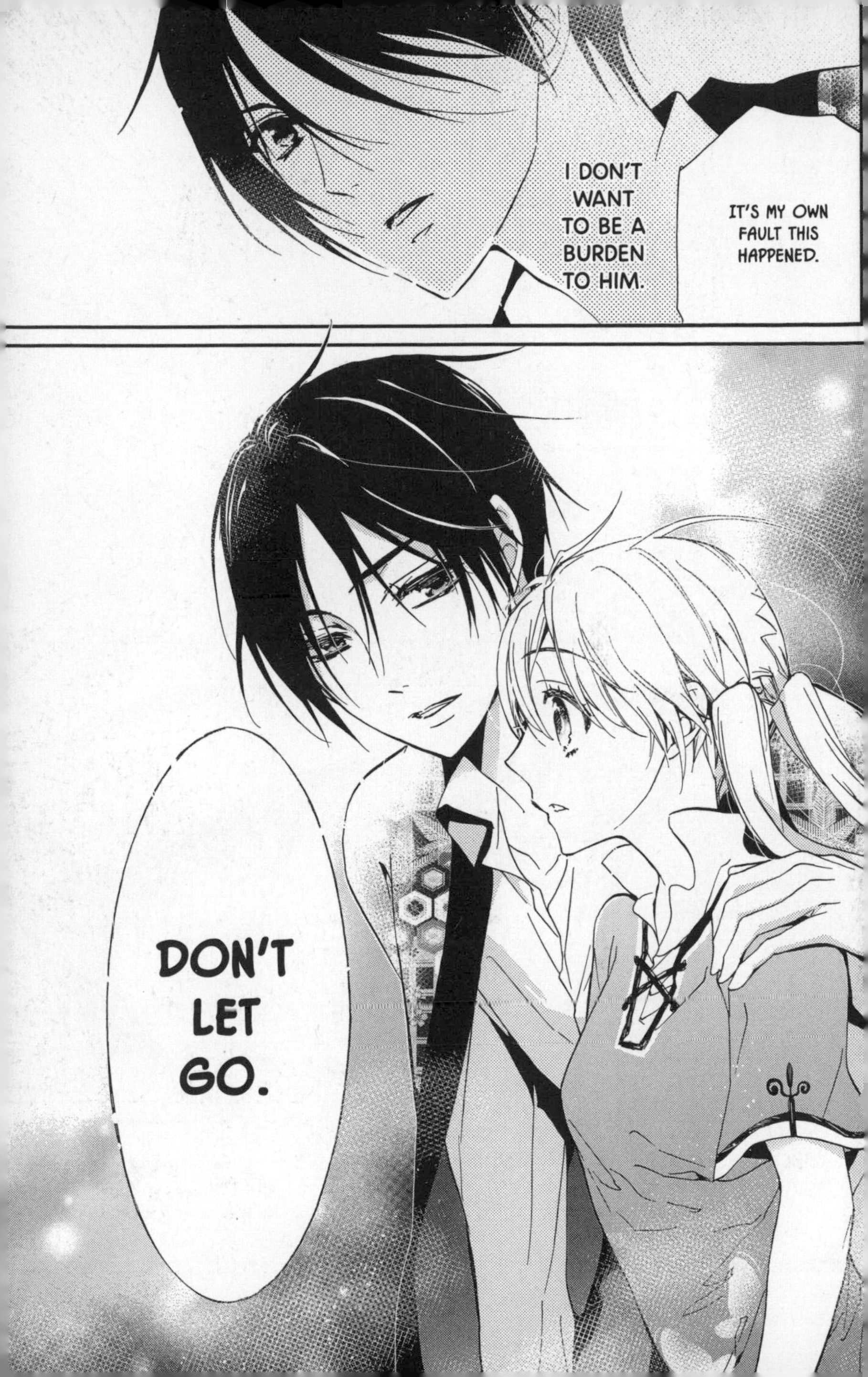
IT'S MY OWN FAULT THIS HAPPENED.
I DON'T WANT TO BE A BURDEN TO HIM.
DON'T LET GO.

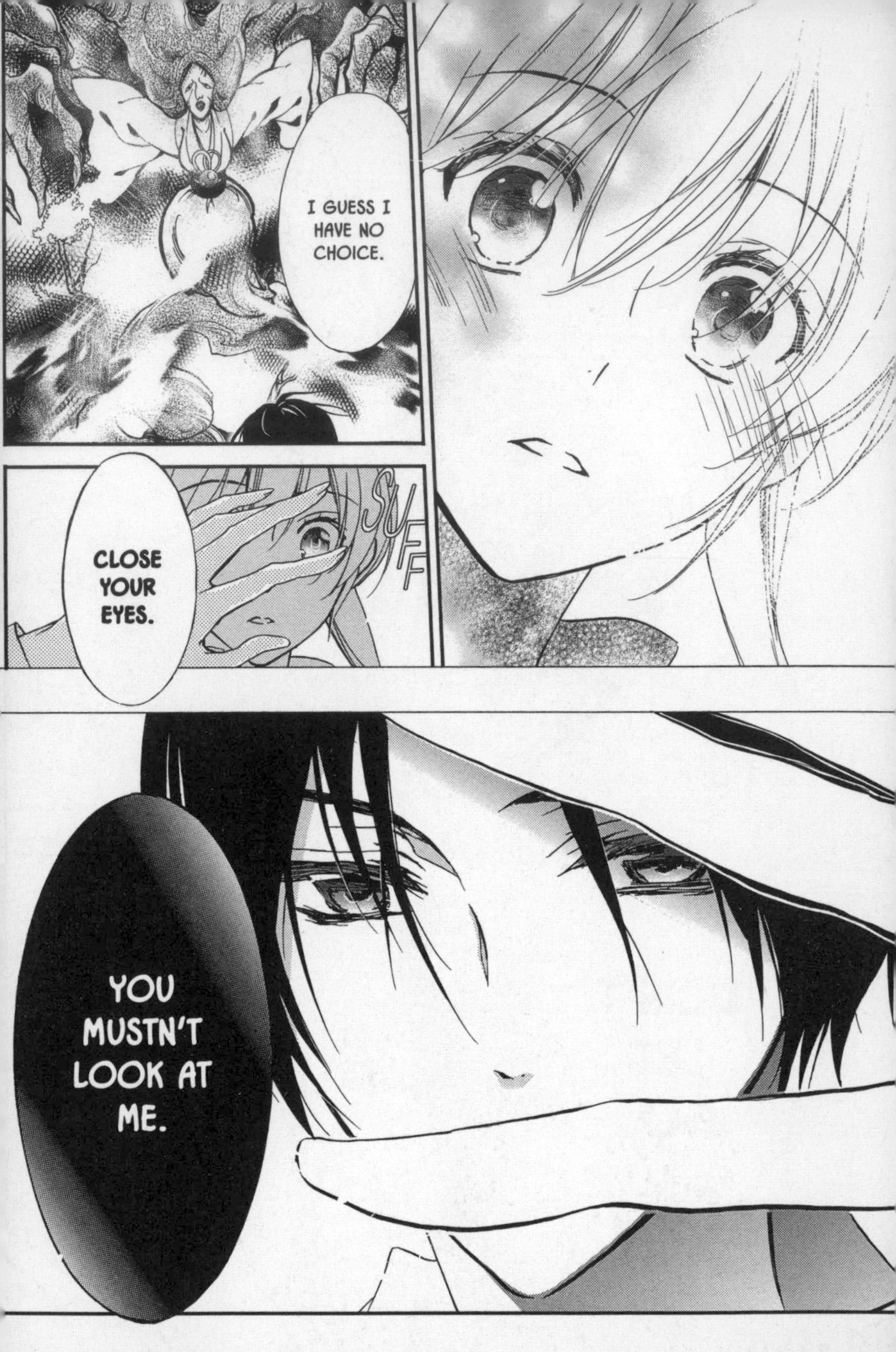
I GUESS I HAVE NO CHOICE.
SUFF
CLOSE YOUR EYES.
YOU MUSTN'T LOOK AT ME.

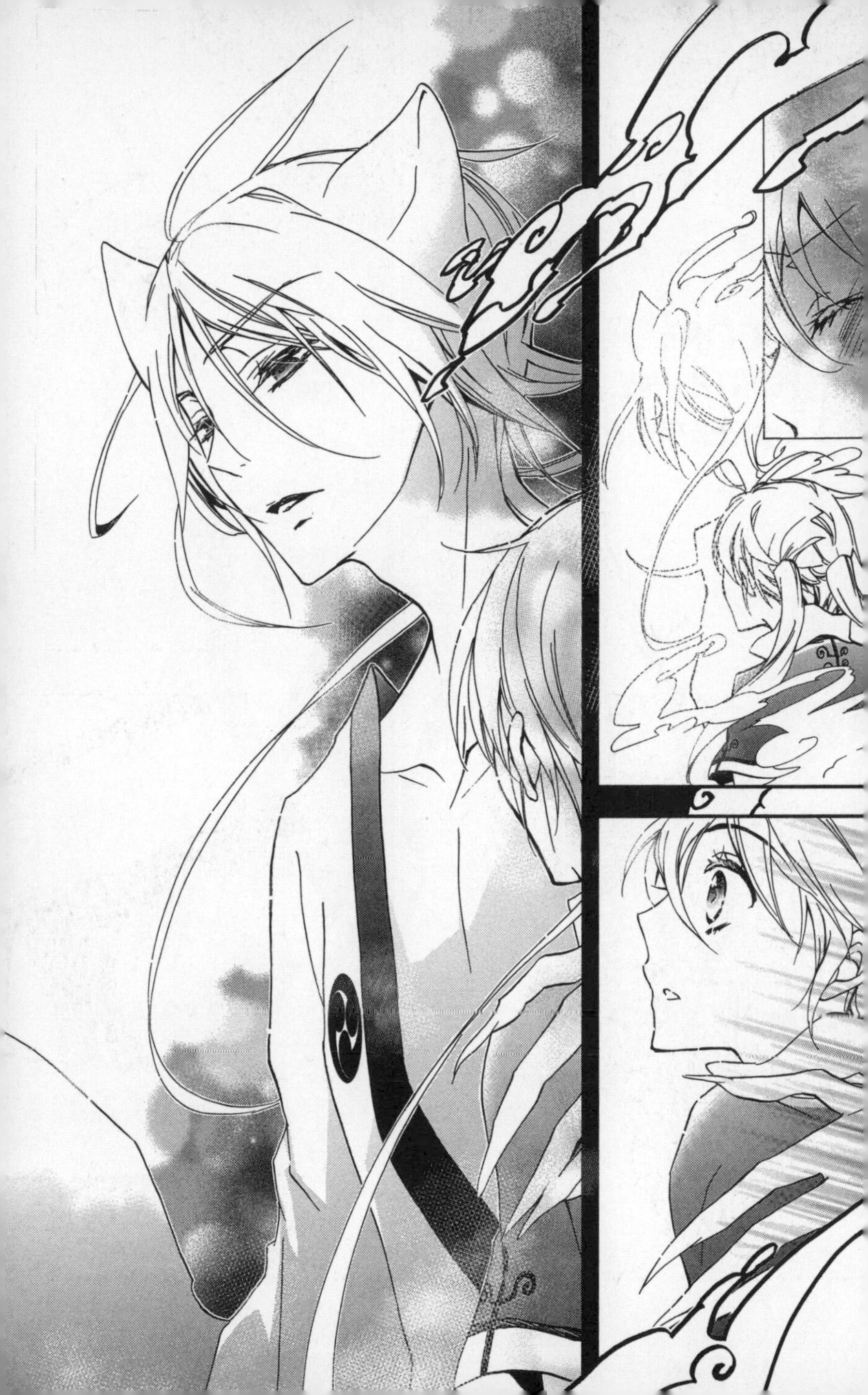

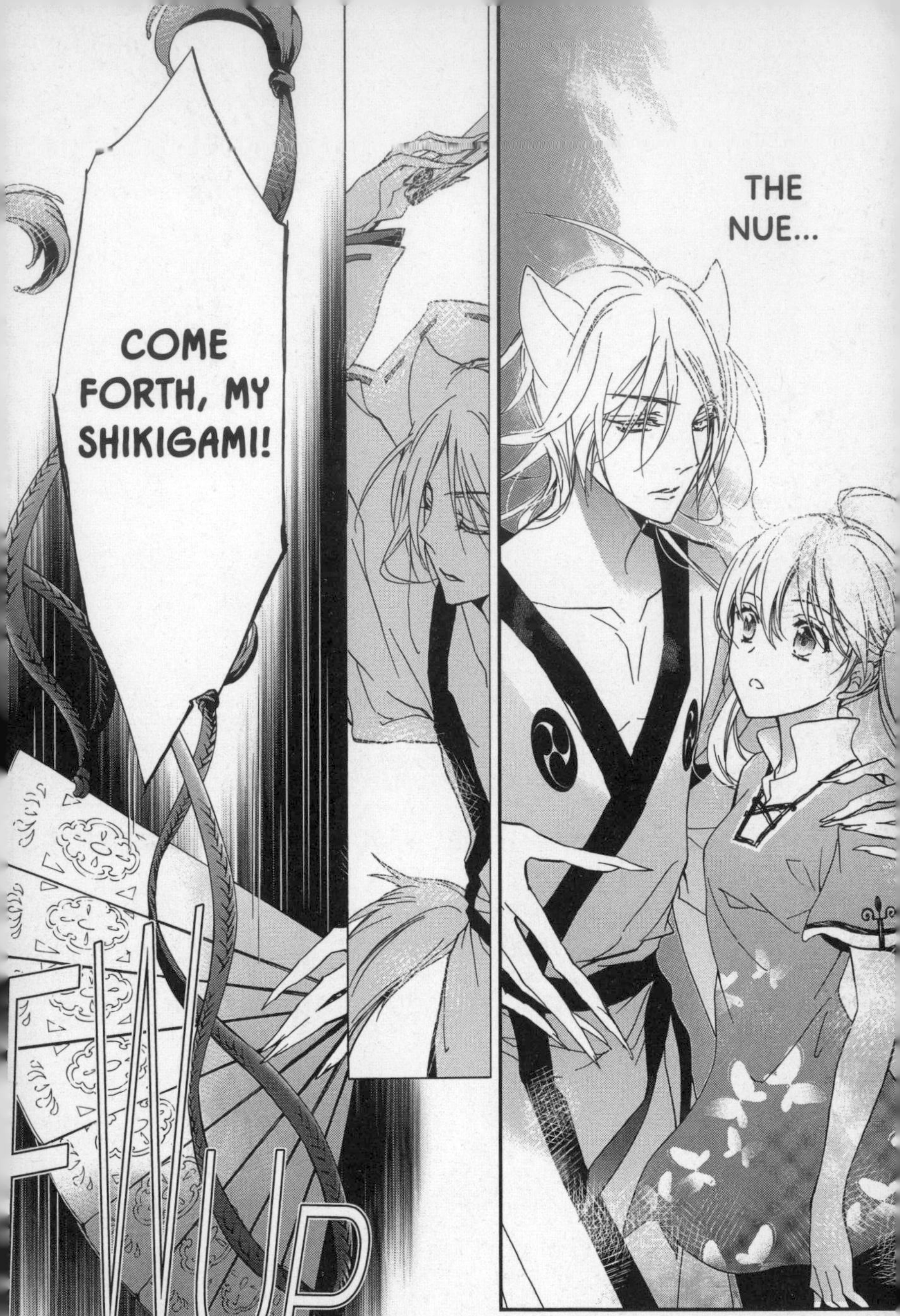
THE NUE...
COME FORTH, MY SHIKIGAMI!
FWUP

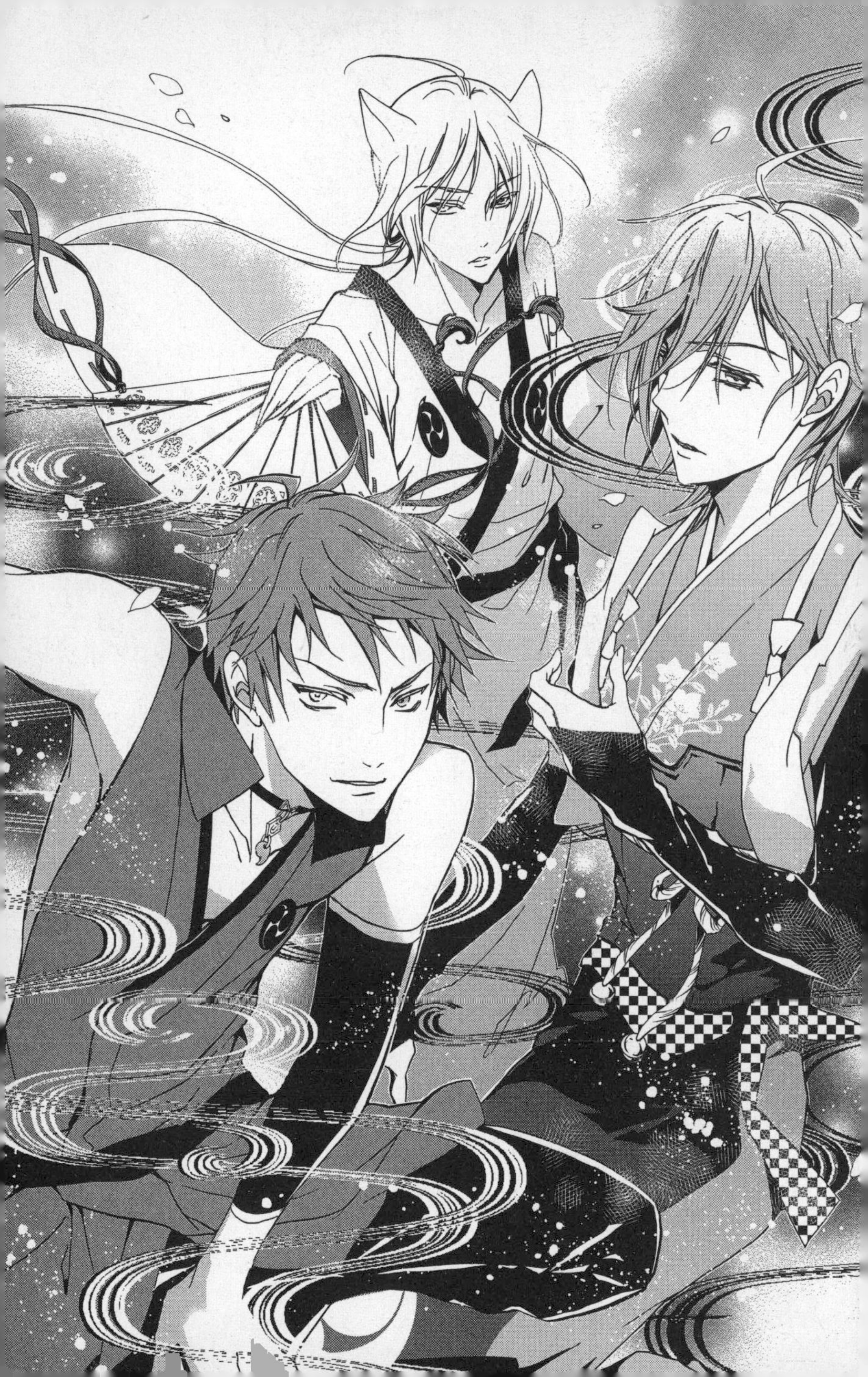

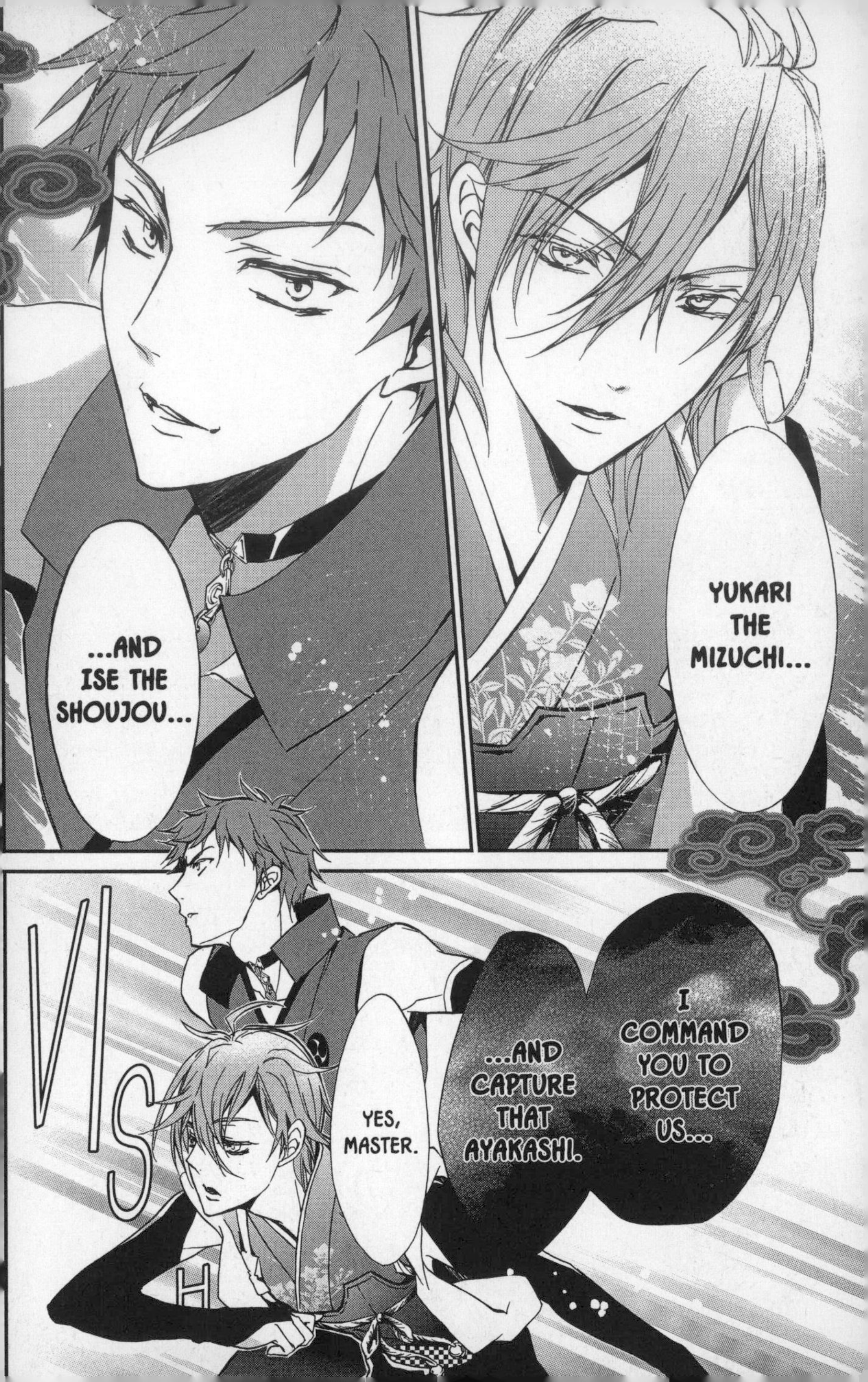
YUKARI THE MIZUCHI...
...AND ISE THE SHOUJOU...
I COMMAND YOU TO PROTECT US...
...AND CAPTURE THAT AYAKASHI.
YES, MASTER.
VISH

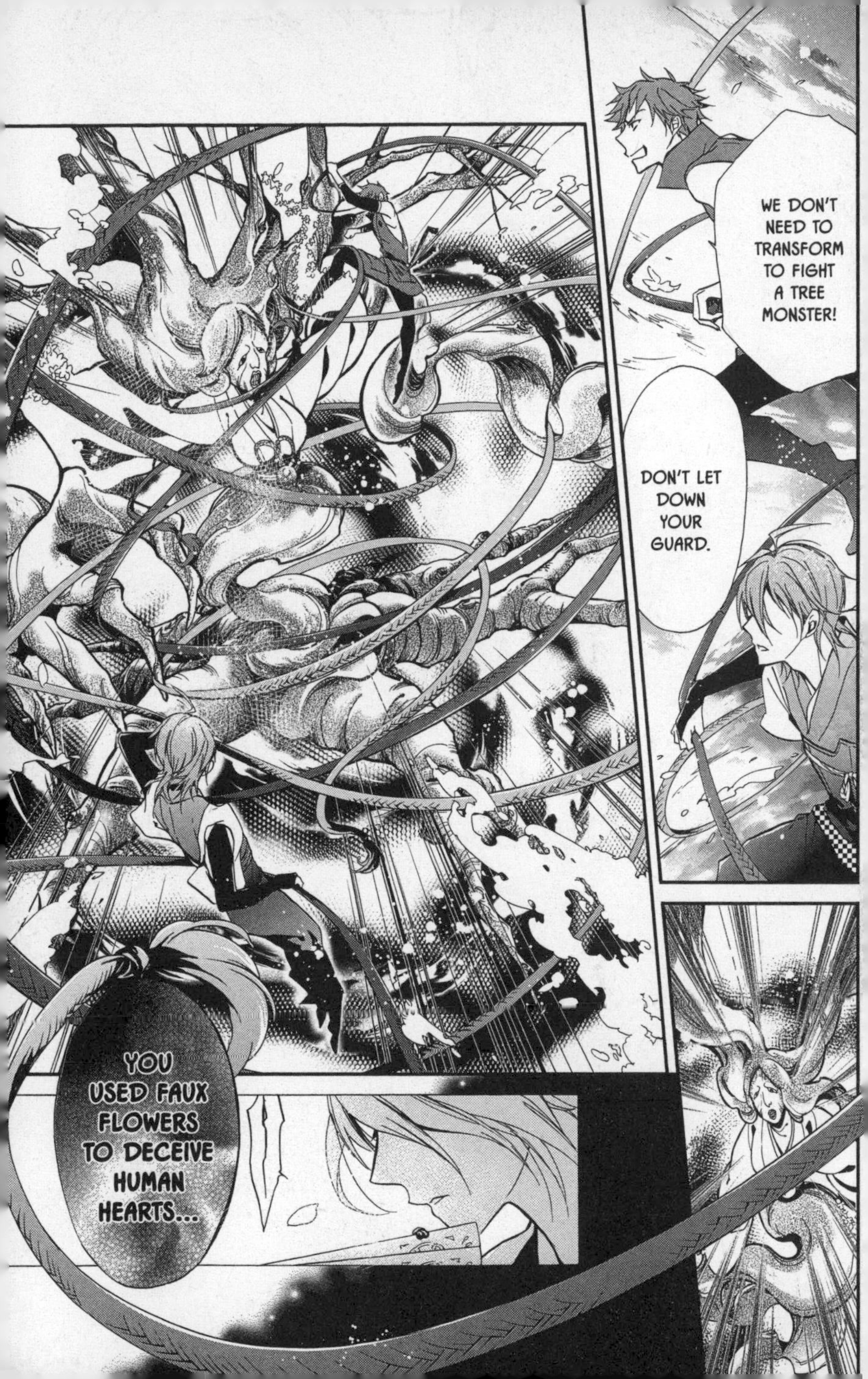
WE DON'T NEED TO TRANSFORM TO FIGHT A TREE MONSTER!
DON'T LET DOWN YOUR GUARD.
YOU USED FAUX FLOWERS TO DECEIVE HUMAN HEARTS...

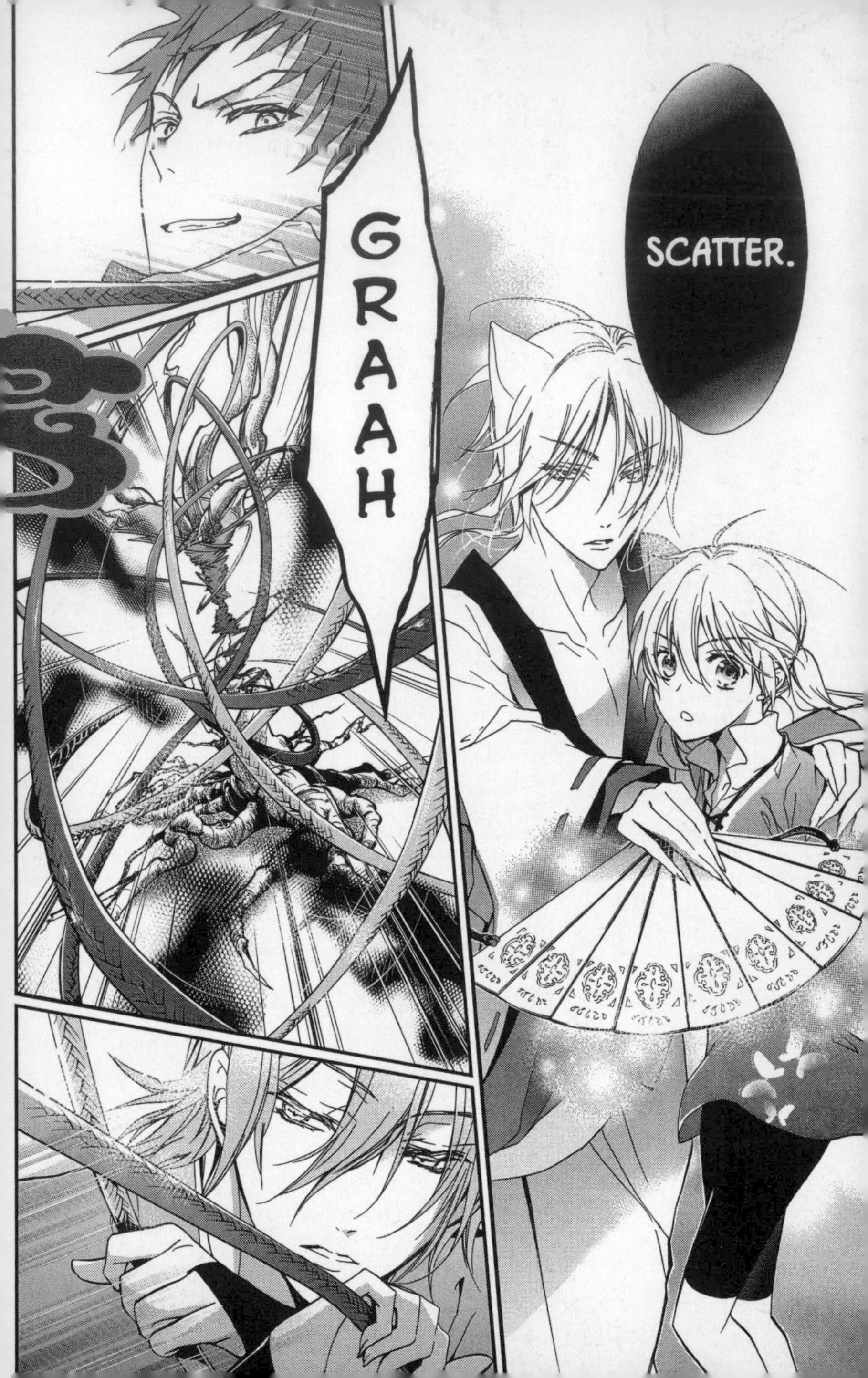
SCATTER.
GRAAH

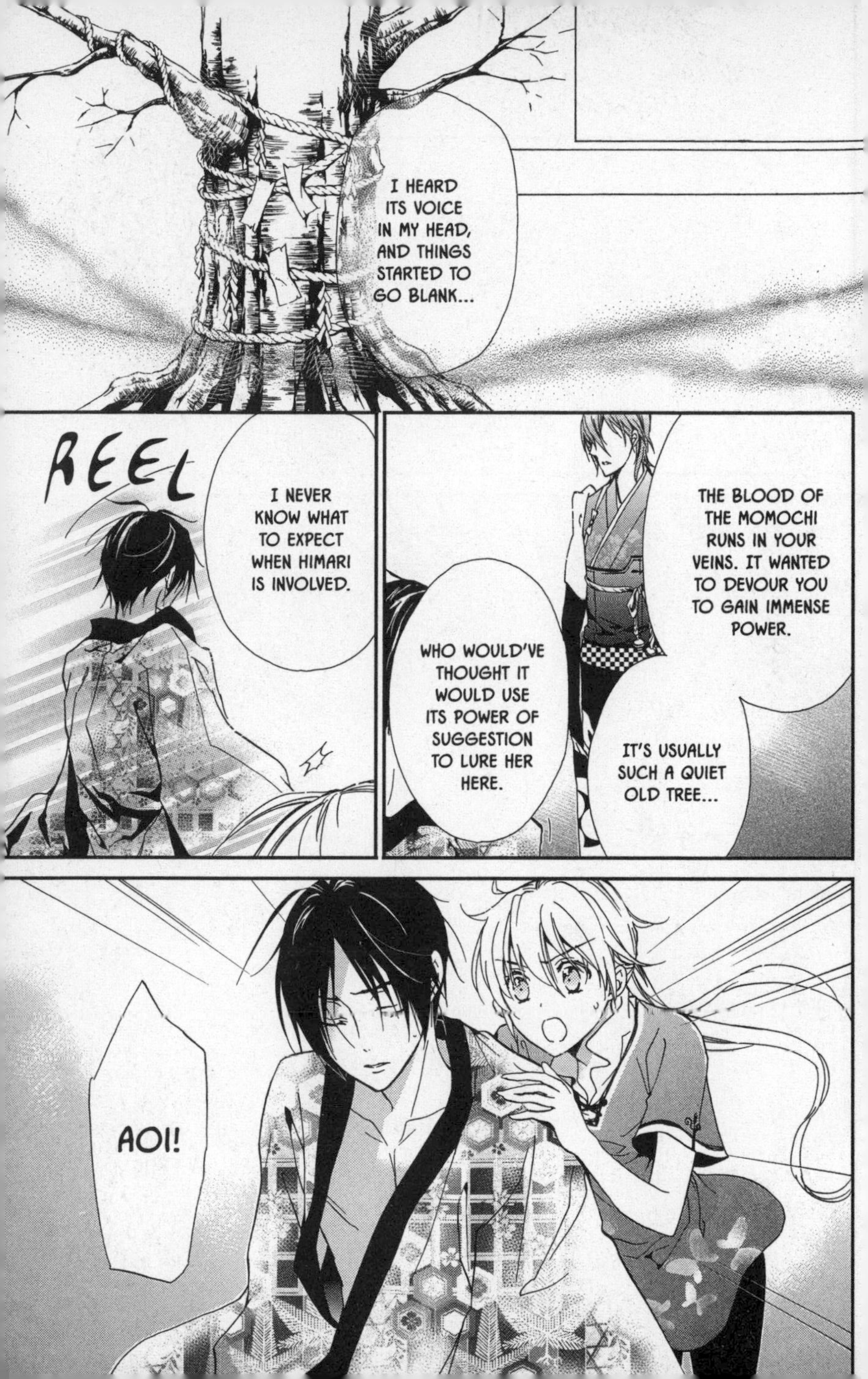
I HEARD ITS VOICE IN MY HEAD, AND THINGS STARTED TO GO BLANK...
THE BLOOD OF THE MOMOCHI RUNS IN YOUR VEINS. IT WANTED TO DEVOUR YOU TO GAIN IMMENSE POWER.
WHO WOULD'VE THOUGHT IT WOULD USE ITS POWER OF SUGGESTION TO LURE HER HERE.
IT'S USUALLY SUCH A QUIET OLD TREE...
I NEVER KNOW WHAT TO EXPECT WHEN HIMARI IS INVOLVED.
REEL
AOI!

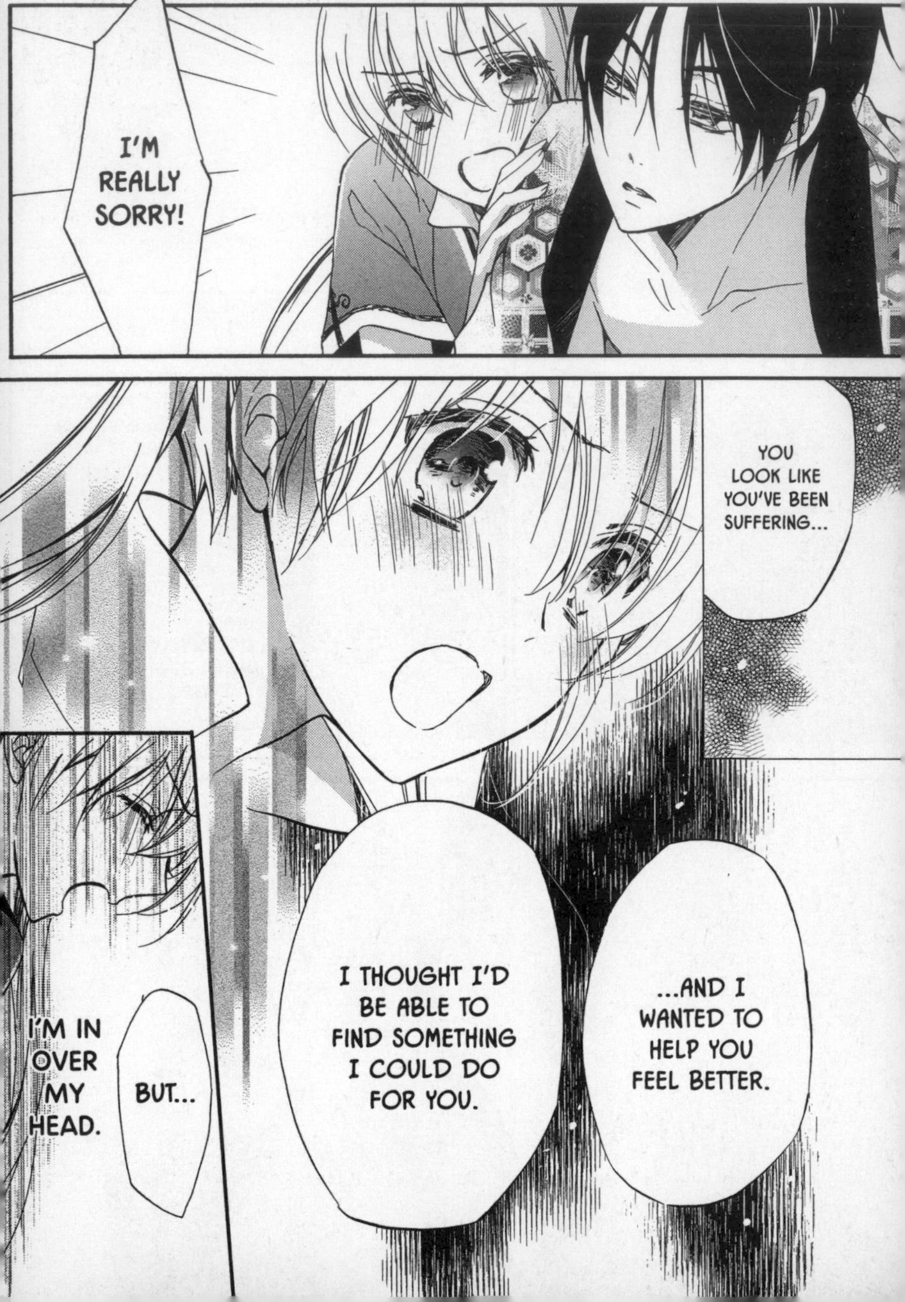
I'M REALLY SORRY!
YOU LOOK LIKE YOU'VE BEEN SUFFERING...
I THOUGHT I'D BE ABLE TO FIND SOMETHING I COULD DO FOR YOU.
...AND I WANTED TO HELP YOU FEEL BETTER.
BUT...
I'M IN OVER MY HEAD.

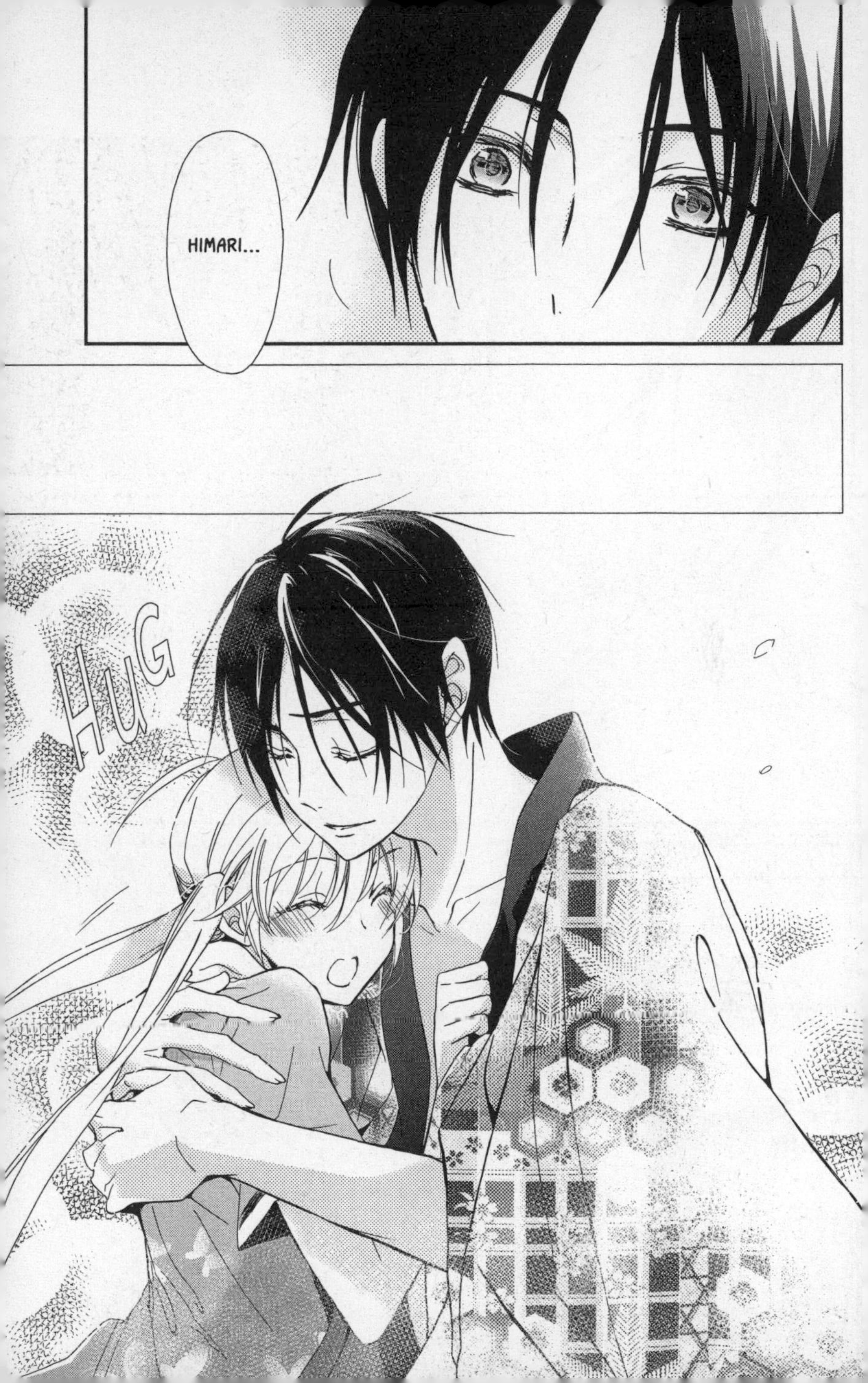
HIMARI...
HUG

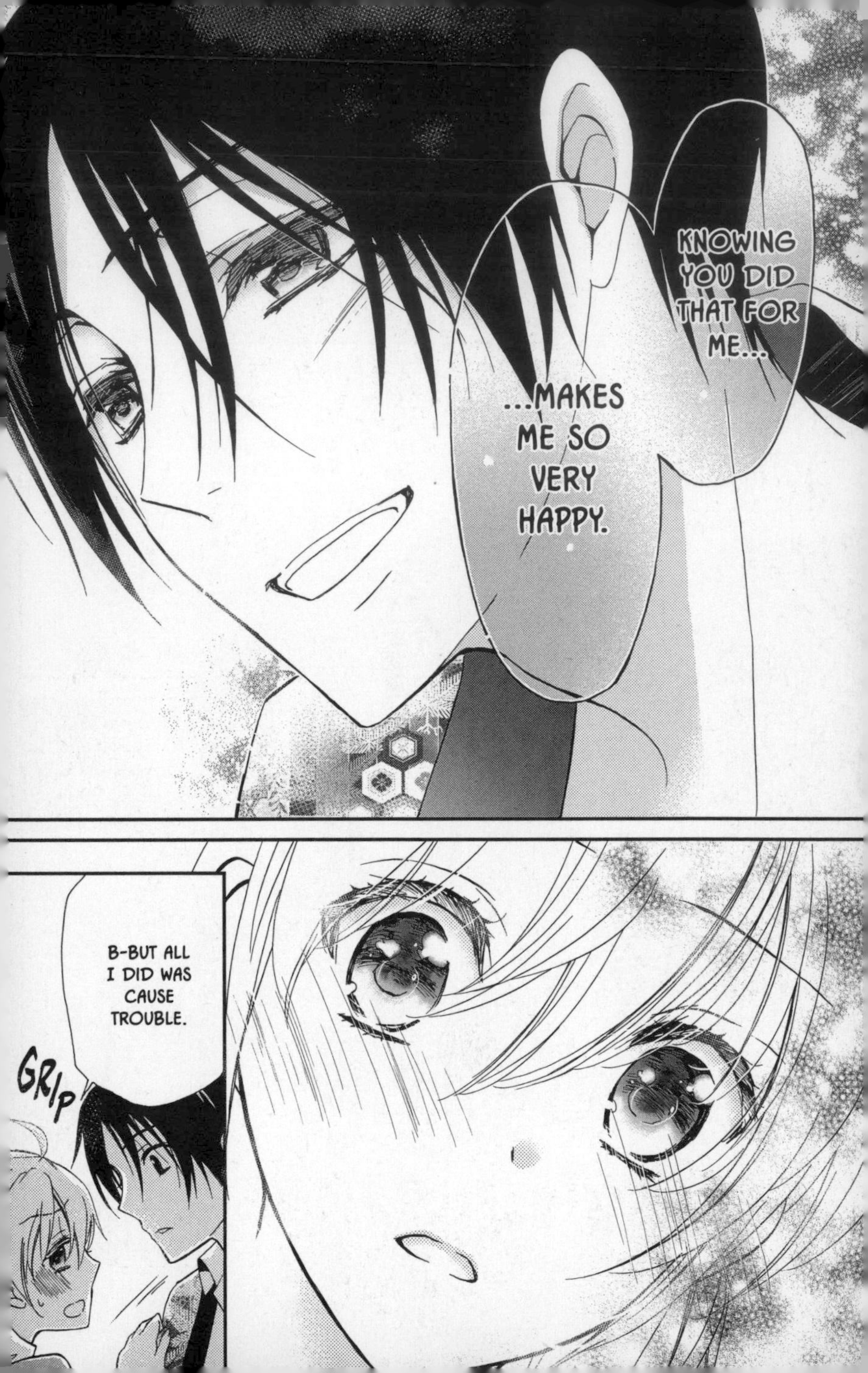
KNOWING YOU DID THAT FOR ME...
...MAKES ME SO VERY HAPPY.
B-BUT ALL I DID WAS CAUSE TROUBLE.
GRIP

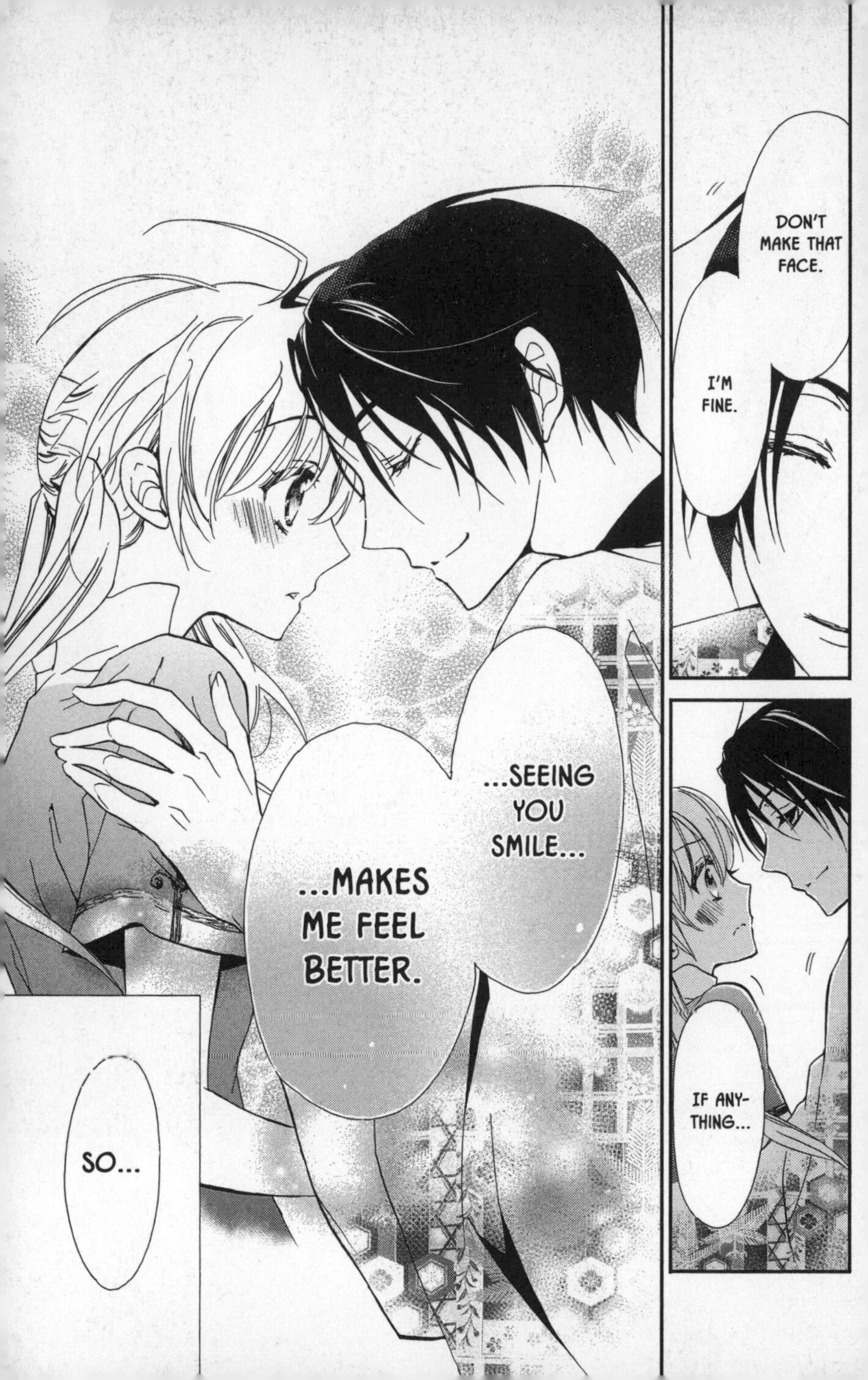
DON'T MAKE THAT FACE.
I'M FINE.
IF ANY-THING...
...SEEING YOU SMILE...
...MAKES ME FEEL BETTER.
SO...

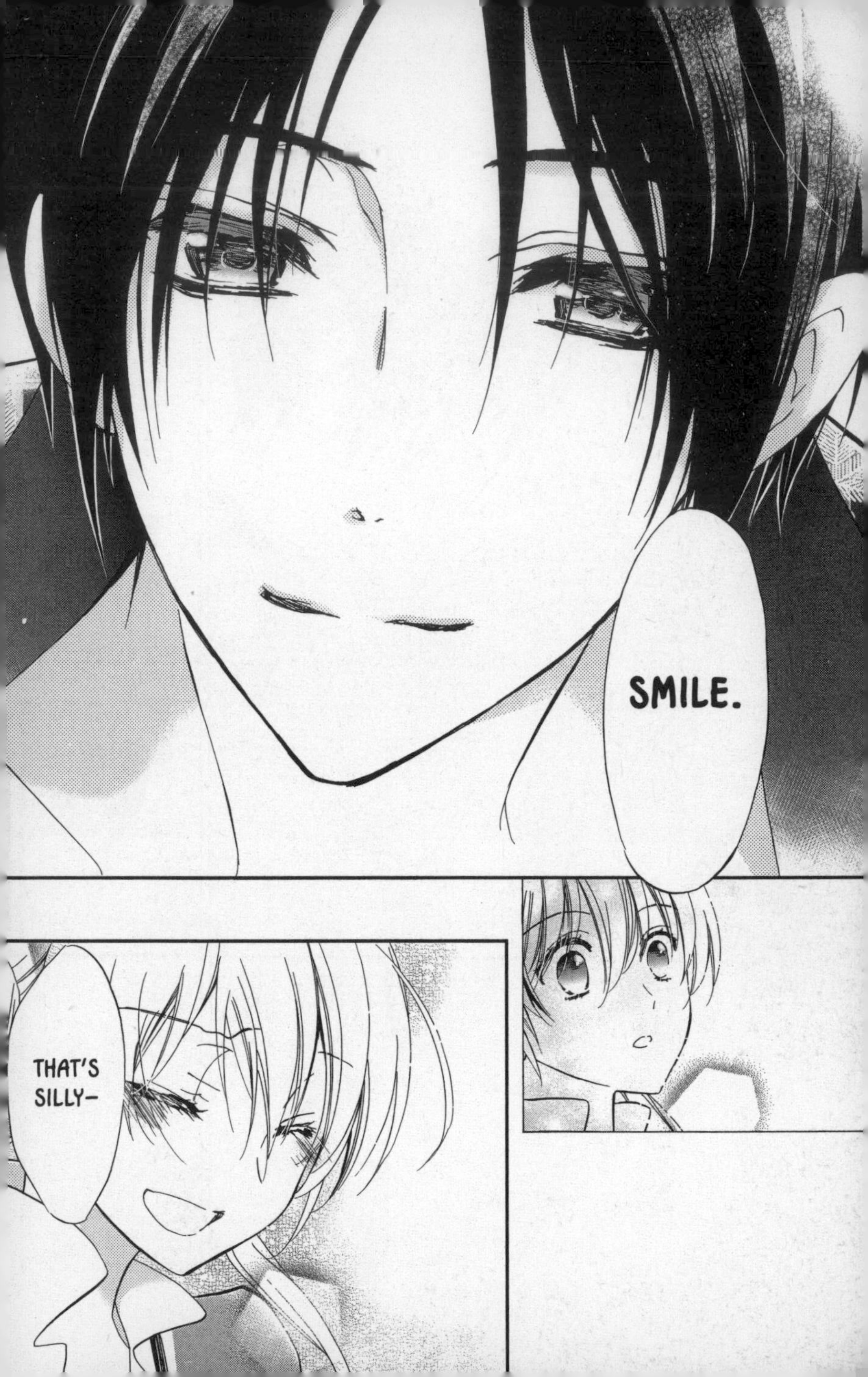
SMILE.
THAT'S SILLY-

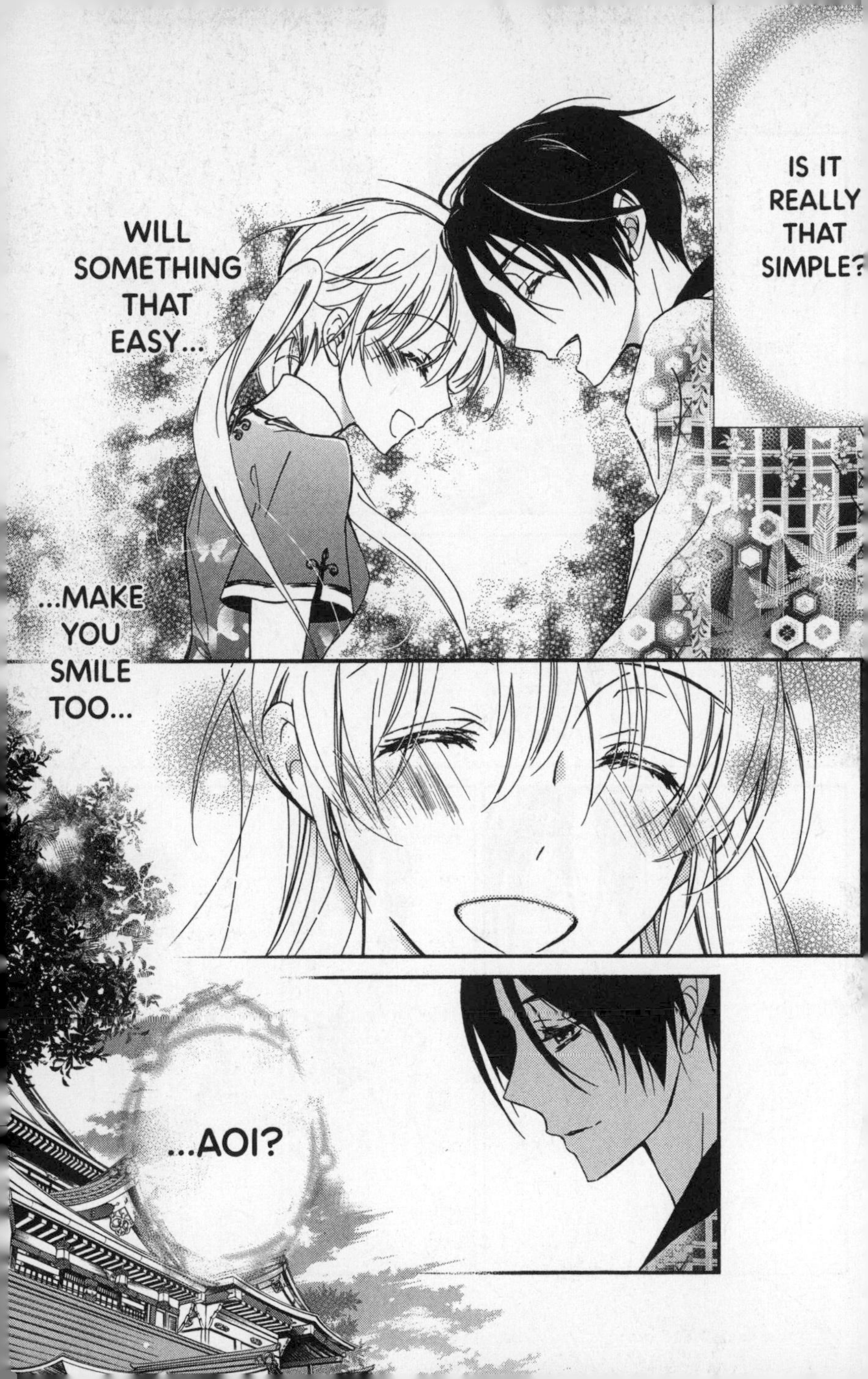
IS IT REALLY THAT SIMPLE?
WILL SOMETHING THAT EASY...
...MAKE YOU SMILE TOO...
...AOI?

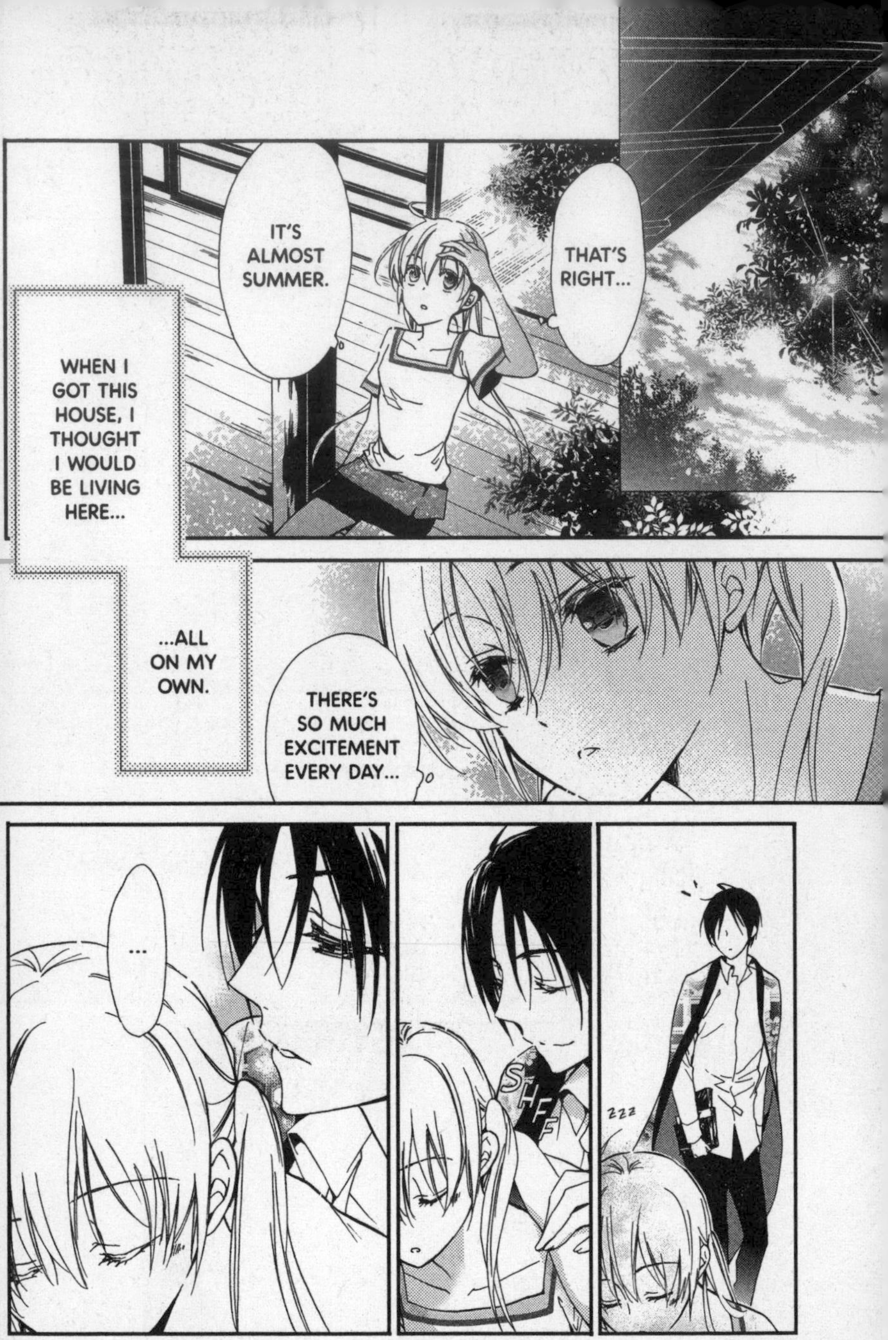
THAT'S RIGHT...
IT'S ALMOST SUMMER.
WHEN I GOT THIS HOUSE, I THOUGHT I WOULD BE LIVING HERE...
...ALL ON MY OWN.
THERE'S SO MUCH EXCITEMENT EVERY DAY...
ZZZ
SHFF
...

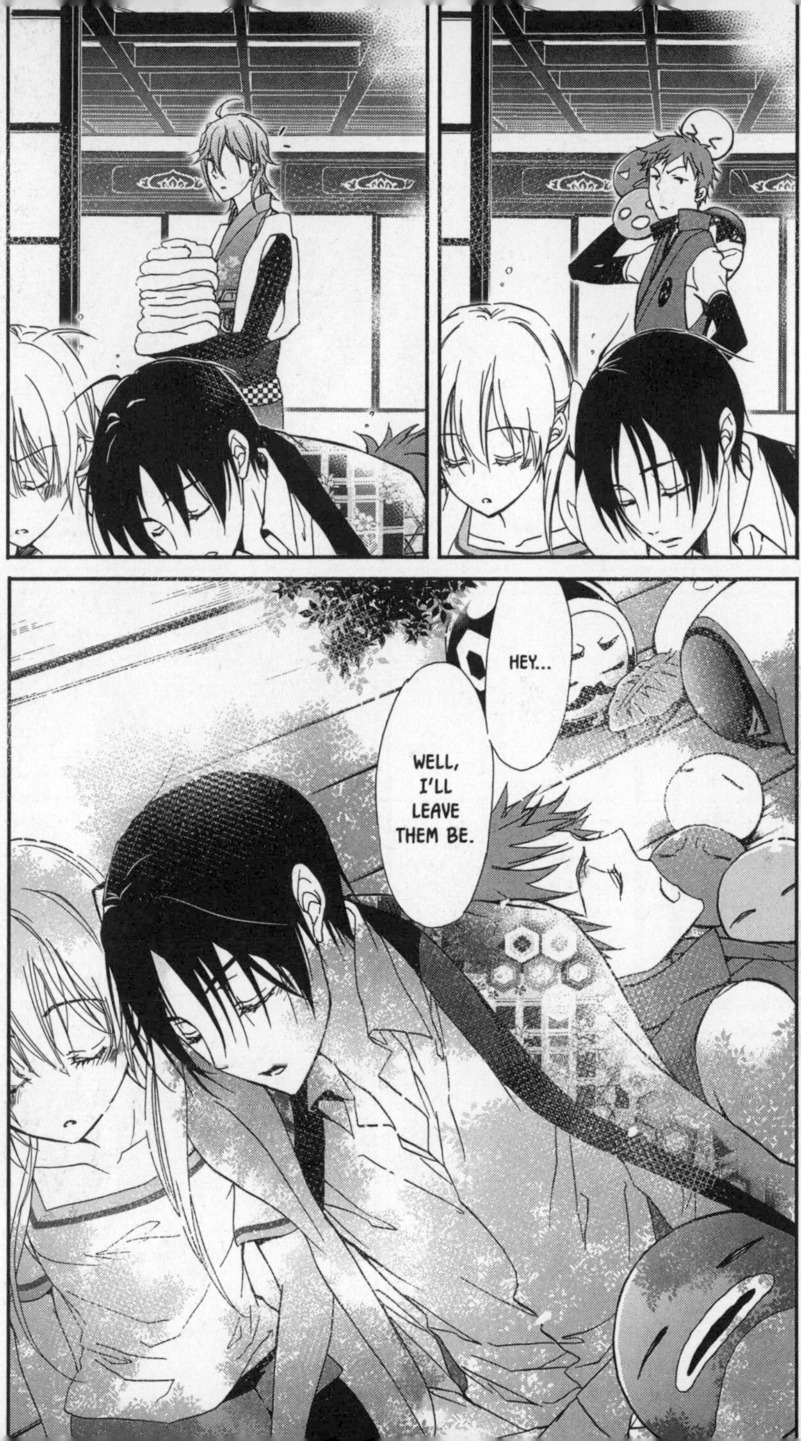
HEY...
WELL, I'LL LEAVE THEM BE.

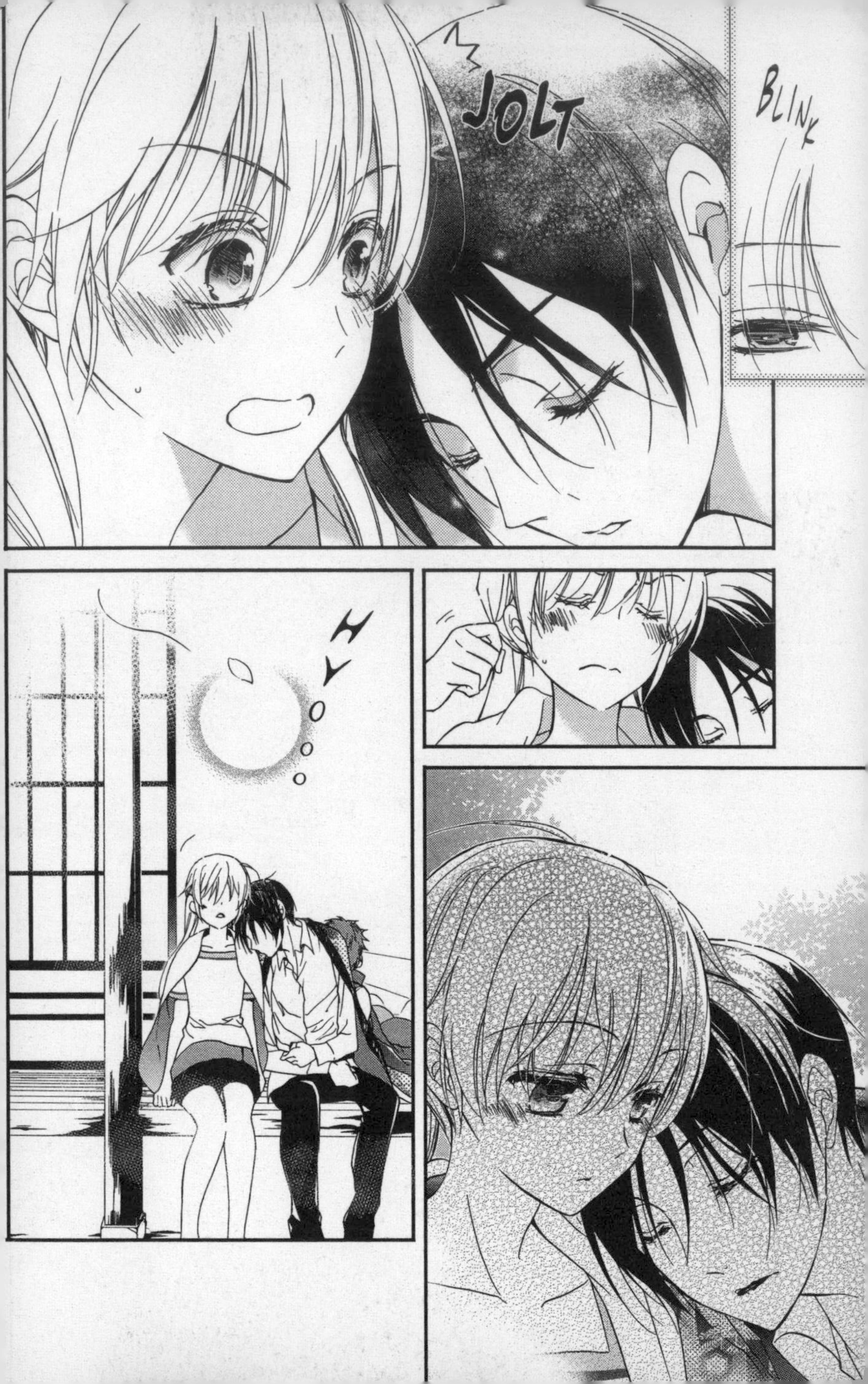
BLINK
JOLT

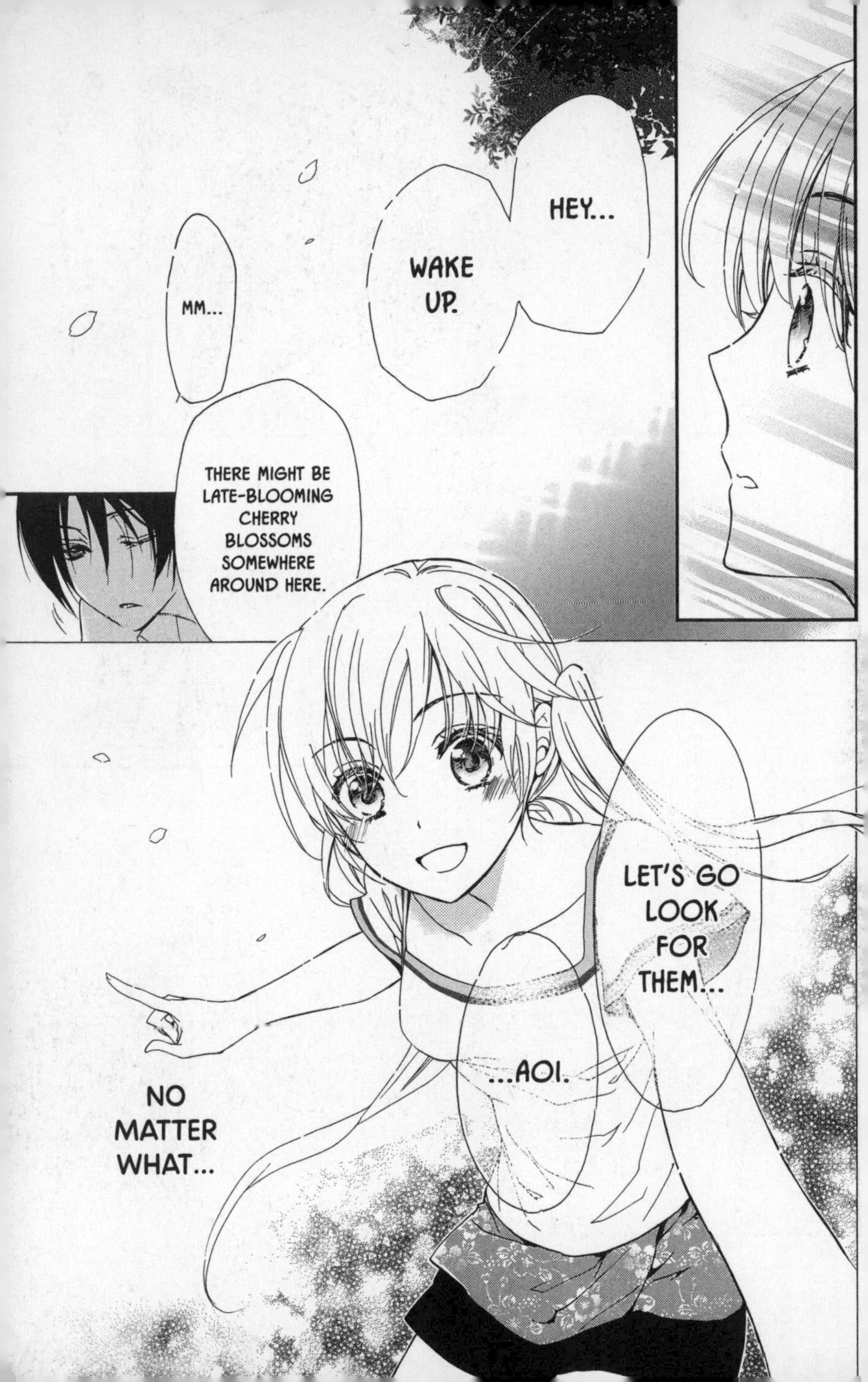
HEY...
WAKE UP.
MM...
THERE MIGHT BE LATE-BLOOMING CHERRY BLOSSOMS SOMEWHERE AROUND HERE.
LET'S GO LOOK FOR THEM...
...AOI.
NO MATTER WHAT...

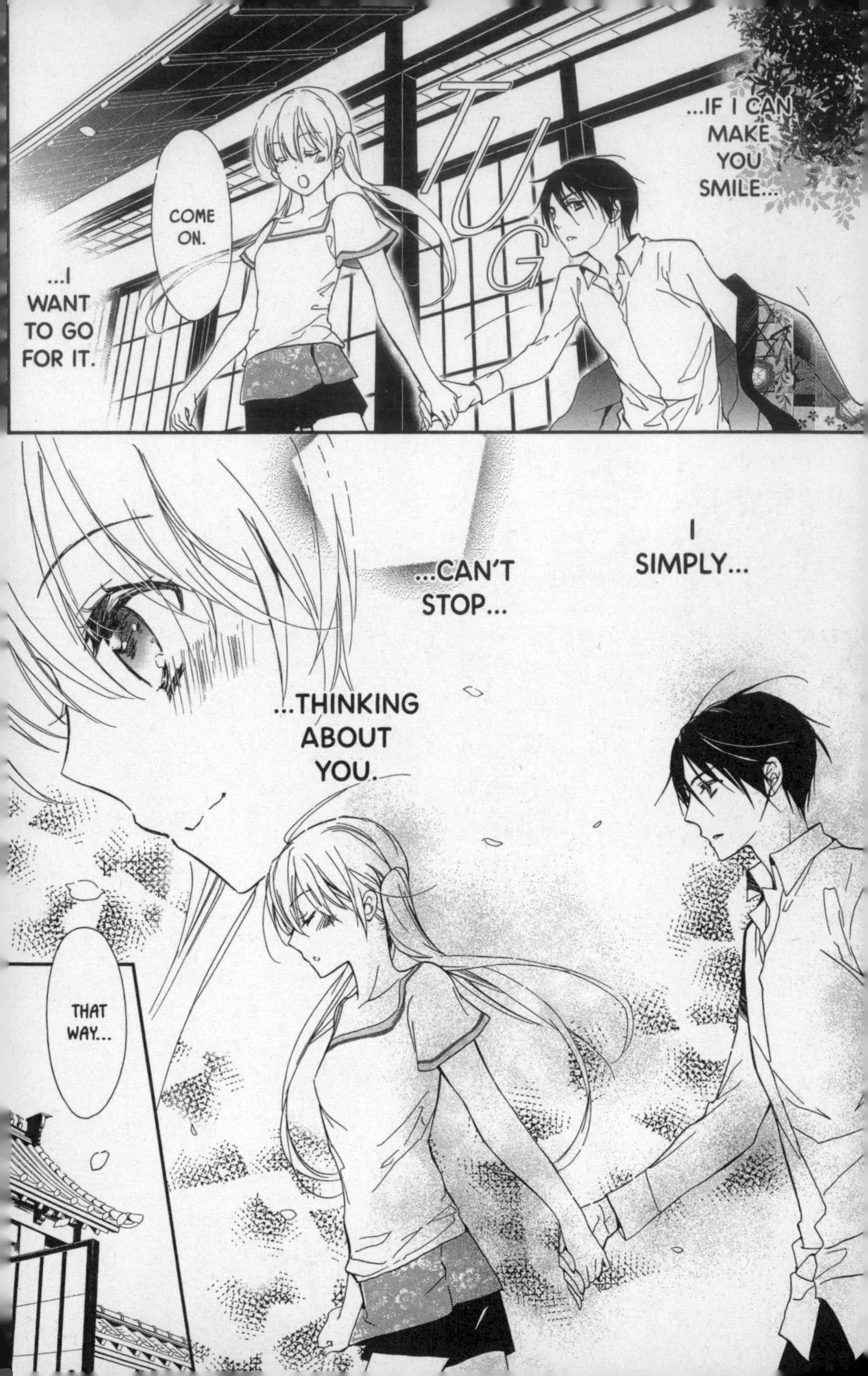
...IF I CAN MAKE YOU SMILE...
TUG
COME ON.
...I WANT TO GO FOR IT.
I SIMPLY...
...CAN'T STOP...
...THINKING ABOUT YOU.
THAT WAY...

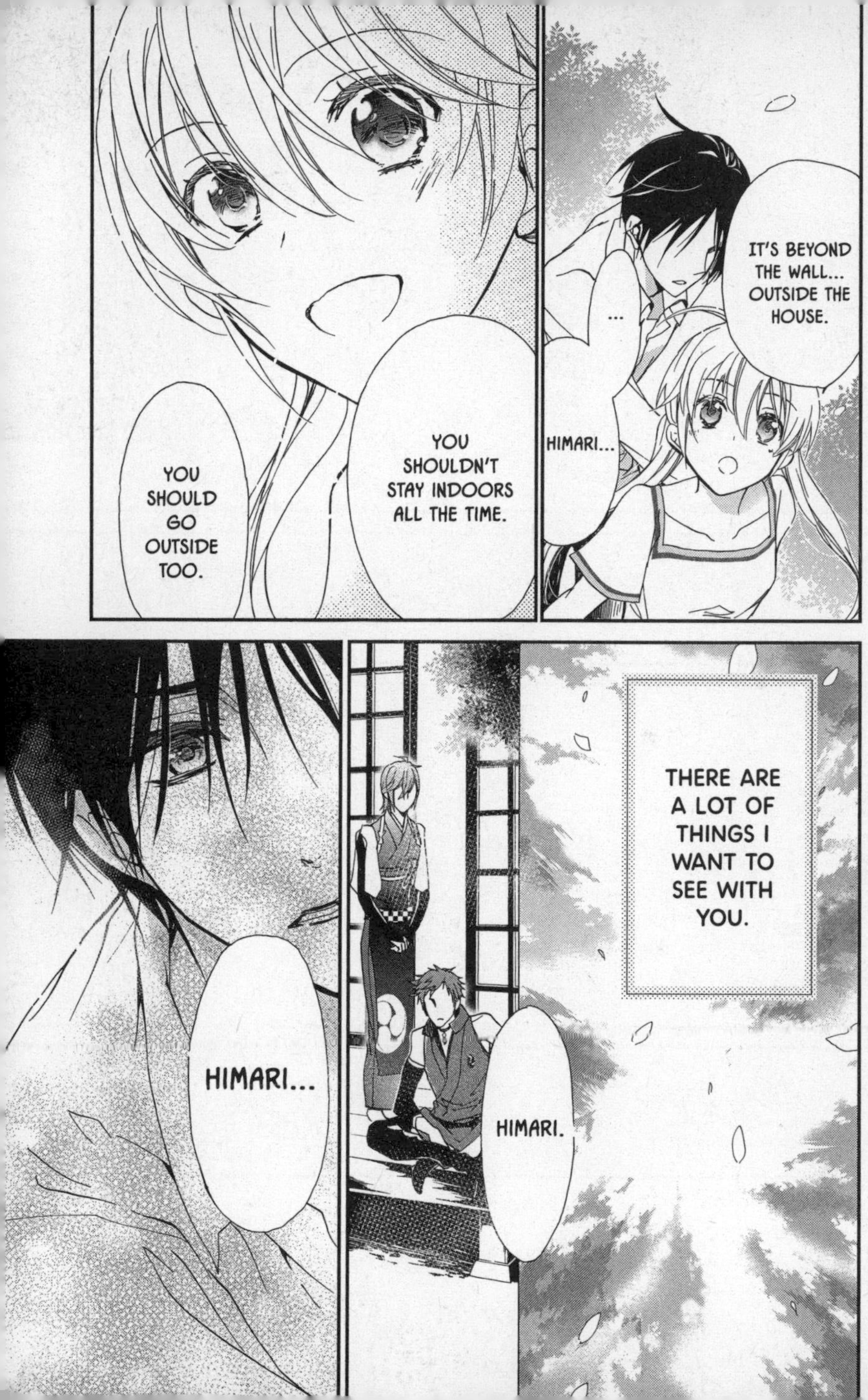
IT'S BEYOND THE WALL... OUTSIDE THE HOUSE.
...
HIMARI...
YOU SHOULDN'T STAY INDOORS ALL THE TIME.
YOU SHOULD GO OUTSIDE TOO.
THERE ARE A LOT OF THINGS I WANT TO SEE WITH YOU.
HIMARI.
HIMARI...

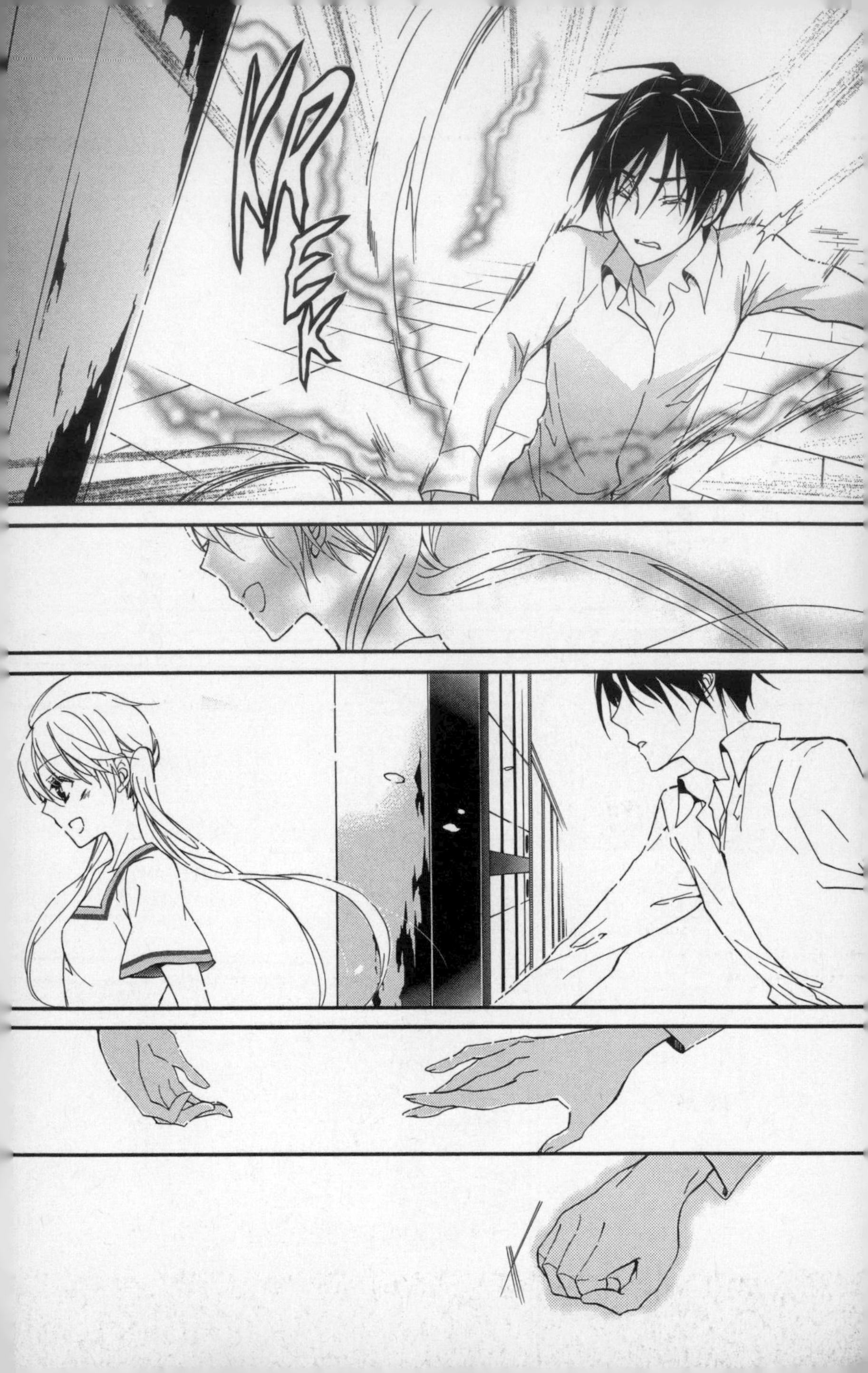
KRAK

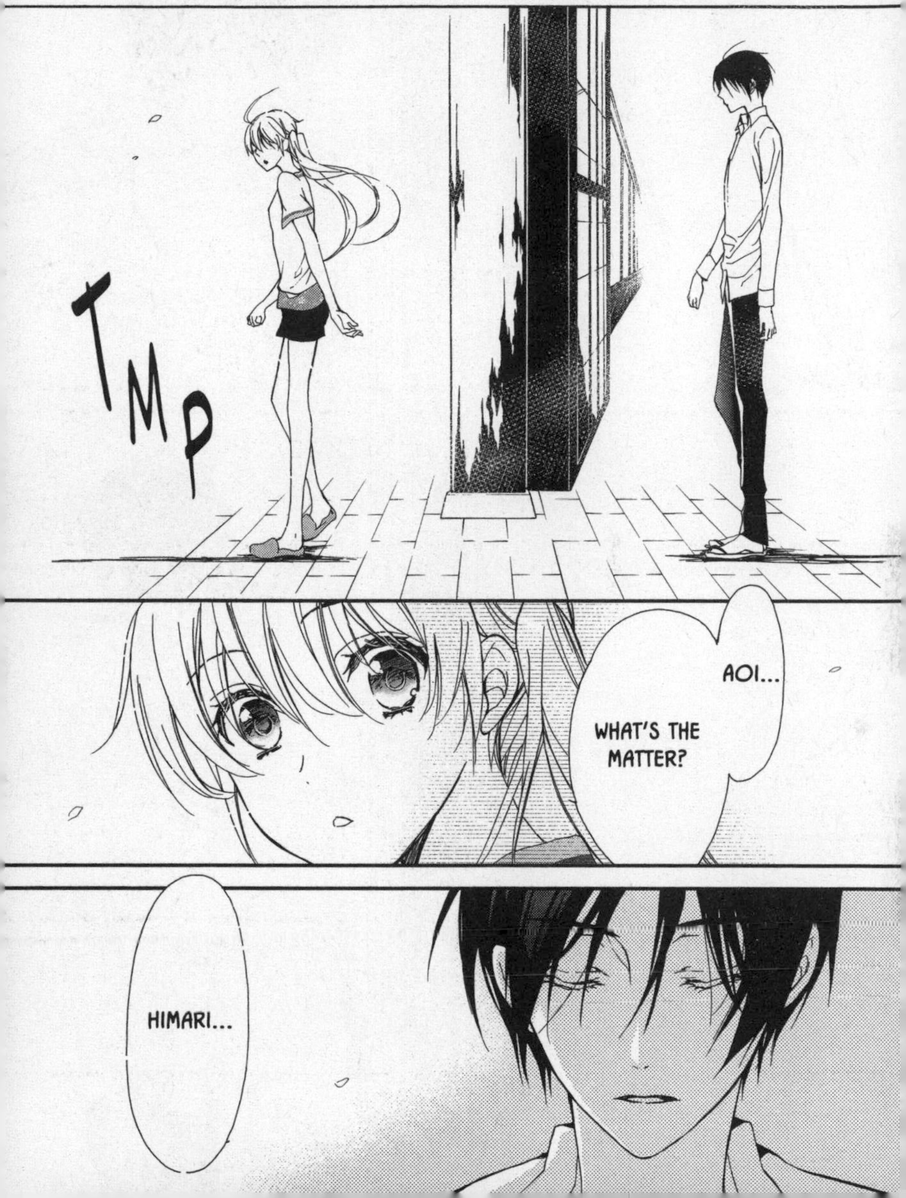
TMP
AOI...
WHAT'S THE MATTER?
HIMARI...

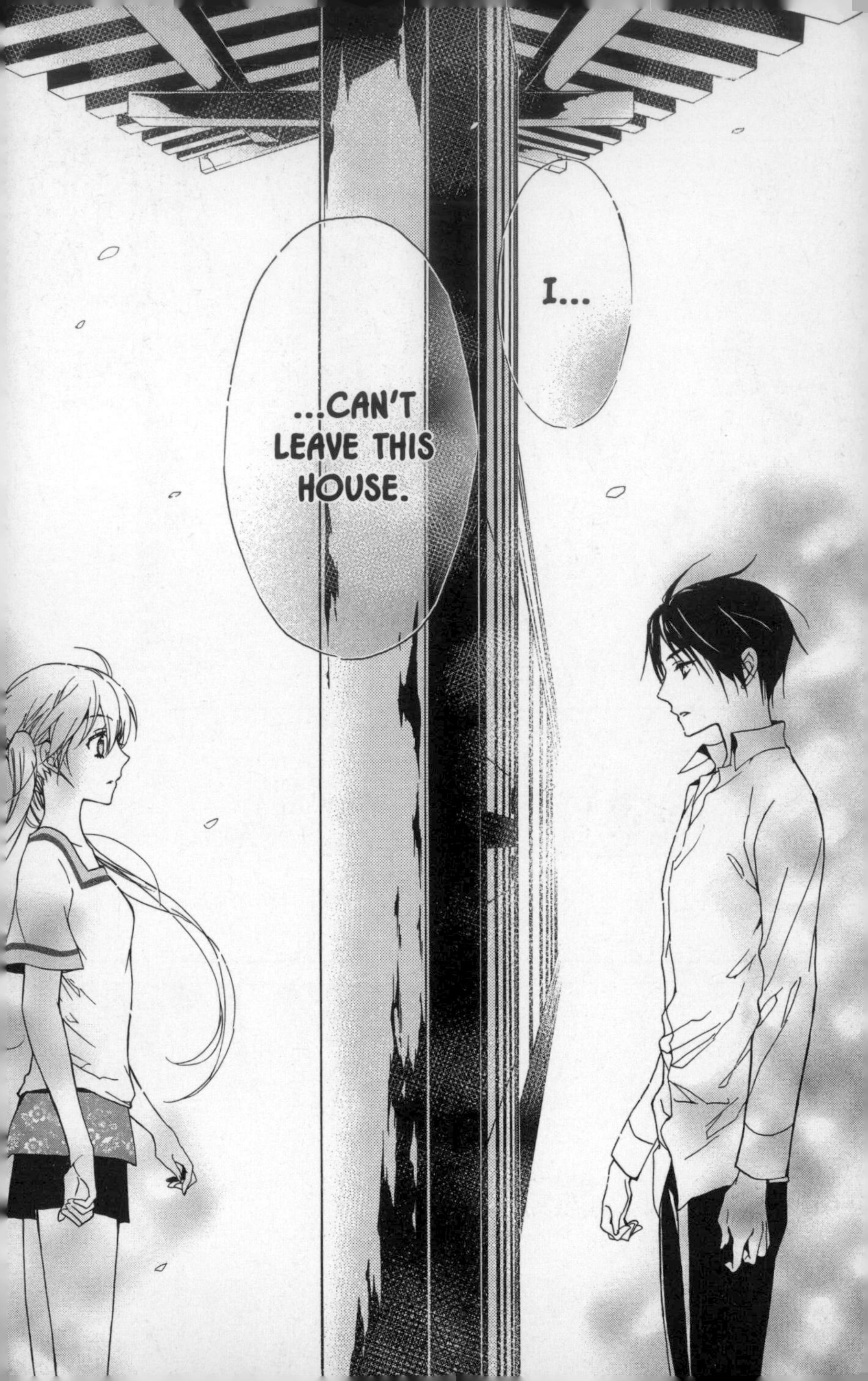
I...
...CAN'T LEAVE THIS HOUSE.

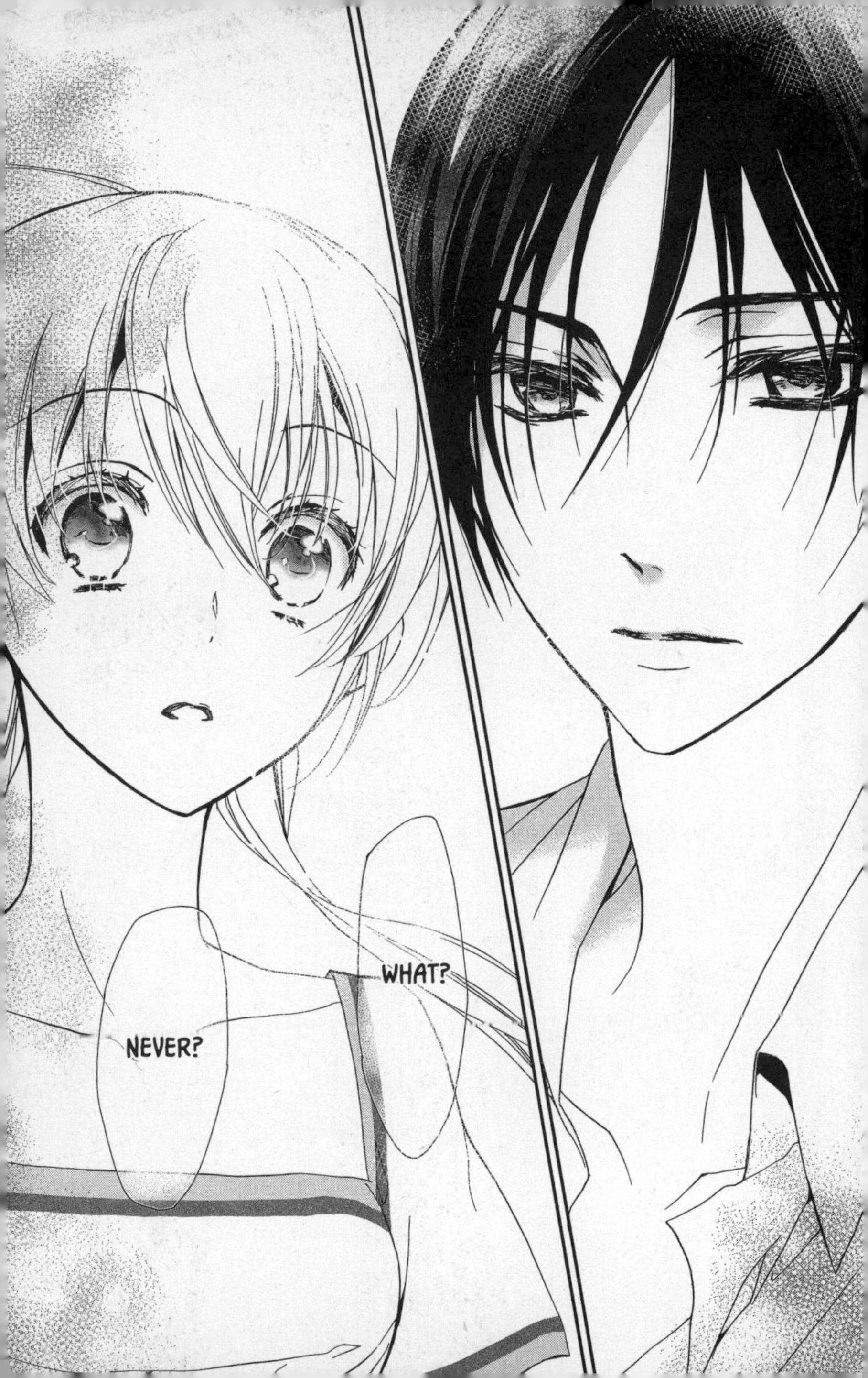
WHAT?
NEVER?

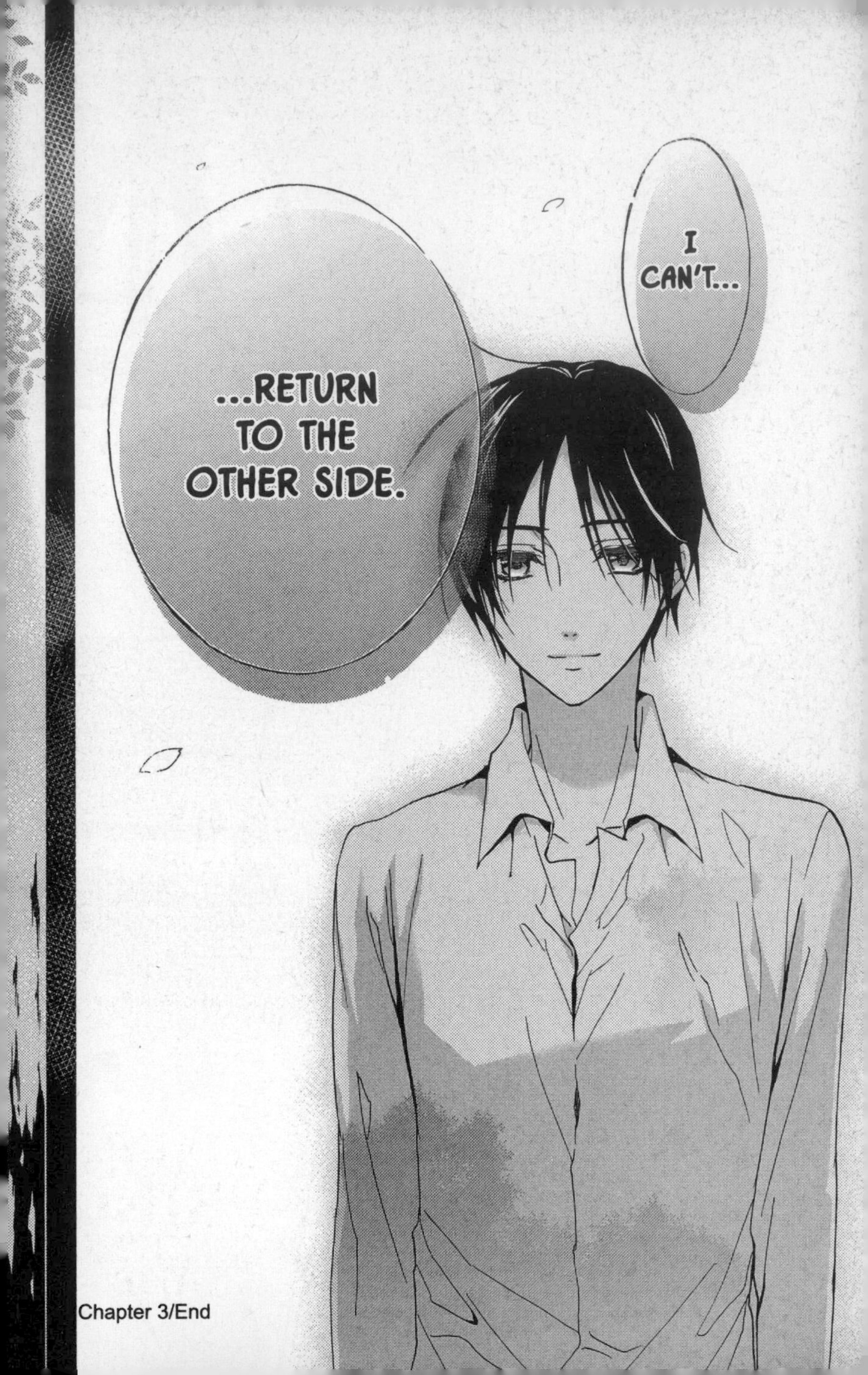
I CAN'T...
...RETURN TO THE OTHER SIDE.
Chapter 3/End

■ What did you think of *The Demon Prince of Momochi House*? When I was little, I'd feel lonely when I was home alone. I was afraid of the dark. I couldn't go to the bathroom alone. I'd always look behind me when I walked home. And mundane noises would make me imagine all kinds of things. Those were the things I was thinking about as I wrote this story.
Please continue to follow the adventures of Himari, Aoi, and this mysterious house!

Aya Shouoto

The DEMON PRINCE of MOMOCHI HOUSE

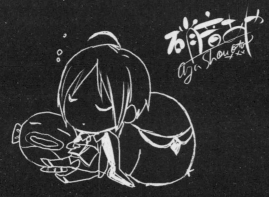

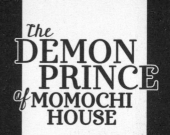

Hello, I'm Aya Shouoto. This is my first "Japanese" style series! I'm a little apprehensive about how I'll do in putting to paper my secret love of things Japanese... But I'm going to do my very best!

-*Aya Shouoto*

Aya Shouoto was born on December 25. Her hobbies are traveling, staying at hotels, sewing and daydreaming. She currently lives in Tokyo and enjoys listening to J-pop anime theme songs while she works.

The Demon Prince of Momochi House

Volume 1
Shojo Beat Edition

Story and Art by Aya Shouoto

Translation JN Productions
Touch-up Art & Lettering Inori Fukuda Trant
Design Fawn Lau
Editor Nancy Thistlethwaite

MOMOCHISANCHI NO AYAKASHI OUJI Volume 1
© Aya SHOUOTO 2013
Edited by KADOKAWA SHOTEN
First published in Japan in 2013 by KADOKAWA CORPORATION, Tokyo.
English translation rights arranged with KADOKAWA CORPORATION, Tokyo.

The stories, characters and incidents mentioned
in this publication are entirely fictional.

No portion of this book may be reproduced or transmitted in any form or
by any means without written permission from the copyright holders.

Printed in the U.S.A.

Published by VIZ Media, LLC
P.O. Box 77010
San Francisco, CA 94107

10 9 8 7 6 5 4 3 2 1
First printing, July 2015

RATED
(T)
FOR
TEEN
PARENTAL ADVISORY
THE DEMON PRINCE OF MOMOCHI
HOUSE is rated T for Teen and is
recommended for ages 13 and up.
ratings.viz.com

Story and Art by **Mayu Shinjo**

AI ORE!
Love Me

The boy (who looks like a girl) meets
girl (who looks like a boy) romance!

Mizuki is the female "prince" of her
all-girls school and the lead guitarist in
an all-girl rock band. Akira is the male
"princess" of his all-boys school and
wants to join her band. Love may be on
his mind, but romance is difficult when
everyone keeps mistaking Mizuki for
a boy and Akira for a girl!

By Mayu Shinjo,
the creator of
Demon Love Spell
and Sensual
Phrase

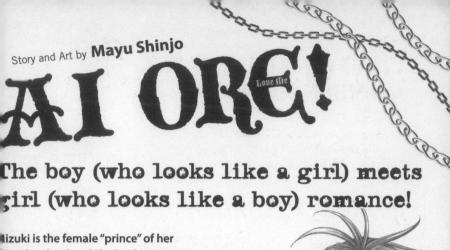

POISON

Check out this sexy and cool
series today. Available now!

viz
media
viz.com

Shojo
Beat

RATED
T+
FOR OLDER
TEEN
ratings.viz.com

Ore wo Utauyori Oreni Oborero! Volume 1
© Mayu SHINJO 2010

Kamisama Kiss

Story and art by **Julietta Suzuki**

What's a newly fledged godling to do?

Now a hit anime series!

Nanami Momozono is alone and homeless after her dad skips town to evade his gambling debts and the debt collectors kick her out of her apartment. So when a man she's just saved from a dog offers her his home, she jumps at the opportunity. But it turns out that his place is a shrine, and Nanami has unwittingly taken over his job as a local deity!

Available now!

viz.com

Shojo Beat

Kamisama Hajimemashita © Julietta Suzuki 2008/HAKUSENSHA, Inc.

Kyoko Mogami followed her true love Sho to Tokyo to support him while he made it big as an idol. But he's casting her out now that he's famous enough! Kyoko won't suffer in silence— she's going to get her sweet revenge by beating Sho in show biz!

Vol. 1 ISBN: 978-1-4215-4226-3

Vol. 2 ISBN: 978-1-4215-4227-0

Vol. 3 ISBN: 978-1-4215-422

Show biz is sweet...but revenge is sweeter!

Skip·Beat!

Story and Art by YOSHIKI NAKAMURA

In Stores Now!

Only **$14.99** for each volume ($16.99 in Canada)

Skip•Beat! © Yoshiki Nakamura 2002/HAKUSENSHA, Inc.

www.viz.com

Don't Hide What's Inside

OTOMEN

by AYA KANNO

Despite his tough jock exterior, Asuka Masamune harbors a secret love for sewing, shojo manga, and all things girly. But when he finds himself drawn to his domestically inept classmate Ryo, his carefully crafted persona is put to the test. Can Asuka ever show his true self to anyone, much less to the girl he's falling for?

Find out in the *Otomen* manga—buy yours today!

Available at your local bookstore or comic store.

OTOMEN © Aya Kanno 2006/HAKUSENSHA, Inc.

www.viz.com

Ouran High School
Host Club
BOX SET

Story and Art by
Bisco Hatori

Escape to the world of the young, rich and sexy

All 18 volumes in a collector's box with an Ouran High School stationery notepad!

In this screwball romantic comedy, Haruhi, a poor girl at a rich kids' school, is forced to repay an $80,000 debt by working for the school's swankiest, all-male club—as a boy! There she discovers just how wealthy the six members are and how different the rich are from everybody else...

www.viz.com

Ouran Koko Host Club © Bisco Hatori 2002/HAKUSENSHA, Inc.

Stop

You may be reading the WRONG WAY!!

IT'S TRUE: In keeping with the original Japanese comic format, this book reads from right to left—so action, sound effects, and word balloons are completely reversed. This preserves the orientation of the original artwork—plus, it's fun! Check out the diagram shown here to get the hang of things, and then turn to the other side of the book to get started!

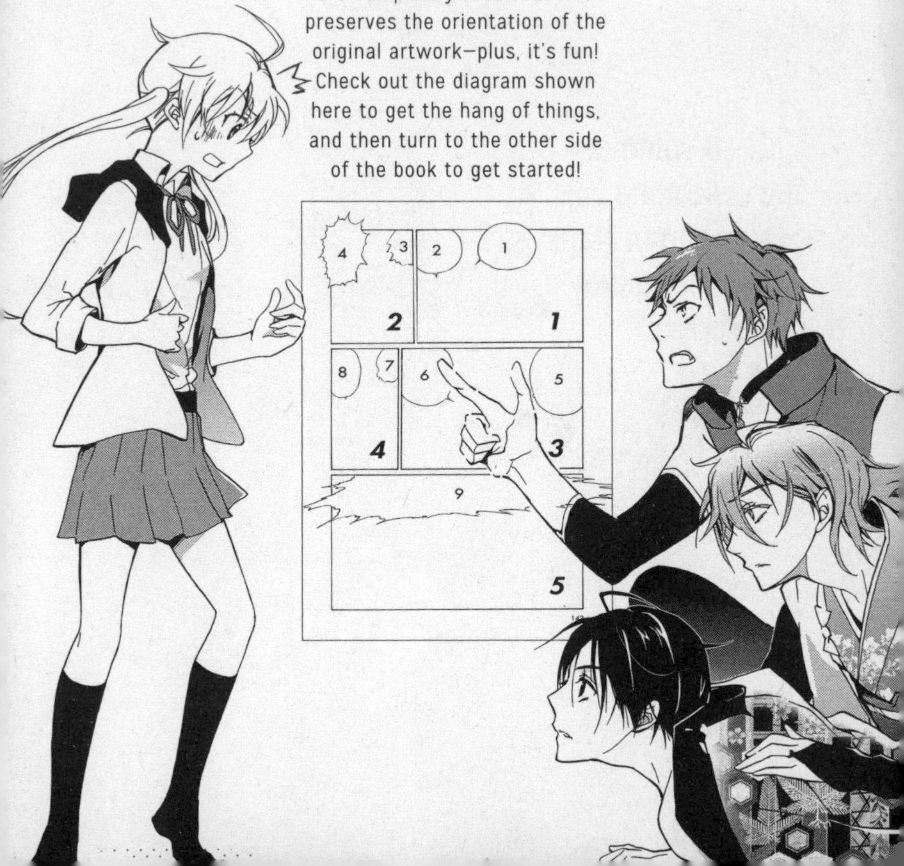